Berlitz®

Burmese

phrase book & dictionary

Berlitz Publishing
New York London Singapore

Contacting the Editors

Every effort has been made to provide accurate information in this publication, but changes are inevitable. The publisher cannot be responsible for any resulting loss, inconvenience or injury. We would appreciate it if readers would call our attention to any errors or outdated information. We also welcome your suggestions; if you come across a relevant expression not in our phrase book, please contact us at: **comments@berlitzpublishing.com**

Printed in China

Editor: Helen Fanthorpe
Translation: updated by Wordbank
Cover Design: Rebeka Davies
Interior Design: Beverley Speight
Picture Researcher: Beverley Speight
Cover Photos: Shutterstock
Interior Photos: APA Corrie Wingate p.1, 12, 18, 25, 27, 28, 30, 31, 33, 34, 47, 50, 54, 57, 61, 67, 69, 81, 84, 94, 106, 108, 109, 110, 111, 113, 123, 126, 129, 131, 133, 135, 136, 138, 143; istockphoto p37, 44, 63, 70, 71, 75, 83, 87, 89, 91, 119, 124, 137, 140, 147, 148, 152, 158.; APA Peter Stuckings p.72; APA A.Nowitz p.92; APA Britta Jaschinski p.39; APA Mina Patria p.43.

Distribution

UK, Ireland and Europe
Apa Publications (UK) Ltd
sales@insightguides.com
United States and Canada
Ingram Publisher Services
ips@ingramcontent.com
Australia and New Zealand
Woodslane
info@woodslane.com.au
Southeast Asia
Apa Publications (SN) Pte
singaporeoffice@insightguides.com

Worldwide
Apa Publications (UK) Ltd
sales@insightguides.com

Special Sales, Content Licensing, and CoPublishing

Discounts available for bulk quantities. We can create special editions, personalized jackets, and corporate imprints. sales@insightguides.com; www.insightguides.biz

Contents

Pronunciation/Consonants 7
Vowels 8
Tones 9
How to use this Book 12

Survival

Arrival & Departure 15
ESSENTIAL 15
Border Control 16

Money 17
ESSENTIAL 17
At the Bank 17

Getting Around 19
ESSENTIAL 19
Tickets 20
Plane 22
Airport Transfer 22
Checking In 23
Luggage 25
Finding your Way 25
Train 26
Departures 27
On Board 27
Bus 28
Jeep / Pick-up Trucks 29
Boat & Ferry 29
Taxi 31
Bicycle, Motorbike & Trishaw 32
Car & Driver 33
Asking Directions 34
Breakdown & Repair 36
Accidents 36

Places to Stay 37
ESSENTIAL 37
Somewhere to Stay 38
At the Hotel 39
Price 41
Preferences 41
Questions 42
Problems 44
Checking Out 45
Domestic Items 46

Communications 47
ESSENTIAL 48
Online 48
Social Media 50
Phone 51
Telephone Etiquette 54
Fax 54
Post 55

Food & Drink

Eating Out **57**
ESSENTIAL 57
Where to Eat 58
Reservations & Preferences 59
How to Order 61
Cooking Methods 62
Dietary Requirements 63
Dining with Children 64
How to Complain 65
Paying 66

Meals & Cooking **67**
Breakfast 67
Appetizers 69
Soup 69
Fish & Seafood 70
Meat & Poultry 70
Vegetables & Staples 71
Fruit 72
Dessert 74
Sauces & Condiments 75
At the Market 75
In the Kitchen 77

Drinks **78**
ESSENTIAL 78
Non-alcoholic Drinks 79
Apéritifs, Cocktails & Liqueurs 80
Beer 80
Wine 81

On the Menu **82**

People

Conversation **97**
ESSENTIAL 97
Language Difficulties 98
Making Friends 100
Travel Talk 100
Personal 101
Work & School 102
Weather 103

Romance **104**
ESSENTIAL 104
The Dating Game 105
Accepting & Rejecting 106
Getting Intimate 107
Sexual Preferences 107

Leisure Time

Sightseeing **109**
ESSENTIAL 109
Tourist Information 109
On Tour 110
Seeing the Sights 111
Religious Sites 113

Shopping **114**
ESSENTIAL 114
At the Shops 114
Ask an Assistant 116
Personal Preferences 117
Paying & Bargaining 118
Making a Complaint 118
Services 119
Hair & Beauty 120
Antiques 121
Clothing 121
Colors 122
Clothes & Accessories 123
Fabric 124
Shoes 125
Sizes 126
Newsagent & Tobacconist 126
Photography 127
Souvenirs 128

Sport & Leisure **130**
ESSENTIAL 130
Watching Sport 130
Playing Sport 132
At the Beach/Pool 133
Out in the Country 134

Going Out **136**
ESSENTIAL 136
Entertainment 136
Nightlife 138

Special Requirements

Business Travel **141**
ESSENTIAL 141
On Business 142

Traveling with Children **144**
ESSENTIAL 144
Out & About 144
Baby Essentials 146
Babysitting 147
Health & Emergency 147

Disabled Travelers **148**
ESSENTIAL 148
Asking for Assistance 148

In an Emergency

Emergencies **151**
ESSENTIAL 151

Police **152**
ESSENTIAL 152
Crime & Lost Property 153

Health **155**
ESSENTIAL 155
Finding a Doctor 155
Symptoms 156
Conditions 157
Treatment 157
Hospital 158
Dentist 159
Gynecologist 159
Optician 160
Payment & Insurance 160
Pharmacy 161
ESSENTIAL 161
What to Take 161
Basic Supplies 163

The Basics **164**
Grammar 164
Numbers 168
ESSENTIAL 168
Ordinal Numbers 169
Time 170
ESSENTIAL 170
Days 170
ESSENTIAL 170
Dates 171
Months 171
Seasons 171
Holidays & Festivals 172
Conversion Tables 173
Kilometers to Miles Conversions 173
Measurement 174
Temperature 174
Oven Temperature 174

Dictionary

English-Burmese Dictionary 176
Burmese-English Dictionary 201

Pronunciation

This section is designed to make you familiar with the sounds of Burmese using our simplified phonetic transcription. You'll find the pronunciation of the Burmese letters and sounds explained below, together with their 'imitated' equivalents. This system is based on sounds of familiar Burmese words and is used throughout the phrase book.
Burmese is a tonal language, but it is relatively easy to pronounce. The Burmese simplified pronunciation we are using is the John Okell method.

Consonants

Character	Pronunciation	Symbol	Example	Pronunciation
က	c as in 'car'	ká	ကား	kà
ခ	k as in 'key'	k'a	ခါး	k'à
ဂ / ဃ	g as in 'gather'	gá	ဂီတ	gi-tá
င	ng as in 'sing'	ngá	ငါး	ngà
စ	s as in 'spell'	sá	စု	sú
ဆ	s as in 'sardine'	s'á	ဆီ	s'i
ဇ / ဈ	z as in 'zebra'	zá	ဈေး	zè
ည	ny as in 'nude'	nyá	ညီ	nyi
ဋ / တ	t as in 'star'	tá	တား	tà
ဌ / ထ	t as in 'team'	t'á	ထီး	t'ì
ဍ / ဎ / ဒ / ဓ	d as in 'dare'	dá	ဓား	dà
ဏ / န	n as in 'no'	ná	နာ	na
ပ	p as in 'speak'	pá	ပဲ	pèh
ဖ	p as in 'peak'	p'á	ဖား	p'à
ဗ / ဘ	b as in 'bar'	bá	ဘဲ	bèh
မ	m as in 'more'	má	မိုး	mò
ယ / ရ	y as in 'yarn'	yá	ရော	yàw
လ / ဠ	l as in 'love'	lá	လာ	la

ဝ	w as in 'way'	wá	ဝါ	wa
သ	th as in 'that'	thá	သိ	thi
ဟ	h as in 'hero'	há	ဟင်း	hìn
အ	a as in 'martini'	á	အား	à

Vowels

Burmese vowel sounds should be easy for speakers of English and other European languages to pronounce. They occur in open, nasalised and stopped forms. See also Tones (p.9) as tones also affect the way in which vowels are constructed.

Open	Pronunciation
i	as the 'i' in 'marine'
e	as the 'e' in 'hey'
eh	as the 'e' in 'bet'
a	as the 'a' in 'father
aw	as the 'aw' in British 'law'
o	as the 'o' in 'go'
u	as the 'oo' in 'zoo

Nasalisation of vowels is similar to that found in French. You can approximate this by putting a weak **'n'** at the end of such a syllable. This nasalisation is indicated by **n** after the vowel, as in **ein**, **'house'.**

Nasalised	Pronunciation
in	as the 'in' in 'sin'
ein	as the 'ain' in 'pain'
an	as the 'an' in 'man'
oun	as the 'oan' in 'moan'
un	as the 'un' in 'junta'
ain	as the 'ine' in 'line'
aun	as the 'own' in 'brown'

The stopped vowels are pronounced as short syllables, cut off at the end by a sharp catch in the voice. This is known as a glottal stop.

stopped	Pronunciation
iq	as the 'it' in 'sit'
eiq	as the 'ate' in 'late'
eq	as the 'et' in 'bet'
aq	as the 'at' in 'mat'
ouq	as the 'oat' in 'boat'
uq	as the 'oot' in 'foot'
aiq	as the 'ight' in 'might'
auq	as the 'out' in 'stout'

Tones

Every syllable has one of five alternatives: **creaky high tone; plain high tone: low tone; stopped syllable;** or **reduced (weak) syllable.**

Remember that in Burmese, the tone of a word can change its meaning!

Creaky High Tone

This is made with the voice tense, producing a high-pitched and relatively short creaky sound, as with words like **'heart'** and **'squeak'.** It is indicated by an acute accent over the vowel, *for example* **ká, 'dance'.**

for example: dance က ká

Plain High Tone

The pitch of the voice starts quite high, then falls for a fairly long time, as with words like **'squeal', 'car'** and **'way'**. It is indicated by a grave accent over the vowel, for example, **kà** which, conveniently, is the Burmese word for **'car'.**

for example: car ကား kà

Low Tone

The voice is relaxed, stays at a low pitch for a fairly long time, and does not rise or fall in pitch. It is indicated by no accent over the vowel, *for example* **ka, 'shield'.**

for example: shield ကာ ka

Stopped Syllable

This is a very short syllable, on a high pitch, cut off at the end by a sharp catch in the voice (a glottal stop). This is like the sound, **'uh-oh',** or the Cockney pronunciation of **'t'** in a word like **'bottle'.** If you have trouble with this sound, try replacing it with a **'t',** but keep the syllable short. It is indicated in this book by a **q** after the vowel, *for example* **kaq, 'join'.** Note that the **q** is not pronounced.

for example: join ကပ် kaq

A Burmese vowel is written using a symbol or combination of symbols above, below or after the consonant that it follows. Tones also affect the way vowels are constructed.

To prevent confusion with other consonants, there is sometimes more than one way of writing the same vowel. *For example*, if you added ာ (a) to ပ (p), it would become ပာ which is the same symbol as for **h**, so instead it is written as ပါ.

Creaky High		Plain High		Low	
–	á	–ား/ –ါး	à	–ာ/ –ါ	a
–ိ	í	–ီး	ì	–ီ	i
–ု	ú	–ူး	ù	–ူ	u
ေ–့	é	ေ–း	è	ေ–	e
–ဲ့	éh	–ဲ	èh	–ယ်	eh
–ို့	ó	–ိုး	ò	–ို	o
ေ–ာ့	áw	ေ–ာ/ ေ–ါ	àw	ေ–ာ်/ ေ–ါ်	aw

The different forms here indicate whether the nasalised/stopped vowel is based on **n** (န), **m** (မ), **p** (ပ) stopped or **t** (တ).

Nasalised		Stopped	
−င် / −ဉ်	in	−စ်	iq
−ိန် / −ိမ်	ein	−ိတ် / −ိပ်	eiq
		−က်	eq
−မ် / −န / −ံ	an	−တ် / −ပ်	aq
−ုန် / −ုမ် / −ုံ	oun	−ုတ် / −ုပ်	ouq
−ွန် / −ွမ် / −ွံ	un	−ွတ် / −ွပ်	uq
ေ−ာင်	aun	−ိုက်	aiq
−ိုင်	ain	ေ−ာက်	auq

How to use this Book

Sometimes you see two alternatives separated by a slash. Choose the one that's right for your situation.

ESSENTIAL

I'm on vacation/business. ကျွန်တော်/ကျွန်မ အပန်းဖြေခရီးထွက်လာတာ/ အလုပ်ကိစ္စနဲ့လာတာ ပါ။ *cănaw* **m**/*cămá* **f** *ăpàn-p'ye-k'äyì t'weq-la-da/ălouq keiq-sá-néh la-da-ba.*

I'm going to… ကျွန်တော်/ကျွန်မ… ကို သွားမလို့။ *cănaw* **m** /*cămá* **f***…go thwá-mă-ló.*

I'm staying at the…Hotel. ကျွန်တော်/ကျွန်မ… ဟိုတယ်မှာ နေနေတယ်။ *cănaw* **m**/*cămá* **f***…ho-teh-hma ne-ne-deh.*

Words you may see are shown in YOU MAY SEE boxes.

YOU MAY SEE…

အကောက်ခွန်	customs
အခွန်ကင်းသော ပစ္စည်းများ	duty-free goods
ကြေငြာစရာလိုသော ပစ္စည်းများ	goods to declare

Any of the words or phrases listed can be plugged into the sentence below.

Tickets

A…ticket. …လက်မှတ်တစ်စောင် *…leq-hmaq dă-zaun*

one-way အသွား *ă-thwà*

round-trip [return] အသွားအပြန် *ă-thwà-ă-pyan*

first class ပထမတန်း *pă-t'ă-má-dàn*

economy class ရိုးရိုးတန်း *yò-yò-dàn*

Burmese phrases appear in purple.

Read the simplified pronunciation as if it were English. For more on pronunciation, see page 7.

Departures

Is this the track [platform]/ train to…?	ဒီလမ်းကြောင်း (ပလက်ဖောင်း)/ ရထားက … ကို သွားတာလား။ *Di-làn-jaùn-(păleq-p´aùn)/ yătà-gá…go thwà-da-là?*
Where is track [platform]…?	…လမ်းကြောင်း (ပလက်ဖောင်း) က ဘယ်မှာလဲ။ *…làn-jaùn-(păleq-p´aùn) gá beh-hma-lèh?*
Where do I change for...?	…ကိုသွားဖို့ ကျွန်တော်/ ကျွန်မ ဘယ်နေရာမှာ ပြောင်းရမလဲ။ *…go-thwà-bó-cănaw* **m** */cămá* **f***-beh-ne-ya-hma-pyaùn-ya-măléh?*

For Tickets, see page 20.

If you are a man, use the masculine form, marked as ***m***; if you are a woman, use the feminine form, marked as ***f***

Related phrases can be found by going to the page number indicated.

Before and after exchanging money, ensure that all bills are clean, unmarked and undamaged (i.e. no creases, rips, tears or holes) as otherwise you may have troub

Information boxes contain relevant country, culture and language tips.

Expressions you may hear are shown in You May Hear boxes.

YOU MAY HEAR…

ခင်ဗျား/ရှင် အင်္ဂလိပ်စကားပြောသလား။ *k´ămyà* **m***/shin* **f** *-ìn-găleiq-zăgà-pyàw-dhălà?* — Do you speak English?

Color-coded side bars identify each section of the book.

Survival

Arrival & Departure 15
Money 17
Getting Around 19
Places to Stay 37
Communications 47

Arrival & Departure

ESSENTIAL

I'm on vacation/ business.	ကျွန်တော်/ကျွန်မ အပန်းဖြေခရီးထွက်လာတာ/ အလုပ်ကိစ္စနဲ့လာတာ ပါ။ *cănaw* **m**/*cămá* **f** *ăpàn-p'ye-k'ăyì t'weq-la-da / ălouq keiq-sá-néh la-da-ba.*
I'm going to…	ကျွန်တော်/ကျွန်မ…ကို သွားမလို့။ *cănaw* **m** / *cămá* **f** … *go thwá-mă-ló.*
I'm staying at the…Hotel.	ကျွန်တော်/ကျွန်မ… ဟိုတယ်မှာ နေ နေတယ်။ *cănaw* **m**/*cămá* **f** … *ho-teh-hma ne-ne-deh.*
I'm staying at the…guesthouse.	ကျွန်တော်/ကျွန်မ အခု… ဧည့်ရိပ်သာမှာ နေနေတယ်။ *cănaw* **m**/*cămá* **f** *ăk'ú … éh-yeiq-tha-hma ne-ne-deh*

YOU MAY HEAR…

ကျေးဇူးပြုပြီး ခင်ဗျားရဲ့/ရှင့်ရဲ့ နိုင်ငံကူးလက်မှတ် ပေးပါ။ *cè-zù pyú-bì k'ămyà-yéh* **m** /*shin-yéh* **f** *-nain-ngan-kù leq-hmaq pè-ba.*	Your passport, please.
ခင်ဗျား/ရှင် ဒီကို လာလည်ရတဲ့အကြောင်းရင်းက ဘာလဲ။ *k'ămyà* **m** / *shin* **f** *di-go la-leh-yá-déh ăcàun-yìn-gá ba-lèh?*	What's the purpose of your visit?
ခင်ဗျား/ရှင် အခု ဘယ်မှာ နေနေလဲ။ *k'ămyà* **m** /*shin* **f** *-ăk'ú beh-hma ne-ne-lèh?*	Where are you staying?
ခင်ဗျား/ရှင် ဘယ်လောက်ကြာကြာ နေမှာလဲ။ *k'ămyà* **m** /*shin* **f** *-beh-lauq-ca-ja ne-hma-le?*	How long are you staying?
ခင်ဗျား/ရှင် ဒီမှာ ဘယ်သူနဲ့လာတာလဲ။ *k'ămyà* **m** /*shin* **f** *-di-hma bă-dhu-néh la-da-lèh?*	Who are you here with?

Border Control

I'm just passing through.	ကျွန်တော်/ကျွန်မ ခဏ ဖြတ်သန်းရုံဖြတ်သန်း သွားတာပါ။ *cănaw* **m** */cămá* **f** *k´ăná-p'yaq-than-youn-p'yaq-than-thwà-da-ba.*
I'd like to declare…	ကျွန်တော်/ကျွန်မ … ကြေညာချင်ပါတယ်။ *cănaw* **m** */ cămá* **f** *…ce-nya-jin-ba-deh.*
I have nothing to declare.	ကျွန်တော်/ကျွန်မမှာ ကြေညာစရာ ဘာမှမရှိပါဘူး။ *cănaw-* **m** */cămá-* **f** *… hma ce-nya-ză-ya ba-hmá mă-shí-ba-bù.*

YOU MAY HEAR…

ကြေညာစရာ တစ်ခုခုပါသလား။ *ce-nya-ză-ya tă-k'ú-gú pa-dhă-là?*	Anything to declare?
ဒီဟာအတွက် ခင်ဗျား/ရှင် ဂျူတီ (အခွန်) ဆောင်ရမယ်။ *di-ha ătweq k'ămyà* **m** */ shin* **f** *duty(ăk'un) s'aun-yá-meh.*	You must pay duty on this.
ဒီအိတ်ကို ဖွင့်ပြပါ။ *di-eiq-ko p'wín-pyá-ba.*	Open this bag.

YOU MAY SEE…

အကောက်ခွန်	customs
အခွန်ကင်းသော ပစ္စည်းများ	duty-free goods
ကြေညာစရာလိုသော ပစ္စည်းများ	goods to declare
ကြေညာစရာမပါရှိပါ	nothing to declare
နိုင်ငံကူးလက်မှတ် ထိန်းချုပ်ရေး	passport control
ရဲ	police

Money

ESSENTIAL

Where's…?	… က ဘယ်နေရာမှာလဲ။ …*gá beh-ne-ya-hma-lèh?*
the ATM	ငွေအလိုအလျောက်ထုတ်ပေးစက် *ngwe-ă-lo-ă-lyauq t'ouq-pè-seq*
the bank	ဘဏ် *ban*
the currency exchange office	ငွေလဲလှယ်ပေးသောရုံ *ngwe lèh-hleh-pè-dhàw-yoùn*
When does the bank open/close?	ဘဏ်က ဘယ်အချိန်တွေမှာ ဖွင့်/ပိတ် သလဲ။ *ban-gá beh ă-c'ein-dwe-hma p'wín-/peiq-thă-lèh?*
I'd like to change dollars/ pounds sterling into Kyat.	ကျွန်တော်/ကျွန်မ ဒေါ်လာ/ပေါင်စတာလင်ကိုကျပ်နဲ့လဲချင်ပါတယ်။ *cănaw* **m**/*cămá* **f** *daw-la/paun să-ta-lin-go caq-néh lèh-jin-ba-deh.*
I'd like to cash traveler's cheques.	ကျွန်တော်/ကျွန်မ ခရီးသွားချက်လက်မှတ်ကို ပိုက်ဆံနဲ့လဲချင်ပါတယ်။ *cănaw* **m**/*cămá* **f** *k'ă-yì-thwà c'eq-leq-hmaq-ko paiq-s'an-néh lèh-jin-ba-deh.*

At the Bank

I'd like to change money.	ကျွန်တော်/ကျွန်မ ပိုက်ဆံလဲချင်ပါတယ်။ *cănaw* **m** /*cămá* **f** *paiq-s'an lèh-jin-ba-deh.*
What's the exchange rate/fee?	ငွေလဲလှယ်နှုန်း/ငွေလဲလှယ်ခက ဘယ်လောက်လဲ။ *ngwe-lèh-hleh -hnòun/ngwe-lèh-hleh-gá -gá bălauq-lèh?*
I think there's a mistake.	ဒီမှာ အမှားအယွင်းတစ်ခုရှိတယ်လို့ ကျွန်တော်/ကျွန်မ ထင်ပါတယ်။ *di-hma ăhmà-ăywìn tă-k'ú shí-deh-ló cănaw* **m**/ *cămá* **f** *t´in-ba-deh*
I lost my traveler's cheques.	ကျွန်တော်/ကျွန်မရဲ့ ခရီးသွားချက်လက်မှတ်တွေ ပျောက်သွားတယ်။ *cănaw* **m** /*cămá* **f** *yéh k'ă-yì-thwà c'eq-leq-hmaq-twe-pyauq-thwà-deh.*

My card… ကျွန်တော်/ကျွန်မ ရဲ့ ကတ် *cănaw* ***m****/cămá* ***f*** *yéh kaq.*
was lost ပျောက်သွားခဲ့တယ်။ *pyauq-thwà-géh-deh.*
was stolen အခိုးခံခဲ့ရတယ်။ *ă-k´ò k'an-géh-yá-deh.*
doesn't work အလုပ် မလုပ်ဘူး။ *ă-louq mă-louq-p'ù.*
The ATM ate my card. ကျွန်တော်/ကျွန်မရဲ့ကတ်ကို ငွေအလိုအလျောက်ထုတ်ပေးစက်က စားသွားတယ်။ *cănaw* ***m****/cămá yéh kaq-ko ngwe-ă-lo-ă-lyauq t'ouq-pè-zeq-gá sà-thwà-deh.*

For Numbers, see page 168.

ATMs are few and far between in Myanmar, and can only really be found in major cities, so make sure to have plenty of US dollars on you on arrival. You can use dollars to pay for hotels, air and rail fares, entry into major sights and for travel agents; for everything else, you will need to exchange some dollars into the local **Kyat**.

YOU MAY SEE…

The official currency in Burma is the **Kyat (K)**.
Notes: **K1, Ks 5, 10, 20, 50, 100, 200, 500 and 1000**

Before and after exchanging money, ensure that all bills are clean, unmarked and undamaged (i.e. no creases, rips, tears or holes) as otherwise you may have trouble using them, even in banks and currency exchange offices. US dollars can be exchanged also. Credit and debit cards and travelers checks are hardly accepted anywhere.

Getting Around

ESSENTIAL

How do I get to town? မြို့ထဲကို ကျွန်တော်/ကျွန်မ ဘယ်လိုရောက်နိုင်မလဲ။ *myó-dèh-go cănaw* ***m****/cămá* ***f*** *beh-lo yauq-nain-mă-lèh?*

Where's…? …က ဘယ်နေရာမှာလဲ။ *…gá beh-ne-ya-hma-lèh?*

- the airport လေဆိပ် *le-zeiq*
- the train station ရထားဘူတာရုံ *yă-t'à bu-da-youn*
- the bus station ဘတ်စ်ကားဂိတ် *baq-săkà-geiq*
- the riverboat jetty မြစ်တွင်းသွား စက်လှေ (သင်္ဘော) ဆိပ်ခံဘောတံတား *myiq-twìn-dhwà seq-hle (thìn-bàw) s'eiq-k'an-bàw-tă-dà*

Is it far from here? အဲဒီနေရာက ဒီကနေ ဝေးသလား။ *èh-di-ne-ya-gá di-gá-ne wè-dhă-là?*

Where do I buy a ticket? ကျွန်တော်/ကျွန်မ လက်မှတ်တစ်စောင် ဘယ်နေရာမှာ ဝယ်ရမလဲ။ *cănaw* ***m*** */cămá* ***f*** *leq-hmaq dă-zaun beh-ne-ya-hma weh-yá-mă-lèh?*

A one-way/ return-trip ticket to… …ကိုသွားတဲ့ အသွားတစ်ကြောင်း/အသွားအပြန် လက်မှတ် *…go thwà-déh ă-thwà dă-jàun / ă-thwà-ă-pyan leq-hmaq*

How much? ဘယ်လောက်ကျသလဲ။ *beh lauq cá-dhă-lèh?*

Which gate/line? ဘယ်ဂိတ်/လိုင်း လဲ။ *beh geiq-/làin- lèh?*

Which platform? ဘယ်ပလက်ဖောင်းလဲ။ *beh pă-leq-p'àun-lèh?*

Where can I get a taxi? ကျွန်တော်/ကျွန်မ အငှားကား ဘယ်နေရာမှာ ရနိုင်မလဲ။ *cănaw* ***m****/cămá* ***f*** *ă-hngà-kà beh-ne-ya-hma yá-nain-mă-lèh?*

Take me to this address. ကျွန်တော်/ကျွန်မကို ဒီလိပ်စာဆီ ပို့ပေးပါ။ *cănaw* ***m****/cămá* ***f*** *-go di-leiq-sa-s'i pó-pè-ba.*

Can I have a map? ကျွန်တော်/ကျွန်မ မြေပုံတစ်ခု ရနိုင်မလား။ *cănaw* ***m****/cămá* ***f*** *mye-boun tă-k'ú yá-nain-mă-là?*

Tickets

When's… to …? … က … ကို ဘယ်အချိန်ထွက်တာလဲ။ *…gá …go beh ă-ćein t'weq-ta-lèh?*

the (first) bus/ boat (ပထမ) ဘတ်စ်ကား/စက်လှေ *(pă-t'ă-má) baq-săkà-/ seq-hle*

the (next) flight (နောက်ထွက်မည့်) လေယာဉ် *(nauq-t'weq-méh/myí) le-yin*

the (last) train (နောက်ဆုံး) ရထား *(nauq-s'òun) yă-t'à*

Where do I buy a ticket? ကျွန်တော်/ကျွန်မ လက်မှတ်တစ်စောင် ဘယ်နေရာမှာ ဝယ်ရမလဲ။ *cănaw* ***m****/cămá* ***f*** *leq-hmaq dă-zaun beh-ne-ya-hma weh-yá-mă-lèh?*

One/Two ticket(s) please. ကျေးဇူးပြုပြီး လက်မှတ် တစ်စောင်/နှစ်စောင်ပေးပါ။ *cè-zù pyú-bì leq-hmaq dă-zaun / hnă-saun pè-ba.*

For today/tomorrow. ဒီနေ့။မနက်ဖြန် အတွက် *di-né / mă-neq-p'yan ă-t'weq*

A…ticket. … လက်မှတ်တစ်စောင် … *leq-hmaq dă-zaun*

one-way အသွား *ă-thwà*

return trip အသွားအပြန် *ă-thwà-ă-pyan*

first class ပထမတန်း *pă-t'ă-má-dàn*

business class အထူးတန်း *ă-t'ù-dàn*

economy class ရိုးရိုးတန်း *yò-yò-dàn*

How much?	ဘယ်လောက်ကျသလဲ။ *beh-lauq cá-dhă-lèh?*
Is there a discount for...?	... အတွက် ဈေးလျှော့ပေးတာ ရှိသလား။ *... ă-tweq zè sháw-pè-da shí-dhă-là?*
children	ကလေးတွေ *k'ă-lè-dwe*
students	ကျောင်းသားတွေ *càun-dhà-dwe*
senior citizens	အသက်အရွယ်ကြီးသူတော *ă-theq-a-yweh cì-dhu-dwe*
tourists	ကမ္ဘာလှည့်ခရီးသွားတွေ *găba-hlèh-k´ăyì-dhwà-dwe*
The express bus/ express train, please.	ကျေးဇူးပြုပြီး အထူးဘတ်စ်ကား/အထူးရထား ပေးပါ။ *cè-zù pyú-bì ă-t'ù baq-săkà-/ ă-t'ù yă-t'à pè-ba.*
The local bus/train, please.	ကျေးဇူးပြုပြီး ဒေသတွင်းသွား ဘတ်စ်ကား/ရထား ပေးပါ။ *cè-zù pyú-bì de-thá-dwìn-dhwà baq-săkà-/yă-t'à pè-ba.*
I have an e-ticket.	ကျွန်တော်/ကျွန်မ မှာ အီး လက်မှတ်တစ်စောင် ရှိတယ်။ *cănaw* ***m****/cămá* ***f*** *-hma ì-leq-hmaq dă-zaun shí-deh.*
Can I buy...	ကျွန်တော်/ကျွန်မ ... ဝယ်လို့ ရနိုင်မလား။ *cănaw* ***m****/cămá* ***f*** *... weh-ló yá-nain-mă-là?*
a ticket on the bus/train?	ဘတ်စ်ကား/ရထား ပေါ်မှာ လက်မှတ်တစ်စောင် *baq-săkà/yă-t'à -baw-hma leq-hmaq dă-zaun.*
the ticket before boarding?	ဘတ်စ်ကား/ရထား ပေါ်မတက်ခင် လက်မှတ် *baq-săkà-/yă-t'à -baw mă-teq-k'in- leq-hmaq*
How long is this ticket valid?	လက်မှတ်က ဘယ်လောက်ကြာကြာ တရားဝင်လဲ။ *leq-hmaq-ká bă-lauq ca-ja tă-yà win-lèh?*
Can I return on the same ticket?	ဒီလက်မှတ်နဲ့ပဲ ပြန်လာလို့ရနိုင်မလား။ *di-leq-hmaq-néh-bèh pyan-la-ló yá-nain-mă-là?*
I'd like to... my reservation.	ကျွန်တော်/ကျွန်မရဲ့ ကြိုတင်နေရာယူထားတာကို ... ချင်ပါတယ်။ *cănaw* ***m*** */cămá* ***f*** *-yéh co-tin-ne-ya-yu-t'á-da-go ... ćin-ba-deh.*
cancel	ဖျက် *p'yeq-*
change	ပြောင်း *pyàun-*
confirm	အတည်ပြု *ă-ti pyú-*

For Time, see page 170.

Plane

Airport Transfer

How much is a taxi to the airport?	လေဆိပ်ကို အငှားကားခ ဘယ်လောက်ကျလဲ။ *le-zeiq-ko ă-hngà-kà-gá bă-lauq cá-léh?*
To…Airport, please.	ကျေးဇူးပြုပြီး … လေဆိပ်ကိုပို့ပေးပါ။ *cè-zù pyú-bì … le-zeiq-ko pó-pè-ba.*
My airline is…	ကျွန်တော်/ ကျွန်မရဲ့ လေကြောင်းလိုင်းက … ဖြစ်တယ်။ *cănaw* **m**/*cămá* **f** *-yéh le-jàun-làin-gá … p'yiq-teh.*
My flight leaves at…	ကျွန်တော်/ကျွန်မရဲ့ လေယာဉ်က … အချိန် ထွက်မှာဖြစ်တယ်။ *cănaw* **m**/*cămá* **f***-yéh le-yin-gá … ă-c'ein- t´weq-hma p'yiq-teh.*
I'm in a rush.	အရေးကြီးနေတယ်။ *cănaw* **m**/*cămá* **f** *ă-yè cì-ne-deh.*
Can you take an alternate route?	ခင်ဗျား/ ရှင် တခြားရွေးစရာ လမ်းကြောင်းတစ်ခုကနေ သွားနိုင်မလား။ *k'ămy* **m** */shin* **f** *-tă-c'à ywè-ză-ya làn-jàun tă-k'ú-gá-ne thwà-nain-mălèh.*
Can you drive faster/slower?	ခင်ဗျား/ ရှင် ပိုပြီးမြန်မြန်။ပိုပြီးနှေးနှေး မောင်းနိုင်မလား။ *k'ămyà* **m** */shin* **f** *- po-bì myan-myan / po-bì hnè-hnè màun-nain-mă-là?*

YOU MAY HEAR…

ခင်ဗျား/ ရှင် ဘယ်လေကြောင်းလိုင်းနဲ့ သွားမှာလဲ။ *k'ămyà* **m** */shin* **f** *beh le-jàun-laìn-néh thwà-hma-lèh?*	What airline are you flying?
ပြည်တွင်း ဒါမှမဟုတ် ပြည်ပ လား။ *pyi-dwìn da-hmá-mă-houq pyi-pá là?*	Domestic or International?
ဘယ် တာမနယ်လ် လဲ။ *k'ămyà* **m**/*shin* **f** *beh ta-mă-nel lèh?*	What terminal?

YOU MAY SEE...

ဆိုက်ရောက်	arrivals
ထွက်ခွာ	departures
ခရီးသွားအိတ်ထုတ်ယူရန်	baggage claim
လုံခြုံရေး	security
ပြည်တွင်း လေယာဉ်များ	domestic flights
ပြည်ပ လေယာဉ်များ	international flights
ချက်ခ်အင် (လေယာဉ်ပေါ်တက်ရန်လက်မှတ်ယူသည့်နေရာ)	check-in desk
ထွက်ခွာဂိတ်များ	departure gates

Checking In

Where's check-in?	ချက်ခ်အင် လုပ်တဲ့နေရာက ဘယ်မှာလဲ။ *c'eq-in louq-téh-ne-ya-gá-beh-hma-lèh?*
My name is...	ကျွန်တော်/ ကျွန်မရဲ့ နာမည်က ... ဖြစ်တယ်။ *cănaw **m**/cămá **f**-yéh nan-meh-gá ... p'yiq-teh.*
I'm going to...	ကျွန်တော်/ ကျွန်မ ... ကို သွားမလို့။ *cănaw **m**/cămá **f**... go thwà-măló.*
I have...	ကျွန်တော်/ ကျွန်မမှာ ... ပါတယ်။ *cănaw **m**/cămá **f** -hma ... pa-deh.*
one suitcase	ခရီးဆောင်အိတ် တစ်လုံး *k'ăyì-zaun-eiq tăloùn*
two suitcases	ခရီးဆောင်အိတ် နှစ်လုံး *k'ăyì-zaun-eiq hnă-loùn*
one piece	တစိတ်တပိုင်း *dăzeiq-dăbaìn*
How much luggage is allowed?	အိတ်အလေးချိန် ဘယ်လောက်ခွင့်ပြုသလဲ။ *eiq ă-lè-jein bălauq-k'wín pyú-dhălèh?*
Is that pounds or kilos?	အဲ့ဒါ ပေါင် ဒါမှမဟုတ် ကီလို လား။ *éh-da-gá paun da-hmá-mă-houq ki-lo lá?*
Which terminal?	ဘယ် တာမနယ်လ် မှာလဲ။ *beh ta-mă-nel-hma-lèh?*
Which gate?	ဘယ်ဂိတ်လဲ။ *beh geiq-lèh?*

I'd like a window/ an aisle seat. ကျွန်တော်/ ကျွန်မ ပြတင်းပေါက်ဖက်ကထိုင်ခုံ။ အစွန်ဖက်ကထိုင်ခုံ တစ်ခုံလိုချင်ပါတယ်။ *cănaw* **m**/*cămá* **f** *bă-dìn-bauq-p'eq-ká t'ain-goun / ă-sun-beq-ká t'ain-goun tă-lòun lo-jin-ba-deh.*

When do we leave/arrive? ကျွန်တော် / ကျွန်မ တို့ ဘယ်အချိန် ထွက်။ရောက် မှာလဲ။ *cănaw* **m**/*cămá* **f** *dó beh ă-c'ein t'weq-/yauq-hma-lèh?*

Is the flight delayed? လေယာဉ်က နောက်ကျတာလား။ *le-yin-gá nauq-cá-ta-là?*

How late? ဘယ်လောက် နောက်ကျမှာလဲ။ *bă-lauq nauq-cá-hma-lèh?*

YOU MAY HEAR...

နောက်တစ်ယောက် *nauq tă-yauq* — Next!

ကျေးဇူးပြုပြီး ခင်ဗျားရဲ့/ ရှင့်ရဲ့ နိုင်ငံကူး လက်မှတ်/လက်မှတ် ပြပါ။ *cè-zù pyú-bì k'ămyà-yéh* **m**/ *shín-yéh* **f**-*nain-ngan-kù leq-hmaq/ leq-hmaq pyá-ba.* — Your ticket/passport, please.

ခင်ဗျား/ ရှင့် ခရီးသွားအိတ်တစ်ခုခု အပ်မှာလား။ *k'ămyà* **m**/ *shín* **f** *k'ăyì-dhwà eiq tăk'ú-k´ú áq-hma-là?* — Are you checking any luggage?

ဒီအိတ်က လက်ဆွဲအိတ် (လက်ကကိုင်သွားဖို့အိတ်) လုပ်ဖို့အတွက် တော်တော်ကြီးနေတယ်။ *di-eiq-ká leq-s'wèh-eiq (leq-ká kain-dhwà-bó eiq) louq-p'ó-ătweq taw-taw cì-ba-deh.* — That's too large for a carry-on [piece of hand luggage].

ဒီအိတ်ကို ခင်ဗျားဘာသာ/ ရှင့်ဘာသာ ထည့်တာလား။ *di-eiq-ko k'ămyà -ba-dha* **m**/ *shin-b-dha* **f** *-t'éh-da-là?* — Did you pack these bags yourself?

တစ်ယောက်ယောက် က ခင်ဗျား/ ရှင် သယ်သွားဖို့ တစ်ခုခု ပေးလိုက်သလား။ *tăyauq-yauq-ká k'ămyà theh-dhwà-bó tă-k'ú-kú pè-laiq-dhălà?* — Did anyone give you anything to carry?

ခင်ဗျားရဲ့/ ရှင့်ရဲ့ ဖိနပ်တွေကို ချွတ်ပါ။ *k'ămyà-yéh* **m**/*shin-yéh* **f** *p'ănaq-twe-ko c'uq-pa.* — Take off your shoes.

အခု လေယာဉ်ပေါ်တက်နေပြီ။... *ăk'ú... le-yin-baw teq-ne-byi.* Now boarding...

Luggage

Where is/are…? …က/ တွေက ဘယ်နေရာမှာလဲ
…gá/dwe-gá- beh-ne-ya-hma-lèh?

the luggage trolleys ခရီးသွားအိတ်တင် လက်တွန်းလှည်းတွေ
k'ă-yì-dhwà eiq-tin-leq-tùn-hlèh-dwe.

the baggage claim ခရီးသွားအိတ် ထုတ်ယူတဲ့နေရာ
k'ă-yì-dhwà eiq-t´ouq-yu-déh-ne-ya

My luggage has been lost/stolen. ကျွန်တော်ရဲ့ / ကျွန်မရဲ့ ခရီးသွားအိတ် ပျောက်သွားတယ်/ ခိုးယူခံရတယ်။ *cănaw-yéh* ***m****/ cămá-yéh* ***f*** *k'ă-yì-dhwà eiq-pyauq-thwà-deh/ kò-yu-k´an-yá-deh*

My suitcase is damaged. ကျွန်တော်ရဲ့/ ကျွန်မရဲ့ ခရီးဆောင်အိတ် ပျက်စီးသွားတယ်။
cănaw-yéh ***m****/cămá-yéh* ***f****- k'ă-yì-zaun–eiq-pyeq-sì-dwèh-deh*

Finding your Way

Where is/are…? …တွေက ဘယ်နေရာမှာလဲ
…dwe-gá-beh-ne-ya-hma-lèh?

the currency exchange ငွေကြေးလဲလှယ်တဲ့နေရာ
ngwe-cè-lèh-hleh-déh-ne-ya

the exit ထွက်ပေါက် *t´weq-pauq*

the taxis အငှားကားတွေ *ăhngà-kà-dwe*

Is there…into town? မြို့ထဲကို သွားတဲ့… ရှိသလား။
Myó-dèh-go-thwà-téh…shí-dhălà?

a bus ဘတ်စ်ကား တစ်စီး *baq-săkà-dăsì*

a train ရထား တစ်စီး *yătà-dăsì*

For Asking Directions, see page 34.

Train

Where's the train station?	ရထားဘူတာရုံက ဘယ်မှာလဲ။ *yătà-bu-ta-youn-gá-bèh-hma-lèh?*
How far is it?	အဲဒါက ဘယ်လောက်ဝေးသလဲ။ *Èh-da-gá-beh-lauq-wè-dhălèh?*
Where is/are…?	… က/ တွေက ဘယ်နေရာမှာရှိလဲ။ *…gá/dwe-gá-beh-ne-ya-hma-shí-lèh*
the ticket office	လက်မှတ်ရုံ *leq-hmaq-youn*
the information desk	စုံစမ်းမေးမြန်းရန်နေရာ *soun-zàn-mè-myàn-yan-ne-ya*
the platforms	ပလက်ဖောင်းတွေ *păleq-p´ăùn-dwe*
Can I have a schedule [timetable]?	ကျွန်တော်/ ကျွန်မ ခရီးစဉ် တစ်ခု ရနိုင်မလား။ *cănaw* **m**/*cămá* **f**- *k'ăyì-zin tăk´ú-ya-nain-mălà?*
How long is the trip?	ခရီးက ဘယ်လောက်ကြာမှာလဲ။ *k'ăyì-gá-beh-lauq-ca-hma-lèh?*
Is it a direct train?	ဒါက တိုက်ရိုက် ရထားလား။ *Da-gá-daiq-yaiq-yătà-là?*
Do I have to change trains?	ကျွန်တော်/ ကျွန်မ ရထားပြောင်းစီး ရမှာလား။ *cănaw* **m**/*cămá* **f**- *yatà-pyaùn-si-yá-mălà?*
Is the train on time?	ရထားက အချိန်မှန် ထွက်မှာလား။ *yătà-gá- ăćein-hman- t´weq-hma-là?*

YOU MAY SEE…

ပလက်ဖောင်းများ	platforms
စုံစမ်းမေးမြန်းရန်	information
ကြိုတင်နေရာယူရန်	reservations
စောင့်ဆိုင်းရန်နေရာ	waiting room
ဆိုက်ရောက်	arrivals
ထွက်ခွာ	departures

Departures

Which track [platform] to…?	… ကိုသွားဖို့ ဘယ်လမ်းကြောင်း (ပလက်ဖောင်း)လဲ။ *…go-thwà-bó-beh-làn-jaùn (păleq-p´aùn-) lèh?*
Is this the track [platform]/ train to…?	ဒီလမ်းကြောင်း (ပလက်ဖောင်း)/ရထားက… ကို သွားတာလား။ *di-làn-jaùn-(păleq-p´aùn)/ yătà-gá...go thwà-da-là?*
Where is track [platform]…?	… လမ်းကြောင်း (ပလက်ဖောင်း)က ဘယ်မှာလဲ။ *…làn-jaùn-(păleq-p´aùn) gá beh-hma-lèh?*
Where do I change for…?	… ကိုသွားဖို့ ကျွန်တော်/ ကျွန်မ ဘယ်နေရာမှာ ပြောင်းရမလဲ။ *…go-thwà-bó- cănaw* **m** */cămá* **f** *beh-ne-ya-hma-pyaùn-ya-măléh?*

On Board

Can I sit here/open the window?	ကျွန်တော်/ ကျွန်မ ဒီနေရာမှာ ထိုင်လို့ရနိုင်မလား။ ပြတင်းပေါက်ဖွင့်လို့ ရနိုင်မလား။ *cănaw* **m***/cămá* **f** *di-ne-ya-hma-t´ain-ló-yá-nain-mălà?*
That's my seat.	ဒါက ကျွန်တော်/ ကျွန်မ ရဲ့ထိုင်ခုံ *cănaw* **m***/cămá* **f** *yéh- t´ain-k´oun*
Here's my reservation.	ဒီမှာ ကျွန်တော်/ ကျွန်မ ရဲ့ကြိုတင်နေရာယူထားတာပါ။ *di-hma-cănaw* **m***/cămá* **f** *yéh-co-tin-ne-ya-yu-t´à da-ba.*

YOU MAY HEAR...

ကျေးဇူးပြုပြီး လက်မှတ်ပြပါ။ *Cè-zù-pyú-byì- leq-hmaq-pyá-ba* — Tickets, please.

ခင်ဗျားရှင်... မှာ ပြောင်းရလိမ့်မယ်။ *...k´myà* ***m****/shin* ***f****...hma-pyaùn-yà-leín-meh.* — You have to change at...

နောက်မှတ်တိုင်... *Nauq-hmaq-tain* — Next stop...

Bus

Where's the bus station? ဘတ်စ်ကားဂိတ် က ဘယ်မှာလဲ။ *baskà-geiq-gá-beh-hmăléh?*

How far is it? အဲဒါက ဘယ်လောက်ဝေးလဲ။ *Èh-da-gá- beh-louq-wè-lèh?*

How do I get to...? အဲဒီ...နေရာကို ကျွန်တော်/ကျွန်မ ဘယ်လိုရောက်နိုင်မလဲ။ *Èh-di...ne-ya-go-cănaw* ***m****/cămá* ***f****-beh-lo-youq-nain-mălèh?*

Is this the bus to...? ဒီဘတ်စ်ကားက...ကိုသွားတဲ့ဘတ်စ်ကားလား။ *di- baskà-gá...go-thwà-dèh- baskà-là?*

Can you tell me when to get off? ဘယ်နေရာမှာ ဆင်းရမလဲဆိုတာ ကျွန်တော်/ကျွန်မကို ခင်ဗျားပြောပြနိုင်မလား။ *beh-ne-ya-hma-sìn-ya-mălèh-so-da-cănaw* ***m****/cămá* ***f*** *-go-k´amya-pyàw-pyà-nain-mălèh?*

Do I have to change buses? ကျွန်တော်/ကျွန်မ ဘတ်စ်ကားတွေ ပြောင်းစီးရမှာလား။ *cănaw* ***m****/cămá* ***f****-baskà-dwe-pyaùn-sì-ya-mălèh?*

Stop here, please! ကျေးဇူးပြုပြီး ဒီနေရာမှာရပ်ပေးပါ။ *cè-zù-pyú-byì-di-ne-ya-hma-yáq-pè-ba*

YOU MAY SEE...

ဘတ်စ်ကားမှတ်တိုင် — bus stop

ဘတ်စ်ကားရပ်ရန်တောင်းဆိုပါ။ — request stop

ဝင်ပေါက်/ထွက်ပေါက် — entrance/exit

သင့်ရဲ့လက်မှတ်ကို တုံးထုပါ။ — stamp your ticket

Jeep / Pick-up Trucks

Where's the jeep station?	ဂျစ်ကားဂိတ် က ဘယ်နေရာမှာလဲ။ *cè-zù-pyú-byì-jiq-kà-qeiq-kà-beh-ne-ya-hmalèh?*
Is this the jeep to…?	ဒီဂျစ်ကားက…ကို သွားတာလား။ *di-jiq-kà…go-thwà-da-là?*
What time are you leaving?	ခင်ဗျား/ ရှင် ဘယ်အချိန်ထွက်မှာလဲ။ *k'ămyà-***m***/shin* **f** *beh-ăćein-t´weq-hmalèh?*
What time will we get there?	အဲဒီကို ကျွန်တော်/ ကျွန်မ တို့ ဘယ်အချိန်ရောက်မှာလဲ။ *Èh-di-go- cănaw* **m***/cămá* **f** *dó-beh-ăćein-youq-mălèh?*
Is this my stop?	ဒီဟာက ကျွန်တော်/ ကျွန်မ ဆင်းရမည့် မှတ်တိုင်လား။ *di-ha-gà-cănaw* **m***/cămá* **f** *s'ìn-yá-méh* *(myí)-hmaq-tain-lèh?*
Where are we?	ကျွန်တော်/ ကျွန်မ တို့ အခုဘယ်နေရာမှာလဲ။ *cănaw* **m***/cămá* **f** *dó-ăkú-beh-ne-ya-hma-lèh?*

Boat & Ferry

When is the boat/ ferry to…?	…ကိုသွားတဲ့ စက်လှေ(သင်္ဘော)/ ဇက် က ဘယ်အချိန်လဲ။ *…go-thwà-déh-seq-hleh(thàìn-bàw)/ zeq-ká-beh-* *ăćein-lèh?*
What time is the next sailing?	နောက်ထွက်မဲ့သင်္ဘောက ဘယ်အချိန်လဲ။ *nauq-t´weq-méh(myí)- thìn-bàw-ga-beh-ăćein-lèh?*

Can I book a seat/cabin?	ကျွန်တော်/ကျွန်မ ထိုင်ခုံတစ်ခုံ/အခန်းတစ်ခန်း ကြိုတင်ဘွတ်ကင်ယူလို့ရနိုင်မလား။ *cănaw* ***m****/cămá-****f*** *t´ain-g´oun/tă-k´oun/ăk´àn-tă-k´àn-co-tin-buq--kin-yu-ló-ya-nain-mălà?*
How long is the crossing?	ကူးတာ ဘယ်လောက်ကြာမှာလဲ။ *kù-da-beh-lauq-ca-hmalèh?*

For Tickets, see page 20.

YOU MAY SEE…

အသက်ကယ်လှေများ	life boats
အသက်ကယ်အင်္ကျီ	life jackets

Myanmar has more than 3000 miles (5000km) of navigable river, with multiple route and vessel options: you can travel in local slowboats in basic 'deck class' with monks, soldiers, mothers and their children and even chickens, or go 'first class' on the upper deck with benches and a table (in both of the latter instances, bring mosquito repellant and blankets), or take faster, more modern or even luxury tourist cruisers.

Taxi

Where can I get a taxi?	အငှားကားတစ်စီး ကျွန်တော်/ ကျွန်မ ဘယ်နေရာမှာ ရနိုင်မလဲ။ *Ăhngà-kà-dazì- Cănaw* **m**/*cămá* **f**-*beh-ne-ya-hma- yá-nain-mălèh?*
Can you send a taxi?	အငှားကားတစ်စီး ခင်ဗျား/ ရှင် ပို့ပေးနိုင်မလား။ *Ăhngà-kà-dăzì-k´ămya* **m**/*shin* **f**-*pó-pè-nain-mălà*
Do you have the number for a taxi?	အငှားကားခေါ်တဲ့ ဖုန်းနံပါတ် ခင်ဗျား/ ရှင့် ဆီမှာ ရှိသလား။ *Ăhngà -kà-k´aw-déh-p´oùn-nan-baq-k´ămya* **m**/*shin* **f**-*s'i-hma- shi-dhălà?*
I'd like a taxi now/ for tomorrow at...	အငှားကားတစ်စီး အခု/ မနက်ဖြန်... အချိန်မှာ လိုချင်ပါတယ်။ *ăhngà-kà-dăzì-ăk´ću/măneq-p´yan...ăćein-hma-lo-jin-ba-deh*
Pick me up at...	ကျွန်တော်/ ကျွန်မ ကို.... အချိန်မှာ လာကြိုပေးပါ။ *cănaw* **m**/*cămá* **f**-*go...ăcein-hma- la-co-pè-ba.*
I'm going to...	ကျွန်တော်/ ကျွန်မ .... ကို သွားမလို့။ *cănaw* **m**/*cămá* **f**...*go- thwà-mălό*
this address	ဒီလိပ်စာ *di-leiq-sa*
the airport	လေဆိပ် *lezeiq*
the bus/train station	ဘတ်စ်ကားဂိတ်/ ဘူတာရုံ *baqsăkà-geiq/bu-da-youn*
the river boat jetty	မြစ်တွင်းသွားစက်လှေ (သင်္ဘော) ဆိပ်ခံဘောတံတား *myiq-twìn-thwà-swq-hle (thin-baw) s'eiq-k´an-baw-dădà*
the ferry	ဇက် *zeq*
I'm late.	ကျွန်တော်/ ကျွန်မ နောက်ကျနေတယ်။ *cănaw* **m**/*cămá* **f** *nauq-cá-ne-deh*
Can you drive faster/slower?	ခင်ဗျား/ ရှင် ပိုပြီးမြန်မြန်/ ပိုပြီးနှေးနှေး မောင်းနိုင်မလား။ *k´ămyà* **m**/*shin* **f** *po-byi-myan-myan/po-byi-hnè-hnè maùn-nain-mălà?*
Stop/Wait here.	ဒီနေရာမှာ စောင့်ပါ/ ရပ်ပါ။ *di-ne-ya-hma-saún-ba/yauq-pa*
How much?	ဘယ်လောက်ကျလဲ။ *beh-louq-cá-lèh*
You said it would cost...	ဒါက ... လောက်ကျမယ်လို့ ခင်ဗျား/ ရှင် ပြောခဲ့တယ်။ *da-gá...lauq-cá-meh-ló-k´ămya* **m**/*sjom* **f** *pyàw-géh-deh*

YOU MAY HEAR…

ဘယ်ကိုသွားမှာလဲ။ *beh-go-thwà-hma-lèh?*	Where to?
လိပ်စာက ဘာလဲ။ *leìq-sa-gá-ba-lèh?*	What's the address?
ညဖက်/လေဆိပ် အတွက် အပိုကြေးပေးရတာတစ်ခု ရှိတယ်။ *nyá-baq/le-z´eiq-ătweq-ăpo-jè-pè-yá-da-tăk´ ú-shí-deh*	There's a nighttime/ airport surcharge.

Keep the change.	ပြန်အမ်းငွေကို ယူထားလိုက်ပါ။ *pyan-àn-ngwe-go-yu-t´à-laiq-pb*

Bicycle, Motorbike & Trishaw

I'd like to hire…	ကျွန်တော်/ကျွန်မ…ငှား ချင်တယ်။ *cănaw* **m**/*cămá* **f**… *hngà-jin-deh*
a bicycle	စက်ဘီးတစ်စီး *seq-beìn-dăzì*
a moped	စက်တပ်ထားတဲ့ဆိုင်ကယ်တစ်စီး *seq-taq-t´à-déh-s'ain-keh-dăzì*
a motorcycle	မော်တော်ဆိုင်ကယ် *maw-taw-s'ain-keh*
a trishaw	ဆိုက်ကားတစ်စီး *s'aiq-kà-dăzì*
How much to go to…?	…ကိုသွားဖို့ ဘယ်လောက်ကျလဲ။ *…go-thwà-bó-beh-lauq-cá-lèh?*

How much per day/week? တစ်ရက်/ တစ်ပတ် ကို ဘယ်လောက်ကျလဲ။ *tăyeq/dăbaq-ko-beh-lauq-cá-lèh?*

Do you have a helmet/lock? ခင်ဗျား/ ရှင့် မှာ ဟဲလ်မက်ဦးထုပ်/ သော့ခလောက် ရှိသလား။ *k´ămya* **m**/*shin* **f** *hma-hèh-meq-ouq-t´ouq-/thaw-gălauq-shí-dhălà?*

I have a puncture/ flat tyre. ကျွန်တော့်/ ကျွန်မ ရဲ့ ဘီးပေါက်သွားတယ်/ ဘီးပြားနေတယ်။ *cănaw* **m**/*cămá* **f** *yéh-bèin-pauq-thwà-deh/ bèin-pyà-ne-deh*

Car & Driver

Where's the car hire? ကားငှားတဲ့နေရာက ဘယ်မှာလဲ။ *kà-hngà-déh-ne-ya-gá-beh-hma-lèh?*

How much…? …ကို ဘယ်လောက်ကျလဲ။ *…go-beh-lauq-cá-lèh?*

per day/week တစ်ရက်/ တစ်ပတ် *tăyeq/dăbaq*

to go to… …ကိုသွားဖို့ *… go-thwà-bó*

Are there any discounts? ဈေးလျှော့တာတစ်မျိုးမျိုး ရှိသလား။ *zè-sháw-da-tămyò-myò-shí-dhălà?*

What time are we leaving? ကျွန်တော်/ ကျွန်မ တို့ ဘယ်အချိန်ထွက်မှာလဲ။ *cănaw* **m**/*cămá* **f** *dó-beh-ăćein-t´weq-hma-lèh?*

What time will we get there? အဲဒီကို ကျွန်တော်/ ကျွန်မ တို့ ဘယ်အချိန်ရောက်မှာလဲ။ *Èh-di-go- Cănaw* **m**/*cămá* **f** *dó-beh-ăćein-yauq-hma-lèh?*

Asking Directions

Is this the way to…? ဒီလမ်းက…ကို သွားတဲ့လမ်းလား။ *di-làn-gá…go-thwà-déh-làn-là?*

How far is it to…? …ကို ဘယ်လောက်ဝေးလဲ။ *…go-beh-lauq-wè-lèh?*

Where's…? …က ဘယ်နေရာမှာလဲ။ *…gá-beh-be-ya-hma-lèh.*

…Street …လမ်း *…làn*

this address ဒီလိပ်စာ *di-leiq-sa*

Can you show me on the map? ခင်ဗျား/ ရှင် ကျွန်တော့်/ ကျွန်မ ကို မြေပုံပေါ်မှာပြနိုင်မလား။ *k´ămya* **m**/*shin* **f** *cănaw* **m**/*cămá* **f** *go-mye-boun-baw-hma-pyá-nain-mălà?*

I'm lost. ကျွန်တော်/ ကျွန်မ လမ်းပျောက်နေတယ်။ *cănaw* **m**/*cămá* **f** *làn-pyaq-ne-deh.*

YOU MAY HEAR…

ရှေ့တည့်တည့် *shé-téh-téh* straight ahead

ဘယ်ဖက် *beh-beq* left

ညာဖက် *nya-beq* right

လမ်းထောင့်ချိုးနားမှာ *làn-daún-jò-nà-hma* around the corner

ဆန့်ကျင်ဖက် *s'án-cin-beq* opposite

နောက်မှာ *nauq-hma* behind

ကပ်လျက် *kaq-hlyeq* next to

ပြီးရင် *pyì-yìn* after

မြောက်/ တောင် *myauq/taun* north/south

အရှေ့/အနောက် *ăshé/ănauq* east/west

မီးပွိုင့်မှာ *mì-pwaín-hma* at the traffic light

လမ်းဆုံတဲ့နေရာမှာ *làn-s'oun-déh-ne-ya-hma* at the intersection

YOU MAY SEE...

ရပ်။	stop
ရပ်ပါ။	yield
ကား မရပ်ရ။	no parking
တစ်လမ်းမောင်း	one way
မဝင်ရ	no entry
မည်သည့်ယာဉ်မှ ဝင်ခွင့်မပြု	no vehicles allowed
ဖြတ်မသွားရ	no passing
ရှေ့တွင် ယာဉ်ကြောအချက်ပြမီး ရှိသည်။	traffic signals ahead
ထွက်ပေါက်	exit

Breakdown & Repair

My ... broke down/ won't start. ကျွန်တော်/ ကျွန်မ ရဲ့...ပျက်သွားတယ်။ စက်နှိုးလို့မရဘူး။ *cănaw* ***m****/cămá* ***f*** *yèh...pyeq-thwà-deh/seq-hnò-ló-măyá-bù*

Can you fix it (today)? ခင်ဗျား/ ရှင် ဒါကို (ဒီနေ့) ပြင်ပေးလို့ရနိုင်မလား။ *k´ămyà* ***m****/shin* ***f*** *da-go (di-né) pyin-bè-ló-yá-nain-mălà?*

When will it be ready? အဲဒါက ဘယ်အချိန် အဆင်သင့်ဖြစ်မလဲ။ *Èh-da-gá-beh-ăćein-ăs'in-dhín-p´yiq-mălèh?*

How much? ဘယ်လောက်ကျသလဲ။ *Beh-lauq-cá-dhălèh?*

Accidents

There was an accident. မတော်တဆထိခိုက်မှုတစ်ခု ဖြစ်ခဲ့တယ်။ *mătaw-tăs'á-t´í-k´aiq-hmú-tăk´ú-p´yiq-k´éh-deh*

Call an ambulance/ the police. လူနာတင်ကားတစ်စီး။ရဲ ကို ခေါ်ပါ။ *lu-na-tin-kă-dăzì/yèh-go-k´aw-ba*

Places to Stay

ESSENTIAL

Can you recommend a hotel?	ခင်ဗျား/ ရှင် ဟိုတယ်တစ်ခု ညွှန်းပေးနိုင်မလား။ *k´ămyà **m**/shin **f** ho-teh-tăk´u-hnyùn-pè-nain-mălà?*
I made a reservation.	ကျွန်တော်/ ကျွန်မ ကြိုတင်အခန်းယူမှု လုပ်ခဲ့တယ်။ *cănaw **m**/cămá **f** co-tin-ăk´àn-yu-hmú-louq-k´éh-deh.*
My name is…	ကျွန်တော်ရဲ့/ ကျွန်မရဲ့ နာမည်က … ဖြစ်ပါတယ်။ *cănaw-yéh **m**/cămá-yéh **f** nan-mehgá… p´yiq-pa-deh*
Do you have a room…?	ခင်ဗျား/ ရှင့် မှာ … အခန်းတစ်ခန်း ရှိသလား။ *k´ămyà **m**/shin **f** hma…ăk´àn-tăk´àn-shí-dhălà?*
for one/two	လူ တစ်ယောက်။နှစ်ယောက်အတွက် *lu-tăyauq/hnăyauq-ătweq*
with a bathroom	ရေးချိုးခန်းတစ်ခု တွဲပါတဲ့ *ye-ćo-gàn-tăk´ú-twèh-pa-déh*
with air conditioning	လေအေးပေးစက်ပါတဲ့ *le-è-pè-zeq-pa-déh*
For…	… အတွက် *…ătewq*
tonight	ဒီနေ့ *di-né*
two nights	နှစ်ရက် *hnăyeq*
one week	တစ်ပတ် *dăbaq*
How much?	ဘယ်လောက်ကျသလဲ။ *beh-lauq-cá-dhălèh?*
Is there anything cheaper?	ဒီ့ထက်ဈေးသက်သာတာရှိသလား။ *di-t´eq-zé-theq-tha-da-shí-dhălà?*
When's checkout?	ဟိုတယ်က ချက်ခ်အောက် ထွက်ပေးရတဲ့အချိန်က ဘယ်အချိန်လဲ။ *ho-teh-gá-ćeq-auq-t´weq-pè-yà-déh-ăćein-gá-beh-ăćein-lèh?*
Can I leave this in the safe?	ကျွန်တော်/ ကျွန်မ ဒါကို မီးခံသေတ္တာထဲမှာ ထားခဲ့လို့ရနိုင်မလား။ *cănaw **m**/cămá **f** da-go-mì-gan-thiq-ta-t´èh-hma-t´a-géh-ló-yá-nain-mălà?*

Can I leave my bags?	ကျွန်တော့်/ ကျွန်မ ရဲ့ အိတ်ကို ထားခဲ့လို့ရမလား။ *cănaw* **m**/*cămá* **f** *yèh-eiq-ko-t´à-géh-ló-yá-mălà?*
Can I have my bill/ a receipt?	ကျွန်တော့်ရဲ့/ ကျွန်မရဲ့ ငွေတောင်းခံလွှာ။ ငွေဖြတ်ပိုင်းတစ်စောင် ရနိုင်မလား။ *cănaw* **m**/*cămá* **f** *yèh-ngwe-taùn-k´an-hlwa/ngwe-p´yaq-pain-dăzaun-yà-nain-mălà?*
I'll pay in cash/by credit card.	ကျွန်တော်/ ကျွန်မ ပိုက်ဆံနဲ့။အကြွေးဝယ်ကတ်နဲ့ ငွေချေမယ်။ *cănaw* **m**/*cămá* **f** *paiq-s'an-néh/ăcwè-weh-kaq-néh-ngwe-će-meh*

Options for places to lay your head include guesthouses in local family homes, hotels and resorts. Hotel prices vary greatly from the cheap and cheerful to expensive, luxury five-star hotels and resorts that will have all the comforts of home. Camping is officially forbidden by the government.

Somewhere to Stay

Can you recommend…?	ခင်ဗျား/ ရှင်… ညွှန်းပေးနိုင်မလား။ *k´ămyà* **m**/*shin* **f**…*hmyùn-pè-nain-mălà?*
a hotel	ဟိုတယ်တစ်ခု *ho-teh-tăk´ú*
a guesthouse (B&B)	ဧည့်ရိပ်သာတစ်ခု *éh-yeiq-tha-tăk´ú*
a resort	အပမ်းဖြေနေရာတစ်ခု *éh-yeiq-tha-tăk´ú?*
What is it near?	အဲဒါက ဘာနဲ့ နီးသလဲ။ *Èh-da-gá-ba-néh-nì-dhălèh?*
How do I get there?	အဲဒီကို ကျွန်တော် /ကျွန်မ ဘယ်လိုရောက်နိုင်မလဲ။ *Èh-di-go- cănaw* **m**/*cămá* **f** *beh-lo-yauq-nqin-mălèh?*

At the Hotel

I reserved a room. ကျွန်တော်/ ကျွန်မအခန်းတစ်ခန်း ကြိုတင်ယူခဲ့တယ် ။ *cănaw* **m**/*cămá* **f** *ăk´àn-tăk´àn-co-tin-yu-géh-deh*

I have a reservation. ကျွန်တော်/ ကျွန်မ မှာ ကြိုတင်အခန်းယူထားတာတစ်ခု ရှိတယ်။ *cănaw* **m**/*cămá* **f** *co-tin-ăk´àn-yu-t´à-da-tăk´ú-shí-deh*

My name is… ကျွန်တော်/ ကျွန်မ ရဲ့ နာမည်က…ဖြစ်ပါတယ်။ *cănaw* **m**/*cămá* **f** *yéh-nan-meh-gá… p´yiq-pa-deh.*

Do you have a room…? ခင်ဗျား/ ရှင် တို့မှာ… အခန်းတစ်ခန်း ရှိသလား။ *k´ămyà* **m**/*shin* **f** *dó-hma…ăk´àn-tăk´àn-shí-dhălà?*

- with a toilet အိမ်သာ *èin-dha*
- shower ရေးချိုးခန်းတစ်ခုပါတဲ့ *ye-ćò-gàn-tăk´ú-pa-dèh*
- with air conditioning လေအေးပေးစက်ပါတဲ့ *le-è-pè-zeq-pa-déh*
- that's smoking ဆေးလိပ်သောက်လို့ရတယ် *s'è-leiq-thauq-ló-yá-deh*
- non-smoking ဆေးလိပ်သောက်လို့မရဘူး။ *s'è-leiq-thauq-ló-măyá-bù*

For… …အတွက် …*ătweq*

- tonight ဒီည *di-nyá*
- two nights နှစ်ည *hnănyá*
- a week တစ်ပတ် *dăbaq*

Do you have…? ခင်ဗျား/ ရှင့် မှာ …ရှိသလား။ *k´ămyà* **m**/*shin* **f** *hma…shí-dhălà?*

a computer	ကွန်ပျူတာ တစ်လုံး *kun-pyu-ta-tăloùn*
(wireless) internet service	(ကြိုးမဲ့) အင်တာနက်ဝန်ဆောင်မှု *(cò-méh) in-ta-neq-wun-s'aun-hmú*
room service	အခန်းတွင်းဝန်ဆောင်မှု *ăk´àn-dwin-wun-s'aun-hmú*
a pool	ရေကူးကန်တစ်ခု *ye-kú-gan-tăk´ú*
a mosquito net	ခြင်ထောင်တစ်လုံး *ćin-daun-tăloùn*
I need…	ကျွန်တော်/ ကျွန်မ… လိုအပ်တယ်။ *cănaw* ***m****/cămá* ***f****… lo-aq-teh*
an extra bed	အိပ်ယာအပိုတစ်ခု *eiq-ya-ăpo-tăk´ú*
a cot	ကလေးအိပ်ယာ *k´ălè-eiq-ya*
a crib	ကလေးပုခက် *k´ălè-păk´eq*
Are there…?	… တွေ ရှိသလား။ *…dwe-shí-dhălà?*
pillows	ခေါင်းအုံးတွေ *gaùn-oùn-dwe*
sheets	အိပ်ယာခင်းတွေ *eiq-ya-k´ìn-dwe*
towels	တဘက်တွေ *dhăbeq-twe*
Can I have the keys?	ကျွန်တော်/ ကျွန်မ သော့တွေ ရနိုင်မလား။ *cănaw* ***m****/cămá* ***f*** *tháw-dwe-yá-nain-mălà?*

YOU MAY HEAR…

ခင်ဗျား/ ရှင့် ရဲ့ နိုင်ငံကူးလက်မှတ်/ အကြွေးဝယ်ကတ်ကျေးဇူးပြုပြီးပေးပါ။ *k´ămyà* ***m****/shin* ***f*** *yèh-nain-ngan-kù-leq-hmaq/ ăcwè-kaq-cè-zù-pyú-bì-pè-ba*	Your passport/ credit card, please.
ဒီပုံစံကိုဖြည့်ပါ။ *di-poun-zan-go-p´yé-ba*	Fill out this form.
ဒီနေရာမှာ ဆိုင်းထိုးပါ။ *di-ne-ya-hma-s'aìn-t´ò-ba*	Sign here.
ငွေကြေးသာလျှင် *ngwe-cè-dha-hlyin*	Cash only.

For Numbers, see page 168.

Price

How much per night/ week?	တစ်ည/တစ်ပတ် ကို ဘယ်လောက်ကျသလဲ။ *tănyá/dăbaq-ko-beh-lauq-cá-dhă-léh?*
Does that include breakfast/tax?	ဒီထဲမှာ နံနက်စာ။အခွန် ပါပြီးသားလား။ *di-t´èh-hma-nan-neq-sa/ăk´un-pa-byi-dhà-là?*
Are there any discounts?	ဈေးလျှော့ပေးတာတစ်ခုခု ရှိသလား။ *zè-shàw-pè-da-tăk´ú-shí-dhălà?*

Preferences

Can I see the room?	ကျွန်တော်/ကျွန်မ အခန်းကို ကြည့်လို့ရမလား။ *cănaw* **m**/*cămá* **f** *ăk´àn-go-cí-ló-yá-mălà?*
I'd like a . . . room.	ကျွန်တော်/ကျွန်မ . . . အခန်း တစ်ခန်းလိုချင်တယ်။ *cănaw* **m**/*cămá* **f** *ăk´àn-tăk´ăn-lo-jin-deh*
better	ပိုကောင်းတဲ့ *po-kaùn-déh*
bigger	ပိုကျယ်တဲ့ *po-ceh-déh*
cheaper	ပိုပြီးဈေးသက်သာတဲ့ *po-byì-zè-theq-tha-déh*
quieter	ပိုပြီးတိတ်ဆိတ်တဲ့ *po-byì-zè-teiq-s'eiq-déh*
I'll take it.	ကျွန်တော်/ကျွန်မ အဲဒါကို ယူမယ်။ *cănaw* **m**/*cămá* **f** *èh-da-go-yu-meh*
No, I won't take it.	ကျွန်တော်/ကျွန်မ အဲ့ဒါကို မယူဘူး။ *cănaw* **m**/*cămá* **f** *èh-da-go-măyu-bù*

Questions

Where is/are...?	...က/တွေက ဘယ်နေရာမှာလဲ။ *...gá/dwe-gá-beh-ne-ya-hma-lèh?*
the bar	ဘား *bà*
the bathrooms	အိမ်သာတွေ *ein-dha-dwe*
the elevator [lift]	ဓာတ်လှေကား *daq-hle-gá*
the gym	အားကစားလုပ်တဲ့နေရာ *à-găzà-louq-téh-ne-ya*
the pool	ရေကူးကန် *ye-kù-gan*
I'd like...	ကျွန်တော်/ကျွန်မ... လိုချင်တယ်။ *cănaw* ***m****/cămá* ***f****...lo-jin-deh*
a blanket	စောင်တစ်ထည် *saun-tăt´eh*
an iron	မီးပူတစ်လုံး *mì-bu-tăloùn*
the room key/key card	အခန်း *ăk´àn* သော့/သော့က *thaw/thaw-kaq*
a pillow	ခေါင်းအုံးတစ်လုံး *gaùn-oùn-tăloùn*
soap	ဆပ်ပြာ *s'aq-pya*
toilet paper	အိမ်သာသုံးစက္ကူ *eìn-dha-thoùn-seq-ku*
a towel	တဘက်တစ်ထည် *dhăbeq-tăt´eh*
Do you have an adapter for this?	ဒီဟာအတွက် ခင်ဗျား/ရှင့် မှာ သင့်တော်တဲ့လျှပ်စစ်မီးခေါင်း ရှိသလား။ *di-ha-ătweq-k´ămyà* ***m****/shin* ***f****-hma-thín-taw-déh-hlay-siq-mì-gaùn-shí-dhălà?*
How do you turn on the lights?	လျှပ်စစ်မီး ခင်ဗျား/ရှင်ဘယ်လိုဖွင့်သလဲ။ *hlaq-sin-mì-k´ămyà* ***m****/shin-* ***f*** *beh-lo-p´wín-dhălèh?*
Can you wake me at...?	ခင်ဗျား/ရှင် ကျွန်တော့်/ကျွန်မ ကို ... အချိန်မှာ နှိုးပေးနိုင်မလား။ *k´ămya* ***m****/shin* ***f****-cănaw* ***m****/cămá* ***f****-go...ăcein-hma-hnò-pè-nain-mălà?*

Can I leave this in the safe?
ကျွန်တော်/ကျွန်မ ဒါကို မီးခံသေတ္တာထဲမှာ ထားခဲ့လို့ရနိုင်မလား။
cănaw ***m****/cămá* ***f*** *da-go-mì-gan- thiq-ta-dèh-hma-t´à-géh-ló-yá-nain-mălà?*

Can I have my things from the safe?
ကျွန်တော်ရဲ့/ကျွန်မရဲ့ပစ္စည်းတွေကို မီးခံသေတ္တာထဲက ယူလို့ရနိုင်မလား။ *cănaw* ***m*** *yéh/cămá* ***f*** *yèh pyiq sì-dwe-go-mì-gan-thiq-ta-dèh-gá-yuló-yá-nain mălà?*

Can you store this for me?
ခင်ဗျား/ရှင် ဒါကို ကျွန်တော်/ကျွန်မ အတွက် သိမ်းထားပေးလို့ ရနိုင်မလား။ *k´ămya* ***m****/shin* ***f*** *da-go-cănaw* ***m****/cămá* ***f*** *ătweq-theìn-t´à-pè-ló-yá-nain-mălà?*

Is there mail /a message for me?
ကျွန်တော်/ကျွန်မ အတွက် စာ/သတင်းတစ်ခု ရှိသလား။
cănaw ***m****/cămá* ***f*** *ătweq-sa/dhădin-tăk´ú-shí-dhălà?*

Do you have a laundry service?
ခင်ဗျားတို့မှာ/ရှင်တို့မှာ အဝတ်လျှော်ပေးတဲ့ ဝန်ဆောင်မှု ရှိသလား။ *k´ămya-dó-hma* ***m****/shin-dó-hma* ***f*** *ăwuq-shaw-pè-déh-wun-s'aun-hmú-shí-dhălà?*

YOU MAY SEE...

တွန်းပါ/ဆွဲပါ	push/pull
အိမ်သာ	bathroom [toilet]
ရေချိုးခန်း	showers
ဓာတ်လှေကား	elevator [lift]
လှေကား	stairs
အဝတ်လျှော်ဆိုင်	laundry
မနှောင့်ယှက်ပါနှင့်	do not disturb
မီးအရေးပေါ်တံခါးပေါက်	fire door
(အရေးပေါ်) ထွက်ပေါက်	emergency/fire exit
အိပ်ရာမှနှိုးပေးခြင်း	wake-up call

Problems

There's a problem.	ပြဿနာတစ်ခု ရှိနေတယ်။ *pyaq-thăna-tăk´ú-shí-ne-deh*
I lost my key/ key card.	ကျွန်တော်ရဲ့/ ကျွန်မရဲ့ သော့။သော့ကဒ် ပျောက်သွားတယ်။ *cănaw-yèh* **m**/*cămá-yèh* **f**/*thaw/thaw-kaq-pyauq-thwà-deh*
I've locked my key/ key card in the room.	ကျွန်တော်ရဲ့/ ကျွန်မရဲ့ သော့။သော့ကဒ်ကို အခန်းထဲထည့်ပိတ်မိတယ်။ *cănaw-yèh* **m**/*cămá-yèh* **f**/ *thaw/thaw-kaq go-ăk´àn-dèh-t´éh-peiq-mí-deh*
There's no hot water/toilet paper.	အခန်းထဲမှာ ရေပူ။အိမ်သာသုံးစက္ကူ မရှိဘူး။ *ăk´àn-dèh-hma-ye-pu/ein-dha-thoùn-seq-ku-măshí-bù*
The room is dirty.	အခန်းက ညစ်ပတ်တယ်။ *ăk´àn-gá-nyiq-paq-teh*
There are bugs in the room.	အခန်းထဲမှာ ကြမ်းပိုးတွေ ရှိတယ်။ *ăk´àn-dèh-hma-jăpò-dwe-shí-deh*
How does… work?	…က ဘယ်လို အလုပ် လုပ်တာလဲ။ *…gá-beh-lo-ălouq-louq-ta-lèh?*
the air conditioning	လေအေးပေးစက် *le-è-pè-seq*
the fan	ပန်ကာ *pan-ga*
the light	လျှပ်စစ်မီး *hlyaq-siq-mì*
the TV	တီဗွီ *ti-bwi*
the toilet	အိမ်သာ *ein-dha*
…doesn't work.	…က အလုပ် မလုပ်ဘူး။ *…gá-ălouq-mălouq-bù*
…is broken.	…က ပျက်နေတယ်။ *… gá- pyeq-ne-deh*
Can you fix it?	အဲဒါကို ခင်ဗျား/ ရှင် ပြင်ပေးနိုင်သလား။ *Èh-da-go-k´ămyà-shin-pyin-bè-nain-dhălà?*
I'd like another room.	ကျွန်တော်/ ကျွန်မ တခြားအခန်းတစ်တစ်ခု လိုချင်တယ်။ *cănaw* **m**/*cămá* **f** *tăcà-ăk´àn-tăk´ú-lo-jin-deh*

Checking Out

When's checkout?	ဟိုတယ်က ချက်ခ်အောက် ထွက်ပေးရတာ ဘယ်အချိန်လဲ။ *ho-teh-gá-ćeq-auq-t´weq-pè-yá-da-beh-ăćein-lèh?*
Can I leave my bags here until. . .?	ကျွန်တော်ရဲ့/ ကျွန်မရဲ့ အိတ်ကို . . . အထိ ချန်ထားခဲ့လို့ရမလား။ *cănaw-yèh* **m***/cămá-yèh* **f** *eiq-ko. . . ăt´í-ćan-t´à-k´éh-ló-yá-mălà?*
Can I have an itemized bill/ a receipt?	အမျိုးအမည်တစ်ခုချင်းစီခွဲပြထားတဲ့ ငွေတောင်းခံလွှာ။ ငွေလက်ခံဖြတ်ပိုင်းတစ်စောင် /ကျွန်တော်။မ ရနိုင်မလား။ *Ămyò-ămyi-tăk´ú-jìn-zi-k´wèh-pyá-t´à-déh-ngwe-taùn-k´an-hlwa/ngwe-leq-k´an-p´yaq-paìn-dăzaun-cănaw* **m***/cămá* **f** *yá-nain-mălà?*
I think there's a mistake.	အမှားတစ်ခု ရှိနေတယ်လို့ ထင်တယ်။ *Ăhmà-tăk´ú-shí-ne-deh-ló-t´in-deh*
I'll pay in cash/by credit card.	ကျွန်တော်/ ကျွန်မ ပိုက်ဆံနဲ့။ အကြွေးဝယ်ကဒ်နဲ့ငွေချေမယ်။ *cănaw* **m***/cămá* **f** *paiq-s'an-néh/ăcwè-weh-kaq-néh-ngwe-će-meh*

There is a mandatory 10 percent tax levied on all hotel bills. Luxury hotels may charge an additional 10 percent.

Domestic Items

I need…	ကျွန်တော်/ကျွန်မ…ကို လိုအပ်တယ်။ *cănaw* **m**/*cămá* **f**…*go-lo-aq-teh*
an adapter	သင့်တော်တဲ့ လျှပ်စစ်မီးခေါင်း *thin-taw-déh-hlaq-siq-mì-gaùn*
bin bags	အမှိုက်အိတ်တွေ *ăhmaiq-eiq-twe*
a bottle opener	ပုလင်းဖွင့်တံ တစ်ချောင်း *pălin-p´wín-dan-tăćaùn*
a can opener	သံဗူးဖွင့်တဲ့အရာ တစ်ခု *than-bù-p´wín-déh-ăya-tăk´ú*
cleaning supplies	သန့်ရှင်းရေးပစ္စည်းတွေ *than-shìn-yè-pyiq-sì-dwe*
a corkscrew	ဖောက်တံဝက်အူ *p´auq-tan-weq-u*
detergent	ဆပ်ပြာမှုန့် *s'aq-pya-hmoún*
dishwashing liquid	ပန်းကန်ဆေးဆပ်ပြာရည် *băgan-s'è-s'aq-pya-ye*
a light bulb	လျှပ်စစ်မီးသီးတစ်လုံး *hlyaq-sìq-mì-dhì-tăloùn*
matches	မီးခြစ်တွေ *mì-jiq-twe*
a mosquito net	ခြင်ထောင်တစ်လုံး *ćin-daun-tăloùn*
mosquito repellant	ခြင်ပြေးဆေး *ćin-pyè-zè*
napkins	လက်သုတ်ပုဝါတွေ *leq-thouq-pàwa-dwe*
paper towels	စက္ကူပုဝါတွေ *seq-ku-păwa-dwe*
scissors	ကပ်ကြေး *kaq-cè*

YOU MAY SEE…

သောက်ရေ	drinking water

Communications

ESSENTIAL

Where's an internet cafe?	အင်တာနက်ကော်ဖီဆိုင် တစ်ဆိုင် ဘယ်နေရာမှာရှိလဲ။ *in-ta-neq-kaw-p´i-zain-tăs'ain-beh-ne-ya-hma-shí-lèh?*
Can I access the internet/check my email?	ကျွန်တော်/ ကျွန်မ အင်တာနက် ဆက်သွယ်လို့ရမလား။ ကျွန်တော်/ ကျွန်မ ရဲ့အီးမေးလ် စစ်လို့ရမလား။ *cănaw **m**/cămá **f** inta-neq-s'eq-thweh-ló-yá-mălà/ cănaw **m**/cămá **f** yèh-ì-mè-sìq-ló-yá-mălèh?*
How much per half hour/hour?	နာရီဝက်/ တစ်နာရီ ကို ဘယ်လောက်ကျသလဲ။ *na-yi-ewq-tăna-yi-go-beh-lauq-cá-dhălèh?*
How do I connect/ log on?	ကျွန်တော်/ ကျွန်မ ဘယ်လိုဆက်သွယ်ရမလဲ/ ဝင်ရမလဲ။ *cănaw **m**/cămá **f** beh-lo-s'eq-thweh-yá-mălèh/ win-yá-mălèh?*
A phone card, please.	ကျေးဇူးပြုပြီး တယ်လီဖုန်းကတ်တစ်ခု ပေးပါ။ *cè-zu-pyú-byì-teh-li-p´oùn-kaq-tăk´ú-bè-ba*
Can I have your phone number?	ခင်ဗျား/ ရှင့် ရဲ့ ဖုန်းနံပါတ် ကျွန်တော်/ ကျွန်မ ရနိုင်မလား။ *k´ămyà **m**/shin **f** yèh-p´oùn-nan-baq-cănaw **m**/cămá **f** yá-nain-mălà?*
Here's my number/email.	ဒီမှာ ကျွန်တော်/ ကျွန်မ ရဲ့ ဖုန်းနံပါတ်/ အီးမေးလ်။ *di-hma-cănaw **m**/cămá **f**-yèh-p´oùn-nan-baq/ì-mè*
Call me.	ကျွန်တော့်/ ကျွန်မ ဆီကို ဖုန်းခေါ်ပါ။ *cănaw **m**/cămá **f** zi-go-p´oùn-k´aw-ba.*
Email me.	ကျွန်တော့်/ ကျွန်မ ဆီကို အီးမေးလ်ပို့ပါ။ *cănaw **m**/cămá **f** zi-go-i-mè-pó-ba*
Hello. This is...	ဟယ်လို၊ ကျွန်တော်/ ကျွန်မ က... ပါ။ *heh-lo-cănaw **m**/cămá **f** gá...ba*
Can I speak to...?	ကျွန်တော်/ ကျွန်မ... နဲ့ စကားပြောလို့ရနိုင်မလား။ *cănaw **m**/cămá **f**...néh-zăgà-pyàw-ló-yá-nain-mălà?*

Can you repeat that?	ခင်ဗျား/ ရှင် ဒါကို ပြန်ပြောပြနိုင်မလား။ *k´ămyà* **m**/*shin* **f** *da-go-pyan-pyàw-byá-ló-yá-nain-mălà?*
I'll call back later.	ကျွန်တော်/ ကျွန်မ နောက်မှ ပြန်ခေါ်မယ်/ *cănaw* **m**/*cămá* **f** *nauq-hmá-pyan-k´aw-meh.*
Bye.	ဘိုင်းဘိုင်။ *baìn-b´ain*
Where's the post office?	စာတိုက်က ဘယ်မှာလဲ။ *Sa-daiq-ká-beh-hma-lèh?*
I'd like to send this to…	ခင်ဗျား/ ရှင် ဒါကို ပြန်ပြောပြနိုင်မလား။ *cănaw* **m**/*cămá* **f** *da-go....go-pó-jin-deh*

Online

Where's an internet cafe?	အင်တာနက်ကော်ဖီဆိုင် တစ်ဆိုင် ဘယ်မှာရှိသလဲ။ *in-ta-neq-kaw-p´i-zain-tăs'ain-beh-hma-shí-dhălèh?*
Does it have wireless internet?	အဲဒီဆိုင်မှာ ဝိုင်ယာမဲ့ (ကြိုးမဲ့) အင်တာနက် ရှိသလား။ *Èh-di-s'ain-hma-wain-ya-yéh-(cò-méh) in-ta-neq-shí-*
dhălà?	
What is the WiFi password?	ဝိုင်ဖိုင် လျှို့ဝှက်နံပါတ်က ဘာလဲ။ *wain-p´ain-shó-hweq-nan-baq-ká-ba-lèh?*
Is the WiFi free?	ဝိုင်ဖိုင်က အလကားရသလား။ *wain-p´ain-gá-ălàgà-yá-dhălà?*
Do you have bluetooth?	ခင်ဗျား/ ရှင့် မှာ ဘလူးတုသ် ရှိသလား။ *k´ămyà* **m**/*shín* **f** *hma-bălù-tú-shí-dhălà?*
Can you show me how to turn on/ off the computer?	ခင်ဗျား/ ရှင် ကျွန်တော်/ ကျွန်မ ကို ကွန်ပျူတာ ဘယ်လို ဖွင့်/ပိတ် ရသလဲ ပြနိုင်မလား။ *k´ămyà* **m**/*shin* **f** *cănaw* **m**/*cămá* **f** *go-kun-pyu-ta-beh-lo-p´wíh/peiq-yá-dhăléh-pyá-bain-mălà?*
Can I…?	ကျွန်တော်/ ကျွန်မ … ရနိုင်မလား *cănaw* **m**/*cămá* **f**…*ya-nain-mălá?*
access the internet	အင်တာနက်ဆက်သွယ်လို့ *in-ta-neq-s'eq-thweh-ló*
check my email	အီးမေးလ်စစ်လို့ *ì-mè-siq-ló*

print	ပရင့်ထုတ်လို့ *părín-t´ouq-ló*
plug in/charge my laptop/iPhone/ iPad/ BlackBerry?	ကျွန်တော်/ကျွန်မ ရဲ့ လက်ပ်တော့ပ်ကွန်ပျူတာ။ အိုင်ဖုန်း/အိုင်ပက်ဒ်/ဘလက်ဘယ်ရီဖုန်းကို ကြိုးတပ်/ဓာတ်အားသွင်းလို့ *cănaw* ***m****/cămá* ***f*** *yéh-leq- táw-kun-pyu-ta/ain-p´oùn/ ain-peq/băleq-behri-p´oùn-go-cò-taq/daq-à-thuìn-ló*
How much per hour/half hour?	နာရီဝက်/တစ်နာရီကို ဘယ်လောက်ကျသလဲ။ *na-yi-weq-tănayi-go-beh-lauq-cá-dhălèh?*
How do I…?	ကျွန်တော်/ကျွန်မ… ဘယ်လို လုပ်ရမလဲ။ *cănaw* ***m****/cămá* ***f****…beh-lo-louq-yá-mălèh?*
connect/ disconnect	ဆက်သွယ်ဖို့။ဖြတ်တောက်ဖို့ *s'eq-thweh-bó/p´yaq-tauq-p´ó*
log on/off	လော့ဂ် ဝင်/ထွက်ဖို့ *láw win/t´weq-p´ó*
type this symbol	ဒီသင်္ကေတကို … ရိုက်ထည့်ရမလဲ။ *di- thin-ke-tá-go…yaiq-t´éh-yá-mălèh?*
What's your email?	ခင်ဗျား/ရှင့် ရဲ့ အီးမေးလ် က ဘာလဲ။ *k´ămyà* ***m****/shin* ***f*** *yéh-ì-mè-gá-ba-léh?*
My email is…	ကျွန်တော်/ကျွန်မ ရဲ့ အီးမေးလ်က … ဖြစ်တယ်။ *cănaw* ***m****/cămá* ***f*** *yéh-ì-mè-gá…p´yiq-teh*
Do you have a scanner?	ခင်ဗျား/ရှင့် ဆီမှာ စကန် လုပ်တဲ့စက်တစ်ခု ရှိလား။ *k´ămyà* ***m****/shin* ***f*** *zi-hma-săkan-louq-téh-seq-tăk´ú-*

shí-là?

Social Media

Are you on Facebook/ Twitter?	ခင်ဗျား/ ရှင် ဖေ့စ်ဘွတ်ခ်/ တွစ်တာပေါ်မှာ ရှိသလား။ *k´ămyà* ***f****/shin* ***f*** *p´é-buq/twiq-ta-baw-hma-shí-dhălà?*
What's your username?	ခင်ဗျား/ ရှင့် ရဲ့ အသုံးပြုသူအမည် (ယူဆာနိမ်း) က ဘာလဲ။ *k´ămyà* ***m****/shín* ***f*** *yéh-ăthoùn-pyú-dhu-ămyi (yu-s'a-neìn) gá-ba-léh?*
I'll add you as a friend.	ခင်ဗျား/ ရှင့် ကို သူငယ်ချင်းအနေနဲ့ ကျွန်တော်/ ကျွန်မ ထည့်လိုက်မယ်။ *k´ămyà* ***m****/shín* ***f*** *go-thăngeh-jìn-ăne-néh- cănaw* ***m****/cămá* ***f*** *t´éh-laiq-meh.*
I'll follow you on Twitter.	ခင်ဗျား/ ရှင့် နောက်ကို တွစ်တာပေါ်ကနေ ကျွန်တော်/ ကျွန်မ လိုက်ကြည့်မယ်။ *k´ămyà* ***m****/shín* ***f*** *nauq-ko-twiq-ta-baw-gá-ne-cănaw* ***m****/cămá* ***f*** *laiq-cí-meh.*
Are you following...?	ခင်ဗျား/ ရှင် ... ကို လိုက်ကြည့်နေသလား။ *k´ămyà* ***m****/shin* ***f****...go-laiq-cí-ne-dhălà?*
I'll put the pictures on	ဓာတ်ပုံတွေကို ဖေ့စ်ဘွတ်ခ်/ တွစ်တာ ပေါ်မှာ ကျွန်တော်/ ကျွန်မ တင်လိုက်မယ်။ *Daq-poun-dwe-go-p´é-buq/ twiqta-baw-hma-t´éh-hma-cănaw* ***m****/ cămá* ***f*** *tin-laiq-meh.*
I'll tag you in pictures.	ဓာတ်ပုံတွေထဲမှာ ခင်ဗျား /ရှင့် နာမည် ကျွန်တော်/ ကျွန်မ တပ်ပေးလိုက်မယ်။ *Daq-poun-dwe-t´éh-hma-*

Internet access is readily available in Yangon and Mandalay and in busy tourist centres. Elsewhere, you may struggle as only 25% of the Burmese have a dependable electricity connection. Connection speeds tend to be too slow for browsing but sending and receiving emails should be possible. Wifi is standard in most high end hotels.

YOU MAY SEE…

ပိတ်ပါ	close
ဖျက်ပါ	delete
အီးမေးလ်	email
ထွက်ပါ	exit
အကူအညီ	help
ချက်ချင်းလက်ငင်း သတင်းပေးပို့မှု	instant messenger
အင်တာနက်	internet
လော့ဂ် အင်	log in
(သတင်း) အသစ်	new (message)
အဖွင့်။အပိတ်	on/off
ဖွင့်ပါ	open
ပရင့်ထုတ်ပါ	print
သိမ်းပါ	save
ပို့ပါ	send
အသုံးပြုသူအမည် (ယူဆာနိမ်း)/ လျှို့ဝှက်နံပါတ် (စာသား)	username/password
ကြိုးမဲ့ အင်တာနက်	wireless internet

k´ămyà ***m****/shín* ***f****-nan-meh-cănaw* ***m****/cămá* ***f****-taq-pé-laìq-mah.*

Phone

A phone card/prepaid phone, please.	ကျေးဇူးပြုပြီးဖုန်းကတ်/ ဖုန်းငွေကြိုသွင်းကတ် တစ်ကတ် ပေးပါ။ *Cè-zu-pyú-byì-p´oùn-kaq/ p´oùn-ngwe-co-thwìn-kaq-dăkaq-pè-ba.*
How much?	ဘယ်လောက်ကျသလဲ။ *Bălauq-cá-dhăléh?*
Where's the pay phone?	ပိုက်ဆံပေးပြောရတဲ့ဖုန်းက ဘယ်နေရာမှာလဲ။ *Paiq-s'an-pè-pyàw-yá-dèh-p´oùn-gá-beh-ne-ya-hma-léh?*
What's the area / country code for…?	…အတွက် နိုင်ငံ/ဒေသကုဒ်နံပါတ်က ဘာလဲ။ *…ătweq-nain-ngan-de-thà-kouq-nan-baq-ká-ba-lèh?*

What's the number?	စုံစမ်းမေးမြန်းဖို့အတွက် ဖုန်းနံပါတ်က ဘယ်လောက်လဲ။ *Soun-zàn-mè-myàn-bó-ătweq-p´oùn-nan-baq-ká-bălauq-lèh?*
I'd like the number for...	...အတွက် ဖုန်းနံပါတ် လိုချင်ပါတယ်။ *...ătweq-p´oùn-nan-baq-lo-jin-ba-deh*
I'd like to call collect [reverse the charges].	ကျွန်တော်/ကျွန်မ ကော်လက်ဖုန်း ဖုန်းခေါ်ချင်တယ်။ *cănaw* ***m****/cămá* ***f*** *kaw-leq-p´oùn- p´oùn-k´aw-jin-deh*
My phone doesn't work here.	ကျွန်တော့်/ကျွန်မ ရဲ့ဖုန်းက ဒီနေရာမှာ အလုပ်မလုပ်ဘူး။ *cănaw* ***m****/cămá* ***f*** *yèh- p´oùn-gá-di-ne-ya-hma-ălouq-mălouq-bù.*
What network are you on?	ဘယ်ကွန်ရက်ပေါ်မှာ ရှိတာလဲ။ *beh-kun-yeq-paw-hma-shí-da-lèh?*
Is it 3G?	အဲဒါက 3G လား။ *Èh-da-gá-thărì-ji-là?*
I have run out of credit/minutes.	ကျွန်တော့်/ကျွန်မ မှာ အကြွေး/မိနစ် ကုန်သွားပြီ။ *cănaw* ***m****/cămá* ***f*** *hma-ăcwè-mí-niq-koun-dhwà-bi*
Can I buy some credit?	ကျွန်တော်/ကျွန်မ အကြွေးနည်းနည်း ဝယ်လို့ရမလား။ *cănaw* ***m****/cămá* ***f*** *ăcwè-nèh-nèh-weh-ló-yá-mălà?*
Do you have phone charger?	ခင်ဗျား/ရှင့် ဆီမှာ တယ်လီဖုန်းအားသွင်းတဲ့ကြိုး ရှိသလား။ *k´ămyà* ***m****/shín* ***f*** *zi-hma-teh-li-p´oùn-ă-thwìn-déh-cò-shí-dhălà?*
Can I have your number?	ခင်ဗျား/ရှင့် ရဲ့ ဖုန်းနံပါတ် ကျွန်တော်/ကျွန်မ ရနိုင်မလား။ *k´ămyà* ***m****/shin* ***f*** *yéh-p´oùn-nan-baq-*

*cănaw **m**/cămá **f** yá-nain-mălà?*

Here's my number. ဒီမှာ ကျွန်တော်/ ကျွန်မ ရဲ့ ဖုန်းနံပါတ်
*di-hma-cănaw **m**/cămá **f** yéh-p´oùn-nan-baq*

Please call/text me. ကျေးဇူးပြုပြီး ကျွန်တော့်/ ကျွန်မ ကို ဖုန်းခေါ်ပါ။ မက်ဆေ့ချ်ပို့ပါ။ *cè-zu-pyú-byì- cănaw **m**/cămá **f** go-p´oùn-k´aw-ba/meq-sé-pó-ba*

I'll call/text you. ခင်ဗျား/ ရှင့် ဆီကို ကျွန်တော်/ ကျွန်မ ဖုန်းခေါ်လိုက်မယ်။မက်ဆေ့ချ် ပို့လိုက်မယ်။
*k´ămyà **m**/shín **f** zi-go- cănaw **m**/cămá **f** p´oùn-k´aw-laiq-meh/meq-s'é-pó-laiq-meh*

YOU MAY HEAR…

ဘယ်သူ စကားပြောနေတာလဲ။
bădhu zăgá pyàw-ne-da-lèh?
Who's calling?

ကိုင်ထားပါ။ *kain-t'à-ba.*
Hold on.

သူ့ ဆီ ကျွန်တော်/ ကျွန်မ လွှဲပေးလိုက်ပါမယ်။
*thú-s'i cănaw **m**/cămá **f** hlwèh-pè-laiq-pa-meh.*
I'll put you through. to him/her.

သူ ဒီမှာမရှိဘူး။တခြားလိုင်းပေါ်မှာ ပြောနေတယ်။
thú di-hma măshí-bù / tă-c'à laìn-baw-hma pyàw-ne-deh.
He/She is not here/on another line.

ခင်ဗျား/ ရှင် သတင်းတစ်ခု ချန်ခဲ့ချင်သလား။
*k'ămyà **m**/shin **f** -thădìn tăk'ú c'an-géh-jin-dhă-là?*
Would you like to leave a message?

နောက်မှ/ ဆယ်မိနစ်ကြာရင် ပြန်ခေါ်လိုက်ပါ။
nauq-hmá / s'eh mí-niq ca-yin pyan-k'aw-laiq-pa.
Call back later/in ten minutes.

ခင်ဗျား/ ရှင့် ကို သူ ပြန်ခေါ်လို့ရနိုင်မလား။
*k'ămyà **m**/shìn **f** go thu pyan-k'aw-ló yá-nain-mă-là?*
Can he/she call you back?

ခင်ဗျား/ ရှင့် ရဲ့ ဖုန်းနံပါတ်က ဘယ်လောက်လဲ။
*k'ămyà **m**/shin **f** yèh p'oùn-nan-baq-ká bă-lauq-lèh?*
What's your number?

There is currently no international GSM roaming facility for mobile phones in Myanmar. The best option for making local and international calls is to purchase a local SIM card and top up card for around US$20.

For Numbers, see page 168.

Telephone Etiquette

Hello. This is…	ဟယ်လို၊ ကျွန်တော် / ကျွန်မ က… ပါ။ *heh-lo-cănaw* **m**/*cămá* **f**-*gá…ba*
Can I speak to…?	ကျွန်တော်/ ကျွန်မ… နဲ့စကားပြောလို့ ရနိုင်မလား။ *cănaw* **m**/*cămá* **f**…*néh-zăgà-pyàw-ló-yà-nain-mălà?*
Extension…	လိုင်းခွဲနံပါတ်… *lain-gwéh-nan-baq…*
Speak louder/ more slowly, please.	ကျေးဇူးပြုပြီး စကားကျယ်ကျယ်/ ပိုပြီးနှေးနှေး ပြောပေးပါ။ *cè-zu-pyú-byì-zăkà-ceh-ceh/po-byì-hnè-hnè-pyàw-bè-ba*
Can you repeat that?	ခင်ဗျား/ ရှင် ပြန်ပြောပြလို့ရနိုင်မလား။ *k´ămyà* **m**/*shin* **f**-*pyan-pyăw-ló-yá-nain-mălà?*
I'll call back later.	ကျွန်တော်/ ကျွန်မ နောက်မှ ပြန်ခေါ်လိုက်မယ်။ *cănaw* **m**/*cămá* **f** *nauq-hmá-pyan-k´aw-laiq-meh*
Bye.	ဘိုင်းဘိုင်။ *bàin-bain*

Fax

Can I send/receive a fax here?	ဒီနေရာကနေ ကျွန်တော်/ ကျွန်မ ဖက်စ် ပို့လို့/ လက်ခံလို့ ရနိုင်မလား။/လက်ခံလို့ ရနိုင်မလား။ *di-ne-ya-gá-ne cănaw* **m**/*cămá* **f** *p´eq pó-/ló-leq-k'an-ló-yá-nain-mălà?*
What's the fax number?	ဖက်စ် နံပါတ်က ဘယ်လောက်လဲ။ *pèq-nan-baq-ká bă-lauq-lèh?*
Please fax this to…	ကျေးဇူးပြုပြီး ဒါကို… ဆီ ဖက်စ်ပို့ပေးပါ။ *cè-zù pyú-bì da-go …s'i pèq pó-pè-ba.*

The Central Telegraph Office is located one block east of the Sule Pagoda on Mahabandoola Street and is open from 8:00 a.m. until 9:00 p.m., Monday to Saturday, and from 8:00 a.m. to 9:00 p.m. on Sundays and public holidays.

Post

Where's the post office /mailbox?	စာတိုက်/စာတိုက်ပုံး ဘယ်နေရာမှာရှိလဲ။ *sa-daiq / sa-daiq-pòun beh-ne-ya-hma shí-lèh?*
A stamp for this postcard/letter to…	…သို့ ဒီပို့စ်ကတ်/ဒီစာအတွက် တံဆိပ်ခေါင်းတစ်ခု *…thó-di pósăkaq/di-sa ătweq dă-zeiq-gaùn tăk'ú*
Where's the post office/mailbox?	စာတိုက်/စာတိုက်ပုံး ဘယ်နေရာမှာရှိလဲ။ *sa-daiq / sa-daiq-pòun beh-ne-ya-hma shí-lèh?*
A stamp for this postcard/letter to…	…သို့ ဒီပို့စ်ကတ်/ဒီစာအတွက် တံဆိပ်ခေါင်းတစ်ခု *…thó-di pósăkaq/di-sa ătweq dă-zeiq-gaùn tăk'ú*
How much?	ဘယ်လောက်ကျလဲ။ *bă-lauq cá-lèh?*
Send this package	ဒီအထုပ်ကို လေယာဉ်နဲ့/အမြန်ချောပို့နဲ့ ပို့ပေးပါ။ *di ă-t'ouq-ko le-yin-néh/ă-myan-c'àw-pó-néh pó-pè-ba.*
A receipt, please.	ကျေးဇူးပြုပြီး ငွေလက်ခံဖြတ်ပိုင်းပေးပါ။ *cè-zù pyú-bì ngwe leq-k'an p'yaq-pàin pè-ba.*

YOU MAY HEAR…

အခွန်ကြေညာရန်ပုံစံကို ဖြည့်ပါ။ *ăk'un ce-nya-yan poun-zan-go p'yé-ba.*	Fill out the customs declaration form.
တန်ဖိုး ဘယ်လောက်ရှိလဲ။ *tan-bó bă-lauq shí-lèh?*	What's the value?
အထဲမှာ ဘာရှိလဲ။ *ă-t'èh-hma- ba shí-lèh?*	What's inside?

Food & Drink

Eating Out 57
Meals & Cooking 67
Drinks 78
On the Menu 82

Eating Out

ESSENTIAL

Can you recommend a good restaurant/bar? ခင်ဗျား/ရှင် စားသောက်ဆိုင်/ဘား ကောင်းကောင်း တစ်ခု ညွှန်းပေးနိုင်မလား။
k'ămyà ***m****/shin* ***f*** *sà-thauq- s'ain/ bà- kàun- gàun- tă-k'ú hnyu`n-pè- nain-mălà?*

Is there a traditional /an inexpensive restaurant nearby? အနီးအနားမှာ ရိုးရာ/ဈေးမကြီးတဲ့ စားသောက်ဆိုင်တစ်ဆိုင်ရှိသလား။
ăni-ăn à-mha-yò-ya/ zè- măcì- déh- sà-thauq- s'ain- tă s'ain- shí-dhălà?

A table for…, please. ကျေးဇူးပြုပြီး လူ … ယောက်စာ စားပွဲတစ်လုံး ပေးပါ။
cè-zù pyú-byí- lu… yauq-sa-zăbwèh- tă-lòun- pè-ba.

Can we sit…? … ကျွန်တော်/ကျွန်မ တို့ ထိုင်လို့ရနိုင်မလား။
cănaw ***m****/cămá* ***f*** *dó- t'ain- ló- yá-nain-mălà?*

here/there ဒီမှာ/ဟိုမှာ *di-hma/Ho-hma*

outside အပြင်မှာ *Ăpyin-hma*

in a non-smoking area ဆေးလိပ်သောက်ခွင့်မပြုတဲ့နေရာမှာ
s'è-leiq-thauq-k'wín-măpyu'- déh -ne-ya-hma

I'm waiting for someone. ကျွန်တော်/ကျွန်မ တစ်ယောက်ယောက်ကိုစောင့်နေတာ။
cănaw ***m****/ cămá* ***f*** *tă-yauq-yauq-go-saún-ne-da.*

Where are the toilets? အိမ်သာဘယ်မှာရှိလဲ။ *ein-dha-beh-hma- shí- lèh?*

The menu, please. ကျေးဇူးပြုပြီး အစားအသောက်အမည်စာရင်း ပေးပါ။
cè-zù pyú-byì-ăsà-ăthauq-ămyi-săyin- bè-ba

What do you recommend? ဘာစားဖို့ ခင်ဗျား/ရှင် တိုက်တွန်းမလဲ။
ba-sà-bó-k'ămyà ***m****/shin* ***f*** *taiq-twu`n- mălèh?*

I'd like… ကျွန်တော်/ကျွန်မ … လိုချင်ပါတယ်။
cănaw ***m****/ cămá* ***f****… lo-jin-ba-deh.*

Some more…, please. ကျေးဇူးပြုပြီး … နည်းနည်းထပ်ပေးပါ။
cè-zù pyú- byì…nèh-nèh-t'aq-pè-ba.

Enjoy your meal!	ခင်ဗျား/ရှင် အရသာခံ စားပါ။ *k'ămyà* **m**/*shin* **f** *ăyádha k'an-zà-ba.*
The check [bill], please.	ကျေးဇူးပြုပြီး ကုန်ကျငွေစာရင်း (ငွေတောင်းခံလွှာ) ပေးပါ။ *cè-zù pyú- byì-koun-cá-ngwe-săyin (ngwe-tau`n-k'an-hlwa) pè ba.*
Is service included?	ဝန်ဆောင်မှုပါပြီးသားလား။ *wun-saun-hmú- pa-bì-dhà-là?*
Can I pay by credit card/have a receipt?	ကျွန်တော်/ကျွန်မ အကြွေးဝယ်ကတ်နဲ့ငွေချေလို့ ရနိုင်မလား။/ငွေလက်ခံဖြတ်ပိုင်းတစ်စောင် ရနိုင်မလား။ *cănaw* **m**/ *cămá* **f** *ăćwè-weh-kaq-néh-ngwe će-ló-yá-nain-mălá?/ngwe-leq-k'an p'yaq-pain tăzaun yá-nain-mălà?*

Where to Eat

Can you recommend…?	ခင်ဗျား/ရှင် … ညွှန်းပေးနိုင်မလား။ *k'ămyà* **m**/*shin* **f**… *hnyu`n-pè-nain-mălà?*
a restaurant	စားသောက်ဆိုင်တစ်ဆိုင် *sà-thauq- s'ain- tă s'ain*
a bar	အရက်ဆိုင်တစ်ဆိုင် *ăyeq-s'ain- tă s'ain*
a café	ကော်ဖီဆိုင်တစ်ဆိုင် *kaw-p´i-s'ain- tă s'ain*
a fast food place	အမြန်အစားအစာ ရနိုင်တဲ့နေရာတစ်ခု *ămyan-ăsà-àsa-yá-nain- déh-ne-ya-tăk'ú*
a cheap restaurant	ဈေးသက်သာတဲ့ စားသောက်ဆိုင်တစ်ဆိုင် *zè-theq-tha-déh-sà-thauq- s'ain- tă s'ain*
an expensive restaurant	ဈေးကြီးတဲ့ စားသောက်ဆိုင်တစ်ဆိုင် *zè-ci- déh-sà-thauq- s'ain- tă s'ain*
a restaurant with a good view	ရှုခင်းကောင်းတဲ့ စားသောက်ဆိုင်တစ်ဆိုင် *shú-gìn-kaú-déh-sà-thauq- s'ain- tă s'ain*
an authentic/ a non-touristy restaurant	ရိုးရာ/နိုင်ငံခြားခရီးသွားမများတဲ့ စားသောက်ဆိုင်တစ်ဆိုင် *yò-ya/nain-ngan-jà-k´ăyì-thwà-mămyà-déh-sà-thauq-s'ain- tă s'ain*

For authentic, local food, the standard place to eat in most towns is in small, cheap, canteen-like restaurants where vegetarian, meat and seafood curries and rice are the mainstays. Stick to lunchtime to reduce the risk of tummy upsets. In the evenings, rough and ready Chinese-style BBQ joints – **a 'gin zein** – are the most common option. No-frills noodle shops and street stalls offering snacks such as samosas, sweet and savoury pancakes and deep-fried bites are also a Myanmar institution. For international and less spicy options, see Dining with Children on p.64.

Reservations & Preferences

I'd like to reserve	ကျွန်တော်/ကျွန်မ ကြိုတင်နေရာယူချင်ပါတယ်။ *cănaw* **m**/ *cămá* **f** *co-tin-ne-ya-yu-jin-ba-deh.*
a table...	...စားပွဲတစ်လုံး ... *zăbwèm-tălou`n*
for two	နှစ်ယောက်စာ *hnăyauq-sa*
for this evening	ဒီညနေအတွက် *di-nyăne-ătweq*
for tomorrow at...	မနက်ဖြန် ... အချိန်အတွက် *māneq-p´yan...ătweq*
A table for two, please.	ကျေးဇူးပြုပြီး နှစ်ယောက်စာ စားပွဲတစ်လုံး ပေးပါ။ *cè-zù pyú- byì-hnăyauq-sa-zăbwèh-tăloùn-pè-ba*
I have a reservation.	ကျွန်တော်/ကျွန်မ ကြိုတင်နေရာယူထားတာရှိတယ်။ *cănaw* **m**/ *cămá* **f** *co-tin-ne-ya-yu-t´à-da-shí-deh*

My name is…	ကျွန်တော်/ကျွန်မရဲ့နာမည်က … ပါ။ *cănaw* ***m****/ cămá* ***f*** *yéh-nan-meh-gá…ba*
Can we sit…?	ကျွန်တော်/ကျွန်မတို့ … ထိုင်လို့ရမလား။ *cănaw* ***m****/ cămá* ***f*** *dó…-t´ain-ló-yá-mălà?*
here/there	ဒီမှာ/ဟိုမှာ *di-hma/Ho-hma*
outside	အပြင်မှာ *Ăpyin-hma*
in a non-smoking area	ဆေးလိပ်မသောက်ရတဲ့နေရာမှာ *s'è-leiq-măthauq-yá-déh -ne-ya-hma*
by the window	ပြတင်းပေါက်နားမှာ *bădin-bauq-nà-hma*
in the shade	အရိပ်ထဲမှာ *Ăyeiq-t´eh-hma*
in the sun	နေပူထဲမှာ *ne-pu-t´eh-hma*

YOU MAY HEAR…

ခင်ဗျား/ရှင့် မှာ ကြိုတင်နေရာယူထားတာရှိသလား။ *k'ămyà* ***m****/shin* ***f*** *hma-co-tin-ne-ya-yu-t´à-da-shí-dhălà?*	Do you have a reservation?
ဘယ်နှစ်ယောက်လဲ။ *beh-hnăyauq-lèh?*	How many?
ဆေးလိပ်သောက်တဲ့နေရာလား ဒါမှမဟုတ် ဆေးလိပ်မသောက်ရတဲ့နေရာလား။ *s'è-leiq-thauq-déh-ne-ya-là? Da-hmá- măhouq-s'è-leiq-măthauq-yá-déh-ne-ya-là?*	Smoking or non-smoking?
ခင်ဗျား/ရှင် (မှာဖို့) အဆင်သင့်ဖြစ်ပြီလား။ *k'ămyà* ***m****/shin* ***f*** *(hma-bó) ăs'in-dhín-p´yiq-pi-là?*	Are you ready (to order)?
ခင်ဗျား/ရှင် ဘာစားချင်လဲ။ဘာမှာချင်လဲ။ *k'ămyà* ***m****/shin* ***f*** *ba-sà-jin-lèh?/ba-hma-jin-lèh.*	What would you like?
ကျွန်တော်/ကျွန်မ ကတော့… စားဖို့တိုက်တွန်းချင်တယ် *cănaw* ***m****/cămá* ***f*** *gá-dáw…sà-bó-taiq-tùn-jin-deh*	I recommend…
ခင်ဗျား/ရှင် အရသာခံပြီး စားပါ။ *k'ămyà* ***m****/shin* ***f*** *ăyádha k´an-byì-sà-ba.*	Enjoy your meal.

Where are the toilets? အိမ်သာတွေကဘယ်နေရာမှာလဲ။
ein-dha-dwe-gá-beh-ne-ya-hma-lèh?

How to Order

Excuse me, sir/ma'am? ကျွန်တော်/ကျွန်မကို ခွင့်လွှတ်ပါ။
cănaw ***m****/ cămá* ***f*** *go-k´wín-hluq-pa*

We're ready (to order). ကျွန်တော်/ကျွန်မတို့ (မှာဖို့) အဆင်သင့်ဖြစ်ပြီ။
cănaw ***m****/ cămá* ***f*** *dó(hma-bó) as'in-dhín-p´yiq-pi*

The wine list, please. ကျေးဇူးပြုပြီး ဝိုင်အမည်စာရင်းပေးပါ။
cè-zù pyú- byì-wain-ămyi-săyin-pè-ba

I'd like… ကျွန်တော်/ကျွန်မ … ကိုမှာချင်တယ်။
cănaw ***m****/ cămá* ***f****… go-hma-in-deh*

a bottle of… … တစ်ပုလင်း … *dă-bălin*

a carafe of… … တစ်ကရား …*tă-k´ăyà*

a glass of… … တစ်ဖန်ခွက် … *tă-p´an-gweq*

The menu, please. ကျေးဇူးပြုပြီး အစားအသောက်အမည်စာရင်းပေးပါ။
cè-zù pyú- byì-ăsà-ăthaunq-ămyi-săyin-pè-ba

Do you have…? ခင်ဗျား/ရှင်တို့ဆီမှာ … ရှိသလား။
k'ămyà ***m****/shin* ***f*** *dó-s'i-hma…shí dhă-là?*

a menu in English အင်္ဂလိပ်လိုရေးထားတဲ့ အစားအသောက်အမည်စာရင်း
Ìn-găleiq-lo-yè-t´à-déh-ăsă- ăthaunq-ămyi-săyin

a fixed price menu ဈေးနှုန်းအသေသတ်မှတ်ထားတဲ့ အစားအသောက်အမည်စာရင်း
zè-hnoùn-ăthe-thaq-hmaq-t´à-déh-ăsă- ăthaunq-ămyi-săyin

a children's menu ကလေးတွေအတွက်အစားအသောက်အမည်စာရင်း
k´ălè-dwe-ătweq-ăsă- ăthaunq-ămyi-săyin

What do you recommend? ဘာစားဖို့ ခင်ဗျား/ရှင် တိုက်တွန်းမလဲ။
ba-sà-bó-k'ămyà ***m****/shin* ***f*** *taiq-tùn-mălèh?*

What's this? ဒါကဘာလဲ။ *da-gá-ba-lèh?*

What's in it? အဲဒီထဲမှာဘာပါလဲ။ *Èh-di-t´èh-hma-ba-pa-lèh?*

Is it spicy? အဲဒါက စပ်သလား။ *Èh-da-ga-saq-thăla?*

YOU MAY SEE...

ပေးချေရမည့် စုစုပေါင်းအခကြေးငွေ	cover charge
တရားသေသတ်မှတ်ထားသောဈေးနှုန်း	fixed price
(ဒီနေ့အတွက်) အထူးအစားအသောက်စာရင်း	menu (of the day)
ဝန်ဆောင်မှု (မပါ)/ဝန်ဆောင်မှုအပါအဝင်	service (not) included
အထူးဟင်းလျာများ	specials

Without..., please. ကျေးဇူးပြုပြီး... မထည့်ပါနဲ့။
cè-zù-pyú-byì...mătéh-ba-néh

It's to go [take away]. အဲဒါက အပြင်ကိုထုတ်သွားမှာ။
Èh-da-gá-ăpyin-go-t´ouq-thwà-hma

For Drinks, see page 78.

Cooking Methods

baked ဖုတ်ထားသော *p´ouq-t´à-dhàw*

boiled ပြုတ်ထားသော *pyouq-t´à-dhàw*

braised နှပ်ထားသော *hnaq-t´à-dhàw*

breaded ပေါင်မုန့်အမှုန့်ကပ်ထားသော
paun-moún-ăhmoún-kaq-t´à-dhàw

creamed ကရင်မ်ထည့်ထားသော *k'ă-rin-t´èh-t´à-dhàw*

diced အတုံးပုံလှီးထားသော *ătoùn-poun-hlì-t´à-dhàw*

filleted အလွှာလိုက်လှီးထားသော *ăhlwa-laiq-hlì-t´à-dhàw*

fried ကြော်ထားသော *caw-t´à-dhàw*

grilled သားငါးမီးကင်ထားသော *thà-ngà-mì-kin-t´à-dhàw*

poached ကြက်ဥ စသည်ကို ရေနွေးပူပူတွင်ထည့်ပြီးချက်သည်
ceq-ú-sá-dhi-go-ye-nwè-pu-bu-dwin-t´éh-byì-ćeq-thi

roasted ကင်ထားသော *kin-t´à-dhàw*

sautéed အမြန်ကြော်ထားသော *ămyan-caw-t´à-dhàw*

smoked မီးသင်းထားသော *mi-thin-t´à-dhàw*

steamed ရေနွေးငွေ့ပေးထားသော *ye-nwè-ngwé-pè-t´à-dhàw*
stewed ရောပေါင်းနှပ်ထားသော *yàw-paún-hnaq-t´à-dhàw*
stuffed အစာသွပ်ထားသော *ăsa-thuq-t´à-dhàw*

Dietary Requirements

I'm… ကျွန်တော်/ကျွန်မ က … ပါ။
cănaw **m**/ *cămá* **f** *gá... ba*

- diabetic ဆီးချိုရောဂါသည် *s'ì-jo-yàw-ga-dheh*
- lactose intolerant နွားနို့တွင်းပါသောဓာတ်တစ်မျိုးနဲ့ မတည့်
  nwà-nó-dwin-pa-dhàw-daq-tămyò-néh-mătéh
- vegetarian ဟင်းသီးဟင်းရွက်သာစားသူ/အသားမစားသူ
  hìn-dhì-hìn-yweq-tha-sà-dhu/ăthà-măsà-dhu
- vegan တိရိစ္ဆာန်အသွေးအသားမစား
  tăreiqsan-ăthwè-ăthà-măsà

I'm allergic to… ကျွန်တော်/ကျွန်မက … နဲ့ဓာတ်မတည့်ပါ။
cănaw **m**/ *cămá* **f** *gá… néh-daq-mătéh-ba*

I can't eat… ကျွန်တော်/ကျွန်မ … ကိုမစားနိုင်ဘူး။
cănaw **m**/ *cămá* **f**… *go-măsà-nain-bù*

- dairy products နို့နဲ့ နို့ထွက်ပစ္စည်း
  nó-néh-nó-t´weq-pyiq-sì
- gluten ကစီဓါတ် *găzi-daq*

nuts — အခွံမာအသီးများ *ăk´un-ma-ăthì-myà*
pork — ဝက်သား *weq-thà*
shellfish — အခွံမာငါး *ăk´un-ma-ngà*
spicy foods — စပ်တဲ့အစားအစာများ *saq-tèh-ăsà-ăsa-myà*
wheat — ဂျုံ *joun*

Is it halal/kosher? — အဲဒါကဟာလာလုပ်ထားတာလား/ဂျူးလူမျိုးစားနိုင်အောင်ပြင်ထားထာလား *Èh-da-gá-ha-la-louq-t´à-da-là? Jù-lu-myò-sà-nain-aun-pyin-t´à-da-là?*

Do you have…? — ခင်ဗျား/ရှင့် မှာ … ရှိသလား။
k´ămyà **m**/*shin* **f** *hma…shí-dhălà?*

skimmed milk — အဆီထုတ်ထားတဲ့နွားနို့
ăs'i-t´ouq-t´à-déh-nwà-nó
whole milk — အဆီအပြည့်ပါတဲ့နွားနို့
ăs'i-ăpyé-pa-déh-nwà-nó
soya milk — ပဲနို့ *péh-nó*

Dining with Children

Do you have children's portions? — ခင်ဗျား/ရှင် တို့မှာ ကလေးတွေစားနိုင်တဲ့ ပုံစံခွက်အချိုးအစားမျိုး ရှိသလား။
k´ămyà **m**/*shin* **f** *dó-hma-k´ălè-dwe-sà-nain-dèh-poun-zan-gweq-ăćò-ăsà myò shí-dhă-là?*

A highchair/child's seat, please. — ထိုင်ခုံမြင့်/ကလေးထိုင်ခုံ ကျေးဇူးပြုပြီးပေးပါ။
t´ain-goun-myín/k´ăle-t´ain-goun-cè-zù-pyú-byì-pè-ba

Where can I feed/ — ကျွန်တော်/ကျွန်မ ကလေးကို ဘယ်နေရာမှာ အစာကျွေးနိုင်မလဲ/အနှီးလဲပေးနိုင်မလဲ
cănaw **m**/*cămá* **f** *k´ălè-go-beh-ne-ya-hma-ăsa-cwè-nain-mălèh?/ăhnì-lèh-pè-nain-mălèh?*

Can you warm this? — ဒါကို ခင်ဗျား/ရှင် နွေးပေးနိုင်မလား။
da-go-k´ămyà **m**/*shin* **f** *hnwè-pè-nain-mălà?*

For Traveling with Children, see page 144.

How to Complain

When will our food be ready?	ကျွန်တော်/ကျွန်မတို့မှာထားတဲ့အစားတွေ ဘယ်အချိန် အဆင်သင့်ဖြစ်မလဲ။ *cănaw* **m**/*cămá* **f** *dó-hma-t´à-déh-ăsà-dwe-bah-aćein-ăs'in-dhín-pyiq-mălèh?*
We can't wait any longer.	ကျွန်တော်/ကျွန်မတို့ ဒီထက်ပိုပြီးမစောင့်နိုင်တော့ဘူး။ *cănaw* **m**/*cămá* **f** *dó- dí-t´eq-po-byì-măsaún-nain-daw-bù*
We're leaving.	ကျွန်တော်/ကျွန်မတို့ သွားတော့မယ်။ *cănaw* **m**/*cămá* **f** *dó- thaw-dáw-meh*
I didn't order this.	ဒါကို ကျွန်တော်/ကျွန်မ မမှာဘူး။ *da-go-cănaw* **m**/*cămá* **f** *măhma-bù*
I ordered…	ကျွန်တော်/ကျွန်မ မှာတာက … *cănaw* **m**/*cămá* **f** *hma-da-ga…*
I can't eat this.	ကျွန်တော်/ကျွန်မ မှာတာက။ *da-go-cănaw* **m**/*cămá* **f** *măsànain-bù-*
This is too…	ဒါက အရမ်း … တယ်။ *da-gá-ăyàn… deh*
cold/hot	အေး/ပူ *è/pu*
salty/spicy	ငံ/စပ် *ngan/saq*
tough/bland	မာ/ဘာအရသာမှမရှိဘူး။ *ma/ba ăyá-dha-hmá- măshí-bù*
This isn't clean/fresh.	ဒီဟာက မသန့်ရှင်းဘူး/မလတ်ဆတ်ဘူး။ *di-ha-gá-măthán-shìn/mă-laq-s'aq-bù*

Paying

The check [bill], please.
ကျေးဇူးပြုပြီး ကုန်ကျငွေစာရင်း (ငွေတောင်းလွှာ)ပေးပါ။
cè-zù-pyú-byì-koun-cá-ngwe-săyìn (ngwe-taùn-hlwa) pè-ba

Separate checks [bills], please.
ကျေးဇူးပြုပြီး သီးသန့်ငွေတောင်းလွှာများပေးပါ။
cè-zù-pyú-byì- thì-dhán-ngwe-taùn-hlwa-myà-pè-ba

It's all together.
ဒါက အားလုံးပဲ။ *da-gá-à-loùn-bèh*

Is service included?
ဝန်ဆောင်ခ ပါပြီးသားလား။
wun-s'aun-gá-pa-byì-dhà-là?

What's this amount for?
ဒီငွေပမာဏက ဘာအတွက်လဲ။
di-ngwe-pămaná-gá-ba-ătweq lèh?

I didn't have that.
ကျွန်တော်/ကျွန်မ အဲဒါကို မရခဲ့ဘူး။
cănaw **m**/*cămá* **f** *èh-da-go-mă-yá-géh-bù*

I had…
ကျွန်တော်/ကျွန်မ ရခဲ့တာက …
cănaw **m**/*cămá* **f** *yá-géh-da-gá…*

Can I have a receipt/ an itemized bill?
ကျွန်တော်/ကျွန်မ ငွေလက်ခံဖြတ်ပိုင်းတစ်ခု/အမျိုးအမည် တစ်ခုချင်းစီဖော်ပြတဲ့ငွေတောင်းလွှာတစ်ခုရနိုင်မလား။
cănaw **m**/*cămá* **f** *ngwe-leq-k´an-p´yaq-paìn-tăk´ú/ ămyò-ămyi-tă-k´ù-jìn-zi-p´aw-pyá-déh-ngwe-taùn-hlwa-tăk´ú-yá nain-mălà?*

That was delicious!
အဲဒါက အရသာရှိတယ်။ *Èh-da-gá-ăyádha-shí-deh*

I've already paid.
ကျွန်တော်/ကျွန်မ ငွေရှင်းပြီးသွားပြီ။
cănaw **m**/*cămá* **f** *ngwe-shìn- byì-dhwà-bi*

Tipping is not common in Burmese eateries, but it has become the norm in tourist restaurants serving foreigner-oriented meals. As usual, payment with crisp, clean notes is the preferred option. Payment by card is rare, and if available, it will incur a surcharge of at least 4%.

Meals & Cooking

Sampling the country's distinctive hybrid cuisine, which fuses Indian, Chinese and Southeast Asian influences, proves among the highlights of any trip to Burma. This is true even in more remote areas where you'll be limited to cooking that makes few concessions to Western taste buds. For more on Where to Eat, see p.58.

Breakfast

bacon	ဝက်သားခြောက် *weq-thà-jauq*
(cold/hot) cereal	ပြားထားသော ဂျုံစေ့အား နွားနို့ဖြင့်စားခြင်း (အအေး/အပူ) *pyà-t´à-dhàw-joun-zé-à-nwà-nó-p´yín sà jìn (ăè/ăpu)*
coffee/tea…	…ကော်ဖီ/လက်ဖက်ရည် *…kaw-p´ì/lăp´eq-ye*
black	ဘလက်ခ်၊ နွားနို့/နို့မှုန့်မပါပဲ *băleq, nwà-nó-hmoún-măpa-bèh*
decaf	ကာဖိန်းဓာတ်မပါသော *ka-p´eìn-daq-măpa-dhàw*
with milk	နွားနို့နှင့် *nwà-nó-hnín*
with sugar	သကြားနှင့် *dhăjà-hnín*
with artificial sweetener	ဆေးသကြားနှင့် *s'è-hăjà-hnín*
butter	ထောပတ် *t´àw-baq*
bread (loaf)/roll	ပေါင်မုန့် (ပေါင်မုန့်ချောင်း)/ပေါင်မုန့်လုံး *paun-moún (paun-moún-ćaùn)/paun-moún-loùn*
cheese	ချီးစ် *ĉì*
Chinese or Spanish sausage	တရုတ် သို့မဟုတ် စပိန် ဝက်အူချောင်း *tăyouq-dhó- măhouq-săpein-weq-u-jaùn*
chocolate drink	ချောကလက်ဖျော်ရည် *ćàw-kăleq-p´yaw-ye*
cured meat	ဆားနယ်ထားသောအသား *s'à-neh-t´à-dhàw-ăthà*
dosa	တိုရှည် *to-she*

dried fish	ငါးခြောက် *ngăćauq*
dried meat	အသားခြောက် *ăthà-jauq*
...egg	... ဥ *ú*
hard-/soft-boiled	မာမာ/ပျော့ပျော့ ပြုတ်ထားသော *ma ma/pyáw-byáw-pyouq-t´à-dhàw*
fried	ကြော်ထားသော *caw-t´à-dhàw*
omelette	ကြက်ဥမွှေကြော် *ceq-ú-hmwe-jaw*
salted	အငံဖောက်ထားသော *ăngn-p´auq-t´à-dhàw*
scrambled	ခေါက်ကြော်ထားသော *k´auq-caw-t´à-dhàw*
sunny side up	မကြက်တကျက်ကြော်ထားသောကြက်ဥကြော် *măceq-dă-jeq-caw-t´à-dhàw-ceq-ú-jaw*
jam/jelly	ယို။ဂျယ်လီ *yo/jeh-li*
...juice	... ဖျော်ရည် *... p´yaw-ye*
apple	ပန်းသီး *pàn-dhì*
grape	စပျစ်သီး *ză-byiq-thì*
orange	လိမ္မော်သီး *lein-maq-dhì*
pineapple	နာနတ်သီး *na-naq-thì*
margarine	ထောပတ်တု *t´àw-baq-tú*
milk	နွားနို့ *nwà-nó*
oatmeal [porridge]	ကွေကာအုတ် (ဆန်ပြုတ်) *kwe-ka-ouq (s'an-byouq)*
omelet	ကြက်ဥမွှေကြော် *ceq-ú-hmwe-jaw*
pancake	မုန့်ပြားသလက်တစ်မျိုး *moún-pyà-thàleq-tămyò*
rice fried with garlic	ကြက်သွန်ဖြူထမင်းကြော် *ceq-thun-p´yu-t´ămìn-jaw*

A great way to start the day is to have a budget breakfast in a traditional teahouse. Chinese teahouses whip up meaty rice dishes while the Burmese variety tend to stick to noodles – the typical Burmese breakfast. Muslim teahouses specialise in freshly fried lamb, chicken and vegetable samosas.

toast ပေါင်မုန့်မီးကင် *paun-moún-mì-kin*
yogurt ဒိန်ချဉ် *dein-jin*

Appetizers

dosa တိုရှည် *to-she*
egg rolls ကြက်ဥလိပ် *ceq-ú-leiq*
fried peanuts မြေပဲကြော် *mye-bèh-jaw*
spring rolls ကော်ပြန့်လိပ် *kaw-byán-leiq*
salted fish ငါးဆားနယ် *ngăs'ăneh*

Soup

chicken soup ကြက်စွပ်ပြုတ် *ceq-suq-pyouq*
clear soup ဟင်းချိုအကြည် *hìn-jo-ăci*
duck soup ဘဲသားစွပ်ပြုတ် *bèh-dhà-suq-pyouq*
noodle soup ခေါက်ဆွဲပြုတ် *k'auq-s'wèh-pyouq*
seafood soup ပင်လယ်စာစွပ်ပြုတ် *pin-leh-za-suq-pyouq*
sizzling rice soup ရှဲရှဲမြည်နေသော ဆန်စွပ်ပြုတ် *shèh-shèh-myi-ne-dhaw-s'an-suq-pyouq*
Thai soup ယိုးဒယားဟင်းချို *yò-dăyà-hìn-jo*
tomato soup ခရမ်းချဉ်သီးဟင်းချို *k'ăyàn-jin-dhì-hìn-jo*
vegetable soup ဟင်းသီးဟင်းရွက်ဟင်းချို *hìn-dhì-hìn-yweq-hìn-jo*
12-taste soup ၁၂ မျိုးဟင်းချို *S'éh-hnămyò-hìn-jo*

Fish & Seafood

butterfish	ငါးမြင်း *ngàmyì*
carp	ငါးဖယ် *ngăp´eh*
catfish	ငါးခူ *ngăk´u*
cod	ပင်လယ်ငါးကြီး *pin-leh-ngà-jì*
crab	ဂဏန်း *gănàn*
eel	ငါးရှဉ့် *fhngăshín*
grouper	ငါးပတ် *ngăbaq*
mackerel	ငါးကွမ်းရှပ် *ngăkùn-shaq*
milkfish	ငွေရောင်ငါး *ngwe-yaun-ngà*
mussels	ယောက်သွားတစ်မျိုး၊ ခရု *yauq-thwà-tămyò k´ayú*
oyster	ကနုကမာကောင်၊ ယောက်သွား *kănú-kăma-gaun yauq-thwà*
salmon	ဆော်လမွန်ငါး/ပန်းရောင်ရှိသောငါး *s'aw-làmun-ngà/pàn-yaun-shí-dhàw-ngà*
sea bass	ငါးကြင်း *ngăjìn*
shellfish	အခွံမာ ငါးတစ်မျိုး *ăk'un-ma-ngà-tàmyò*
shrimp	ပုစွန်ဆိပ် *băzun-zeiq*
squid	ပြည်ကြီးငါး *pyi-jì-ngà*

Meat & Poultry

bacon	ဝက်သားခြောက် *weq-thà-jauq*
beef	အမဲသား *ămèh-thà*
chicken	ကြက်သား *ceq-thà*
chinese or Spanish sausage	တရုတ် သို့မဟုတ် စပိန်ဝက်အူချောင်း *tăyouq-dhó-măhouq-săpein-weq-u-jaùn*
duck	ဘဲသား *bèh-dhà*
ham	ဝက်ပေါင်ခြောက် *weq-paun-jauq*
lamb	သိုးကလေးသား *thò-gălè-dhà*
liver	အသည်း *ăthèh*
pork	ဝက်သား *weq-thà*
steak	စတိတ်အသား *săteiq-ăthà*

Vegetables & Staples

asparagus	ကညွတ် *kănyuq*
broccoli	ပန်းဂေါ်ဖီ အစိမ်းရောင် *pàn-gaw-bi-ăsèin-yaun*
cabbage	ဂေါ်ဖီထုပ် *gaw-bi-d´ouq*
carrot	မုန်လာဥနီ *moun-la-ú-ni*
cauliflower	ပန်းဂေါ်ဖီ *pàn-gaw-bi-*
celery	တရုတ်နံနံ *tàyouq-nan-nan*
chinese cabbage	တရုတ်ဂေါ်ဖီထုပ် *tàyouq- gaw-bi- d´ouq*
chinese long bean	တရုတ်ပဲတောင့်ရှည် *tàyouq-pèh-daùn-she*
chinese water spinach	တရုတ်ကန်စွန်း *tàyouq-găzùn*
corn	ပြောင်းဖူး *paùn-bù*
eggplant [aubergine	ခရမ်းသီး *k´ăyàn-dhì*
garlic	ကြက်သွန်ဖြူ *ceq-thun-p´yu*
green bean	ပဲသီးစိမ်း *pèh-dhì-zèin*
leaf mustard	မုန်လာရွက် *moun-ka-yweq*
lettuce	ဆလပ်ရွက် *s'ălaq-yweq*
mushroom	မှို *hmo*
noodles	ခေါက်ဆွဲ *k´auq-s'wèh*
olive	သံလွင်သီး *than-lwin-dhì*
pea	ပဲအမျိုးမျိုး *pèh-ămyò-myò*
potato	အာလူး *a-lù*

radish	မုန်လာဥဖြူ *moun-la-ú-byu*
rice	ဆန် *s'an*
red/green pepper	ငရုပ်ပွ အနီ/အစိမ်း *ngăyouq-pwà-ăni/ăìn*
scallion [spring onion]	ကြက်သွန်မြိတ် *ceq-thun-meiq*
seaweed	ပင်လယ်ရေညှိ *pin-leh-ye-hnyí*
soy bean	ပဲပိစပ် *pèh-bí-zaq*
spinach	ဟင်းနုနွယ်ရွက် *hìn-nú-nweh-yweq*
tofu	တိုဖူး/ပဲပြား *to-p´ù/pèh-byà*
tomato	ခရမ်းချဉ်သီး *k´ăyàn-jin-dhì*
vegetable	ဟင်းသီးဟင်းရွက် *hìn-dhì-hìn-yweq*

Fruit

apple	ပန်းသီး *pàn-dhì*
apricot	တရုတ်ဆီးသီး *tàyouq-zì-dhì*
banana	ငှက်ပျောသီး *ngăpyàw-dhì*
cherry	ချယ်ရီသီး *ćeh-ri-dhì*
chinese dates	တရုတ်မက်မန်းသီး *tàyouq-meq-màn-dhì*
fruit	သစ်သီးဝလံများ *thiq-thì-wălan-myà*
grapefruit	ကျွဲကောသီးအသေးတစ်မျိုး *cwèh-gàw-dhì-ăthè-tămyò*
grape	စပျစ်သီး *zăbyiq-thì*

crab apple ဂဏန်းပန်းသီး *gănàn-pàn-dhì*

kiwi ကီဝီသီး *ki-wi-dhì*

lychee လိုင်ချီးသီး(လိုက်ချီးသီး) *lain-ĉi-dhì laiq-ĉi-dhì*

lemon ရှောက်သီး *shauq-thì*

lime သံပရာသီး *than-băya-dhì*

mango သရက်သီး *thăyeq-thì*

longan fruit သဖန်းသီးတစ်မျိုး *thăp´àn-dhì-tămyò*

mandarin orange မန်ဒရင်းလိမ္မော်သီး *man-dărìn-lein-maw-dhì*

melon ဖရဲသီးနွယ်ဝင်အသီး *p´ăyèh-dhì-nweh-win-ăthì*

orange လိမ္မော်သီး *lein-maw-dhì*

peach မက်မုံသီး *meq-moun-dhì*

pear သစ်တော်သီး *thiq-taw-dhì*

pineapple နာနတ်သီး *na-naq-thì*

plum ဆီးသီး *zì-dhì*

pomegranate သလဲသီး *thălèh-dhì*

red bayberry အနီရောင် ဘယ်ရီသီးတစ်မျိုး *ăni-yaun-beh-ri-dhì-tămyò*

strawberry စထရော်ဘယ်ရီသီး *săt´ăraw-beh-ri-dhì*

Dessert

agar-agar	ကျောက်ကျော *cauq-càw*
biscuit/ cookie	ဘီစကစ်/ကွတ်ကီး *bi-săkiq/kuq-kì*
cake	ကိတ်မုန့် *keiq-moún*
deep-fried dough sticks	အီကြာကွေးကြော် *i-ca-kwè-jaw*
fried cake	ကိတ်ကြော် *keiq-caw*
golden rice	ရွှေထမင်း *shwe-t´ămìn*
ice cream	ရေခဲမုန့် *ye-gèh-moùn*
jaggery	ထန်းလျက် *t´àn-lyeq (t´ănyeq)*
jujube plums cooked in jaggery	ဇီးယို *zì-yo*
pancakes	မုန့်ပြားသလက် *moún-pyà-thăleq*
sago/tapioca in syrup	သာကူ/ပလောပီနံပြုတ်ရည် *tha-gu/pălàw-pi-nan*
semolina pudding	ဂျုံကြမ်းပူတင်း၊ မုန့်စိမ်းပေါင်း *joun-jàn-pu-tìn moún-sein-baùn*
shredded coconut	အုန်းသီးမှုန့် *oùn-dhì-moún*
steamed rice pudding	ထမင်းပူတင်း *t´ămin-pu-tìn*
sticky rice cake	ကောက်ညှင်းကိတ်မုန့် *kauq-hnyìn-keiq-moún*
sugar candy	သကြားလုံး *dhăjà-loùn*
sweet fried rice	မုန့်စလင်းထောင့်ကြော် *moún-sălin-daún-caw*
toddy plum sugar cake	ထန်းသီးမုန့် *t´àn-dhì-moún*

Sauces & Condiments

Ketchup ခရမ်းချဉ်သီးအချဉ်ရည် *k´ăyàn-jin-dhì-ăćin-ye*
Mustard မုန်ညှင်းဆီ *moun-hnyìn-zi*
Pepper ငြုပ်ကောင်း *ngăyouq-kaùn*
Salt ဆား *s'à*

At the Market

Where are the baskets? ခြင်းတောင်းတွေက ဘယ်မှာလဲ။ *Ćin-daùn-dwe-gá-beh-hma-lèh?*
Where is…? … က ဘယ်မှာလဲ။ *…gá-beh-hma-lèh?*
I'd like some of that/this ကျွန်တော်/ကျွန်မ ဒီဟာ/ဟိုဟာ နည်းနည်းလောက် လိုချင်တယ်။ *cănaw* ***m****/cămá* ***f*** *lo-jin-deh*
Can I taste it? ဒါကို ကျွန်တော်/ကျွန်မ မြည်းကြည့်လို့ရမလား။ *da-go cănaw* ***m****/cămá* ***f*** *myì kyí-ló-yá-mălà?*
I'd like… ကျွန်တော်/ကျွန်မ … လိုချင်တယ်။ *cănaw* ***m****/cămá* ***f****… lo-jin-deh*

a kilo/half kilo of… …တစ်ကီလို။ကီလိုဝက် … *tăkilo-kilo-weq*
a liter of… … တစ်လီတာ … *tălita*
a piece of… … တစ်စိတ် … *dăzeiq*
a slice of… … တစ်ချပ် … *tăćaq*

More./Less. သိပ်မများ/သိပ်မနည်း *theiq-mămyà*
How much? ဘယ်လောက်ကျလဲ။ *beh-laug-cà-lèh?*
Where do I pay? ကျွန်တော်/ကျွန်မ ဘယ်မှာ ပိုက်ဆံပေးရမလဲ။ *cănaw* ***m****/cămá* ***f*** *beh-hma-paiq-s'an-pè-yà-mălèh?*

i

Myanmar has retained many of the old weights and measures used during British colonial times such as the **lakh** and **viss**. The tin or basket is used to measure quantities of agricultural export goods. The kilogram equivalent differs for rice, sesame and other goods. For Conversion Tables, see page 173.

A bag, please.	ကျေးဇူးပြုပြီး အိတ်တစ်လုံးပေးပါ။ *cè-zù-pyù-byì-eiq-tăloùn-pè-ba*
I'm being helped.	ကျွန်တော်/ကျွန်မ အကူအညီရခဲ့တယ်။ *cănaw **m**/cămá **f** ăku-ănyi-yá-gèh-deh*

For Conversion Tables, see page 173.

YOU MAY HEAR…

ကျွန်တော်/ကျွန်မ ခင်ဗျားကို ကူညီပေးနိုင်မလား။ *cănaw **m**/cămá-k **f**´ămyà-go-ku-ny-pè-nain-malà?*	Can I help you?
ခင်ဗျား/ရှင် ဘာလိုချင်လဲ။ *k´ămyà **m**/shin **f** ba-lo-jin-lèh?*	What would you like?
ဒီ့အပြင်ရောဘာလိုသေးလဲ။ *dí-ăpyin-yàw-b-lo-dhè-lèh?*	Anything else?
ဒါက … ကျပ်/ဒေါ်လာ *da-gá… caq/daw-la*	That's…kyat/ dollars.

YOU MAY SEE…

တကယ်လို့ .... မတိုင်မီ သုံးမယ်ဆိုရင်အကောင်းဆုံးပဲ။	best if used by…
ကယ်လိုရီ (ကစီဓာတ်)	calories
အဆီမပါသော	fat free
ရေခဲသေတ္တာထဲမှာ ဆက်တိုက်အအေးခံထားပါ	keep refrigerated
… နည်းနည်းပါနိုင်တယ်။	may contain traces of...
မိုက်ခရိုဝေ့ဗ်ထဲထည့်ပြီး အပူပေးလို့ရနိုင်တယ်	microwaveable
… မတိုင်မီ အပြီးရောင်းပါ။	sell by…
အသီးအရွက်စားသူများအတွက် သင့်တော်ပါသည်။	suitable for vegetarians

In the Kitchen

bottle opener	ပုလင်းဖွင့်တံ *pălin-p´wín-dan*
bowl	ပန်းကန်လုံး *băgan-loùn*
can opener	သံဗူးဖွင့်တံ *than-bù-p´wín-dan*
chopsticks	အစာစားသောတူ *ăsà-sà-dhàw-tu*
corkscrew	ဝက်အူလှည့်တံ *weq-u-hlèh-dan*
cup	ခွက် *k´weq*
fork	ခက်ရင်း *k´eq-rin (k´ărìn)*
frying pan	ကြော်သည့်ဒယ်အိုး *caw-dhí-deh-ó*
glass	ဖန်ခွက် *p´an-gweq*
(steak) knife	(စတိတ်လှီးသည့်)ဓား *(săteiq-hlì-dhí) dà*
measuring cup/spoon	တိုင်းတာသည့် ခွက်/ဇွန်း *taìn-ta-dhí-k´weq/zùn*
napkin	လက်သုတ်ပုဝါ *leq-thouq-păwa*
plate	ပန်းကန်ပြား *băgan-byà*
pot	အိုး *ó*
spatula	ကော်သည့်အတံ *kaw-dhí-ătan*
spoon	ဇွန်း *zùn*

Drinks

ESSENTIAL

TThe wine list/drink menu, please.	ကျေးဇူးပြုပြီး ဝိုင်အမည်စာရင်း/သောက်စရာအမည်စာရင်း ပေးပါ။ *cè-zù-pyù-byì-wain-ămyi-săyìn/thauq-săya-ămyi-săyìn pè-ba*
What do you recommend?	ဘာသောက်ဖို့ ခင်ဗျား/ရှင် တိုက်တွန်းမလဲ။ *ba-thauq-p´ó-k´ămyà/shin-taiq-tùn-mălèh*
I'd like a bottle/glass of red/white wine.	ဝိုင်နီ/ဝိုင်ဖြူ တစ်ပုလင်း။တစ်ခွက် ကျွန်တော/ကျွန်မ လိုချင်ပါတယ်။ *wain-ni /wain-p´yu-dă-bălín/tăk´weq cănaw* ***m****/cămá* ***f*** *lo-jin-ba-deh*
The house wine, please.	ကျေးဇူးပြုပြီး အိမ်လုပ်ဝိုင် ပေးပါ။ *cè-zù-pyù-byì-ein-louq-wain-pè-ba*
Another bottle/glass, please.	ကျေးဇူးပြုပြီး နောက်ထပ် တစ်ပုလင်း/တစ်ဖန်ခွက် ပေးပါ။ *cè-zù-pyù-byì-nauq-t´aq-da-bălin/tăp´an-gweq-pè-ba*
I'd like a local beer.	ဒေသထွက်ဘီယာတစ်မျိုး ကျွန်တော်/ကျွန်မ လိုချင်ပါတယ်။ *de-thá-t´weq-bi-ya-tămyò-cănaw* ***m****/ cămá* ***f*** *lo-jin-ba-deh*
Can I buy you a drink?	ကျွန်တော်/ကျွန်မ ခင်ဗျား/ရှင့်ကို သောက်စရာတစ်ခုခု ဝယ်တိုက်နိုင်မလား။ *cănaw* ***m****/cămá* ***f*** *k´ămyà* ***m****/ shin* ***f*** *go-thauq-săya-tăk´úgú-weh-taiq-nain-mălà?*
Cheers!	ချီးယားစ် *ĉi-yà*
A coffee/tea, please.	ကျေးဇူးပြုပြီး ကော်ဖီ/လက်ဖက်ရည်တစ်ခွက်ပေးပါ။ *cè-zù-pyù-byì-kaw-p´i/lăp´eq-ye-tă-k´weq-pè-ba*
Black.	ဘလက်ခ်/နွားနို့မပါ *băleq/nwà-nó-măpa*
With…	… နဲ့ *…néh*
milk	နွားနို့ *nwà-nó*
sugar	သကြား *dhăjà*

artificial sweetener	ဆေးသကြား *s'è-hăjà*
A…, please.	ကျေးဇူးပြုပြီး…တစ်ခွက်ပေးပါ။ *cè-zù-pyù-byì… tăk´weq-pè-ba*
juice	ဖျော်ရည် *p´yaw-ye*
soda	ဆိုဒါ *s´o-da*
(sparkling/still) water	(စပါကလင်ပါသော/ရိုးရိုး) ရေ *(săpa-kălin-pa-dhàw/yò-yò) ye*

Non-alcoholic Drinks

coffee	ကော်ဖီ *kaw-p´i*
hot chocolate	ချောကလက်ဖျော်ရည်အပူ *ćàw-kăleq-p´yaw-ye-ăpu*
juice	ဖျော်ရည် *p´yaw-ye*
lemonade	လီမွန်နိတ်ဖျော်ရည် *li-mun-neiq-p´yaw-ye*
milk	နွားနို့ *nwà-nó*
soda	ဆိုဒါ *s'o-da*
(sparkling/still) water	(စပါကလင်ပါသော/ရိုးရိုး) ရေ *(săpa-kălin-pa-dhàw/yò yò)ye*
(iced) tea	လက်ဖက်ရည်(အေး) *lăp´eq ye (è)*

YOU MAY HEAR…

ကျွန်တော်/ကျွန်မ ခင်ဗျား/ရှင့် အတွက် သောက်စရာတစ်ခုခု ယူပေးနိုင်မလား။ *cănaw* ***m****/cămá* ***f*** *k´ămyà* ***m****/shin* ***f*** *ătweq-thauq-săya-tăk´ú-k´ú-yu-pènain-mălà*	Can I get you a drink?
နို့နဲ့ ဒါမှမဟုတ် သကြားနဲ့လား။ *nó-néh-da-hmá-măhouq-dhăjà-néh-là?*	With milk or sugar?
စပါကလင်ပါတဲ့ရေလား ဒါမှမဟုတ် ရိုးရိုးရေလား။ *săpakălin-pa-déh-ye-là?*	Sparkling or still water?

Bottled water is available everywhere (always check the seal before opening) and most restaurants offer freshly squeezed juice.

Apéritifs, Cocktails & Liqueurs

brandy	ဘရန်ဒီအရက် *băran-di-ăyeq*
gin	ဂျင်အရက် *sjin-ăyeq*
rum	ရမ်အရက် *ran-ăyeq*
scotch	စကော့အရက် *săkáw-ăyeq*
tequila	တကီးလားအရက် *tăkì-ăyeq*
vodka	ဗော့ဂါအရက် *báw-ga-ăyeq*
whisky	ဝီစကီအရက် *wi-săki-ăyeq*

Beer

...beer	... ဘီယာ ... *bi-ya*
bottled/draft	ပုလင်း။ရိုးရိုးလောင်းထည့်သော *pălin/yò-yò-laùn-t´éh-dhàw*
dark/light	အရောင်ရင့်။အရောင်ဖျော့ *ăyaun-yín/ăyaun-p´yáw*
lager/pilsener	လက်ဂျာ/ပေလ်စနာ *sjin-ăyeqleq-ja/pe săna*
local/imported	ဒေသထွက်/နိုင်ငံခြား *de-thá-dweq/nain-ngan-jà*
non-alcoholic	မမူးသော/အရက်မပါသော *mămù-dhàw/ăyeq-măpa dhàw*

Consumption of alcohol in general, and beer in particular, is on the rise in Myanmar. Local brands of light larger such as "Mandalay Beer" can be found everywhere, and in the resorts international brands such as San Miguel, Tiger and Singha. Neon-lit "beer stations" where local draught lagers are sold by the pitcher or glass, are the places most locals go for a tipple.

Wine

...wine	... ဝိုင် ...*wain*
red/white	အနီ/အဖြူ *ăni/ăp´yu*
house/table	အိမ်/စားပွဲ *ein/zăbwèh*
dry/sweet	အခါး/အချို *ăk´à/ăćo*
sparkling	စပါကလင် *săpakălin*
champagne	ရှန်ပိန် *shan-pein*
dessert wine	အချိုတည်းသည့်အနေဖြင့်သောက်သောဝိုင် *ăćo-tèh-dhí-ănè-p´yín-thauq-thàw-wain*

Myanmar produces some decent New-world-style wines, grown mostly in the Shan Hills around Pyin U Lwin (Maymo) and Taunggyi (near Inle Lake). Red Mountain (redmountain-estate.com) Sauvignon Blanc and the wines from Myanmar Vineyard (Myanmar-vineyard.com) are particularly successful.

On the Menu

almond	ဗန်ဒါသီး၊ ဗန်ဒါစေ့ *ban-da-dhi ?ban-da-zé*
anchovy	ပုန်းရည်ကြီး *poùn-ye-jì*
aperitif	အစားမစားမီ စားသောက်ကောင်းစေရန်သောက်သောအရက် *ăsà-măsà-mi-sà-thauq-kaùn-ze-yan-thauq-thàw-ăyeq*
apple	ပန်းသီး *pàn-dhì*
apricot	တရုတ်ဆီးသီး *tăyouq-zì-dhì*
artichoke	မျှစ်နှင့်တူသောအမြစ်တစ်မျိုး *hmyiq-hnín-tu-dhàw-ămyiq-tămyò*
artificial sweetener	ဆေးသကြား *sè-dhăjà*
asparagus	ကညွတ် *kănyuq*
avocado	ထောပတ်သီး *t´àw-baq-thì*
banana	ငှက်ပျောသီး *ngăpyàw-dhì*
bass	ငါးကြင်း *ngăjìn*
bay leaf	ဟင်းခတ်အမွှေးအကြိုင်အရွက်တစ်မျိုး *hìn-k´aq-ăhmwè-ăkyain-ăyweq-tămyò*
bean	ပဲစိမ်း *pèh-seìn*
bean sprout	ပဲစိမ်းပင်ပေါက် *pèh-seìn-bin-bauq*
beef	အမဲသား *ămèh-dhà*
beer	ဘီယာ *bi-ya*
beet	သကြားမုန်လာဥ *dhăjà-moun-la-ú*
brandy	ဘရန်ဒီအရက် *băran-di-ăyeq*
bread	ပေါင်မုန့် *paun-moún*
breast (of chicken)	(ကြက်)ရင်အုပ်သား *(ceq) yin-ouq-thà*
broth	အသားပြုတ်ရည် *ăthà-pyouq-ye*
butter	ထောပတ် *t´àw-baq*
buttermilk	ထောပတ်နှင့် နို့ရောထားသော *t´àw-baq-hnín-nó-yàw-t´à-dhàw*
cabbage	ပန်းဂေါ်ဖီ၊ မုန်လာထုပ် *pàn-gaw-bi ? moun-la-douq*

cake — ကိတ် *keiq*
candy [sweets] — သကြားလုံး (အချိုများ) *dhăjà-loùn (ăćo-myà)*
caramel — သကြားသကာရည် *dhăjà-dhăga-ye*
caraway — ကရဝေးရွက် *kărăwè-yweq*
carrot — မုန်လာဥနီ *moun-la-ú-ni*
cashew — သကြားသီး *dhăjà-dhì*
cauliflower — ပန်းဂေါ်ဖီ *pàn-gaw-bi*
celery — တရုတ်နံနံပင် *tăyouq-nan-nan-bin*
cereal — ပြားထားသောဂျုံစေ့ *pyà-t´à-dhàw-joun-zé*
cheese — ချီးစ် *ći*
cherry — ချယ်ရီသီး *ćeh-ri-dhì*
chervil — ပြင်သစ်နံနံပင် *pyin-thiq-nan-nan-bin*
chestnut — သစ်အယ်ပင *thiq-eh-bin*
chicken — ကြက်သား *ćeq-thà*
chickpea — ကုလားပဲ *kălăbèh*
chicory — ချီကိုရီပင် *ći-ko-ri-bin*
chili pepper — စပ်သောငရုပ်ပွ *saq-thàw-ngăyouq-pwà*
chinese dates — တရုတ်မက်မန်း *tăyouq-meq-màn*
chinese liquor — တရုတ်အရက် *tăyouq-ăyeq*
chives — ကြက်သွန်နွယ်ဝင်တစ်မျိုး

	ceq-thun-nweh-win-tămyò
chocolate	ချောကလက် *ćàw-kàleq*
chop	တောက်တောက်စင်းသည် *tauq-tauq-sìn-dhi*
chopped meat	တောက်တောက်စင်းထားသောအသား *tauq-tauq-sìn-t´à-dhàw-ăthà*
cider	သစ်တော်သီးရည် *thiq-taw-dhì-ye*
cilantro [coriander]	တရုတ်ဟင်းမွှေးရွက် *tăyouq-hin-hmwè-yweq*
cinnamon	သစ်ကြံပိုးခေါက် *thiq-jăbò-gauq*
clam	ယောက်သွား *auq-thwà*
clove	လေးညှင်း *lè-hnyìn*
coconut	အုန်းသီး *oùn-dhì*
coconut noodles	အုန်းနို့ခေါက်ဆွဲ *oùn-nó-k´auq-s'wèh*
coconut rice	အုန်းထမင်း *oùn-t´ămìn*
cod	ပင်လယ်ငါးကြီးတစ်မျိုး *pin-leh-ngà-jì-tămyò*
coffee	ကော်ဖီ *kaw-p´i*
cookie [biscuit]	ကွတ်ကီး (ဘီစကစ်) *kuq-kì (bi-săkiq)*
cornmeal	ပြောင်းဖူးမုန့် *paùn-bù-moún*
crab	ဂဏန်း *gănàn*
crabmeat	ဂဏန်းသား *gănàn-dhà*
cracker	ခရက်ကာ *k´ăreq-ka*
cream	ကရင်မ် *k´ărin*
cream, whipped	ကရင်မ် (နို့နှစ်)၊ ခေါက်ပြီးအမြှုပ်ထအောင်ပြုသည် *k´ărin- (nó-hniq) ? k´auq-pyì-ăhmyouq-t´á-aun-pyú-dhi*
cucumber	သခွားသီး *thăk´wà-dhì*
cumin	ဆနွင်း *s'ănwìn*
cured pork	ဆားနယ်ထားသောဝက်သား *s'à-neh-t´à-dhàw-weq-thà*
custard	ကြက်ဥ၊နွားနို့တို့ဖြင့်လုပ်ထားသောမုန့် *ceq-ú ? nwà-nó-dó-p´yín-louq-t´à-dhàw-moún*

dessert wine	အချိုတည်းသည့်အနေဖြင့် သောက်သောဝိုင်ချို *ăćo-tèh-dhí-ăne-p´yín-thauq-thàw-wain-jo*
duck	ဘဲသား *bèh-dhà*
dumpling	ဖက်ထုတ် *pèq-t´ouq*
eel	ငါးရှဉ့် *ngăshín*
egg	ကြက်/ဘဲဥ *ceq/bèh-ú*
pickled egg	အချဉ်တည်ထားသော ကြက်/ဘဲဥ *ăćin-teh-t´à-dhàw-ceq/bèh-ú*
steamed egg pasty	ကြက်/ဘဲဥပြုတ် အစာသွတ် *ceq/bèh-ú-pyouq-ăs'a-thuq*
egg yolk/white	ကြက်/ဘဲဥ အနှစ်/အကာ *ceq/bèh-ú-ăhniq/ăka*
eggplant [aubergine]	ခရမ်းသီး *kăyàn-dhì*
endive	ဒေစီနွယ်ဝင်အရွက်တစ်မျိုး/ဆလပ်တွင်းထည့်သည် *de-si-nweh-win-ăyeq-tămyò/s'ălaq-twìn-t´éh-dhi*
escarole [chicory]	အရွက်ကြီးပြီးအခါးဓာတ်နည်းသော ဒေစီနွယ်ဝင်အရွက်တစ်မျိုး *ăyeq-cì-byì-ăk´à-daq-nèh-dhàw-de-si-nweh-win-ăyweq-tămyò*
fennel	ကြွပ်ပြီးအနည်းငယ်ချိုသောအရွက်တစ်မျိုး *cuq-pyì-ănèh-ngeh-ćo-dhàw-ăyweq-tămyò*
fig	သဖန်းသီး *thăp´àn-dhì*
fish	ငါး *ngà*

french fries — အာလူးချောင်းကြော် *a-lù-jaùn-jaw*
fried rice — ထမင်းကြော် *t´ămìn-jaw*
fritter — ဂျုံဖြင့်မန်ပြီးကြော်ထားသောစားစရာ *joun-p´yín-man-byì-caw-t´à-dhàw-sà-zăya*
fruit — သစ်သီး *thiq-thì*
game — အမဲလိုက်သား/ကစားပွဲ *ămèh-laiq-thà/găzà-bwèh*
garlic — ကြက်သွန်ဖြူ *ceq-thun-byu*
garlic sauce — ကြက်သွန်ဖြူအနှစ်ရည် *ceq-thun-byu-ăhniq-ye*
gherkin — သခွားသီးအသေး *thăk´wà-dhì-ăthè*
giblet — ကြက်၊ ဘဲကလီစာ *ceq ?bèh-kăliza*
gin — ဂျင်အရက် *jin-ăyeq*
ginger — ဂျင်း *jìn*
goat — ဆိတ် *s'eiq*
goat cheese — ဆိတ်နို့မှထုတ်သောချိစ် *s'eiq-nó-hmá-t´ouq-thàw-ĉì*
gooseberry — ဘယ်ရီသီးတစ်မျိုး *beh-ri-dhì-ăthè-tămyò*
grapefruit — ကျွဲကောသီးအသေးတစ်မျိုး *cwèh-gàw-dhì-ăthè-tămyò*
grapes — စပျစ်သီး *zăbyiq-thì*
grass carp — မြက်ငါးဖယ်။ရေချိုငါးတစ်မျိုး *myeq-ngăp´eh/ye-jo-ngà-tămyò*

green bean ပဲသီးစိမ်း *pèh-dhì-zèin*
guava မာလကာသီး *ma-lăka-dhì*
haddock ဟက်ဒေါ့ခ်ဟုခေါ်သည့် ပင်လယ်ငါးတစ်မျိုး *heq-dáw-hú-k´aw-dhí-pin-leh-ngà-tămyò*
hake ဟာကယ်ဟုခေါ်သည့် ပင်လယ်ငါးတစ်မျိုး *ha-keh-hú-k´aw-dhí-pin-leh-ngà-tămyò*
halibut ပင်လယ်ငါးပြားတစ်မျိုး *pin-leh-ngà-pyà-tămyò*
ham ဝက်ပေါင်ကြပ်တင်သား *weq-paun-caq-tin-dhà*
hamburger ဟမ်ဘာဂါ/အသားညှပ်ပေါင်မုန့် *han-ba-ga/ăthà-hnyaq-paun-moún*
hazelnut သစ်အယ်သီး *thiq-eh-dhì*
heart နှလုံး *hnăloùn*
hen ကြက်မ *ceq-má*
herb ဆေးဖက်ဝင်သစ်ဥ၊သစ်ဖု၊သစ်ရွက် *sè-beq-win-thiq-ú ? thiq-p´ú ? thiq-yweq*
herring သေးငယ်သောပင်လယ်ငါးတစ်မျိုး *thè-ngeh-dhàw-pin-leh-ngà-tămyò*
honey ပျားရည် *pyà-ye*
hot dog ဝက်အူချောင်းညှပ်ပေါင်မုန့် *weq-u-jaùn-hnyaq-paun-moún*
ice (cube) ရေခဲ *ye-gèh*
ice cream ရေခဲမုန့် *ye-gèh-moún*
jam ယို/ပေါင်မုန့်နှင့်သုတ်စားသည့်ယို *yo/paun-moún-hnín-thouq-sà-dhí-yo*
jelly ဂျယ်လီ/ကျောက်ကျော *jeh-li/cauq-càw*
juice ဖျော်ရည် *p´yaw*
kidney ကျောက်ကပ် *cauq-kaq*
kiwi ကီဝီသီး *ki-wi-dhì*
lamb သိုးငယ်/သိုးငယ်သား *thò-ngeh/thò-ngeh-dhà*
leek ကြက်သွန်နီတစ်မျိုး *ceq-thun-ni-tămyò*

leg	ခြေထောက် *ćе-dauq*
lemon	ရှောက်သီး *shauq-thì*
lemonade	လီမွန်နိတ်ဖျော်ရည် *li-mun-neiq-p´yaw-ye*
lentil	ပဲနီလေး၊ ပဲဝါလေး *pèh-ni ? pèh-wa-lè*
lettuce	ဆလပ်ရွက် *s'ălaq-yweq*
lime	သံပုရာသီး *than-băya-dhì*
liver	အသည်း *ăthèh*
lobster	ပုဇွန်ထုပ်ကြီး *bàzun-douq-cì*
longan fruit	သဖန်းသီးတစ်မျိုး *thăp´àn-dhì-tămyò*
loin	ပေါင်သား *paun-dhà*
macaroni	အီတလီခေါက်ဆွဲတစ်မျိုး *i-tăli-k´auq-s'wèh-tămyò*
mackerel	ငါးကွမ်းရှပ် *ngăkùn-shaq*
mandarin orange	မန်ဒရင်းလိမ္မော်သီး *man-dărìn-lein-maw-dhì*
mango	သရက်သီး *thàyeq-thì*
margarine	ထောပတ်တု *t´àw-baq-tú*
mayonnaise	အနည်းငယ်ချဉ်သောကရင်မ်တစ်မျိုး *ănèh-ngeh-ćin-dhàw-k´ărin-tămyò*
meat	အသား *ăthà*
melon	ဖရဲသီးနွယ်ဝင်အသီး *p´ăyèh-dhì-nweh-win-ăthì*
milk	နွားနို့/နို့ရည် *nwà-nó/nó-ye*
monkfish	ငါးပုဏ္ဏား *ngăpoun-nà*
mushroom	မှို *hmo*
mussel	ယောက်သွားတစ်မျိုး/ခရုတစ်မျိုး *yauq-thwà-tàmyò/k´ăyú-tămyò*
mutton	သိုးသား *thò-dhà*
noodle	ခေါက်ဆွဲ *k´auq-s'wèh*
nougat	သစ်စေ့ထည့်ထားသောသကြားလုံး *thiq-sé-t´éh-dà-dhàw-dhăjà-loùn*

nutmeg	ဇာတိပ္ဖိုလ်သီး *za-teiq-p´o-dhì*
nuts	အခွံမာသီးများ *ăk´un-ma-dhì-myà*
octopus	ရေဘဝဲ *ye-băwèh*
olive	သံလွင်သီး *than-lwin-dhì*
olive oil	သံလွင်ဆီ *than-lwin-zi*
omelet	ကြက်ဥမွှေကြော် *ceq-ú-hmwe-jaw*
onion	ကြက်သွန်နီ *ceq-thun-ni*
orange	လိမ္မော်သီး *lein-maw-dhì*
organ meat [offal]	ဝမ်းတွင်းသား *wàn(wùn) dwin-dhà*
oyster	ကနုကမာကောင်/ယောက်သွား *kănú-kăma-gaun/yauq-thwá*
pancake	မုန့်ပြားသလက် *moún-pyà-thăleq*
papaya	သင်္ဘောသီး *thin-bàw-dhì*
paprika	ချိုပြီးစပ်သည့် ငရုပ်သီးတစ်မျိုး *ćo-byì-saq-thí-ngàyouq-thì-tămyò*
pastry	ပေစတရီ/ဂျုံဖြင့်လုပ်သည့်မုန့်တစ်မျိုး *pe-sătări/joun-p´yín-louq-thí-moún-tămyò*
peach	မက်မုံသီး *meq-moun-dhi*

peanut	မြေပဲ *mye-bèh*
pear	သစ်တော်သီး *thiq-taw-dhì*
peas	ပဲအမျိုးမျိုး *bèh-ămyò-myò*
pecan	အမျှင်ဓာတ်နှင့်ပရိုတင်းဓာတ်များသည့် အသီးတစ်မျိုး *ăhmyin-daq-hnín-păro-tin-daq-myà-dhí-ăthì-tămyò*
pepper (vegetable)	ငရုပ်ပွ (ဟင်းသီးဟင်းရွက်) *ngăyouq-pwá (hìn-dhì-hìn-yweq)*
pickle	အချဉ်တည်ထားသောအရာ *ăćin-t´à-dhàw-ăya*
pie	ပိုင်။အစာသွတ်ဖုတ်မုန့် *pain/ăsa-thuq-p´ouq-moún*
pineapple	နာနတ်သီး *na-naq-thì*
pizza	ပီဇာ *pi-za*
plum	ဆီးသီး *zì-dhì*
pomegranate	သလဲသီး *thălèh-dhì*
pork	ဝက်သား *weq-thà*
port	ပို့ဝိုင်။ဆိပ်ကမ်း *pó-wain/s'eiq-kàn*
potato	အာလူး *a-lù*
potato chips [crisps]	အာလူးပြားကြော် (အကြွပ်) *ă-lù-byà-jaw (ăćuq)*
poultry	ကြက်သား၊ ဘဲသား *ceq thà ? bèh thà*
prune	ဆီးသီးခြောက် *zì-dhì-jauq*
pumpkin	ရွှေဖယုံသီး *shwe-p´ăyoun-dhì*
quail	ငုံး *ngoùn*
rabbit	ယုန် *youn*
radish	မုန်လာဥဖြူ *moun-la-ú-p´yu*
raisin	စပျစ်သီးခြောက် *zăbyiq-thì-jauq*
red bayberry	အနီရောင်ဘယ်ရီသီးတစ်မျိုး *ăni-yaun-beh-ri-dhì-tămyò*

red cabbage မုန်လာထုတ်နီ
moun-la-douq-ni
rice ဆန် *s'an*
roll အလိပ် *ăleiq*
rum ရမ်အရက် *ran-ăyeq*
salad ဆလပ်/အရွက်စုံ *s'ă-laq/ăyewq-soun*
sardine ငါးသေတ္တာငါး *ngà-thiq-ta-ngà*
sauce အနှစ် *ăhniq*
sausage ဝက်အူချောင်း *weq-u-jaùn*
scallion [spring onion] ကြက်သွန်မိတ် *ceq-thun-meiq*
scallop ပင်လယ်ခုံးကောင်တစ်မျိုး
pin-leh-goùn-gaun-tămyo
scotch ဖျောက်ဖျက်သည်/စကော့အရက်
p´yauq-p´yeq-thi/ săkáw-ăyeq
sea bass ငါးပြေမ *pin-leh-ngă-pye-má*
sea perch ကကတစ်ငါး *ká-gădiq-ngà*
seafood ပင်လယ်စာ *pin-leh-za*
seaweed ပင်လယ်ရေညှိ *pin-leh-ye-hnyí*
shallot ကြက်သွန်ဖြူနံ့ထွက်သည့် ကြက်သွန်နီတစ်မျိုး
ceq-thun-byu-nán-t´weq-thí-ceq-thun-ni-tămyò
shan noodles ရှမ်းခေါက်ဆွဲ *shàn-k´auq-s'wèh*

shank ခြေသလုံး *će-dhăloùn*
shellfish အခွံမာငါးတစ်မျိုး/ခုံးကောင် *ăk´un-ma-ngà-tămyò/goùn-gaun*
sherry ရှယ်ရီအရက် *sheh-ri-ăyeq*
shoulder ပုခုံး *păk´oùn*
shrimp ပုစွန်ဆိပ် *băzun-zeiq*
silver carp ငွေရောင်ငါးဖယ် *ngwe-yaun-ngà-p´eh*
sirloin ပေါင်ရင်းသား၊ အထူးသဖြင့် အမဲပေါင်ရင်းသား *paun-yin-dhà ? ăt´ù-thăp´yín-ămèh-paun-yin-dhà*
snack သွားရည်စာ *thăye-za*
snail ခရု *k´ăyú*
soda ဆိုဒါရည် *so-da-ye*
sole ခြေဖဝါး/ပြားသောငါးတစ်မျိုး *će-p´ăwà/pyà-dhàw-ngà-tămyò*
soup ဟင်းချို *hìn-jo*
sour cream ချဉ်သောကရင်မ် *ćin-dhàw-k´ărin*
soy [soya] ပဲပိစပ် *pèh-bí-zaq*
soy sauce ပဲငံပြာရည်အနှစ် *pèh-ngan-pya-ye-ăhniq*
soybean [soya bean] ပဲပိစပ်ပဲ *pèh-bí-zaq-pèh*
soymilk [soya milk] ပဲနို့ *pèh-nó*
spaghetti အီတလီခေါက်ဆွဲ *i-tăli-k´auq-s'wèh*
spices ဟင်းခတ်အမွှေးအကြိုင်များ *hìn-k´aq-ăhmwè-ăcain-myà*
spinach ဟင်းနုနွယ်ရွက် *hìn-nú-nweh-yweq*
spirits စိတ်နေသဘောထား/ဝိဉာဉ်/အရက်ပြင်းများ *seiq-ne-dhăbàw-dà/wein-nyin/ăyeq-pyìn-myà*
squash သစ်သီးဖျော်ရည် *thiq-thì-p´yaw-ye*
squid ပြည်ကြီးငါး *pyi-jì-ngà*
steak စတိတ်အသား *săteiq-ăthà*

steamed rice	ထမင်း *t´ămìn*
stewed fruit	အသီးရောနှပ် *ăthì-yàw-hnaq*
sticky rice	ကောက်ညှင်းပေါင်း *kauq-hnyìn-baùn*
strawberry	စထရော်ဘယ်ရီသီး *săt´ăraw-beh-ri-dhì*
suckling pig	မွေးကင်းစဝက်ကလေး *mwè-kìn-zá-weq-k´ălè*
sugar	သကြား *dhăjà*
sweets	သကြားလုံးများ/အချိုများ *dhăjà-loùn-myà/ăć0-myà*
sweet and sour sauce	ချိုချဉ်ဟင်းနှစ် *ćo-ćin-hìn-hniq*
sweet corn	ပြောင်းဖူးချို *pyaùn-bù-ćo*
sweet pepper	ငရုပ်ချို *ngăyouq-ćo*
sweet potato	ကန်စွန်းဥ *găzùn-ú*
sweetener	ဆေးသကြား *s'è-dhăjà*
swordfish	ဓါးကဲ့သို့ချွန်သောနှုတ်သီးရှိသည့်ငါး *dà-kéh-thó-ćun-dhàw-hnouq-thì-shí-dhí-ngà*
syrup	သကာရည်/တင်လဲရည် *dhăga-ye/tin-lèh-ye*
tangerine	လိမ္မော်သီးတစ်မျိုး *lein-maw-dhì-tămyò*
tarragon	တာရဂွန်/ဟင်းခတ်အမွှေးအကြိုင်တစ်မျိုး *ta-răgun/hìn-k´aq-ăhmwè-ăcain-tămyò*

tea လက်ဖက်ရည် *lăp´eq-ye*

thyme သိုင်းမ်/ဟင်းခတ်အမွှေးအကြိုင်တစ်မျိုး *thaìn/hin-k´aq-ăhmwè-ăcain-tămyò*

tofu တိုဖူး/ပဲပြား *to-p´ù/pèh-byà*

breaded tofu ပေါင်မုန့်ကဲ့သို့အပြားလုပ်ထားသော တိုဖူး/ပဲပြား *paun-moún-kéh-thó-ăpyà-louq-t´à-dhàw -to-p´ù/pèh-byà*

cold tofu with garlic sauce ကြက်သွန်ဖြူအနှစ်ဆမ်းထားသော တိုဖူး/ပဲပြားအအေး *ceq-thun-byu-ăhniq-s'àn-t´à-dhàw-to-p´ù/pèh-byà*

crushed tofu with pickled egg ဘဲဥချဉ်နှင့် ချေထားသောတိုဖူး/ပဲပြား *bèh-ú-jin-hnín-će-t´à-dhàw-to-p´ù/pèh-byà*

fried, stuffed tofu ကြော်ထားသောအစာသွပ်တိုဖူး/ပဲပြား *caw-t´à-dhaw-ăsa-thuq-to-p´ù/pèh-byà*

spicy tofu တိုဖူး/ပဲပြားအစပ် *to-p´ù/pèh-byà-ăsaq*

sauteed tofu တိုဖူး/ပဲပြားအမြန်ကြော် *to-p´ù/pèh-byà-ămyan-jaw*

tofu in a clay pot မြေအိုးတိုဖူး/ပဲပြား *mye-ò-to-p´ù/pèh-byà*

tofu with fish ငါးနှင့်တိုဖူး/ပဲပြား *ngà-hnín-to-p´ù/pèh-byà*

tofu with meatballs အသားလုံးနှင့်တိုဖူး/ပဲပြား *ăthà-loùn-hnín-to-p´ù/pèh-byà*

tofu with peeled အခွံချွတ်ထားသောပုစွန်ဆိပ်နှင့်တိုဖူး/ပဲပြား *ăkùn-ćuq-t´à-dhàw-băzun-zeiq-hnín- to-p´ù/pèh-byà*

freshwater shimp	
toast	ပေါင်မုန့်မီးကင်သည်/အောင်မြင်စေရန်အရက်မသောက်မီဆိုသောစကား *paun-moún-mì-kin-dhi/aun-myin-ze-yan-ăyeq-măthauq-mi-s'o-dhàw-zăgà*
tomato	ခရမ်းချဉ်သီး *k´ăyàn-jin-dhì*
tongue	လျှာ *sha*
tonic water	ခွန်အားဖြည့်ရေ *k´un-à-p´yé-ye*
tripe	ဝမ်းတွင်းသား *wàn (wùn) dwìn-dhà*
trout	ငါးသလောက် *ngăthălauq*
truffles	အင်ဥ။ မှိုဥ *in-ú/hmo-ú*
tuna	တူနာငါး *tu-na-ngà*
turkey	ကြက်ဆင် *ceq-s'in*
turnip	မုန်လာဥ *moun-la-ú*
vanilla	ဗနီလာ/မွှေးသောသစ်ခွပန်းတစ်မျိုး *băni-la/hmwè-dhaw-thiq-k´wá-pàn-tămyo*
veal	နွားလေးသား *nwà-lè-dhà*
vegetable	ဟင်းသီးဟင်းရွက် *hìn-dhì-hìn-yewq*
vermouth	ရနံ့အရသာပေါင်းထည့်ထားသော ဝိုင်တစ်မျိုး *yănan´-ăyá-dha-paùn-t´éh-t´à-dhàw-wain-tămyò*
vinegar	ရှာလကာရည် *sha-lăka-ye*
vodka	ဗော့ဂါအရက် *báw-ga-ăyeq*
waffle	ဝေဖာ *we-p´a*
walnut	သစ်ကြားသီး *thiq-cà-dhì*
water	ရေ *ye*
watercress	ကန်စွန်းရွက် *găzùn-yweq*
watermelon	ဖရဲသီး *p´ăyèh-dhì*
wheat	ဂျုံ *joun*
whisky	ဝီစကီ *wi-săki*
wine	ဝိုင် *wain*
yogurt	ဒိန်ချဉ် *dein-jin*

People

Conversation 97
Romance 104

Conversation

ESSENTIAL

Hello!/Hi!	ဟယ်လို/ဟိုင်း *hălo, hèh-lo/hain*
How are you?	နေကောင်းလား။ *ne-kaùn-là?*
Fine, thanks.	နေကောင်းပါတယ်၊ ကျေးဇူးပဲ။ *ne-kaùn-ba-deh-cè-zù-bèh*
Excuse me!	ကျွန်တော်/ကျွန်မ ကိုစိတ်မရှိပါနဲ့။ *cănaw* ***m*** */cămá* ***f*** *go-seiq-măshí-ba-néh*
Do you speak English?	ခင်ဗျား/ရှင် အင်္ဂလိပ်စကား ပြောသလား။ *k´ămyà* ***m****/shin* ***f*** *ìn-găleiq-zăgà-pyàw-dhălà?*
What's your name?	ခင်ဗျား/ရှင့် နာမည် ဘယ်လိုခေါ်သလဲ။ *k´ămyà-* ***m****/shín* ***f*** *nan-meh-beh-lo-k´aw-dhălèh?*
My name is...	ကျွန်တော်/ကျွန်မရဲ့နာမည်က ... ပါ။ *cănaw* ***m****/cămá* ***f*** *yèh-nan-meh-gá...ba*
Nice to meet you.	ခင်ဗျား/ရှင့်ကို တွေ့ရတာ ဝမ်းသာပါတယ်။ *k´ămyà* ***m****/shín* ***f*** *go-twè-yá-da-wùn-tha-ba-deh*
Where are you from?	ခင်ဗျား/ရှင် ဘယ်နိုင်ငံကလာတာလဲ။ *k´ămyà* ***m****/shin* ***f*** *beh-nain-ngan-gá-la-da-lèh?*
I'm from the U.S./U.K.	ကျွန်တော်/ကျွန်မက ယူကေ/အမေရိကန် နိုင်ငံကပါ။ *cănaw* ***m****/cămá* ***f*** *gá-yu-ke/Ăme-rí-kan-nain-ngan-gá-ba*
What do you do for a living?	အသက်မွေးဝမ်းကျောင်းဖို့အတွက် ခင်ဗျား/ရှင် ဘာအလုပ်လုပ်လဲ။ *Ătheq-mwè-wàn-caùn-bó-ătweq-k´ămyà* ***m****/shin* ***f*** *ba-ălouq-louq-lèh?*
I work for...	ကျွန်တော်/ကျွန်မ ... အတွက် အလုပ်လုပ်ပါတယ်။ *cănaw* ***m****/cămá* ***f****...ătweq-ălouq-louq-pa-deh.*
I'm a student.	ကျွန်တော်/ကျွန်မက ကျောင်းသားတစ်ယောက်ပါ။ *cănaw* ***m****/cămá* ***f*** *ga- caùn-dhà-tăyauq-pa*

I'm retired.	ကျွန်တော်/ကျွန်မက ပင်စင်ယူထားတာပါ။ *cănaw* ***m****/cămá* ***f*** *gá- pin-sin-yu-t´à-da-ba.*
Do you like…?	ခင်ဗျား/ရှင် … ကိုကြိုက်သလား။ *k´ămyà* ***m*** */shin* ***f****… go-caiq-thălà?*
Goodbye.	ဂွတ်ဘိုင်/နှုတ်ဆက်ပါတယ်။ *guq-bain/hnouq-s'eq-pb-deh.*
See you later.	နောက်မှတွေ့မယ်။ *nauq-hmà-twè-meh*

You should always refer to people by their full title and full name. There are no family names in Burmese culture. Only by way of address can one tell the gender or social status of a Burmese. For example, a man called **Kau Reng** might be addressed as "**U kau Reng**", "**Ko Kau Reng**" or "**Maung Kau Reng**". The title "U" indicated superiority of social or official position, or of age. "**Ko**" is common among men of similar standing and "**Maung**" is used with persons who are younger or of an inferior status, and among children and teenage boys. "**Ko Maung**" may be used if the name is monosyllabic.

Language Difficulties

Do you speak English?	ခင်ဗျား/ရှင် အင်္ဂလိပ်စကားပြောသလား။ *k´ămyà* ***m****/shin* ***f*** *ìn-găleiq-zăgà-pyàw-dhălà?*
Does anyone here speak English?	ဒီမှာရှိတဲ့တစ်ယောက်ယောက် အင်္ဂလိပ်စကားပြောသလား။ *di-hma-shí-déh-tăyauq-yauq-ìn-găleiq-zăgà-pyàw-dhălà?*
I don't speak (much) Burmese.	ကျွန်တော်/ကျွန်မ ဗမာစကား (များများ) မပြောတတ်ဘူး။ *cănaw* ***m****/cămá* ***f*** *băma-zăga (myà-myà) măpyàw-daq-bù*
Can you speak more slowly?	ခင်ဗျား/ရှင် ပိုပြီးဖြည်းဖြည်း ပြောနိုင်မလား။ *k´ămyà* ***m****/ shin* ***f*** *po-byì-p´yè-p´yè-pyàw-nain-mălà?*

Can you repeat that?	ခင်ဗျား/ရှင် အဲဒါကို ထပ်ပြီးပြောပြနိုင်မလား။ *k´ămyà **m**/shin **f** èh-da-go-t´aq-pì- pyàw-nain-mălà?*
Excuse me?	ကျွန်တော်/ကျွန်မကို စိတ်မရှိပါနဲ့။ *cănaw **m**/cămá **f** go-seiq-măshí-ba-néh*
Can you spell it?	ခင်ဗျား/ရှင် ဒါကို စာလုံးပေါင်းပြနိုင်မလား။ *k´ămyà **m**/shin **f** da-go-sa-loùn-paùn-byà-nain-mălà*
Please write it down.	ကျေးဇူးပြုပြီး အဲဒါကို ရေးချပြပါ။ *cè-zù-pyú-byì- èh-da-go-yè-k´yá-pyá-ba*
Can you translate this into English for me?	ဒါကို ကျွန်တော်/ကျွန်မ အတွက် အင်္ဂလိပ်လို ခင်ဗျား/ရှင် ဘာသာပြန်ပေးနိုင်မလား။ *da-go-cănaw **m**/cămá **f** ătweq-ìn-găleiq-lo-k´ămyà/ shin-ba-dha-pyan-bè-nain-mălà?*
What does this/that mean?	အဲဒါ/ဒါက ဘာကိုဆိုလိုတာလဲ။ *Èh-da/da-gá-ba-go-s'o-lo-da-lèh?*
I understand.	ကျွန်တော်/ကျွန်မ နားလည်တယ်။ *cănaw **m**/cămá **f** nà-leh-deh.*
I don't understand.	ကျွန်တော်/ကျွန်မ နားမလည်ဘူး။ *cănaw **m**/cămá **f** nà-măleh-bù*
Do you understand?	ခင်ဗျား/ရှင် နားလည်သလား။ *k´ămyà **m**/shin **f** nà-leh-dhălà*

YOU MAY HEAR…

ကျွန်တော်/ကျွန်မ အင်္ဂလိပ်စကား နည်းနည်းပဲပြောတယ်။ *cănaw **m**/cămá **f** ìn-găleiq-zăgà-nèh-nèh-bèh-pyàw-deh*	I only speak a little English.
ကျွန်တော်/ကျွန်မ အင်္ဂလိပ်စကားမပြောဘူး။ *cănaw **m**/cămá **f** ìn-găleiq-zăgà-măpyàw-bù*	I don't speak English.

Making Friends

Hello!	ဟယ်လို *hălo, Hèh-lo*
Good afternoon.	မင်္ဂလာနေ့လည်ခင်းပါ။ *min-găla-nè-leh-gìn-ba.*
Good evening.	မင်္ဂလာညနေခင်းပါ။ *min-găla-nya-ne-gìn-ba.*
My name is...	ကျွန်တော်/ကျွန်မရဲ့နာမည်က... ပါ။ *cănaw* ***m****/cămá* ***f*** *yèh-nan-meh-gá...ba.*
What's your name?	ခင်ဗျား/ရှင့် နာမည် ဘယ်လိုခေါ်လဲ။ *k'ămyà* ***m****/shin* ***f*** *yèh-nan-meh-beh-lo-k'aw-dhălèh?*
I'd like to introduce you to...	ကျွန်တော်/ကျွန်မ ခင်ဗျား/ရှင့်ကို ... နဲ့ မိတ်ဆက်ပေးချင်တယ်။ *cănaw* ***m****/cămá* ***f*** *k'ămyà* ***m****/shin* ***f*** *go...nèh-meiq-s'eq-pè-jin-deh.*
Pleased to meet you.	ခင်ဗျား/ရှင့်နဲ့တွေ့ရတာ ဝမ်းသာပါတယ်။ *k'ămyà* ***m****/shin* ***f*** *nèh-twè-yá-da-wùn-tha-ba-deh.*
How are you?	နေကောင်းလား။ *ne-kaùn-là?*
Fine, thanks. And you?	ကောင်းပါတယ်၊ ကျေးဇူးပဲ။ ခင်ဗျား/ရှင် ရောနေကောင်းလား။ *ne-kaùn-ba-deh-cè-zù-bèh k'ămyà* ***m****/shin* ***m*** *yàw-ne-kaùn-là?*

Burmese society is characterised by **onana**, the all-pervasive avoidance of doing anything that would offend, cause someone to lose face, or become embarrassed. Elders should always be shown respect and it is considered rude to touch someone's head because it is the highest point of the body. It is also rude to touch another's feet, but worse still to point with the foot or sit with feet pointing at another person. Shoes should be removed when entering homes.

Travel Talk

I'm here...	ကျွန်တော်/ကျွန်မ ဒီကို... လာတာပါ။ *cănaw* ***m****/cămá* ***f****-di-go... la-da-ba*

on business — အလုပ်ကိစ္စ *ălouq-keiq-sá*

on vacation [holiday] — အနားယူအပန်းဖြေဖို့ (အားလပ်ရက်) *ănà-yu-ăpán-p´ye-bó (à-laq-yeq)*

studying — ကျောင်းတက်ဖို့ *caùn-teq-p´ó*

I'm staying for… — ကျွန်တော်/ကျွန်မ… နေမှာပါ။
cănaw ***m****/cămá* ***f****… ne-hma-ba*

I've been here… — ကျွန်တော်/ကျွန်မ ဒီကိုရောက်နေတာ… ရှိသွားပြီ။
cănaw ***m****/cămá* ***f*** *di-go-yauq-ne-da… shí-thwà-bi.*

a day — တစ်ရက် *tăyeq*

a week — တစ်ပတ် *tăbaq*

a month — တစ်လ *tălá*

Where are you from? — ခင်ဗျား/ရှင် ဘယ်ကလာတာလဲ။
k´ămyà ***m****/shin* ***m*** *beh-gá-la-da-lèh?*

I'm from… — ကျွန်တော်/ကျွန်မ… ကလာတာပါ။
cănaw ***m****/cămá* ***f*** *…gá-la-da-ba*

For Numbers, see page 168.

Personal

Who are you with? — ခင်ဗျား/ရှင် ဘယ်သူနဲ့လာတာလဲ။
k´ămyà ***m****/shin* ***f*** *beh-dhu-néh-la-da-lèh?*

I'm here alone. — ကျွန်တော်/ကျွန်မ ဒီကို တစ်ယောက်တည်းလာတာ။
cănaw ***m****/cămá* ***f*** *di-go-tăyauq-t´èh-la-da.*

I'm with… — ကျွန်တော်/ကျွန်မ… နဲ့လာတာ။
cănaw ***m****/cămá* ***f****… néh-la-da.*

my husband/wife — ကျွန်တော်/ကျွန်မရဲ့ ခင်ပွန်း/ဇနီး
cănaw ***m****/cămá* ***f*** *yéh-k´in-bùn/zăni.*

my boyfriend/ girlfriend — ကျွန်တော်/ကျွန်မရဲ့ ယောကျ်ားလေးမိတ်ဆွေ။ မိန်းကလေးမိတ်ဆွေ *cănaw* ***m****/cămá* ***f*** *yèh-yauq-cà-lè-meiq-s'we/meìn-k´ălè-meiq-s'we*

a friend — သူငယ်ချင်းတစ်ယောက် *thăngeh-jìn-tăyauq*

friends — သူငယ်ချင်းတွေ *thăngeh-jìn-dwe*

a colleague	လုပ်ဖော်ကိုင်ဖက်တစ်ယောက် *louq-p´aw-kain-beq-tăyauq*
colleagues	လုပ်ဖော်ကိုင်ဖက်တွေ *louq-p´aw-kain-beq- twe*
When's your birthday?	ခင်ဗျား/ရှင့် ရဲ့မွေးနေ့က ဘယ်တော့လဲ။ *k´ămyà* ***m****/shín* ***f*** *yèh-mwè-nè-gá-beh-dáw-lèh?*
How old are you?	ခင်ဗျား/ရှင့် အသက်ဘယ်လောက်ရှိပြီလဲ။ *k´ămyà* ***m****/shín* ***f*** *ătheq-beh-lauq-shí-bi-lèh?*
I'm…	ကျွန်တော်/ကျွန်မ အသက်… နှစ်ရှိပါပြီ။ *cănaw* ***m****/cămá* ***f*** *ătheq… hinq-shí-ba-bi*
Are you married?	ခင်ဗျာ/ရှင့် အိမ်ထောင်ရှိသလား။ *k´ămyà* ***m****/shin* ***f*** *ein-daun-shí-dhălà?*
I'm…	ကျွန်တော်/ကျွန်မ… *cănaw* ***m****/cămá* ***f****…*
single/in a relationship	အိမ်ထောင်မရှိတစ်ကိုယ်တည်းပါ/တွေ့ဆုံနေတဲ့သူရှိပါတယ် *ein-daun-măshí-tăgo-dèh-ba/Twé-s'oun-ne-déh-dhu-shí-ba-deh.*
engaged	စေ့စပ်ထားပါတယ်။ *sé-zaq-t´à-ba-deh.*
married	အိမ်ထောင်ရှိပါတယ်။ *ein-daun-shí-ba-deh*
divorced	လင်မယားကွာရှင်းထားပါတယ်။ *lin-măyà-kwa-shìn-t´àba-deh*
separated	ကွဲကွာနေပါတယ်။ *kwèh-kwa-ne-ba-deh*
widowed	မုဆိုးဖို/မ ပါ။ *mouq-s'ò-bo/-má-ba*
Do you have children/ grandchildren?	ခင်ဗျား/ရှင့်မှာ သားသမီး၊ မြေးတွေ ရှိသလား။ *k´ămyà* ***m****/shín* ***f*** *hma-thà-thămí-myè-twe-shí-dhălà?*

For Numbers, see page 168.

Work & School

What do you do for a living?	ခင်ဗျား/ရှင် အသက်မွေးဝမ်းကျောင်းဖို့အတွက် ဘာအလုပ် လုပ်သလဲ။ *k´ămyà* ***m*** */ shin* ***f*** *ătheq-mwè-wàn-caùn-bó-ătweq-ba-ălouq-louq-thălèh?*
What are you studying?	ခင်ဗျား/ရှင် ဘာသင်ယူ နေတာလဲ။ *k´ămyà* ***m****/shin* ***f*** *ba-thin-yu-ne-da-lèh*

I'm studying Burmese. ကျွန်တော်/ကျွန်မ ဗမာစာ သင်နေတာ။
cănaw **m**/*cămá* **f** *băma-za-thin-ne-da*

I... ကျွန်တော်/ကျွန်မ... *cănaw* **m**/*cămá* **f**...

work full-/ part-time အချိန်ပြည့် အလုပ်လုပ်ပါတယ်။ *ăćein-byé-ălouq-louq-pa-deh*

am unemployed အလုပ်မရှိပါ။ *ălouq-măshí-ba*

work at home အိမ်မှနေပြီး အလုပ်လုပ်ပါတယ်။
ein-hmà-ne-byì-ălouq-louq-pa-deh

Who do you work for? ခင်ဗျား/ရှင်ဘယ်သူ့အတွက် အလုပ်လုပ်တာလဲ။
k´ămyà **m**/*shin* **f** *beh-dhú-ătweq-ălouq-louq-ta-lèh*

I work for... ကျွန်တော်/ကျွန်မ... အတွက် အလုပ်လုပ်ပါတယ်။
cănaw **m**/*cămá* **f**... *ătweq-ălouq-louq-pa-deh*

Here's my business card. ဒီမှာ ကျွန်တော်/ကျွန်မရဲ့ အလုပ်လိပ်စာကတ်ပါ။
di-hma-cănaw **m**/*cămá* **f** *yéh-ălouq-leiq-sa-kaq-pa*

For Business Travel, see page 141.

Weather

What's the forecast? ခန့်မှန်းချက်က ဘာလဲ။ *k´án-hmàn-jeq-ká-ba-lèh?*

What beautiful/ terrible weather! ဘယ်လောက် လှတဲ့/ဆိုးတဲ့ ရာသီဥတုလဲ။
beh-lauq-hlá-dèh/s'ò-dèh-ya-dhi-ú-dú-lèh?

It's... အခု... *ăk´ú*...

cool/warm အေးတယ်/နွေးတယ် *è-deh/nwé-deh*

cold/hot အေးတယ်/ပူတယ် *è-deh/pu-deh*

humid/ dry စိုစွတ်တယ်/ခြောက်သွေ့တယ် *so-suq-teh/ćauq-thwé-deh*

rainy/sunny မိုးရွာတယ်/နေပူတယ် *mò-ywa-deh/ne-pu-deh*

snowy/icy နှင်းကျတယ်/ရေခဲနေတယ် *hnin-cá-deh/ye-k´èh/ne-deh.*

Do I need a jacket/ an umbrella? ကျွန်တော်/ကျွန်မ ဂျက်ကက်အင်္ကျီတစ်ထည်။ ထီးတစ်ချောင်း လိုမလား။
cănaw **m**/*cămá* **f** *jeq-keq-in-ji-tăt´eh/t´ì-tăćaùn-lo-mălà?*

For Temperature, see page 174.

Myanmar is at its best during the dry and relatively cool period from late November to late February. From March onwards, humidity levels start to build and temperatures start to reach 40ºC (104ºF) by late April. The rains properly erupt in Mid-May and last until October. Travel during this time is problematic: roads are routinely washed away, rail lines flooded and cyclones wreak havoc on the coastal plains and delta area.

Romance

ESSENTIAL

Would you like to go out for a drink/dinner?	ခင်ဗျား/ရှင် တစ်ခုခုသောက်ဖို့/ညစာစားဖို့ အပြင်ထွက်ချင်သလား။ *k´ămyà* **m**/*shin* **f** *t´ăk´ú-k´ú-thauq-p´ó/ nyá-za-sà-bó-ăpyin-t´weq-ćin-dhălà?*
What are your plans for tonight/ tomorrow?	ဒီည/မနက်ဖြန် အတွက် ခင်ဗျား/ရှင့်ရဲ့ အစီအစဉ်တွေက ဘာလဲ။ *di-nyà/măneq-p´yan-ătewq k´ămyà* **m**/*shín* **f** *yéh-ăsin-dwe-gà-ba-lèh?*
Can I have your (phone) number?	ကျွန်တော်/ကျွန်မ ခင်ဗျား/ရှင့် ရဲ့ဖုန်းနံပါတ် ရနိုင်မလား။ *cănaw* **m**/*cămá* **f** *k´ămyà* **m**/*shín* **f** *yéh-p´oùn-bab-baq-yá-nain-mălà?*
Can I join you?	ကျွန်တော်/ကျွန်မ ခင်ဗျား/ရှင်နဲ့အတူလိုက်လို့ရမလား။ *cănaw* **m**/*cămá* **f** *k´ămyà* **m**/*shin* **f** *néh-ătu-laiq-ló-yá-nain-mălà?*
Can I buy you a drink?	ကျွန်တော်/ကျွန်မ ခင်ဗျား/ရှင့်ကို သောက်စရာတစ်ခုခု ဝယ်တိုက်နိုင်မလား။ *cănaw* **m**/*cămá* **f** *k´ămyà* **m**/*shín* **f** *go-thauq-săya-tăk´ú-k´ú-weh-taiq-yá-mălà?*
I love you.	ခင်ဗျား/ရှင့်ကို ကျွန်တော်/ကျွန်မ ချစ်တယ်။ *k´ămyà* **m**/*shín* **f** *go- cănaw* **m**/*cămá* **f** *ćiq-the.*

The Dating Game

Would you like to go out…?	ခင်ဗျား/ရှင် … အပြင်သွားချင်သလား။ *k´ămyà* **m**/*shin* **f**…*ăpyin-thwà-jin-dhălà?*
for coffee	ကော်ဖီသောက်ဖို့အတွက် *kaw-p´i-thauq-p´ó-ătweq*
for a drink	တစ်ခုခုသောက်ဖို့အတွက် *tăk´ú-k´ú- thauq-p´ó-ătweq*
to dinner	ညစာစားဖို့ *nyá-za-sà-bó*
What are your plans for…?	…အတွက် ခင်ဗျား/ရှင့်ရဲ့အစီအစဉ်တွေက ဘာတွေလဲ။ …*ătweq- k´ămyà* **m**/*shín* **f** *yéh-ăsi-ăsin-dwe-gá-ba-dwe-lèh?*
today	ဒီနေ့ *di-né*
tonight	ဒီည *di-nyá*
tomorrow	မနက်ဖြန် *măneq-p´yan*
this weekend	ဒီစနေ တနင်္ဂနွေ ရုံးပိတ်ရက် *di-săne-tănì-gănwe-yoùn-peiq-yeq*
Where would you like to go?	ခင်ဗျား/ရှင် ဘယ်နေရာကို သွားချင်သလဲ။ *k´ămyà* **m**/*shin* **f** *beh-ne-ya-go-thwà-jin-dhălèh?*
I'd like to go to…	ကျွန်တော်/ကျွန်မ… ကိုသွားချင်တယ်။ *cănaw* **m**/*cămá* **f**…*go- thwà-jin-deh*
Do you like…?	ခင်ဗျား/ရှင် … ကိုကြိုက်သလား။ *k´ămyà* **m**/*shin* **f**…*go-ćaiq-thălà?*
Can I have your phone number/ email?	ကျွန်တော်/ကျွန်မ ခင်ဗျား/ရှင့်ရဲ့ ဖုန်းနံပါတ်။ အီးမေးလ် ရနိုင်မလား။ *cănaw* **m**/*cămá* **f** *k´ămyà* **m**/*shín* **f** *yéh-p´oùn-nan-baq/ì-mè-yá-nain-mălà?*
Are you on Facebook/ Twitter?	ခင်ဗျား/ရှင့် ဖေ့စ်ဘွတ်ခ်/တွစ်တာ ပေါ်မှာ ရှိသလား။ *k´ămyà* **m**/*shín* **f** *p´é-buq/twiq-ta-baw-hma-shí-dhălà?*
Can I join you?	ကျွန်တော်/ကျွန်မ ခင်ဗျား/ရှင့် နဲ့ အတူလိုက်လို့ရမလား။ *cănaw* **m**/*cămá* **f** *k´ămyà* **m**/*shin* **f** *néh-ătu-laiq-ló-yá-mălà?*

You're very attractive. ခင်ဗျား/ရှင်က အရမ်းဆွဲဆောင်မှုရှိတယ်။
k´ămyà **m**/*shin* **f** *ga ăyàn-s'wèh-s'aun-hmú-shí-deh*

Let's go somewhere quieter. ပိုပြီးဆိတ်ငြိမ်တဲ့တစ်နေရာရာကို သွားရအောင်။
po-byì-s'eiq-nyein-déh-tăne-ya-ya-go-thwà-yá-aun.

For Communications, see page 47.

Accepting & Rejecting

I'd love to. ကျွန်တော်/ကျွန်မ ကြိုက်ပါတယ်။
cănaw **m**/*cămá* **f** *caiq-pa-deh*

Where should we meet? ကျွန်တော်/ကျွန်မ တို့ ဘယ်နေရာမှာ တွေ့သင့်သလဲ။
cănaw **m**/*cămá* **f** *dó-beh-ne-ya-hma-twé-thín-dhălèh?*

I'll meet you at the bar/your hotel. ကျွန်တော်/ကျွန်မ ခင်ဗျား/ရှင့်ကို ဘားမှာ။ ခင်ဗျား/ရှင်ရဲ့ဟိုတယ်မှာ တွေ့မယ်။
cănaw **m**/*cămá* **f** *k´ămyà* **m**/*shín* **f** *go-bà-hma/ kămyà* **m**/*shin* **f** *yéh-ho-the-hma-twé-meh.*

I'll come by at... ကျွန်တော်/ကျွန်မ ... အချိန် လာခဲ့မယ်။
cănaw **m**/*cămá ...-ăćein-la-géh-meh.*

I'm busy. ကျွန်တော်/ကျွန်မ အလုပ်ရှုပ်နေတယ်။
cănaw **m**/*cămá* **f** *ălouq-shouq-ne-deh*

I'm not interested. ကျွန်တော်/ကျွန်မ စိတ်မဝင်စားပါဘူး။
cănaw **m**/*cămá* **f** *seiq-măwin-zà-ba-bù*

Leave me alone. ကျွန်တော်/ကျွန်မ တစ်ယောက်တည်းနေပါရစေ။
cănaw **m**/*cămá* **f** *tăyauq-t´éh-ne-băyá-ze.*

Stop bothering me! ကျွန်တော်/ကျွန်မ ကိုအနှောင့်အယှက်ပေးနေတာ ရပ်လိုက်တော့။ *cănaw* **m**/*cămá* **f** *go-ăhnaùn-ăsheq-pè-ne-da-yaq-laiq-táw*

For Time, see page 170.

Getting Intimate

Can I hug/kiss you?	ကျွန်တော်/ကျွန်မ ခင်ဗျား/ရှင့်ကို ဖက်လို့/နမ်းလို့ ရနိုင်မလား။ *cănaw* **f**/*cămá* **f** *k´ămyà* **m**/*shín* **f** *go-p´eq-ló/nàn-ló-yá-nain-mălà?*
Yes.	ရပါတယ်။ *yá-ba-deh*
No.	မလုပ်ပါနဲ့။ *mălouq-pa-néh.*
Stop!	ရပ်။ *yaq*
I love you.	ခင်ဗျား/ရှင့် ကို ကျွန်တော်/ကျွန်မ ချစ်တယ်။ *k´ămyà* **f**/*shín* **f** *go- cănaw* **m**/*cămá* **f** *ćiq-the.*

Sexual Preferences

Are you gay?	ခင်ဗျား/ရှင်က လိင်တူဆက်ဆံသူလား။ *k´ămyà* **m**/*shin* **f** *gá-lein-du-s'eq-s'an-dhu-là?*
I'm…	ကျွန်တော်/ကျွန်မ က … ပါ။ *cănaw* **m**/*cămá* **f** *gá…ba.*
heterosexual	လိင်ကွဲဆက်ဆံသူ *lein-gwèh-s'eq-s'an-dhu*
homosexual	လိင်တူဆက်ဆံသူ *lein-du-s'eq-s'an-dhu*
bisexual	လိင်တူ/လိင်ကွဲ နှစ်မျိုးစလုံးဆက်ဆံသူ *lein-du/lein-gwèh-hnămyò-zăloùn- s'eq-s'an-dhu*
Do you like men/women?	ခင်ဗျား/ရှင့် ယောက်ျား/မိန်းမ ကြိုက်သလား။ *k´ămyà* **f**/*shin* **f** *yauq-ćà/meìn-má-caiq-thălà?*

Homosexuality is technically illegal in Myanmar under section 377 of the penal code, and punishable by up to 10 years in prison. Although the law is rarely enforced, be aware that attitudes are conservative and are shrouded in stigma and superstition.

Leisure Time

Sightseeing 109
Shopping 114
Sport & Leisure 130
Going Out 136

Sightseeing

ESSENTIAL

Where's the tourist information office?	နိုင်ငံခြားသားခရီးသွားဧည့်သည် စုံစမ်းမေးမြန်းရေးရုံးက ဘယ်နေရာမှာလဲ။ *nain-ngan-jà-dhà-k'ă-yì-thwà-éhdheh-soun-zàn-mè-myàn-yé-youn-gà-beh-ne-ya-mha-lèh ?*
What are the main sights?	အဓိက ကြည့်နိုင်တဲ့နေရာတွေက ဘာတွေလဲ။ *Ădí-kà-cí-nain-déh-ne-ya-dwe-gà-ba-dwe-lèh ?*
Do you offer tours in English?	ခင်ဗျား/ရှင်တို့ အင်္ဂလိပ်စကားပြောခရီးစဉ်တွေ လုပ်ပေးသလား။ *k'ămyà* **m**/*shin* **f** *dó-ìngăleiq-zăgàpyàw-k'ăyìzin-dwe-louq-pè-dhălà ?*
Can I have a map/guide?	ကျွန်တော်/ကျွန်မ မြေပုံတစ်ခု/ဧည့်လမ်းညွှန်တစ်ခု ရနိုင်မလား။ *cănaw* **m** /*cămà* **f** *mye-boun-tàk'ú/éh-làn-hnyun-tàk'ú-yà-nain-mă-là ?*

Tourist Information

Do you have information on…?	ခင်ဗျား/ရှင့် မှာ … အတွက် အချက်အလက်တွေရှိသလား။ *kămyà* **m**/*shin* **f** *hma … ătweq-ăćeq-ăleq-twe-shí-dhălà ?*
Can you recommend…?	ခင်ဗျား/ရှင် … ညွှန်းပေးနိုင်မလား။ *k'ămyà* **m**/*shin* **f** *… hnyùn-pé-nain-mălà ?*
a bus tour	ဘတ်စ်ကားခရီးတစ်ခု *baqsăkà-k'ăyí-tăk'ú*
an excursion to…	…ကို လေ့လာရေးခရီးတစ်ခု *… go-lè-la-yé-k'ăyì- tăk'ú*
a hot air balloon trip	မီးပုံးပျံခရီးတစ်ခု *mí-boùn-byan-k'ăyì- tăk'ú*
a tour of…	… ခရီးစဉ်တစ်ခု *… k'ăyì-zin- tăk'ú*

The only official source of tourist information is Myanmar Travels & Tours (myanmartravelsandtours.com). They can arrange permits for the more off-track parts of the country open to visitors. They also book airline and rail tickets but do not offer much in the way of practical information, apart from handing out town plans and leaflets.

On Tour

I'd like to go on the excursion to…	… ကို သွားတဲ့လေ့လာရေးခရီးစဉ်တစ်ခု သွားချင်ပါတယ်။ *… go-thwà-dèh-lé-yè-k'ăyì-zin- tăk'ú-thwà-jin-ba-deh*
When's the next tour?	နောက်ထွက်မယ့် ခရီးစဉ်က ဘယ်တော့လဲ။ *nauq-t'weq-méh-k'ăyì-zin-gá-beh-dáw-lèh ?*
Are there tours in English?	ဒီခရီးစဉ်တွေက အင်္ဂလိပ်လိုလား။ *di-k'ăyì-zin-dwe-gá- ìngăleiq-lo-là ?*
Is there an English guide book/audio guide?	အင်္ဂလိပ်လိုလမ်းညွှန်စာအုပ်တစ်အုပ်။ အသံထွက်လမ်းညွှန်တစ်ခု ရှိသလား။ *Íngăleiq-lo-làn-hnyun-saouq-tă ouq / ăthan dweq làn hnyun-tăku-shí-dhălà ?*
What time do we leave/return?	ကျွန်တော်/ကျွန်မ တို့ ဘယ်အချိန် ထွက်/ပြန်ရောက် မလဲ။ *cănaw* **m**/*cămà* **f** *dó-beh-ăćein-t'weq / pyan-yauq-mă lèh ?*

We'd like to see… ကျွန်တော်/ကျွန်မတို့ … ကို ကြည့်ချင်ပါတယ်။ *cănaw* ***m***/*cămà* ***f*** *dó- … go-cí-jin-ba-deh*

Can we stop here…? ကျွန်တော်/ကျွန်မတို့ ဒီနေရာမှာ … ရပ်လို့ရမလား။ *cănaw* ***m***/*cămà* ***f*** *dó-di-neyahma … yaq-ló-yá-mă-là*

to take photos ဓာတ်ပုံရိုက်ဖို့ *daq-poun-yaiq-p'ó*

for souvenirs အမှတ်တရပစ္စည်းဝယ်ဖို့ *ăhmaq-tăyá-piqsì-weh-p'ó*

for the toilets အိမ်သာသွားဖို့ *ein-dha-thwà-p'ó*

Is it disabled-accessible? အဲဒါက မသန်မစွမ်းသူတွေ ဝင်ထွက်လို့ရနိုင်လား။ *Èh-da-gá-mă than măswùn-dhu-dwe-win-t'weq-ló-yá-nain-là*

For Tickets, see page 20.

Seeing the Sights

Where is/ are…? … က။တွေက ဘယ်နေရာမှာလဲ။ *… gá/dwe-gá-beh-ne-ya-hma-lèh*

the botanical gardens ရုက္ခဗေဒဥယျာဉ် *youq k'á-bedá-ú(ú) yin*

the downtown area မြို့လယ်ကောင်ဧရိယာ *myó-leh-gaun-e-rí-ya*

the fountain ရေပန်း *ye-bàn*

the library စာကြည့်တိုက် *sa-cí-daiq*

the market ဈေး *zè*

the museum ပြတိုက် *pyá-daiq*

the old town မြို့ဟောင်း *myó-haùn*

the palace နန်းတော် *nàn-daw*

the park	ပန်းခြ *pàn-jan*
the pagoda	ဘုရား *P'ăyà*
the ruins	အပျက်အစီးတွေ *ăpyeq-ăsi-dwe*
the safari park	ဆာဖာရီပန်းခြံ *S'a-p'a-ri-pàn-jan*
the shopping area	ဈေးဝယ်နိုင်တဲ့ဧရိယာ *zè-weh-nain-déh-e-ríya*
the shrine	ပုထိုး/စေတီ/ဘုရားစင် *Păt'ò/zedi/p'ăyà-zin*
the temple	ဘုရားကျောင်း *p'ăyà-caùn*
the theatre	ဇာတ်ရုံ *zaq-youn*
the town square	မြို့ရင်ပြင် *myó-yin-byin*
the zoological park	တိရစ္ဆာန်ဥယျာဉ် *tăreiq-san-ú(ù) yin*
Can you show me on the map?	ခင်ဗျား/ရှင် ကျွန်တော်/ကျွန်မကို မြေပုံပေါ်မှာ ပြပေးနိုင်မလား။ *k'ămyà* **m**/*shin* **f** /*cănaw* **m**/ *cămà* **f** *go-mye-boun-baw-hma-pyá-pè-nain-mălà?*
It's…	အဲဒါက … *Éh-da-gá* ….
amazing	အံ့သြစရာကောင်းတယ်။ *án-àw-zăya-kaùn-deh*
beautiful	လှပတယ်။ *hlá-pá-deh*
boring	ပျင်းစရာကောင်းတယ်။ *pyìn-zăya-kaùn-deh*
interesting	စိတ်ဝင်စားစရာကောင်းတယ်။ *seiq-win-zà-zàya-kaùn-deh*
magnificent	ခမ်းနားတယ်။ *k'àn-nà-deh*
romantic	ရင်ခုန်စရာကောင်းတယ်။ *yin-k'oun-zàya-kaùn-deh*
strange	ထူးဆန်းတယ်။ *t'ù-s'àn-deh*

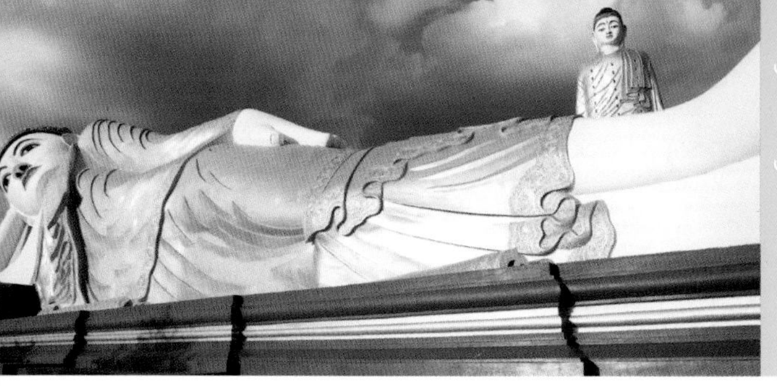

terrible ဆိုးရွားတယ်။ *s'òy-ywà-deh*
ugly ရုပ်ဆိုးတယ်။ *youq-s'ò-deh*
I (don't) like it. အဲဒါကို ကျွန်တော်/ကျွန်မ မကြိုက်ဘူး။
Èh-da-go- cănaw **m***/cămà* **f** *mă-caiq-bù*

For Asking Directions, see page 34.

Religious Sites

Where's…? … က ဘယ်နေရာမှာလဲ။ *…gá-beh-ne-ya-hma-lèh*
the Catholic/Protestant church ကက်သိုလစ်/ပရိုတက်စတင့် ဘုရားရှိခိုးကျောင်း *keqthăliq / Păroteqsătín-p'ăya-shiq-k'ò-caùn*
the monastery ဘုန်းကြီးကျောင်း *p'oùn-jì-caùn*
the mosque ဗလီ *băli*
the shrine ပုထိုး/စေတီ/ဘုရားစင် *păt'ò/zedi/p'ăyà-zin*
the synagogue ဂျူးဘုရားရှိခိုးကျောင်း *jù-p'ăya-shiq-k'ò-caùn*
the temple ဘုရားကျောင်း *p'ăya-caùn*
What time is the service? ဘုရားဝတ်ပြုချိန်က ဘယ်အချိန်လဲ။
p'ăya-wuq-pyú-jein-gá-beh-ăćein-lèh?

Whenever you enter religious grounds, you must remove your shoes and socks. Proper clothing should also be worn at a temple: especially no short skirts for women and no skimpy shorts.

Shopping

ESSENTIAL

Where's the market/ mall?	ဈေး/ဈေးဆိုင်တွေရှိတဲ့အဆောက်အဦးက ဘယ်နေရာမှာလဲ။ *zè / zè-zain-dwe-shí-déh-ăs'ajq-ăù-gá-beh-ne-ya-hma-lèh ?*
I'm just looking.	ကျွန်တော်/ကျွန်မ ကြည့်ရုံ ကြည့်နေတာပါ။ *cănaw* ***m****/cămà* ***f*** *mă-cí youn-cí-ne-da-ba*
Can you help me?	ခင်ဗျား/ရှင် ကျွန်တော်/ကျွန်မ ကို ကူညီနိုင်မလား။ *k'ămyà* ***m****/shin* ***f*** */cănaw* ***m****/cămà* ***f*** *go-ku-nyi-nain-mă là ?*
I'm being helped.	ကျွန်တော်/ကျွန်မ အကူအညီရပါတယ်။ *cănaw* ***m****/cămà* ***f****-ăku-ănyi-yá-ba-deh*
How much?	ဘယ်လောက်ကျလဲ။ *beh-lauq-cá-lèh ?*
That one, please.	ကျေးဇူးပြုပြီး ဒီတစ်ခုပေးပါ။ *cè-zù-pyú-byì-di-tăk'ú-pè-ba*
That's all.	ဒါပဲ။ *da-bèh*
Where can I pay?	ကျွန်တော်/ကျွန်မ ဘယ်နေရာမှာ ငွေချေနိုင်မလဲ။ *cănaw* ***m****/cămà* ***f*** *beh-ne-ya-hma-ngwe-će-nain-mă lèh ?*
Can I pay by credit card?	ကျွန်တော်/ကျွန်မ အကြွေးဝယ်ကတ်နဲ့ ငွေချေနိုင်မလား။ *cănaw* ***m****/cămà* ***f*** *ăcwèweh-kaq-néh-ngwe-će-nain-mălà*
I'll pay in cash.	ကျွန်တော်/ကျွန်မ ပိုက်ဆံလက်ငင်းပေးမယ်။ *cănaw* ***m****/cămà* ***f*** *paiq-s'an-leq-ngìn-pè-meh*
A receipt, please.	ကျေးဇူးပြုပြီး ငွေလက်ခံဖြတ်ပိုင်းတစ်ခု ပေးပါ။ *cè-zù-pyú-byì-ngwe-leq-k'an-p'yaq-paìn-tăk'ú-pè-ba*

At the Shops

Where's...?	... က ဘယ်နေရာမှာလဲ။ ... *gá-beh-ne-ya-hma-lèh ?*
the bank	ဘဏ် *ban*
the market	ဈေး *zè*
the newsstand	သတင်းစာရောင်းတဲ့နေရာ *dhă dìn-za-yaùn-déh-ne-ya*
the night market	ညဈေး *nyá-zè*

the pharmacy	ဆေးဆိုင် *s'è-zain*
Where can I buy…?	ကျွန်တော်/ကျွန်မ… ကို ဘယ်နေရာမှာ ဝယ်လို့ရနိုင်မလဲ။ *cănaw* **m**/*cămà* **f**… *go-beh-ne-ya-hma-weh-ló-yá-nain-mălèh ?*
alcohol [liquor]	အရက် (အရက်ပြင်း) *ăyeq (ăyeq-pyìn)*
antiques	ရှေးဟောင်းပစ္စည်း *shè-haùn-pyiqsì (piqsì)*
books	စာအုပ်တွေ *sa ouq-twe*
clothes	အဝတ်စများ *ă wuq sá-myà*
herbal remedies	ဆေးဖက်ဝင်သစ်သီး၊သစ်ဥ၊သစ်ရွက်မှထုတ်ထားသော အိမ်သုံးဆေးများ *s'è-beq-win-thiq-thì-thiq-ú-thiq-yweq-hmá-t'ouq-t'à-dhàw-ein-dhoún-s'è-myà*
jade	ကျောက်စိမ်း *cauq-sein*
jewelry	လက်ဝတ်ရတနာ *leq-wuq-yă dă na*
groceries	နေ့စဉ်စားသုံးကုန်ပစ္စည်းများ *né-zin-sà-thoùn-koun-pyiq sì(piqsì)-myà*
music	ဂီတ *gi tá*
rubies	ပတ္တမြားများ *bădămyà*
shoes	ရှူးဖိနပ်များ *shù-p'ă naq-myà*
snacks	သွားရည်စာများ *thă ye-za-myà*
souvenirs	အမှတ်တရပစ္စည်းများ *ăhmaq tăyá-pyiqsì-myà*
toys	အရုပ်များ *ăyouq-myà*

Ask an Assistant

When do you open/close?	ခင်ဗျား/ရှင် ဘယ်အချိန် ဖွင့်။ပိတ်သလဲ။ *k'ămyà* ***m****/shin* ***f*** *beh-ăc'ein-p'wín / peiq-thă lèh?*
Where can I pay?	ကျွန်တော်/ကျွန်မ ဘယ်နေရာမှာ ငွေချေနိုင်မလဲ။ *cănaw* ***m****/cămà* ***f*** *beh-neya-hma-ngwe-c'e-nain-mă lèh*
Can you help me?	ခင်ဗျား/ရှင် ကျွန်တော့်/ကျွန်မ ကို ကူညီနိုင်မလား။ *k'ămyà* ***m****/shin* ***f*** */cănaw* ***m****/cămà* ***f*** *go-ku-nyi-nain-mălà*
I'm just looking.	ကျွန်တော်/ကျွန်မ ကြည့်ရုံကြည့်နေတာပါ။ *cănaw* ***m****/cămà* ***f*** *cí youn-cí-ne-da-ba*
I'm being helped.	ကျွန်တော်/ကျွန်မ အကူအညီရပါတယ်။ *cănaw* ***m****/cămà* ***f*** *ăku-ănyi-yá-ba-deh*
Do you have…?	ခင်ဗျား/ရှင် မှာ … ရှိသလား။ *k'ămyà* ***m****/shin* ***f*** *hma… shí-dhă là*
Can you show me…?	ခင်ဗျား/ရှင် ကျွန်တော်/ကျွန်မ ကို … ပြနိုင်မလား။ *k'ămyà* ***m****/shin* ***f*** */cănaw* ***m****/cămà* ***f*** *go- … pyá-bain-mă là*
Can you ship/wrap it?	ခင်ဗျား/ရှင် ဒါကို သင်္ဘောနဲ့တင်ပေးနိုင်မလား။ ထုတ်ပေးနိုင်မလား။ *k'ămyà* ***m****/shin* ***f*** *da-go-thìn bàw-néh-tin-pè-nain-mălà / t'ouq-pè-nain-mălà*
How much?	ဘယ်လောက်ကျသလဲ။ *beh-lauq-cá-thă lèh*
That's all.	ဒါအားလုံးပဲ။ *da-àloùn-bèh*

YOU MAY HEAR…

ကျွန်တော်/ကျွန်မ ခင်ဗျား/ရှင့်ကို ကူညီနိုင်မလား။ *cănaw* ***m****/cămà* ***f****/ k'ămyà* ***m****/shin* ***f*** *go-ku-nyi-nain-mălà*	Can I help you?
ခဏလေးပါ။ *k'ăná-lè-ba*	One moment.
ခင်ဗျား/ရှင် ဘာလိုချင်လဲ။ *k'ămyà* ***m****/shin* ***f*** *ba-lo-ćin-lèh*	What would you like?
ဒါ့အပြင်ရှိသေးလား။ *dá-ăpyin-shí-dhè-là*	Anything else?

YOU MAY SEE...

ဖွင့်သည်/ပိတ်သည်	open/closed
နေ့လည်စာစားချိန် ပိတ်သည်။	closed for lunch
ငွေလက်ခံသူ	cashier
ပိုက်ဆံသာလက်ခံသည်	cash only
အကြွေးဝယ်ကတ်လက်ခံသည်။	credit cards accepted
အလုပ်ချိန်များ	business hours
ထွက်ပေါက်	exit
အစမ်းဝတ်ကြည့်ရန်အခန်း	fitting room

Personal Preferences

I'd like something... ကျွန်တော်/ကျွန်မ... အရာတစ်ခုခု လိုချင်တယ်။ *cănaw* **m**/*cămà* **f**... *ăya-tăk'ú-k'ú-lo-jin-deh*

cheap/expensive ဈေးသက်သာတဲ့/ဈေးကြီးတဲ့ *zè-theq tha-déh / zè-cí-déh*

larger/smaller ပိုကြီးတဲ့/ပိုသေးတဲ့ *po-cí- déh / po-thè-déh*

from this region ဒီဒေသမှထွက်တဲ့ *di-de thá-hmá-t'weq-téh*

Around...Kyat/ dollars. ...ကျပ်/ဒေါ်လာ လောက်ရှိမယ်။ *... caq/daw la-lauq-shí-meh*

Is it real? အဲဒါက အစစ်လား။ *Èdaga-ăsiq-là*

Can you show me this/that? ခင်ဗျား/ရှင် ကျွန်တော်/ကျွန်မ ကို အဲဒါ/ဟိုဟာ ပြနိုင်မလား။ *k'ămyà* **m**/*shin* **f** / *cănaw* **m**/*cămà* **f** *go-èhda / hoha-pyá-nain-mălà*

That's not quite what I want. အဲဒါက ကျွန်တော်/ကျွန်မ လိုချင်တဲ့ဟာလောက် မဟုတ်ဘူး။ *Èhdagá cănaw* **m**/*cămà* **f** *lo-jin-déh-ha-lauq-măhout-bù*

No, I don't like it. မလိုချင်ဘူး၊ ကျွန်တော/ကျွန်မ အဲဒါကို မကြိုက်ဘူး။ *mă lojin-bù cănaw* **m**/*cămà* **f** *èhda-go-măcaiq-bù*

It's too expensive. အဲဒါက အရမ်းဈေးကြီးတယ်။ *Èhdagá-ăyàn-zè-cì-deh*

I have to think about it. ကျွန်တော်/ကျွန်မ အဲဒီအကြောင်း စဉ်းစားမယ်။ *cănaw* **m**/*cămà* **f** *èhdi-ăcaùn-sìn zà-meh*

I'll take it. ကျွန်တော်/ကျွန်မ အဲဒါကိုယူမယ်။ *cănaw* **m**/*cămà* **f** *èhda go-yu-meh*

Paying & Bargaining

How much?	ဘယ်လောက်ကျလဲ။ *beh-lauq-cá-lèh ?*
I'll pay…	ကျွန်တော်/ကျွန်မ … နဲ့ငွေချေမယ်။ *cănaw* **m**/*cămà* **f**… *néh-ngwe-će-meh*
in cash	ပိုက်ဆံ *paiq-s'an*
by credit card	အကြွေးဝယ်ကတ် *ăcwè-weh-kaq*
A receipt, please.	ကျေးဇူးပြုပြီး ငွေလက်ခံဖြတ်ပိုင်းပေးပါ။ *cèzù-pyú-byì-ngwe-leq-k'an-p'yaq-pàain-pè-ba*
That's too much.	အဲဒါက အရမ်းဈေးများတယ်။ *Èhdagá-ăyàn-zè-myà-deh*
I'll give you…	ကျွန်တော်/ကျွန်မ ခင်ဗျား/ရှင့် ကို … ပေးမယ်။ *cănaw* **m**/*cămà* **f** *k'ămyà* **m**/*shin* **f** *go …pè-meh*
I have only… dollars / Kyat.	ကျွန်တော်/ကျွန်မ မှာ … ကျပ်/ဒေါ်လာ ပဲရှိတယ်။ *cănaw* **m**/*cămà* **f** *hma… caq / dawla-bèh-shí-deh*
Is that your best price?	အဲဒါက ခင်ဗျား/ရှင့် ရဲ့ အကောင်းဆုံးဈေးလား။ *Èhdagá- k'ămyà* **m**/*shin* **f** *yéh-ăkaùn-zoùn-zè-là*
Can you give me discount?	ခင်ဗျား/ရှင် ကျွန်တော်/ကျွန်မ ကို ဈေးလျှော့ပေးနိုင်မလား။ *k'ămyà* **m**/*shin* **f** *cănaw* **m**/*cămà* **f** *go-zè-sháw-pè-nain-mălà*

For Numbers, see page 168.

Remember, payment in cash, using crisp, clean, unmarked bills, is always preferred.

Making a Complaint

I'd like…	ကျွန်တော်/ကျွန်မ … လုပ်ချင်ပါတယ်။ *cănaw* **m**/*cămà* **f**… *louq-ćin-ba-deh*
to exchange this	ဒါကို လဲဖို့ *da-go-lèh-bó*
a refund	ငွေပြန်အမ်းဖို့ *ngwe-pyan-àn-bó*
to see the manager	မန်နေဂျာနဲ့တွေ့ဖို့ *man-ne-ja-néh-twé-bó*

YOU MAY HEAR...

ခင်ဗျား/ရှင် ဘယ်လိုငွေချေမှာလဲ။ *k'ămyà* ***m***/ *shin* ***f*** *beh-lo-ngwe-će-hma-lèh*	How are you paying?
ခင်ဗျား/ရှင့် ရဲ့ အကြွေးဝယ်ကတ်က အငြင်းခံရတယ်။ *k'ămyà* ***m***/ *shin* ***f*** *yéh-ăcwè-weh-kaq-ká-ănyìn-k'an-yá-deh*	Your credit card has been declined.
ကျေးဇူးပြုပြီး နိုင်ငံသားကတ် ပြပါ။ *cè-zù-byú-pyì-nain-ngan-dhà-kaq-pyá-ba*	ID please.
ကျွန်တော်/ကျွန်မ တို့ အကြွေးဝယ်ကတ် လက်မခံပါဘူး။ *cănaw /cămà-dó-ăcwè-weh-kaq-leq-măk'an-ba-bù*	We don't accept credit cards.
ကျေးဇူးပြုပြီး ငွေလက်ငင်းသာပေးပါ။ *cè-zù-byú-pyì-ngwe-leq-ngin-dha-pè-ba*	Cash only, please.

Services

Can you recommend...?	ခင်ဗျား/ရှင် ... ညွှန်းပေးနိုင်မလား။ *k'ămyà* ***m***/ *shin* ***f***... *hnyùn-pè-nain-mălà*
a barber	ဆံပင်ညှပ်ဆိုင် တစ်ဆိုင် *zăbin-hnyaq-s'ain-tăs'ain*
a dry cleaner	အဝတ်အခြောက်လျှော်ဆိုင် တစ်ဆိုင် *ăwuq-ăćauq-shaw-zain-tăs'ain*
a hairstylist	ဆံပင်အလှပြင်ဆိုင် တစ်ဆိုင် *zăbin-ăhlá-pyin-zain-tăs'ain*
a laundromat [launderette]	ကိုယ့်ဘာသာ အဝတ်လျှော်၊ မီးပူတိုက်နိုင်တဲ့နေရာ တစ်နေရာ *kó-p'adha-ăwuq-shaw, mì-bu-taiq-nain-déh-ne-ya-tăneya*
a travel agency	ခရီးသွားအေဂျင်စီ တစ်ခု *k'ă yì-thwà-ejinsi-tăk'ú*
Can you...this?	ခင်ဗျား/ရှင် ဒါကို ... ပေးနိုင်မလား။ *k'ămyà* ***m***/ *shin* ***f*** *da-go...pè-nain-mălà*
alter	ပြင်ဆင်/ပြောင်းလဲ *pyin s'in-pyaùn-lèh*
clean	သန့်ရှင်း *than-shìn*
fix	ပြုပြင် *pyú-byin*

press မီးပူတိုက် *mì bu-taiq*

When will it be ready? အဲဒါက ဘယ်အချိန် အဆင်သင့်ဖြစ်မလဲ။ *Èh dagá-beh-ăćein-ăs'in-thín-p'yiq-mă lèh*

Hair & Beauty

I'd like… ကျွန်တော်/ကျွန်မ … ချင်ပါတယ်။ *cănaw* **m**/*cămà* **f**… *ćin-ba-deh*

an appointment for today/tomorrow ဒီနေ့/မနက်ဖြန်အတွက် ချိန်းဆိုမှုတစ်ခုလုပ် *di-né / mă neq-p'yan-ătweq-ćèin-s'o-hmú-tă-kú-louq*

some color/ highlights ဆေးရောင်ဆိုး/တစ်ချို့နေရာတွေမှာ အရောင်နည်းနည်းရင့် *s'è-yaun-s'ò / tăćó-neya-dwe-hma-ăyaun-nèh- nèh-yín*

my hair styled/ blow-dried ကျွန်တော်/ကျွန်မရဲ့ ဆံပင်ကို ပုံသွင်း။ ဆံပင်အခြောက်ခံစက်နဲ့မှုတ် *cănaw* **m**/*cămà* **f** *yéh-zăbin-go-poun-thwìn / zăbin-ăćauq-k'an-zeq-néh-hmouq*

a haircut ဆံပင်ညှပ် *zăbin-hnyaq*

an eyebrow/ bikini wax မျက်ခုံးမွေး/ဘီကီနီဝတ်ရင်ကြည့်ကောင်းအောင် ဖယောင်းတင် *myeq-k'oùn-hmwè / bikini-wuq-yin-cì-kaùn-aun-p'ă yaùn-tin*

a facial မျက်နှာ ချေးချွတ်/ဆေး *myeq-hna-jì-ćuq / s'è*

a manicure/ pedicure လက်သည်း။ခြေသည်း အလှပြင် *leq-thèh / će(ći) thèh-ăhlá-pyin*

a (sports) massage (အားကစားသမားတွေအတွက်) အနှိပ်ခံ *(àgăzà-dhă mà-dwe-ătweq) ăhneiq-k'an*

A trim, please. ကျေးဇူးပြုပြီး တိပေးပါ။ *cè-zù-byú-pyì-tí-pè-ba*

Not too short. သိပ်မတိုပါစေနဲ့။ *theiq-măto-ba-ze-néh*

Shorter here. ဒီနေရာမှာ ပိုပြီးတိုပေးပါ။ *di-neya-hma-po-byì-to-pè-ba*

Do you offer…? ခင်ဗျား/ရှင် တို့ … လုပ်ပေးသလား။ *k'ămyà* **m**/ *shin* **f** *dó … louq-pè-dhă là*

acupuncture အပ်စိုက်ကုသမှု *aq-saiq-kú-thá-hmú*

aromatherapy မွှေးပျံ့သန့်ရှင်းသောလေ ပေးပြီးကုသမှု *hmwè-pyán-thán-shìn-dhàw-le-pè-byì-kú-thá-hmú*

Spas can be found in high-end resorts and luxury hotels.

Antiques

How old is it? ဒါက ဘယ်လောက်အိုဟောင်းနေပြီလဲ။ *da-gá-beh-lauq-o-haùn-ne-byi-lèh*

Do you have anything from the...period? ခင်ဗျား/ရှင့် ဆီမှာ ... ခေတ်က ပစ္စည်းတစ်ခုခု ရှိသလား။ *k'ămyà* ***m****/ shin* ***f*** *s'i-hma ... k'iq-ká-pyiq-sì-tă-k'ú-k'ú-shi-dhă-là*

Do I have to fill out any forms? ကျွန်တော်/ကျွန်မ ပုံစံတစ်ခုခု ဖြည့်ဖို့လိုမလား။ *cănaw* ***m****/cămà* ***f****-poun-zan-tă-k'ú-k'ú-p'é-bó-lo-mă là*

Is there a certificate of authenticity? ဒီဟာ အစစ်အမှန်ဖြစ်ကြောင်းထောက်ခံစာ ရှိသလား။ *di ha-ăsiq-ăhman-p'iq-caùn-t'auq-k'an-za-shí-dhălà*

Can you ship/ wrap it? ခင်ဗျား/ရှင် ဒါကို သင်္ဘောတင်/ထုတ် ပေးနိုင်မလား။ *k'ămyà* ***m****/ shin* ***f*** *da-go-thin bàw-tin / t'ouq-pè-nain-mă là*

Clothing

I'd like... ကျွန်တော်/ကျွန်မ ... လိုချင်တယ်။ *cănaw* ***m****/cămà* ***f****... lo-ćin-deh*

Can I try this on? ကျွန်တော်/ကျွန်မ ဒါကို အစမ်းဝတ်ကြည့်လို့ရမလား။ *cănaw* ***m****/cămà* ***f*** *da-go-ăsàn-wuq-cí-ló-yá-mălà*

It doesn't fit. ဒီဟာက မတော်ဘူး။ *di-ha-gá-mătaw-bù*

It's too… ဒီဟာက အရမ်း … တယ်။ *di-ha-gá-ăyàn … deh*

  big/small ကြီး/သေး *cì / thè*

  short/long တို/ရှည် *to / she*

  tight/loose ကျပ်/ချောင် *caq / ćaun*

Do you have this in size…? ခင်ဗျား/ရှင့် ဆီမှာ ဒီလိုဟာမျိုး ဆိုဒ်/အရွယ် … ရှိသလား။ *k'ămyà* **m**/ *shin* **f** *s'i-hma-di-lo-ha-myò-s'aiq / ăyweh … shí-dhă là*

Do you have this in a bigger/smaller size? ခင်ဗျား/ရှင့်ဆီမှာ ဒီလိုဟာမျိုး ပိုကြီး/ပိုသေးတဲ့ ဆိုဒ်/အရွယ်အစား ရှိသလား။ *k'ămyà* **m**/ *shin* **f** *s'i-hma-di-lo-ha-myò-po-cí-po-thè-dè-s'aiq / ăyweh-shí-dhă là*

For Numbers, see page 168.

YOU MAY HEAR…

ဒီဟာက ခင်ဗျား/ရှင့် အပေါ်မှာ ကြည့်လို့ကောင်းတယ်။ *di-ha-gá-k'ămyà* **m**/ *shin* **f** *ăpaw-hma-cí-ló-kaùn-deh* That looks great on you.

ဒါက ဘယ်လိုတော်မလဲ။ *da-gá-beh-lo-taw-mălèh* How does it fit?

ကျွန်တော်/ကျွန်မ တို့ဆီမှာ ခင်ဗျား/ရှင့် ရဲ့ ဆိုဒ်/အရွယ်အစား မရှိဘူး။ *cănaw* **m**/*cămà* **f** *dó-s'i-hma k'ămyà* **m**/ *shin* **f** *yéh-s'aiq / ăyweh-ăsà-măshí-bù* We don't have your size.

Colors

I'd like something… ကျွန်တော်/ကျွန်မ … အရောင်တစ်ခုခု ကိုကြိုက်တယ်။ *cănaw* **m**/*cămà* **f**… *ăyaun-tăk'úk'ú-go-caiq-teh*

  beige အညိုဖျော့ဖျော့ *ănyo-p'yáw-p'yáw*

  black အနက်/အမဲ *ăneq / ămáh*

  blue အပြာ *ăpya*

  brown အညို *ănyo*

green	အစိမ်း *ăsein*
gray	မီးခိုး *mì-gò*
orange	လိမ္မော် *lein-maw*
pink	ပန်းရောင် *pàn-yaun*
purple	ခရမ်း *k'ăyàn*
red	အနီ *ăni*
white	အဖြူ *ăp'yu*
yellow	အဝါ *ăwa*

Clothes & Accessories

a backpack	ကျောပိုးအိတ် တစ်လုံး *càw-pò-eiq-tă loùn*
a belt	ခါးပတ် တစ်ခု *găbaq-tăk'ú*
a bikini	ဘီကီနီ/အမျိုးသမီးရေကူးဝတ်စုံ တစ်စုံ *bikini / ămyò-thămì-ye-kù-wuq-soun-tă zoun*
a blouse	အမျိုးသမီးဝတ် အပေါ်အင်္ကျီ/ဘလောက်အင်္ကျီ တစ်ထည် *ămyò-wuq-ăpaw-ìnji / bălauq-ìnji-tăt'eh*
a bra	ဘရာစီယာ တစ်ထည် *bă ra-si-ya-tă-t'eh*
briefs [underpants]/	ဘောင်းဘီတို *baùn-bi-to*
panties [knickers]	ပင်တီ *pinti*
a coat	ကုတ်အင်္ကျီ တစ်ထည် *kouq-ìn ji-tă-t'eh*
a dress	ဂါဝန် တစ်ထည် *ga-wun-tă-t'eh*
a hat	ဦးထုပ် တစ်လုံး *ouq-t'ouq-tă-loùn*
a htamein (sarong)	ထမိန် တစ်ထည် *t'ă mein tă-t'eh*
a jacket	အပေါ်ဝတ်ဂျက်ကက် တစ်ထည် *ăpaw-wuq-jeq keq-tă-t'eh*
jeans	ဂျင်းဘောင်းဘီ *jin-baùn-bi*
a longyi (for man)	ပုဆိုး တစ်ထည် *păs'ò-tă-t'eh*
a longyi (for woman)	လုံချည် တစ်ထည် *lo ji-tă-t'eh*
pyjamas	ညအိပ်အင်္ကျီ (ပဂျားမား) *nyá-eiq-ìn-ji (pă jà mà)*
pants [trousers]	ဘောင်းဘီရှည် *baùn-bi-she*
pantyhose [tights]	ခြေအိတ်ဘောင်းဘီရှည် *će(ći) eiq-baùn-bi-she*
a purse [handbag]	လက်ကိုင်အိတ် *leq-kain-eiq*
a raincoat	မိုးကာအင်္ကျီ တစ်ထည် *mò-ga-ìn-ji-tă t'eh*

a scarf	လည်စီး တစ်ခု *leh-zi-tă k'ú*
a shirt	ရှပ်အင်္ကျီ တစ်ထည် *shaq-ìn-ji-tă t'eh*
shorts	ဘောင်းဘီတို *baùn-bi-to*
a skirt	စကပ် တစ်ထည် *să kaq-tă t'eh*
socks	ခြေအိတ်များ *će(ći) eiq-myà*
a suit	ဆု(တ်)တစ်စုံ၊ ဘောင်းဘီရှည် နှင့် အပေါ်ဝတ်ကုတ် တစ်စုံ *s'ú-tă zoun-baùn-bi-she-hnín-ăpaw-wuq-kouq-tă zoun*
sunglasses	နေကာမျက်မှန် *ne-ga-myeq-hman*
a sweater	ဆွယ်တာအနွေးထည် တစ်ထည် *s'weh-ta-ănwè-deh-tăt'eh*
a sweatshirt	အားကစားဝတ်ဆွယ်တာ တစ်ထည် *ă găzà-wuq-s'weh-ta-tăt'eh*
a swimsuit	ရေကူးဝတ်စုံ တစ်စုံ *ye-kù-wuq-soun-tă zoun*
a T-shirt	တီရှပ် တစ်ထည် *ti-shaq-tă t'eh*
a tie	နက်တိုင် တစ်ခု *neq-tain-tă k'ú*
underwear	အတွင်းခံ *ă twin-gan*

Fabric

I'd like…	ကျွန်တော်/ကျွန်မ … လိုချင်တယ်။ *cănaw* **m**/*cămà* **f**… *lo-ćin-deh*
cotton	ကော်တွန်/ချည်စ *kaw-tun / ći-zá*
denim	ဒီနင်/ဂျင်းစလိုမျိုး အစ *din in / jín-zá-lo-myò-ă sá*

The **longyi** is somewhat a symbol of national identity, worn everyday by both men and women. When worn by a man it is known as a **pasoe**, and when worn by a woman it is known as a **htamein**. It is a kilt-like piece of cloth worn from the waist to the ankle, similar to the Malaysian sarong. It is traditionally worn with the **eingyi**, a transparent blouse which is worn with a round-collared, long-sleeved jacket. Men tie theirs with a knot in front while women tie theirs to the side, tucked into a black waistband called a **htet sint**, sewn into the waist of the **longyi**.

lace	ဇာ *za*
leather	သားရေစ *thă-ye-zá*
linen	လီနင်စ *li nin-zá*
silk	ပိုးစ *pò-zá*
wool	သိုးမွေးစ *thò-mwè-zá*
Is it machine washable?	ဒါက အဝတ်လျှော်စက်နဲ့ လျှော်လို့ရသလား။ *da-ga-ăwuq-shaw-zeq-néh-shaw-ló-yá-dhă là*

Shoes

I'd like…	ကျွန်တော်/ကျွန်မ … လိုချင်တယ်။ *cănaw* **m**/*cămà* **f**… *lo-ćin-deh*
high-heels/flats	ခုံမြင့်/ပြား ဖိနပ် *k'oun'-myín / pyà-p'ănaq*
loafers	စွပ်ရချွတ်ရလွယ်တဲ့ ဘွတ်ဖိနပ် *suq-yá-ćuq-yá-lweh-déh-buq-p' ănaq*
sandals	ကွင်းထိုးဖိနပ် *gwìn-dò-p' ănaq*
shoes	ရှူးဖိနပ် *shù-p' ănaq*
slippers	ခြေညှပ်ဖိနပ *će(ći)-hnyaq-p' ănaq*
sneakers	အားကစားစီးဖိနပ် *à gă zà-sì-p' ănaq*
Size…	ဆိုဒ်နံပါတ် … ။ *s'aiq-nan-baq …*

For Numbers, see page 168.

Sizes

small (S) — အသေး *ăthè*
medium (M) — အလယ်အလတ် *ăleh-ălaq*
large (L) — အကြီး *ăcì*
extra large (XL) — ပိုကြီး *ăpo-cì*
petite — သေးသွယ်သူများအတွက် *thè-thweh-dhu-myà-ătweq*
plus size — ပိုပိုပြီးကြီးသော *po-po-byì-cì-dhàw*

Newsagent & Tobacconist

Do you sell English-language newspapers? — ခင်ဗျား အင်္ဂလိပ်ဘာသာစကားနဲ့သတင်းစာ ရောင်းသလား။ *gá-k'ămyà-ìngăleiq-badha-zăgà-néh-dhă-dìn-za-yaùn-dhă là?*

I'd like… — ကျွန်တော်/ကျွန်မ … လိုချင်တယ်။ *cănaw* **m**/*cămà* **f***… lo-ćin-deh*

- candy [sweets] — သကြားလုံး (ချိုချဉ်များ) *dhă-jà-loùn(ćo-ćin-myà)*
- chewing gum — ပီကေ *pi-ke*
- a chocolate bar — ချောကလက်ချောင်းတစ်ချောင်း *ćàw-kă leq-ćaùn-tă ćaùn*
- a cigar — ဆေးပြင်းလိပ်တစ်လိပ် *s'è-byìn-leiq-tă leiq*
- a pack/carton of cigarettes — စီးကရက် တစ်ဗူး/တစ်ကာတွန်း *s'ì-kă req-tă bù / tă ka-tùn*

a lighter	ဓာတ်မီးခြစ်တစ်လုံး *daq-mì-jiq-tăloùn*
a magazine	မဂဇင်းတစ်စောင် *meq gă zìn-dă zaun*
matches	သစ်သားမီးခြစ် *thiq-thà-mì-jiq*
a newspaper	သတင်းစာတစ်စောင် *dhă dìn zà-dă zaun*
a pen	ဘောပင်တစ်ချောင်း *bàw pin-tăćaùn*
a postcard	ပို့စကတ်တစ်ခု *pó să kaq-tă k'ú*
a road/town map of…	… လမ်း/မြို့ရဲ့မြေပုံတစ်ခု *… làn / myó-yéh-mye-boun-tă k'ú*
stamps	တံဆိပ်ခေါင်းများ *dă zeiq gaùn-myà*

Photography

I'd like…camera.	ကျွန်တော်/ကျွန်မ … ကင်မရာတစ်လုံး လိုချင်တယ်။ *cănaw* ***m****/cămà* ***f****… kin măra-tă loùn-lo-ćin-deh.*
an automatic	အော်တိုမက်တစ်/အလိုအလျောက် *awtomeq / ălo-ăhlauq*
a digital	ဒစ်ဂျစ်တယ် *diq-jiq-teh*
a disposable	တစ်ခါသုံး *tă k'a-thoùn*
I'd like…	ကျွန်တော်/ကျွန်မ … လိုချင်တယ်။ *cănaw* ***m****/cămà* ***f****… lo-ćin-deh*
a battery	ဘက်ထရီတစ်လုံး *beq t'ă ri-tă loùn*
a memory card	မမ်မိုရီကတ်/မှတ်ဉာဏ်ကတ် *man-mo ri-kaq / hmaq-nyan-kaq*
Can I print digital photos here?	ကျွန်တော်/ကျွန်မ ဒီမှာ ဒစ်ဂျစ်တယ်ဓာတ်ပုံ ကူးလို့ရမလား။ *cănaw* ***m****/cămà* ***f*** *di-hma-diq jiq the-daq-poun-kù-ló-yá-m cănaw* ***m****/cămà* ***f*** *là?*

Be careful not to photograph military or government buildings, soldiers, police or officials, as it is strictly forbidden.

Souvenirs

Can I see this/that?	ကျွန်တော်/ကျွန်မ ဒီဟာ/ဟိုဟာကို ကြည့်လို့ရမလား။ *cănaw* **m**/*cămà* **f** *di ha/ho ha-go-cí-ló-yá-mă là*
I'd like…	ကျွန်တော်/ကျွန်မ … လိုချင်တယ်။ *cănaw* **m**/*cămà* **f**… *lo-ćin-deh*
a bracelet	လက်ကောက်တစ်ရံ *leq-kauq-tă yan*
a brooch	ရင်ထိုးတစ်ခု *yin-dò-dă-k'ú*
ceramics	ကြွေထည်များ *cwe-deh-myà*
a clock	နာရီတစ်လုံး *na yi-tă-loùn*
a doll	အရုပ်မတစ်ရုပ် *ă youq-má-tă youq*
earrings	နားကပ်။နားကွင်းများ *nă gaq / nă gwìn-myà*
jewelry	လက်ဝတ်ရတနာ *leq-wuq-yădăna*
a key ring	သော့ချိတ် တစ်ကွင်း *tháw-jeiq-dă gwin*
lacquerware	ယွန်းထည် *yún-deh*
a marionette	ကြိုးဆွဲ ရုပ်သေးတစ်ရုပ် *cò-zwèh-youq-thè-tă-youq*
a necklace	လည်ဆွဲတစ်ခု *leh-zwèh-tăk'ú*
a postcard	ပို့စကတ်တစ်ခု *pó să kaq-tă k'ú*
pottery	မြေအိုး *mye-ò*
a puppet	လက်ထိုး/တုတ်ထိုး ရုပ်သေးရုပ်တစ်ရုပ် *leq-t'ò / douq-t'ò-youq-thè-youq-tă youq*
a ring	လက်စွပ်တစ်ကွင်း *leq-suq-dăgwìn*

a statue	ရုပ်ထုတစ်ခု *youq-t'ú-tăk'ú*
a tapestry	ရွှေချည်ထိုး/ငွေချည်ထိုး တစ်ထည် *shwe-ji-t'ò / ngwe-ji-t'ò-tă teh*
a T-shirt	တီရှပ်တစ်ထည် *ti-shaq-tă t'eh*
a toy	အရုပ်တစ်ရုပ် *ă youq-tă youq*
a watch	လက်ပတ်နာရီတစ်လုံး *leq-paq-na-yi-tă-loùn*
I'd like…	ကျွန်တော်/ကျွန်မ … လိုချင်တယ်။ *cănaw* ***m****/cămà* ***f****… lo-ćin-deh*
copper	ကြေးနီ *cè-ni*
diamonds	စိန်တွေ *sein-dwe*
jade	ကျောက်စိမ်း *cauq-sein*
white/yellow gold	ရွှေဖြူ/ရွှေဝါ *shwe-byu / shwe-wa*
pearls	ပုလဲတွေ *pă lèh-dwe*
pewter	ခဲနှင့် သံဖြူရောစပ်ထားသော သတ္တု *k'èh-hnín-than-byu-yàw-saq-t'à-dhàw-thaq-tú*
platinum	ပလက်တီနမ် *pă leq ti nan*
rubies	ပတ္တမြားတွေ *bă dă myà-dwe*
sterling silver	စတာလင်ငွေ *să ta-lin-ngwe*
Is this real?	အဲဒါက အစစ်လား။ *Èh-da-gá-ăsiq-là*
Can you engrave it?	အဲဒီအပေါ်မှာ ခင်ဗျား/ရှင် စာထွင်းရေးနိုင်မလား။ *È-di-ă paw-hma-k'ămyà* ***m****/ shin* ***f*** *sa-t'win-yè-nain-mălà*

Nearly everywhere you visit in Myanmar will have markets (**zei**) selling traditional handicrafts. Upscale hotels usually have souvenir boutiques also. Another rich source of items to take home is the concessions lining the stairways to Buddhist pagodas, which specialize in religious paraphernalia such as incense, prayer beads and mini Buddhas.

Sport & Leisure

ESSENTIAL

When's the game?	ကစားပွဲက ဘယ်အချိန်လဲ။ *gă zà pwèh-gá-beh-ăćwin-lèh*
Where's...?	... က ဘယ်နေရာမှာလဲ။ *... gă-beh-ne-ya-hma-lèh*
the beach	ကမ်းခြေ *kàn-je*
the park	ပန်းခြံ *pàn-jan*
the pool	ရေကူးကန် *ye-kù-gan*
Is it safe to swim here?	ဒီမှာ ရေကူးတာ လုံခြုံစိတ်ချရရဲ့လား။ *di-hma-ye kù-da-loun-ćoun-seiq-ćá-yá-yéh-là*
Can I hire clubs?	ကျွန်တော်/ကျွန်မ ကလပ်တွေ (ဂေါက်ရိုက်တံတွေ) ငှားလို့ရနိုင်လား။ *cănaw* **m**/*cămà* **f** *kă laq-twe (gauq-yaiq- tan-dwe) hngà-ló-yá-nain-là*
How much per hour/day?	တစ်နာရီ/တစ်ရက်ကို ဘယ်လောက်ကျလဲ။ *Tă na yi / tă yeq-ko-beh-lauq-cá-lèh*
How far is it to...?	... ကို ဘယ်လောက်ဝေးလဲ။ *... ko-beh-lauq-wè-lèh*
Show me on the map, please.	ကျေးဇူးပြုပြီး ကျွန်တော့်/ကျွန်မကို မြေပုံပေါ်မှာ ပြပါ။ *cè zù-pyú-byi- cănáw* **m**/*cămá* **f** *go-mye-boun-baw-hma-pyá-ba*

Watching Sport

When's...(game/ race/tournament)?	... (ကစားပွဲ/ပြိုင်ပွဲ/ယှဉ်ပြိုင်ပွဲ) က ဘယ်အချိန်လဲ။ *... (gă zà bwèh / pyain-bwèh) gá-beh-ăćein-lèh*
the bando [kickboxing]	ဗန်တို (ခြေထောက်နှင့်ကန် လက်သီးနှင့်ထိုး) *ban-to (će-dauq-hnín-kan-leq-thì-hnín-t'ò)*
the boxing	လက်ဝှေ့ထိုးပွဲ *leq-hwé-t'ò-bwèn*

the chinlone	ခြင်းလုံး *ĉin-loùn*
the soccer [football]	ဘောလုံးပွဲ (ဘောလုံးကန်ပွဲ) *bàw-loùn-bwèh(bàw-loùn-kan-bwèh)*
Who's playing?	ဘယ်သူတွေ ကစားမှာလဲ။ *beh-dhu-dwe-găzà-hma-lèh?*
Where's the stadium?	အားကစားရုံက ဘယ်မှာလဲ။ *ă-gă-ză-youn-gá- beh-hma-lèh?*
Can I place a bet?	ကျွန်တော်/ကျွန်မ လောင်းကြေးထပ်လို့ ရနိုင်မလား။ *cănaw* **m**/*cămá* **f** *laùn-jè-taq-ló-yá-nain-mălà?*

For Tickets, see page 20.

Burmese boxing can be viewed throughout the country at temple festivals and there are regular matches in Mandalay. Boxers may use any part of their bodies in attacking their opponent and the winner is he who draws first blood. For a more relaxed national sport, non-competitive, skilful **Chinlone** games are held across the country and traditionally involve a rattan ball being passed between groups of six people through a graceful and stylish combination of martial arts and dance moves.

Playing Sport

Where is...?	... က ဘယ်မှာလဲ။ *...gá-beh-hma-lèh?*
the golf course	ဂေါက်ကွင်း *gauq-kwìn*
the park	ပန်းခြံ *pàn-jan*
How much per...	... ကို ဘယ်လောက်ကျလဲ။ *...ko-beh-lauq-cá-lèh?*
day	တစ်ရက် *tă yeq*
hour	တစ်နာရီ *tă na-yi*
game	တစ်ပွဲ *tă bwèh*
round	ကွင်းတစ်ပတ် *kwìn-dă-baq*
Can I rent [hire]...?	ကျွန်တော်/ကျွန်မ ... ငှားလို့ရနိုင်မလား။ *cănaw* **m**/*cămá* **f**...*hngà-ló-yá-nain-mălà?*
some clubs	ဂေါက်သီးရိုက်တဲ့ကလပ်တစ်ချို့ *gauq-thì-yaiq-téh-kălaq-tăcó*
some equipment	ကိရိယာတန်ဆာပလာတစ်ချို့ *kăríya-dăzapăla-tăcó*
We'd like to go...	ကျွန်တော်/ကျွန်မတို့ ... သွားချင်တယ်။ *cănaw* **m**/*cămá* **f** *dó... thaw-jin-deh*
cycling	စက်ဘီးစီး *seq-beìn-sì*
diving	ကားမောင်း *kà-maùn*
hot air ballooning	မီးပုံးပျံစီး *mì-boùn-byan-sì*
snorkelling	ရေမျက်နှာပြင်အပေါ်ယံရေငုပ်တာ *yé-myeq-hna-byin-ăpawyan-ye-ngouq-ta*
trekking	လမ်းလျှောက်ခရီးရှည် *làn-hlauq-k'ăyì-she*
white water rafting	မြစ်ရေစီးကြမ်းထဲမှာဖောင်စီး *myiq-ye-sè-jàn-dèh-hma-p'aun-sì*

Bicycles can be hired easily and cheaply and are an excellent way to see the country. Trekking is also easily undertaken. Itineraries can be arranged through a tour operator.

At the Beach/Pool

Where's the beach/pool?	ကမ်းခြေ/ရေကူးကန် က ဘယ်နေရာမှာလဲ။ *kàn-je/ye-kù-gan-gá-beh-neya-hma-lèh?*
Is there a...?	အဲဒီမှာ ... တစ်ခု ရှိသလား။ *Èh-di-hma...tăk'ú-shí-dhălà?*
kiddie pool	ကလေးငယ်တွေအတွက်ရေကူးကန် *k'ălè-ngeh-dwe-ătweq-yekù-gan*
pool	ရေကူးကန် *yekù-gan*
lifeguard	သက်စောင့် *theq-saún*
Is it safe...?	...စိတ်ချရရဲ့လား။ *...seiq-ćá-yá-yèh-là?*
to swim	ရေကူးဖို့ *yekù-bó*
to dive	ရေငုပ်ဖို့ *ye-ngouq-p'ó*
for children	ကလေးတွေအတွက် *k'ălè-dwe-ătweq*
I'd like to hire...	ကျွန်တော်/ကျွန်မ ... ငှားချင်တယ်။ *cănaw* **m**/*cămá* **f***...hngà-jin-deh*
diving equipment	ရေငုပ်ရာမှာသုံးတဲ့ ကိရိယာတန်ဆာပလာ *ye-ngoug-ya-hma-thoùn-dèh-kăríya-dă za pă la.*
snorkeling equipment	ရေမျက်နှာပြင်အပေါ်ယံငုပ်ရာမှာသုံးတဲ့ ကိရိယာတန်ဆာပလာ *ye-myaq-hna-byin-ăpaw-yan-ngouq-ya-hma-thoùn-déh-kăríya-dă za pă la.*

For…hours.	… နာရီ အတွက် *…na-yi-ătweq*
Are there lessons?	သင်တန်းတွေရှိလား။ *thin-dàn-dwe-shí-là?*
I'm a beginner.	ကျွန်တော်/ကျွန်မက အခုမှစမှာ။ *cănaw* **m**/*cămá* **f** *gá-ăk'ú-hmá-sá-hma*
I'm experienced.	ကျွန်တော်/ကျွန်မမှာ အတွေ့အကြုံရှိတယ်။ *cănaw* **m**/*cămá* **f** *hma-ătwé-ăcoun-shí-deh*

Out in the Country

A map of…, please.	… ရဲ့ မြေပုံတစ်ခု ကျေးဇူးပြုပြီးပေးပါ။ *…yé-mye-boun-tăk'ú-cè-zú-pyú-byì-pè-ba*
this region	ဒီဒေသ *di-de-thá*
the walking routes	လမ်းလျှောက်တဲ့လမ်းကြောင်းတွေ *làn-hlauq-téh-làn-jaùn-dwe*
the bike routes	စက်ဘီးစီးတဲ့လမ်းကြောင်းတွေ *seq-beìn-sì-déh-làn-jaùn-dwe*
the trails	တောလမ်းတွေ *tàw-làn-dwe*
Is it…?	အဲဒါက … လား။ *Èh-da-gá…là?*
easy	လွယ်ကူ *lweh-ku*
difficult	ခက်ခဲ *k'eq-k'èh*
far	ဝေးလံ *wè-lan*
steep	မတ်စောက် *maq-sauq*
How far is it to…?	… ကို ဘယ်လောက်ဝေးလဲ။ *… ko-beh-lauq-wè-lèh?*
I'm lost.	ကျွန်တော်/ကျွန်မ လမ်းပျောက်နေတယ်။ *cănaw* **m**/*cămá* **f** *làn-pyauq-ne-deh*
Where's…?	… က ဘယ်နေရာမှာလဲ။ *…ká-beh-neya-hma-lèh*
the bridge	တံတား *dă da*

the cave	လှိုင်ဂူ *hlain-gu*
the field	ကွင်းပြင် *kwìn-byin*
the hill	တောင်ကုန်း *taun-goùn*
the mountain	တောင် *taun*
the nearest village	အနီးဆုံးရွာ *ănì-zoùn-ywa*
the viewpoint	ရှုခင်းကြည့်တဲ့နေရာ/ဗျူးပွိုင့် *shú-gìn-cí-déh-neya/byù-pwaín*
the park	ပန်းခြံ *pàn-jan*
the path	လမ်းကြောင်း *làn-jaùn*
the peak	ထိပ်ဖျား *t'eiq-p'yá*
the picnic area	ပျော်ပွဲစားတဲ့နေရာ *pyaw-bwèh-zà-déh-ne-ya.*
the river	မြစ် *myiq*
the sea	ပင်လယ် *pin-leh*
the valley	တောင်ကြား *taun-jà*
the waterfall	ရေတံခွန် *ye-dà-gun*

Going Out

ESSENTIAL

What's there to do at night?	အဲဒီနေရာမှာ ညဖက်ကို ဘာလုပ်လို့ရသလဲ။ *Èh-di-ne-ya-hma-myá-beq-ko-ba-louq-ló-yá-dhălèh?*
Do you have a program of events?	ခင်ဗျား/ရှင့်မှာ ပွဲတွေအတွက် အစီအစဉ်စာရွက်တစ်ခု ရှိသလား။ *k´ămyà* **m**/*shin* **f** *hma-pwèh-dwe-ătwweq-ăsi-ăzin-sa-yweq-tăk´ú-shí-dhălà?*
What's playing tonight?	ဒီည ဘာပြမှာလဲ။ *di-nyá-ba-pyá-hma-lèh?*
Where's…?	… က ဘယ်နေရာမှာလဲ။ *…gá-beh-neya-hma-lèh?*
the downtown area	မြို့လည်ကောင်ဧရိယာ *myó-leh-gaun-eríya.*
the bar	ဘား/အရက်ဆိုင် *bà/ăyeq-s'ain*
the dance club	ကတဲ့ကလပ် *ká-déh-kălaq*

Entertainment

Can you recommend…?	ခင်ဗျား/ရှင် … ညွှန်းပေးနိုင်မလား။ *k´ămyà* **m**/*shin* **f***…hnyùn-pè-nain-mălá?*
a concert	ဂီတပွဲတစ်ပွဲ *gi-tá-pwèh-dăbwèh*
a karaoke bar	ကာရာအိုကေဘား တစ်ခု *ka ra o ke-bà-tăk´ú*
a movie	ရုပ်ရှင်တစ်ကား *youq-shin-dă-gà*
a play	ပြဇာတ်တစ်ခု *pyá zaq-tăk´ú*
a pwe (traditional dance / music)	ပွဲ (ရိုးရာအက/ဂီတ) တစ်ပွဲ *pwèh (yò ya ăká/gitá) dă bwèh*
a show	ပြပွဲတစ်ခု *pyá-pwèh-tă-k´ú*
When does it start/end?	အဲဒါက ဘယ်အချိန် စ/ပြီး တာလဲ။ *Èh da gá-beh-ăćein-sá/pyí-da-lèh?*

How long is it? အဲဒါက ဘယ်လောက်ကြာသလဲ။
Èh da gá-beh-lauq-ca-dhă-lèh?

How much are tickets? လက်မှတ်တွေက ဘယ်ဈေးလဲ။
leq hmaq-twe-gá-beh-zè-lèh?

What's the dress code? ဝတ်စုံကုဒ်/အမှတ်အသားက ဘာလဲ။
ဘယ်လိုဝတ်စုံဝတ်ရမလဲ။
wuq soun-kouq/ăhmaq-ăthà-gà-ba lèh/beh lo-wuq soun-wuq-yá-mălèh?

For Tickets, see page 20.

Recitals of classical Burmese music and dance (**pwe)** and puppet shows (www.mandalaymarionettes.com) can be seen during festival times on the city streets or pagoda grounds or in the theatres in Yangon.

Alternatively, the famous Moustache Brothers' traditional satirical show is worth seeing. It is somewhat of an institution in Mandalay and features a type of traditional theatre known as **yeint** that combines clowning with dance and puppetry. It is staged by three moustachioed locals who were imprisoned for poking fun at the government. They're now only allowed to perform for foreigners.

Nightlife

What's there to do at night?
အဲဒီမှာ ညဖက်ကို ဘာလုပ်လို့ရသလဲ။
Èh di-hma-nyá-beq-ko-ba-louq-ló-yá-dhălèh?

Can you recommend…?
ခင်ဗျား/ရှင် … ညွှန်ပေးနိုင်မလား။
k´ămyà **m**/*shin* **m**… *hnyun-pè-nain-mălà?*

a bar
ဘားတစ်ခု/အရက်ဆိုင်တစ်ဆိုင်
bà-tăk´ú/ăyeq-s'ain-tă-s'ain

a show
ပြပွဲ တစ်ပွဲ
pyá-bwèh-tă-bwèh.

some traditional dance/ music
ရိုးရာ အက/ဂီတပွဲတစ်ချို့
yò-ya-ăká/gitá-pwèh-tăćó

Is there live music?
လူကိုယ်တိုင်ထိုင်ဆိုတဲ့ ဂီတ ရှိသလား။
Lu-ko-dain-t´ain-so-déh-gitá-shí-dhălà?

How do I get there?
ကျွန်တော်/ကျွန်မ အဲဒီနေရာကို
ဘယ်လိုရောက်နိုင်မလဲ။
cănaw **m**/*cămá* **f** *èh-di-neya-go-beh lo-youq-nain-mălèh?*

Is there a charge?
ဝင်ကြေးကောက်တာရှိလား။
win-jè-kauq-ta-shí-là?

Let's go dancing.
သွားကရအောင်။
thaw-ká-yá-aun

Aside from a half dozen nightclubs, evening entertainment tends to be low-key and limited to male-dominated beer gardens, downbeat karaoke dives and old-style teashops. Outside of the main cities, everything shuts down by 9:00p.m., or earlier.

Is this area safe at night?	အဲဒီဧရိယာက ညဖက်ကို လုံခြုံစိတ်ချရရဲ့လား။ *èhdi-eríya-gá-nyá-beq-ko-loun-joun-seiq-ćà-yà-yéh-là?*

Special Requirements

Business Travel 141

Traveling with Children 144

Disabled Travelers 148

Business Travel

ESSENTIAL

I'm here on business. ကျွန်တော်/ကျွန်မ ဒီကို အလုပ်ကိစ္စနဲ့လာတာပါ။
cănaw **m**/*cămá* **f** *di-go-ălouq-keiq-sá-néh-la-da-ba*

Here's my card. ဒီမှာ ကျွန်တော်/ကျွန်မရဲ့ လိပ်စာကတ်ပါ။
di-hma-cănaw **m**/*cămá* **f** *yèh-ălouq-leiq-sa-kaq-pa*

Can I have your card? ကျွန်တော်/ကျွန်မ ခင်ဗျား ရှင့်ရဲ့ လိပ်စာကတ် ရနိုင်မလား။
cănaw **m**/*cămá* **f** *k'ămyà* **m**/*shin* **f** *yéh-leiq-sa-kaq-yá-nain-mălà?*

I have a meeting with… ကျွန်တော်/ကျွန်မမှာ မှာ… နဲ့ တွေ့ဖို့ရှိတယ်။
cănaw **m**/*cămá* **f** *hma…néh-twé-bó-shí-deh.*

Where's…? …က ဘယ်နေရာမှာလဲ။ *…gà- beh-ne-ya-hma-lèh*

the business center လုပ်ငန်းသုံးစင်တာ *louq-ngàn-dhoùn-sin-ta*

the convention hall စည်းဝေးခန်းမ *sì-wè-k´àn-má*

the meeting room အစည်းအဝေးခန်း *ăsì-wè-ăwè-k´àn*

When on business in Burma there are a few points to remember: attire should be conservative – lightweight suits with ties for men, and knee-length or longer skirts for women are appropriate; business cards are widely used. When exchanging business cards, take a moment to read it before popping it in your pocket and always use both hands to present and receive them. Handshakes are the conventional greeting, but do not offer your hand to a woman until invited to do so.

On Business

I'm here for…	ကျွန်တော်/ကျွန်မ ဒီကို … အတွက် လာတာပါ။ *cănaw* **m**/*cămá* **f** *di-go…ătweq-la-da-ba.*
a seminar	နှီးနှောဖလှယ်ပွဲတစ်ခု *hnì-hnàw-p´ăleh-bwèn-tăk´ú*
a conference	ကွန်ဖရင့်တစ်ခု *kun-p´ă-rín-tă-k´ú*
a meeting	အစည်းအဝေးတစ်ခု *ăsì-wè-ăwè- tă-k´ú*
My name is…	ကျွန်တော်/ကျွန်မ ရဲ့နာမည်က…ပါ။ *cănaw* **m**/*cămá* **f** *yéh-na-myi (nan-meh)-gá…ba*
May I introduce my colleague…	ကျွန်တော်/ကျွန်မ ရဲ့ လုပ်ဖော်ကိုင်ဖက်… နဲ့ မိတ်ဆက်ပေးပါရစေ။ *cănaw* **m**/*cămá* **f** *yéh-louq-p´aw-kain-beq…néh-meiq-s'eq-pè-băyá-ze.*
I have a meeting/an appointment with…	ကျွန်တော်/ကျွန်မ မှာ … နဲ့ အစည်းအဝေး။ ချိန်းဆိုထားတာ တစ်ခု ရှိပါတယ်။ *cănaw* **m**/*cămá* **f** *hma…néh-ăsìăwè/ćèin-s'o-t´à-da-tăk´ú-shí-ba-deh.*
I'm sorry I'm late.	ကျွန်တော်/ကျွန်မ နောက်ကျတဲ့အတွက် ဝမ်းနည်းပါတယ်။ *cănaw* **m**/*cămá* **f** *nauq-cá-déh-ătweq-wùn-nèh-ba-deh.*
I need an interpreter.	ကျွန်တော်/ကျွန်မ စကားပြန်တစ်ယောက် လိုအပ်ပါတယ်။ *cănaw* **m**/*cămá* **f** *zăgăbyan-tăyauq-lo-aq-pa-deh.*
You can contact me at the…Hotel.	ခင်ဗျား/ရှင် ကျွန်တော်/ကျွန်မ ကို… ဟိုတယ်မှာ ဆက်သွယ်နိုင်ပါတယ်။ *k'ămyà* **m**/*shin* **f** *cănaw* **m**/*cămá* **f** *go…hoteh-hma-s'eq-thweh-nain-ba-deh.*

I'm here until…	ကျွန်တော်/ကျွန်မ ဒီမှာ…အထိ ရှိမယ်။ *cănaw* ***m****/cămá* ***f*** *di-hma…ăt´í-shí-meh.*
I need to…	ကျွန်တော်/ကျွန်မ…လိုအပ်တယ်။ *cănaw* ***m****/cămá* ***f****… lo-aq-teh.*
make a call	ဖုန်းတစ်ခါခေါ်ဖို့ *p´oùn-tăk´a-k´aw-bó*
make a photocopy	မိတ္တူတစ်စောင်ကူးဖို့ *meiqtu-dăzaun-kù-bó*
send an email	အီးမေးလ်တစ်စောင် ပို့ဖို့ *ì-mè-dăzaun-pó-bó*
send a fax	ဖက်စ်တစ်စောင် ပို့ဖို့ *p´eqsà-dăzaun-pó-bó*
send a package (for next-day delivery)	(နောက်တစ်ရက်မှာ ပို့နိုင်ဖို့အတွက်) အထုတ်တစ်ထုတ် ပို့ဖို့ *(nauq-tăyeq-hma-pó-nain-bó-ătweq) ăt´ouq-tăt´ouq-pó-bó*
It was a pleasure to meet you.	ခင်ဗျား/ရှင် နဲ့တွေ့ခဲ့ရတာ နှစ်သက်စရာကောင်းပါတယ်။ *k´ămyà* ***m****/shin* ***f*** *néh twè-k'éh-ya-da nhit-theq-sa-yar kaùn-ba-deh.*

YOU MAY HEAR…

ခင်ဗျား/ရှင် မှာ ချိန်းထားတာ ရှိသလား။ *k'ămyà* ***m****/shin* ***f*** *hma-ćein-t´à-da-shí-dhălà.*	Do you have an appointment?
ဘယ်သူနဲ့လဲ။ *beh-dhu-néh-leh?*	With whom?
သူက အစည်းအဝေးခန်းထဲမှာ။ *thu-gá-ăsì-ăwè-gàn-dèh-hma.*	He/She is in a meeting.
ကျေးဇူးပြုပြီး ခဏလောက်စောင့်ပါ။ *cè-zù-pyú-byì-k´ănà-lauq-saún-ba.*	One moment, please.
ထိုင်ခုံမှာ ထိုင်ပါ။ *t´ain-goun-hma-t´ain-ba*	Have a seat.
ခင်ဗျား/ရှင် တစ်ခုခု သောက်မလား။ *k'ămyà* ***m****/shin* ***f*** *tăkú-k´ú-thauq-mălà?*	Would you like something to drink?
လာရောက်တဲ့အတွက် ခင်ဗျား/ရှင့် ကို ကျေးဇူးတင်ပါတယ်။ *la-yauq-téh-ătweq-k'ămyà* ***m****/shin* ***f*** *go-cè-zù-tin-ba-deh.*	Thank you for coming.

Traveling with Children

ESSENTIAL

Is there a discount for kids? ကလေးတွေအတွက် ဈေးလျှော့ပေးတာ ရှိသလား။ *k'ălè-dwe-ătweq-zè-sháw-pé-da-shí-dhălà?*

Can you recommend a babysitter? ခင်ဗျား/ရှင် ကလေးထိန်းတစ်ယောက် ညွှန်ပေးနိုင်မလား။ *k'ămyà* **m**/*shin* **f** *k´ălè-dein-tăyauq-hnyun-pè-nain-mălà?*

Do you have a child's seat/highchair? ခင်ဗျား/ရှင့် မှာ ကလေးထိုင်ဖို့. ထိုင်ခုံ။ထိုင်ခုံမြင့် တစ်ခု ရှိသလား။ *k'ămyà* **m**/*shin* **f** *hma-k´ălé-t´ain-bó-t´ain-goun/t´ain-goun-myín-tăk´ú-shí-dhălà?*

Where can I change the baby? ကျွန်တော်/ကျွန်မ ကလေးအနှီး ဘယ်နေရာမှာ လဲပေးနိုင်မလဲ။ *cănaw* **m**/*cămá* **f** *k´ălè-ăhnì-beh-ne-ya-hma-lèh-pè-nain-mălèh?*

Out & About

Can you recommend something for kids? ကလေးတွေအတွက် ခင်ဗျား/ရှင် တစ်ခုခု ညွှန်ပေးနိုင်မလား။ *k´ălè-dwe-ătweq-k'ămyà* **m**/*shin* **f** *tăk´ú-k´ú-hnyun-pè-nain-mălà?*

Where's...? ...က ဘယ်နေရာမှာလဲ။ *...gá-beh-ne-ya-hma-lèh*

the kiddie [paddling] pool ကလေး (ယက်နိုင်တဲ့) ရေကူးကန် *k'ălè (yeq-nain-déh) ye-kù-gan*

the park ပန်းခြံ *pàn-jan*

the puppet show ရုပ်သေးပွဲ *youq-thè-bwèh*

the market ဈေး *zè*

the zoological gardens တိရစ္ဆာန်ဥယျာဉ် *tăreiqs'an-ù(ú)yin*

the safari park ဆာဖာရီ ဥယျာဉ် *s'ap´ari-ù(ú)yin*

Are kids allowed?	ကလေးတွေကို ဝင်ခွင့်ပြုသလား *k´ălè-dwe-go-win-k´wín-pyú-dhălà?*
Is it safe for kids?	အဲဒါကလေးတွေအတွက် စိတ်ချရရဲ့လား။ *èh-da-gá-k´ălè-dwe-ătweq-seiq-ćá-yá-yèh-là?*
Is it suitable for... year olds?	အဲဒါက အသက်... နှစ်ရှိတဲ့ ကလေးတွေအတွက် သင့်လျော်ရဲ့လား။ *Èh-da-gá-ătheq...hniq-shí-déh-k´ălè-dwe-ătweq-thín-taw-yéh-là?*

For Numbers, see page 168.

YOU MAY HEAR...

ဘယ်လောက် ချစ်စရာကောင်းလိုက်လဲ။ *beh-lauq-ćiq-săya-kaùn-laiq-lèh?*	How cute!
သူ့ ရဲ့နာမည်က ဘယ်လိုခေါ်လဲ။ *thú-yéh-nan-meh (na-myi) gá-beh-lo-k´aw-lèh?*	What's his/her name?
သူ့ အသက်က ဘယ်လောက်ရှိပြီလဲ။ *thú-ătheq-ká-beh-lauq-shí-byi-lèh?*	How old is he/she?

Baby Essentials

Do you have…?	ခင်ဗျား/ရှင့် မှာ… ရှိသလား။ *k'ămyà* **m**/*shin* **f** *hma…shí-dhă-là?*
a baby bottle	ကလေးနို့ဗူး *k'ălè-nó-bù*
baby food	ကလေးအစားအစာ *k'ălè-ăsà-ăsa*
baby wipes	ကလေးအညစ်အကြေးသုတ်ဖတ် *k'ălè-ănyiq-ăcè-thouq-p´aq*
a car seat	ကားထိုင်ခုံတစ်ခုံ *kà-t´ain-goun-tă-k´oun.*
a children's menu/portion	ကလေးအစားအစာ အမည်စာရင်း/အချိုးအစား *k'ălè-ăsà-ăsa-ămyi-săyìn/ăćò-ăsà*
a child's seat/ highchair	ကလေးထိုင်ခုံ/ထိုင်ခုံမြင့် တစ်လုံး *k'ălè-t´ain-goun/t´ain-goun-myín-tăloùn*
a crib/cot	ပုခက်/ကလေးအိပ်ရာကုတင် တစ်လုံး *păkeq/k´ălè-eiq-ya-gădin-tă-loùn*
diapers [nappies]	ကလေးအောက်ခံအနှီး (သေးခံ) *k'ălè-auq-k´an-ăhnì (thè-gan)*
formula	ဖော်မြူလာ *p´aw-myu-la*
a pacifier [dummy]	နို့သီးခေါင်း/ကိုက်စရာတစ်ခု (အရုပ်) *nó-dhì-gaùn/kaiq-săya-tăk´ú (ăyouk)*
a playpen	ကလေးငယ်များကစားနိုင်သော နေရာ *k'ălè-ngeh-myà-găzà-nain-dhăw-ne-ya*
a stroller [pushchair]	လမ်းလျှောက်ရင်းတွန်းနိုင်သော လက်တွန်းလှည်း (လက်တွန်းထိုင်ခုံ) *làn-shauq-yìn-tùn-nain-dhàw-leq-tùn-hlèh (leq-tùn-t´ain-goun)*
Can I breastfeed the baby here?	ကျွန်မ ကလေးကို ဒီနေရာမှာ နို့တိုက်လို့ရနိုင်မလား။ *cămá-k´ălè-go-di-ne-ya-hma-nó-taiq-ló-yá-nain-mălà?*
Where can I breastfeed /change the baby?	ကျွန်မ ဘယ်နေရာမှာ ကလေးကို နို့တိုက်နိုင်မလဲ/ အနှီးလဲပေးနိုင်မလဲ။ *cămá-beh-ne-ya-hma-k´ălè-go-nó-taiq-nain-mălèh/ăhnì-lèh-pè-nain-mălèh?*

For Dining with Children, see page 64.

Traveling with children is not easy with the hot and humid climate, and the disposal (and purchase) of diapers outside of the main cities may be difficult due to the non-existent refuse collection.

Babysitting

Can you recommend a babysitter?
ခင်ဗျား/ရှင် ကလေးထိန်းတစ်ယောက်ညွှန်ပေးနိုင်မလား။
k'ămyà **m**/*shin* **f** *k´ălè-deìn-tăyouq-hnyun-pè-nain mălà?*

How much do you/they charge?
ခင်ဗျား/ရှင်သူတို့က ပိုက်ဆံ ဘယ်လောက်ယူတာလဲ။
k'ămyà **m**/*shin* **f** *thu-dó-gá-paiq-s'an-beh-lauq-yu-da-lèh?*

I'll be back at…
ကျွန်တော်/ကျွန်မ… အချိန်မှာ ပြန်လာခဲ့မယ်။
cănaw **m**/*cămá* **f**…*ăćein-hma-pyan-la-géh-meh*

If you need to contact me, call…
တကယ်လို့ ခင်ဗျား/ရှင် ကျွန်တော်/ကျွန်မကို ဆက်သွယ်ဖို့လိုအပ်ရင်… ကိုခေါ်လိုက်ပါ။
dă-geh-ló-k'ămyà **m**/*shin* **f** *cănaw* **m**/*cămá* **f**-*go-s'eq-thweh-bó-lo-aq-yin… go-k´aw-laiq-pa*

For Time, see page 170.

Health & Emergency

Can you recommend a pediatrician?
ခင်ဗျား/ရှင် ကလေးအထူးကုဆရာဝန်တစ်ယောက် ညွှန်ပေးနိုင်မလား။ *k'ămyà* **m**/*shin* **f** *k´ălè-ăt´ù-kù-s'ăya-wun-tăyauq-hnyun- pè-nain-mălà?*

My child is allergic to…
ကျွန်တော်/ကျွန်မ ရဲ့ ကလေးက… နဲ့ ဓာတ်မတဲ့ဘူး။
cănaw **m**/*cămá* **f** *yéh-k´ălè-gá… néh-daq-mătéh-bù*

My child is missing.
ကျွန်တော်/ကျွန်မ ရဲ့ကလေး ပျောက်နေတယ်။
cănaw **m**/*cămá* **f** *yéh- k´ălè-pyauq-ne-deh.*

Have you seen a boy/girl?
ခင်ဗျား/ရှင် ယောကျ်ားကလေး/မိန်းကလေး တစ်ယောက်တွေ့မိသလား။ *K'ămyà* **m**/*shin* **f** *yauq-cà-gălè/meìn-k´ălè-tăyauq-twè-mí- dhălà?*

For Police, see page 152.

Disabled Travelers

ESSENTIAL

Is there…? အဲဒီမှာ… ရှိသလား။ *Èh-di-hma…shí-dhălà?*

access for the disabled မသန်းမစွမ်းသူတွေ ဝင်ထွက်နိုင်တဲ့နေရာ *măthan-măswùn-dhu-dwe-win-t´weq-nain-déh-ne-ya*

a wheelchair ramp ဘီးတပ်ထိုင်ခုံ တက်နိုင်သောဆင်ခြေလျှော *beìn-taq-t´ain-goun-teq-nain-dhàw-s'in-je-shàw*

a disabled-accessible toilet မသန်မစွမ်းသူတွေ တက်နိုင်တဲ့ အိမ်သာ *măthan-măswùn-dhu-dwe-teq-nain-déh-ein-dha*

I need… ကျွန်တော်/ကျွန်မ… လိုအပ်ပါတယ်။ *cănaw* **m**/*cămá* **f**… *lo-aq-pa-deh*

assistance အကူအညီ *ăku-ănyi*

an elevator [a lift] ဓာတ်လှေကားတစ်စင်း *daq-hle-gà-dăzin*

a ground-floor room မြေညီထပ်အခန်းတစ်ခန်း *mye-nyi-daq-ăk´àn-tăkàn*

Asking for Assistance

I'm… ကျွန်တော်/ကျွန်မ… *cănaw* **m**/*cămá* **f**...

disabled မသန်မစွမ်းပါ။ *măthan-măswùn-ba*

visually impaired အမြင်အာရုံမကောင်းပါ။ *ămyin-a-youn-mă-kaùn-ba*

deaf နားမကြားပါ ။ *nà-mă-cà-ba*

hearing impaired အကြားအာရုံ ချွတ်ယွင်းနေပါတယ်။ *ăcà-a-youn-ćuq-ywìn-ne-ba-deh.*

unable to walk far/use the stairs လမ်းဝေးဝေးမလျှောက်နိုင်ပါ/ လှေကားထစ်များအသုံးမပြုနိုင်ပါ *làn-wè-wè-mă-shauq-nain-ba/hle-gă-diq-myà-ăthoùn-mă-pyú-nain-ba*

Please speak louder.	ကျေးဇူးပြုပြီး စကားပိုပြီးကျယ်ကျယ်ပြောပါ။ *cè-zù-pyú-byì-zăgà-po-byì-ceh-ceh-pyàw-ba*
Can I bring my wheelchair?	ကျွန်တော်/ကျွန်မ ရဲ့ ဘီးတပ်ထိုင်ခုံ ယူလာလို့ရနိုင်မလား။ *cănaw* **m**/*cămá* **f** *yèh-bein-taq-t´ain-goun-yu-la-ló-yá-nain-mălà?*
Are guide dogs permitted?	လမ်းပြခွေးတွေကို ခေါ်လာခွင့်ပြုသလား။ *làn-pyà-k´wè-dwe-go-k´aw-la-gwín-pyú-dhălà?*
Can you help me?	ခင်ဗျား/ရှင် ကျွန်တော်/ကျွန်မ ကိုကူညီနိုင်မလား။ *kămyà* **m**/*shin* **f** *cănaw* **m**/*cămá* **f** *go-ku-nyi-nain-mălà?*
Please open/ hold the door.	ကျေးဇူးပြုပြီး တံခါးဖွင့်ပေးပါ/ကိုင်ပေးထားပါ။ *cè-zù-pyú-byì-dăgà-p´wín-pè-ba/kain-pè-t´à-ba.-*

For Health, see page 155.

In an Emergency

Emergencies	151
Police	152
Health	155
The Basics	164

Emergencies

ESSENTIAL

Help! ကူညီကြပါဦး။
ku-nyi-jába-oùn

Go away! ထွက်သွား။
t´weq-thwà

Stop, thief! သူခိုး၊ ရပ်လိုက်။
thăkò, yaq-laiq

Get a doctor! ဆရာဝန်တစ်ယောက်ခေါ်ပါ။
śăya-wun-tăyauq-k´aw-ba

Fire! မီးလောင်နေတယ်။
mì-laun-ne-deh

I'm lost. ကျွန်တော်/ကျွန်မ လမ်းပျောက်နေတယ်။
cănaw **m**/*cămá* **f**-*làn-pyauq-ne-deh*

Can you help me? ခင်ဗျား/ရှင် ကျွန်တော်/ကျွန်မကို ကူညီနိုင်မလား။
k'ămyà **m**/*shin* **f** *cănaw* **m**/*cămá* **f**
-go-ku-nyi-nain-mălà?

In an emergency, dial:
199 for the police
199 for an ambulance
191 for a fire

Police

ESSENTIAL

Call the police! ရဲကိုခေါ်ပါ။ *yèh-go-k´aw-ba*

Where's the police station? ရဲစခန်း ဘယ်မှာလဲ။ *yèh-săk´àn-beh-hma-lèh*

There was an accident/attack. မတော်တဆထိခိုက်မှု/တိုက်ခိုက်မှုတစ်ခု ဖြစ်ခဲ့တယ်။ *mătaw-tăśá-t´í-k´aiq-hmú-taiq-k´aiq-hmú-tăk´ú-p´yiq-k´éh-deh*

My child is missing. ကျွန်တော်/ကျွန်မရဲ့ ကလေးပျောက်နေတယ်။ *cănaw* **m**/*cămá* **f** *yéh-k´ălé-pyauq-ne-deh*

I need... ကျွန်တော်/ကျွန်မမှာ...လိုအပ်နေတယ်။ *cănaw* **m**/*cămá* **f** *hma...lo-aq-ne-deh*

  an interpreter စကားပြန်တစ်ယောက် *zăgăbyan-tăyaq*

  to make a phone call. ဖုန်းတစ်ခါ ခေါ်ဖို့ *pòun-tăk´a-k´aw-bò*

I'm innocent. ကျွန်တော်/ကျွန်မမှာ အပြစ်မရှိပါဘူး *cănaw* **m**/*cămá* **f** *hma-ăpyiq-măshí-ba-bù*

YOU MAY HEAR...

ဒီပုံစံကို ဖြည့်ပါ။ *di-poun-zan-go-p´yé* — Fill out this form.

သင့်ရဲ့မှတ်ပုံတင်ကို ပြပါ။ *thin´yéh-hmaq-poun-tin-go-pyá-ba* — Your ID, please.

ဘယ်အချိန်/ဘယ်နေရာမှာ ဖြစ်ခဲ့တာလဲ။ *beh-ăćein/beh-ne-ya-hma-p´yiq-k´éh-da-lèh?* — When/Where did it happen?

သူဘယ်လိုပုံစံရှိသလဲ။ *thu-beh-bo-poun-zan-shi-deălèh?* — What does he/she look like?

Superiors are addressed as **"Ah Ko Gyi"**, **"Ko Gyi"** or **"saya"** (teacher). **"Saya"** is also used for medical doctors. Monks are addressed as **"Sayada"** (venerable), **Ashin** (reverence) or **Kodaw** (Your Reverence) — the latter most often used by a layman addressing a monk. Military officers are called **Bo**.

Crime & Lost Property

I need to report…	ကျွန်တော်/ကျွန်မ…ကို သတင်းပို့ဖို့လိုအပ်နေတယ်။ *cănaw* ***m****/cămá* ***f****…go-dhădin-pó-bó-lo-aq-ne-deh*
a mugging	လုယက်မှုတစ်ခု *lú-yeq-hmú-tăk´ú*
a rape	မုဒိန်းမှုတစ်ခု *mădeìn-hmú-tăk´ú*
a theft	ခိုးဝှက်မှုတစ်ခု *k´ó-hweq-hmú-tăk´ú*
I was mugged.	ကျွန်တော်/ကျွန်မ လုယက်ခံခဲ့ရတယ်။ *cănaw* ***m****/cămá* ***f*** *lú-yeq-hmú-k´an-géh-yá-deh.*
I was robbed.	ကျွန်တော်/ကျွန်မ ဓါးပြတိုက်ခံခဲ့ရတယ်။ *cănaw* ***m****/cămá* ***f*** *dămyá-taiq-k´an-géh-yá-deh.*
I lost…	ကျွန်တော့်/ကျွန်မ ရဲ့ …ပျောက်ဆုံးခဲ့တယ်။ *cănaw* ***m****/cămá* ***f*** *…pyauq-sòun-géh-deh*
…was stolen.	…အခိုးခံခဲ့ရတယ်။ *…ăk´ò-k´an-géh-yé-deh*
My backpack	ကျွန်တော/ကျွန်မရဲ့ ကျောပိုးအိတ် *cănaw* ***m****/cămá* ***f*** *yéh-càw-pò-eiq*
My bicycle	ကျွန်တော့်/ကျွန်မရဲ့ စက်ဘီး *cănaw* ***m****/cămá* ***f*** *yéhseq-beìn*
My camera	ကျွန်တော့်/ကျွန်မရဲ့ ကင်မရာ *cănaw* ***m****/cămá* ***f*** *yéh-kin-măra*
My computer	ကျွန်တော့်/ကျွန်မရဲ့ ကွန်ပျူတာ *cănaw* ***m****/cămá* ***f*** *yéh-kun-pyu-ta*

My credit card	ကျွန်တော့်/ကျွန်မရဲ့ အကြွေးဝယ်ခွင့်ကတ် *cănaw* ***m***/*cămá* ***f*** *yéh-ăcwè-weh-gwín-kaq*
My jewelry	ကျွန်တော့်/ကျွန်မရဲ့ လက်ဝတ်ရတနာ *cănaw* ***m***/*cămá* ***f*** *yéh-leq-wuq-yădăna*
My money	ကျွန်တော့်/ကျွန်မရဲ့ ပိုက်ဆံ *cănaw* ***m***/*cămá* ***f*** *yéh-paiq-śan*
My passport	ကျွန်တော့်/ကျွန်မရဲ့ နိုင်ငံကူးလက်မှတ် *cănaw* ***m***/*cămá* ***f*** *yéh-nain-ngn-kù-leq-hmaq*
My purse [handbag]	ကျွန်တော့်/ကျွန်မရဲ့ ပိုက်ဆံအိတ် (လက်ကိုင်အိတ်) *cănaw* ***m***/*cămá* ***f*** *yéh-paiq-śan-eiq (leq-kain-eiq)*
My traveler's cheques	ကျွန်တော့်/ကျွန်မရဲ့ ခရီးသွားချက်လက်မှတ်များ *cănaw* ***m***/*cămá* ***f*** *yéh-k´ăyì-thwà-ćeq-leq-hmq-myà*
My wallet	ကျွန်တော့်/ကျွန်မရဲ့ အိတ်ဆောင်ပိုက်ဆံအိတ် *cănaw* ***m***/*cămá* ***f*** *yéh-eiq-śan-paiq-śan-eiq*
I need a police report.	ကျွန်တော်/ကျွန်မရဲ့ သတင်းမှတ်ချက်တစ်ခု လိုအပ်တယ်။ *cănaw* ***m***/*cămá* ***f*** *yéh-dhădìn-hmaq-ćeq-tăk´ú-lo-aq-teh*
Where is the British/ American/Irish embassy?	ဗြိတိန်/အမေရိကန်/အိုင်ယာလန် သံရုံး ဘယ်နေရာမှာလဲ။ *byí-tein/ămeríkan/ain-ya-lan-than yoùn-beh-ne-ya-hma-lèh?*

Health

ESSENTIAL

I'm sick. ကျွန်တော်/ကျွန်မ နေမကောင်းဘူး။
cănaw **m**/*cămá* **f** *ne-mă-kaùn-bù*

I need an English-speaking doctor. ကျွန်တော်/ကျွန်မ အင်္ဂလိပ်စကားပြောတဲ့ဆရာဝန် တစ်ယောက်လိုအပ်တယ်။ *cănaw* **m**/*cămá* **f** *in-găleiq-zăgà-pyàw-déh-śăya-wun-tăyauq-lo-aq-teh.*

It hurts here. ဒီနေရာက နာတယ်။ *di-ne-ya-gá-na-deh*

Finding a Doctor

Can you recommend a doctor/dentist? ခင်ဗျား/ရှင် ဆရာဝန်/သွားဆရာဝန် တစ်ယောက်ဆီ ညွှန်ပေးနိုင်မလား။ *kămyà* **m**/*shin* **f** *śăya-wun/thaw-śăya-wun-tăyauq-śi-hnyun-pè-nain-mălà?*

Can the doctor come here? ဆရာဝန် ဒီနေရာကို လာနိုင်မလား။
śăya-wun-di-ne-ya-go-la-nain-mălà?

I need an English-speaking doctor. ကျွန်တော်/ကျွန်မ အင်္ဂလိပ်စကားပြောတဲ့ဆရာဝန် တစ်ယောက် လိုအပ်တယ်။ *cănaw* **m**/*cămá* **f** *in-găleiq-zăgà-pyàw-déh-śăya-wun-tăyauq-lo-aq-teh.*

What are the office hours? ရုံးချိန်တွေက ဘယ်အချိန်တွေလဲ။
yoùn-jein-dwe-gá-beh-ăćein-dew-lèh?

I'd like an appointment for… ကျွန်တော်/ကျွန်မ ချိန်းဆိုမှုတစ်ခု…အတွက် ယူလိုတယ်။
cănaw **m**/*cămá* **f** *ćeìn-śo-hmú-tăk´ú…ătewq-yu-lo-deh*

today ဒီနေ့ *di-né*

tomorrow မနက်ဖြန် *măneqp´yan*

as soon as possible တတ်နိုင်သလောက် မြန်မြန်
taq-nain-dhălauq-myan-myan

It's urgent. ဒီဟာက အရမ်းအရေးကြီးတယ်။
di-ha-gá-ăyàn-ayè-ci-deh

Symptoms

I'm bleeding. ကျွန်တော်/ကျွန်မ သွေးထွက်နေတယ်။ *cănaw* ***m****/cămá* ***f****- thwè-t´weq-ne-deh*

I'm constipated. ကျွန်တော်/ကျွန်မ ဝမ်းချုပ်နေတယ်။ *cănaw* ***m****/cămá* ***f*** *wàn-ćouq-ne-deh*

I'm dizzy. ကျွန်တော်/ကျွန်မ ခေါင်းမူးနေတယ်။ *cănaw* ***m****/cămá* ***f*** *gaùn-mù-ne-deh*

I'm nauseous. ကျွန်တော်/ကျွန်မ အန်ချင်နေတယ်။ *cănaw* ***m****/cămá* ***f****-an-jin-ne-deh*

I'm vomiting. ကျွန်တော်/ကျွန်မ အန်နေတယ်။ *cănaw* ***m****/cămá* ***f*** *an-ne-deh*

It hurts here. ဒီနေရာက နာတယ်။ *di-ne-ya-gá-na-deh*

I have… ကျွန်တော်/ကျွန်မ မှာ…ရှိတယ်။ *cănaw* ***m****/cămá* ***f****...hma-shí-deh*

- an allergic reaction ဓာတ်မတဲ့မှုတစ်ခု *daq-mătéh-hmú-tăk´ú*
- chest pain ရင်ဘတ်အောင့်မှု *yin-baq-aún-hmú*
- cramps ဗိုက်။ကြွက်းသား နာမှု *baiq-cweq-thà-na-hmú*
- diarrhea ဝမ်းလျှောမှု *wàn-shàw-hmú*
- an earache နားကိုက်မှု *nà-kaiq-hmú*
- a fever အဖျား *ăp´yà*
- pain နာကျင်မှု *nà-cin-hmú*
- a rash အရေပြားနီရဲမှု *ăye-byà-ni-yèh-hmú*
- a sprain အဆစ်လွဲပြီးနာကျင်မှု *ăśiq-lwèh-byì-na-cin-hmú*
- some swelling ရောင်ရမ်းမှု နည်းနည်း *yaun-yăn-hmú-néh-néh*
- a sore throat လည်ချောင်းနာကျင်မှု *leh-jaùn-na-cin-hmú*
- a stomach ache ဗိုက်နာမှု *baiq-na-hmú*

I've been sick for…days. ကျွန်တော်/ကျွန်မ နေမကောင်းဖြစ်နေတာ…ရက်ရှိသွားပြီ။ *cănaw* ***m****/cămá* ***f*** *ne-măkaùn-p´yq-ne-da... yeq-shí-thwà-by*

For Numbers, see page 168.

Conditions

I'm…	ကျွန်တော်/ကျွန်မ *cănaw* ***m****/cămá* ***f***
anemic	သွေးအားနည်းနေတယ်။ *thwè-à-nèh-ne-deh*
asthmatic	ရင်ကျပ်နေတယ်။ *yin-caq-ne-deh*
diabetic	ဆီးချိုရောဂါရှိတယ်။ *sì-jo-yăw-ga-shí-deh*
I'm epileptic.	ကျွန်တော်/ကျွန်မမှာ အတက်/ဝက်ရူးပြန် ရောဂါရှိတယ်။ *cănaw* ***m****/cămá* ***f*** *hma-ăteq-weq-yù-pyan-yàw-ga-shí-deh*
I'm allergic to	ကျွန်တော်/ကျွန်မ…နဲ့ ဓာတ်မတဲ့မှုရှိတယ်။ *cănaw* ***m****/cămá* ***f****…néh- daq-măteh-hmú-shí-deh*
antibiotics/	ပဋိဇီဝဆေးများ။ *pătí-zi-wá-śè-myà*
penicillin.	ပင်နယ်စလင် *pin-neh-sălin*
I have…	ကျွန်တော်/ကျွန်မမှာ…ရှိတယ် *cănaw* ***m****/cămá* ***f****-hmar…shí-deh*
arthritis	အဆစ်ရောင်ရမ်းနာကျင်မှု *ăśiq-yaun-yàn-na-cin-hmú*
a heart condition	နှလုံးရောဂါအခြေအနေတစ်ခု *hnăloùn-yàw-ga-ăće-ăne-tăk´ú*
high/low blood pressure	သွေးဖိအား မြင့်/နိမ့် မှု *thwè-p´í-à-myín-hmú*
I'm on…	ကျွန်တော်/ကျွန်မ…ကို စားနေတယ်။ *cănaw* ***m****/cămá* ***f****…go-sà-ne-deh*

For Meals & Cooking, see page 67.

Treatment

Do I need a prescription/medicine?	ကျွန်တော်/ကျွန်မ ဆေးအညွှန်း/ဆေးတစ်မျိုး လိုမလား။ *cănaw* ***m****/cămá* ***f*** *śè-ăhnyùn-/śè-tămyò-lo-mălà?*
Can you prescribe a generic drug [unbranded medication]?	ခင်ဗျား/ရှင် သာမန်ဆေးအမည်ကွဲတစ်မျိုး ညွှန်းပေးနိုင်မလား။ *kămyà* ***m****/shin* ***f*** *tha-man-śè-ăhnyùn/śè-tămyò hnyùn-pè-nain-mălà?*

Can you prescribe a herbal treatment?	ခင်ဗျား/ရှင် ရိုးရာသစ်ဖုသစ်ဥတွေနဲ့ကုသမှုတစ်ခု ညွှန်းပေးနိုင်မလား။ *kămyà* **m**/*shin* **m** *yò-ya-thiq-p´ú-dwe-néh-kú-thá-tăk´ú-hnyùn-pè-nain-mălà?*
Where can I get it?	ဒါကို ကျွန်တော်/ကျွန်မ ဘယ်နေရာမှာ ရနိုင်မလဲ။ *da-go-cănaw* **m**/*cămá* **f** *beh-ne-ya-hma-yá-nain-mălèh?*

For What to Take, see page 161.

YOU MAY HEAR…

ဘာ မှား/ဖြစ် လို့လဲ။ *ba-hmà/p´yiq-ló-lèh?*	What's wrong?
ဘယ်နေရာမှာ နာတာလဲ။ *beh-ne-ya-hma-na-da-lèh?*	Where does it hurt?
ဒီနေရာမှာ နာသလား။ *di-ne-ya-hma-na-dhălà?*	Does it hurt here?
ခင်ဗျား/ရှင် ဆေးသောက်နေသလား။ *kămyà* **m**/*shin* **f** *śe-thauq-ne-dhălà?*	Are you on medication?
ခင်ဗျား/ရှင် တစ်ခုခုကို ဓာတ်မတည့်တာ ရှိသလား။ *kămyà* **m**/*shin* **f** *tăk´ú-gú-go-daq-măte´h-da-shí-dhălà?*	Are you allergic to anything?
ပါးစပ် ဟပါ။ *băzaq-há-ba*	Open your mouth.
အသက်ပြင်းပြင်းရှူပါ။ *Ătheq-pyìn-pyìn-shu-ba*	Breathe deeply.
ကျေးဇူးပြုပြီး ချောင်းဆိုးပါ။ *cè-zù-pyú-byì-ćaùn-śò-ba*	Cough, please.
ဆေးရုံကိုသွားပါ။ *Śe-youn-go-thwà-ba*	Go to the hospital.

Hospital

Notify my family, please.	ကျေးဇူးပြုပြီး ကျွန်တော်/ကျွန်မ မိသားစုကို အသိပေးပေးပါ။ *cè-zù-pyú-byì-cănaw* **m**/*cămá* **f** *mí-thà-zú-ăthí-pè-bè-ba.*
I'm in pain.	ကျွန်တော်/ကျွန်မ နာနေတယ်။ *cănaw* **m**/*cămá* **f** *na-ne-deh*

I need a doctor/nurse.	ကျွန်တော်/ကျွန်မ ဆရာဝန်။ သူနာပြုတစ်ယောက်လိုအပ်တယ်။ *cănaw* **m**/*cămá* **f** *śăya-wun/thu-na-pyú-tăyauq-lo-aq-teh*
When are visiting hours?	လူနာတွေ့ခွင့်ရတာ ဘယ်အချိန်တွေလဲ။ *lu-na-twé-gwín-yá-da-beh-ăćein-dwe-lèh?*
I'm visiting	ကျွန်တော်/ကျွန်မ...ကိုလာတွေ့တာပါ။ *cănaw* **m**/*cămá* **m**...*go-la-twé-da-ba*

Dentist

I have...	ကျွန်တော်/ကျွန်မ မှာ... ရှိနေတယ်။ *cănaw* **m**/*cămá* **f** *hma...shí-ne-deh*
a broken tooth	ကျိုးနေတဲ့သွားတစ်ချောင်း *cò-ne-déh-thwà-tăćaùn*
a lost filling	သွားဖာထားတာ ပြုတ်သွားမှု *thwa-p´a-t´à-da-pyouq-thwà-hmú*
a toothache	သွားကိုက်မှု *thwà-kaiq-hmú*
Can you fix this denture?	ခင်ဗျား/ရှင် ဒီသွားတုကို ပြင်ပေးနိုင်မလား။ *kămyà* **m**/*shin* **f** *di-thwà-dú-go-pyin-pè-nain-mălà?*

Gynecologist

I have cramps/ a vaginal infection.	ကျွန်မမှာ ကိုက်ခဲမှုများ/မိန်းမကိုယ်မှာ အနာဝင်မှု ရှိနေတယ်။ *cămá-hma-kaiq-k´èh-hmú-myà/ meìn-măgo-hma-ăna-win-hmú-shí-ne-deh.*
I missed my period.	ကျွန်မ ရာသီမလာဘူး။ *cămá-ya-dhi-măla-bù*
I'm on the Pill.	ကျွန်မ ကိုယ်ဝန်တားဆေးသောက်နေတယ်။ *cămá-ko-wun-tà-zè-thauq-ne-deh*
I'm (...months) pregnant.	ကျွန်မ ကိုယ်ဝန် (... လ) ရှိနေတယ်။ *cămá-ko-wun (...lá) shí-ne-deh*
I'm not pregnant.	ကျွန်မမှာ ကိုယ်ဝန်မရှိဘူး။ *cămá-hma-ko-wun-măshí-bù*
My last period was...	ကျွန်မ နောက်ဆုံးရာသီလာတဲ့ရက်က ... ဖြစ်တယ်။ *cămá-nauq-śoùn-ya-dhi-la-déh-yeq-ká...p´yiq-teh*

For Numbers, see page 168.

Optician

I lost… ကျွန်တော်/ကျွန်မ … ပျောက်သွားတယ်။ *cănaw* **m**/*cămá* **f**…*pyauq-thwà-deh*

a contact lens မျက်ကပ်မှန်များ *meq-kaq-hman-myà*

my glasses ကျွန်တော်/ကျွန်မရဲ့မျက်မှန် *cănaw* **m**/*cămá* **f** *yéh-myeq-hman*

a lens မှန်များ *hman-myà*

Payment & Insurance

How much? ဘယ်လောက်ကျလဲ။ *beh-lauq-cá-lèh?*

Can I pay by credit card? ကျွန်တော်/ကျွန်မ အကြွေးဝယ်ကတ်နဲ့ငွေချေလို့ရမလား။ *cănaw* **m**/*cămá* **f** *ăcwè-weh-kaq-néh-ngwe-će-ló-yá-mălà?*

I have insurance. ကျွန်တော့်/ကျွန်မမှာ အာမခံရှိတယ်။ *cănaw* **m**/*cămá* **f** *hma-a-má-gan-shí-deh*

I need a receipt for my insurance. ကျွန်တော့်/ကျွန်မရဲ့ အာမခံအတွက်ငွေလက်ခံဖြတ်ပိုင်းလိုအပ်တယ်။ *cănaw* **m**/*cămá* **f** *yéh-a-má-gan-ătweq-mgwe-leq-k´an-p´yaq-paìn-lo-aq-teh*

Pharmacy

ESSENTIAL

Where's the pharmacy?	ဆေးဆိုင် ဘယ်နေရာရှိလဲ။ *Śè-zain-beh-ne-ya-shí-lèh?*
What time does it open/close?	အဲဒီဆိုင်က ဘယ်အချိန် ဖွင့်/ပိတ် သလဲ။ *Èh-di-sain-gá-be-ăćein-p´wín/peiq-thălèh?*
What would you recommend for…?	ဘာလုပ်ဖို့အတွက် သင့်တိုက်တွန်းမလဲ။ *ba-louq-p´ó-ătweq-thin-taiq-tùn-mălèh?*
How much do I take?	ကျွန်တော်/ကျွန်မ ဘယ်လောက် သောက်ရမလဲ။ *cănaw* **m**/*cămá* **f** *beh-louq-thauq-yá-măleh?*
I'm allergic to…	ကျွန်တော်/ကျွန်မ … နဲ့ဓာတ်မတဲ့ဘူး။ *cănaw* **m**/*cămá* **f**…*néh-daq-mătéh-bù?*

Yangon has several pharmacies, all with 24-hour counters. Outside Yangon, pharmacies are few and far between.

What to Take

How much do I take?	ကျွန်တော်/ကျွန်မ ဘယ်လောက် သောက်ရမလဲ။ *cănaw* **m**/*cămá* **f** *beh-lauq-thaug-yá-mălèh?*
How often?	ဘယ်နှစ်ကြိမ်သောက်ရမလဲ။ *beh-hnăcein-thauq-yá-mălèh?*
Is it safe for children?	အဲ့ါက ကလေးတွေအတွက် ဘေးကင်းရဲ့လား။ *Èh-di-sain-gá-beh-ăcein-p´wín/peiq-thălèh?*
I'm taking…	ကျွန်တော်/ကျွန်မ … ကို သောက်နေတယ်။ *cănaw* **m**/*cămá* **f**…*go-thauq-ne-deh*
Are there side effects?	ဘေးထွက်ဆိုးကျိုးတွေ ရှိသလား။ *bè-t´weq-śò-jò-dwe-shí-dhălà?*

I need something for...	...အတွက် ကျွန်တော်/မ ဆေးတစ်မျိုးမျိုး လိုအပ်တယ်။ ...ătewq-cănaw **m**/cămá **f** śè-tămyò-myò-lo-aq-teh
a cold	အအေးမိခြင်း ăè-mí-jìn
a cough	ချောင်းဆိုးခြင်း ćaùn-śò-jìn
diarrhea	ဝမ်းလျှောခြင်း wàn-shăw-jìn
a headache	ခေါင်းကိုက်ခြင်း gaùn-kaiq-ĉìn
insect bites	အင်းဆက်အကိုက်ခံရခြင်း ìn-s´eq-ăkaiq-k´an-yá-jìn
mosquito bites	ခြင်ကိုက်ခံရခြင်း ćin-kaiq-k´an-yá-jìn
motion sickness	ခရီးသွားရင်းမူးဝေအော့အန်ခြင်း kyăì-thwà-yìn-mù-we-áw-an--jìn
a sore throat	လည်ချောင်းနာခြင်း leh-jaùn-na-jìn
sunburn	နေလောင်ခြင်း ne-laun-jìn
a toothache	သွားကိုက်ခြင်း thwà-jìn
an upset stomach	ဗိုက်ပျက်မှု baiq-pyeq-hmú

YOU MAY SEE...

တစ်ရက်ကို တစ်ကြိမ်/သုံးကြိမ်	once/three times a day
ဆေးလုံး	tablet
ဆေးစက်	drop
လက်ဖက်ရည်ဇွန်း	teaspoon
အစား	...meals
စားပြီး	after
မစားမီ	before
နဲ့အတူ	with
အစာအိမ်ထဲမှာ ဘာအစာမှမရှိဘဲ	on an empty stomach
တစ်လုံးလုံးကို မျိုချလိုက်ပါ။	swallow whole
မူးဝေမှု ဖြစ်ကောင်း ဖြစ်စေနိုင်တယ်။	may cause drowsiness
မမျိုချပါနဲ့။	do not ingest

Basic Supplies

I'd like... ကျွန်တော်/ကျွန်မ... လိုချင်ပါတယ်
cănaw **m**/*cămá* **f**...*lo-jin-ba-deh*

acetaminophen [paracetamol] ပါရာစီတမော (အဆီတာမီနိုဖန်) *pa-ya-si-tămàw (ăśi-ta-mi-no-p´an)*

antiseptic cream ပိုးသတ်ဆေးကရင်မ် *pò-thaq-śè-k´ărin*

aspirin အက်စ်ပရင် *eq-săpărin*

band-Aid [plasters] ပလာစတာ (ဘန်းဒိတ်) *pălasăta (bàn-deiq)*

bandages ပတ်တီးများ *paq-tì-myà*

a comb ဘီးတစ်ချောင်း *bì-tăćaùn*

condoms ကွန်ဒုံးများ *kun-doùn-mya*

contact lens solution မျက်ကပ်မှန်ဆေးရည် *myeq-kaq-hma-śè-ye*

deodorant ချွေးနံ့ပျောက်ဆေး *ćwè-nán-pyauq-sè-ye*

a hairbrush ခေါင်းဖီးဘရပ်ရှ်တစ်ခု *gaùn-p´ì-băraq-tăkú*

hairspray ဆံပင်ဖျန်းဆေး *zăbin-p´yàn-śè*

ibuprofen အိုင်ဗျူပရိုဖန် (အကိုက်အခဲပျောက်ဆေး)
ain-byu-păro-p´an (ăkaiq-ăk´eh-pyauq-śè)

insect repellent အင်းဆက်ပြေးတဲ့ဆေး *ìn-śeq-pyè-déh-śè*

lotion လိမ်းဆေး *leìn-zè*

moisturizing cream အစိုဓာတ်ထိမ်း ကရင်မ် *ăso-daq-teìn-kărin*

a nail file လက်သည်းတိုက်တဲ့ တံစဉ်း *leq-thèh-taiq-téh-dăzìn*

a needle and thread အပ်တစ်ချောင်းနဲ့ အပ်ချည် *aq-tăćaùn-néh-aq-ći*

a (disposable) razor (တစ်ခါသုံး) မုတ်ဆိတ်ရိတ်တံတစ်ချောင်း
(tăk´a-thoùn) mouq-śeiq-yeiq-tan-tăćaùn

razor blades မုတ်ဆိတ်ရိတ် ဓါးများ *mouq-śeiq-yeiq-dà-myà*

sanitary napkins [pads] အမျိုးသမီး လစဉ်သုံးပဝါများ (ပက်ဒ်များ)
ămyò-dhămì-lá-zin-thoùn-păwa-myà (peq-myà)

scissors ကပ်ကြေး *kaq-ćè*

shampoo/conditioner ခေါင်းလျှော်ရည်/ဆံပင်ပျော့ဆေး
gaùn-shaw-ye/ zăbin-pyáw-zè

soap ဆပ်ပြာ *śaq-pya*

sunscreen	နေလောင်ကာကရင်မ် *ne-laun-ka-kárin*
tampons	တမ်ပွန်များ (အမျိုးသမီးသုံးပစ္စည်း) *tan-pun-myà (ămyò-dhàmì-thoùn-pyiq-sí)*
tissues	တစ်ရှူး *tiq-shù*
toilet paper	အိမ်သာသုံးစက္ကူ *ein-dha-thoùn-seq-ku*
toothpaste	သွားတိုက်ဆေး *thaw-daiq-śè*

For Baby Essentials, see page 146.

Thanaka is the yellowish-white paste that most women and girls daub on their faces and arms. It is made from the bark of trees and is worn to protect fragile complexions from the darkening and dehydrating effects of the sun. Its fragrance is similar to that of sandalwood. It is also believed to cure acne and act as an antiseptic.

The Basics

Grammar

Burmese is a tonal language but it is a relatively simple language to learn to speak as the different tones can easily be differentiated. Grammatical rules are few and are easy to learn.

Word Order

Sentence formation follows the subject + object + verb (as opposed to the English pattern of subject + object + verb).

e.g. My name is… *cănaw* **m**/*cămá* **f** *yèh-nan-meh-gá.....ba.*
The room is dirty. *ăk´àn-gá-nyiq-paq-teh*

There are subject and object markers but as with many languages, sometimes the subject and even the object may be left out if the situation permits.
If in doubt, there is no harm in spelling it out in full to avoid misunderstanding.

Verbs

Particles are also added to verbs to indicate tense, but you will pick these up as you become more familiar with the phrases used in the book. There is no inflection of the verb to agree with tense or numbers.

There are three main tense particles:

Present/past tense	Future	Completed action
teh/deh	*meh*	*pi/bi*

Articles

There is no article corresponding to 'the' or 'a/an' in Burmese.
For example:

A house by the riverside *myi nabei: ga. ein.*

This can be broken down as follows:

house *ein*
by the side of *na bei: ga*
river *myi*

To indicate a specific object, the demonstrative adjective di (this, these) or ho (that, those) is placed before the noun it qualifies, e.g.

That house *ho ein*
This river *di myi*

Nouns

There is no need for declension of nouns to agree with number or gender.

To indicate a plural, the appropriate suffix must be used: add *twe/dwe* after the noun, where the noun does not change, and the *twe* or *dwe* simply indicates its plurality:

For example:

a friend	*thăngeh-jìn-tăyauq*
friends	*thăngeh-jìn-dwe*
a colleague	*louq-p´aw-kain-beq-tăyauq*
colleagues	*louq-p´aw-kain-beq- twe*

Similarly, a particle indicating gender may be affixed to a noun in order to define whether it is feminine or masculine, e.g. ခွေး for males, or ခွေးမ for females.

For example:

male dog ခွေး   female dog ခွေးမ

Personal Pronouns

The important thing to remember here is that the sex of the speaker determines which pronoun is used for 'I', 'we', 'you' (sing.) and 'you' (pl). For example, a man will use **cănaw** and a woman will use **cămà**. You masculine is **k'ămyà**. You feminine is **shin**.

For example:

My name is...	*cănaw* **m**/ *cămá* **f** *yéh-nan-meh-gá.....ba*
What's your name?	*k´ămyà* **m**/*shin* **f** *yèh-nan-meh-beh-lo-k´aw-dhălèh?*

	male speaker		female speaker	
I	*cănaw*	ကျွန်တော်	*cămá*	ကျွန်မ
you (sg)	*k'ămyà*	ခင်ဗျား	*shin*	ရှင်
he/she/it	*thu*	သူ	*thu*	သူ
we	*cănaw-dó*	ကျွန်တော်တို့	*cămá-dó*	ကျွန်မတို့
you (pl)	*k'ămyà-dó*	ခင်ဗျားတို့	*shin-dó*	ရှင်တို့
they	*thu-dó*	သူတို့	*thu-dó*	သူတို့

Adjectives

Adjectives come after the noun and often act as the verb, i.e. they replace the verb as the meaning is explicit without the use of a verb:

For example:

red	*ăni-yaun*
a red sweater	*ăni-yaun-śweh-ta*
the car is red	*kà-ga-ăni-yaun (-p'yiq-teh)*

where *p'yiq-teh* is the verb "is" in this instance and can be left out.

Imperatives

You will notice the frequent use of the particle *pa/ba*, added to the end of sentences. This particle makes the sentence more polite (although it is not necessary to use it all the time).

For example:

Go!	*k'ămyà* **m** *thwà-ba!*	Polite version male speaker
	shin **f** *thwà-ba!*	Polite version female speaker
Go!	*thwà!*	Direct version

Negation

To form a negative, simply put *mă-* before the verb, and *p'ù/bù* at the end of the sentence, replacing the tense particle *teh/deh*.

I didn't order this.	*da-go-cănaw* **m**/*cămá* **f** *măhma-bù*
I ordered…	*cănaw* **m**/*cămá* **f** *hma-da-ga…*

Numbers

ESSENTIAL

0 zero သုံည *thoun-nyá*
1 one တစ် *tiq*
2 two နှစ် *hniq*
3 three သုံး *thoùn*
4 four လေး *lè*
5 five ငါး *ngà*
6 six ခြောက် *ćauq*
7 seven ခုနှစ် *k´un-hniq*
8 eight ရှစ် *shiq*
9 nine ကိုး *kò*
10 ten တစ်ဆယ် *tăs'eh*
11 eleven ဆယ့်တစ် *s'éh tiq*
12 twelve ဆယ့်နှစ် *s'éh-hniq*
13 thirteen ဆယ့်သုံး *s'éh-thoùn*
14 fourteen ဆယ့်လေး *s'éh-lè*
15 fifteen ဆယ့်ငါး *s'éh-ngà*
16 sixteen ဆယ့်ခြောက *s'éh-ćauq*
17 seventeen ဆယ့်ခုနစ *s'éh-k´un-hniq*
18 eighteen ဆယ့်ရှစ် *s'éh-shiq*
19 nineteen ဆယ့်ကိုး *s'éh-kò*
20 twenty နှစ်ဆယ် *hnăs'eh*
21 twenty-one နှစ်ဆယ့်တစ် *hnăs'eh-tiq*
22 twenty-two နှစ်ဆယ့်နှစ် *hnăs'eh-hniq*
30 thirty သုံးဆယ် *thoùn-zeh*
31 thirty-one သုံးဆယ့်တစ် *Thoùn-zéh-tiq*
40 forty လေးဆယ် *lè-zeh*
50 fifty ငါးဆယ် *ngà-zeh*

60	sixty ခြောက်ဆယ် *ćauq-śeh*
70	seventy ခုနစ်ဆယ် *k´un-nă śeh*
80	eighty ရှစ်ဆယ် *shiq-śeh*
90	ninety ကိုးဆယ် *kò-śeh*
101	one hundred and one တစ်ရာ့တစ် *tăyá-tiq*
200	two hundred နှစ်ရာ *hnăyá*
500	five hundred ငါးရာ *ngăyá*
1,000	one thousand တစ်ထောင် *tăt´aun*
10,000	ten thousand တစ်သောင်း *tăthaùn*
1,000,000	a million တစ်သန်း *tăthàn*

Ordinal Numbers

first	ပထမ *păt´ămá*
second	ဒုတိယ *dútíyá*
third	တတိယ *tătíyá*
fourth	စတုတ္ထ *sădouqt´á*
fifth	ပဉ္စမ *pyinsămá*
once	တစ်ကြိမ် *dăjein*
twice	နှစ်ကြိမ် *hnăjein*
three times	သုံးကြိမ် *thoùn-jein*

Time

ESSENTIAL

What time is it?	ဘယ်အချိန်ရှိပြီလဲ။ *beh-ăćein-shí-bì-lèh*
It's midday.	အခုနေ့လည် *ăk´u-né-leh*
At midnight.	ညသန်းခေါင်မှာ *nyá-dhăgaun-hma*
From one o'clock two o'clock.	တစ်နာရီ မှ နှစ်နာရီ *tănayi-hmá-hnănayi*
Five past three.	သုံးနာရီ ထိုးပြီးလို့ ငါးမိနစ် *thoùn-na-yi-t´ò-byì-ló-ngà-mí-niq*
A quarter to ten.	လေးနာရီထိုးဖို့ဆယ့်ငါးမိနစ် *lè-na-yi-t´ò-bó-śéh-ngà-mí-niq*
5:30 a.m./p.m.	မနက်/ညနေ ငါးနာရီ *măneq/nyăne-ngà-na-yi*

Days

ESSENTIAL

Monday	တနင်္လာနေ့ *tănìnla-né*
Tuesday	အင်္ဂါနေ့ *inga-né*
Wednesday	ဗုဒ္ဓဟူးနေ့ *bouqdăhù-né*
Thursday	ကြာသပတေးနေ့ *cathăbădè-né*
Friday	သောကြာနေ့ *thauqea-né*
Saturday	စနေနေ့ *săne-né*
Sunday	တနင်္ဂနွေနေ့ *tănìngănew-né*

Dates

yesterday — မနေ့က *mănégá*
today — ဒီနေ့ *di-né*
tomorrow — မနက်ဖြန် *măneq-p´yan*
day — ရက် *yeq*
week — ရက်သတ္တပတ် *yeq-thaqdăbaq*
month — လ *lá*
year — နှစ် *hniq*
Happy New Year! — ပျော်စရာနှစ်သစ်ပါ။ *pyaw-zăya-hniq-thiq-pa*
Happy Birthday! — ပျော်စရာမွေးနေ့ပါ။ *pyaw-zăya-mwè-né-pa*

Months

January — ဇန်နဝါရီလ *zan-năwari-lá*
February — ဖေဖော်ဝါရီလ *p´ep´awwari-lá*
March — မတ်လ *maq-lá*
April — ဧပြီလ *ebyi-lá*
May — မေလ *me-lá*
June — ဇွန်လ *zun-lá*
July — ဇူလိုင်လ *zulain-lá*
August — ဩဂုတ်လ *ăwgouq-lá*
September — စက်တင်ဘာလ *seq-tin-ba-lá*
October — အောက်တိုဘာလ *oauq-to-ba-lá*
November — နိုဝင်ဘာလ *no-win-ba-lá*
December — ဒီဇင်ဘာလ *di-zin-ba-lá*

Seasons

spring — နွေဦးရာသီ *nwe-ú-ya-dhi*
summer — နွေရာသီ *nwe-ya-dhi*
autumn — ဆောင်းဦးရာသီ *śaùn-ú-ya-dhi*
winter — ဆောင်းရာသီ *śaùn-ya-dhi*

Holidays & Festivals

January

Independence Day – 4 January

Kachin Manao Festival (Kyitkyina, Kachin)

Ananda Pagoda Festival (Bagan, Mandalay)

Month-long religious celebration.

Naga New Year (Sagaing)

February

Maha Muni Pagoda Festival (Mandalay)

Salone Festival (Tanintharyi Region)

March

Shwedagon Pagoda Festival (Yangon)

Kakku Pagoda Festival (Inle)

April

Thingyan Water Festival (Country wide).

Thanaka Grinding Festival (Rakhine)

Shwemawdaw Pagoda Festival (Bago)

Myanmar New Year Festival (Countrywide)

May

Wesak (Buddha's Birthday)

Chinlone Festival, Mahanumi Pagoda, Mandalay

August

Taungbyon Festival, near Mandalay

September

Tooth Relic Ceremony, Pyay

October
Kyaikhtiyo Pagoda Festival (Mon State)
Phaung Daw U Festival (Inle Lake)

November
Matho Thingan (Yangon)

December
Kayin New Year Festival

Conversion Tables

When you know	Multiply by	To find
ounces	28.3	grams
pounds	0.45	kilograms
inches	2.54	centimeters
feet	0.3	meters
miles	1.61	kilometers
square inches	6.45	sq. centimeters
square feet	0.09	sq. meters
square miles	2.59	sq. kilometers
pints (U.S./Brit)	0.47/0.56	liters
gallons (U.S./Brit)	3.8/4.5	liters
Fahrenheit	-32, / 1.8	Celsius
Celsius	+32 , x 1.8	Fahrenheit

Kilometers to Miles Conversions	
1 km = 0.62 miles	**20 km** = 12.4 miles
5 km = 3.1 miles	**50 km** = 31 miles
10 km = 6.20 miles	**100 km** = 62 miles

Colonial Weights & Measures in Use

1 viss (peith-tha)	1.633g / 3.6 lbs
2 tical	16.33 g
1 cubit (tong)	0.457 metres / 18 ins
1 span (htwa)	0.23 metres / 9 ins
1 furlong	201 metres / 659ft
1 lakh	100,000 units
1 crore	100 lakh

Measurement

1 gram	**= 1000 milligrams**	= 0.035 oz.
1 kilogram (kg)	**= 1000 grams**	= 2.2 lb
1 liter (l)	**= 1000 milliliters**	= 1.06 U.S./0.88
1 centimeter	**= 10 millimeters**	= 0.4 inch (cm)
1 meter (m)	**= 100 centimeters**	= 39.37 inches/ 3.28 ft.
1 kilometer	**= 1000 meters**	= 0.62 mile (km)

Temperature

-40°C = -40°F	**-1°C** = 30°F	**20°C** = 68°F
-30°C =-22°F	**0°C** = 32°F	**25°C** = 77°F
-20°C = -4°F	**5°C** = 41°F	**30°C** = 86°F
-10°C = 14°F	**10°C** = 50°F	**35°C** = 95°F
-5°C = 23°F	**15°C** = 59°F	

Oven Temperature

100° C = 212° F	**177° C** = 350° F
121° C = 250° F	**204° C** = 400° F
149° C = 300° F	**260° C** = 500° F

Dictionary

English–Burmese 176
Burmese–English 201

English – Burmese

A

able တတ်တယ် *taq-teh*

about လောက/ နီးပါး *lauq / nì-bà*

above ကျော်ကျော်/ အထက် *caw-jaw / ăt'eq*

accept *v* **(approval)** လက်ခံ/ ခွင့်ပြု **leq-k´an/ k´wí-pyú**

access *n* လက်လှမ်းမှီ *leq-hlàn-hmi*

accessory အပိုပစ္စည်း *ăpo-pyiq-sì*

accident မတော်တဆထိခိုက်မှု *mătaw-tăs'-t'í-k´aiq-hmú*

account ငွေစာရင်း *ngwe-zăyìn*

ache ကိုက်ခဲမှု *kaiq-k'èh-hmú*

acupuncture အပ်စိုက်ကုသမှု *aq-saiq-kú-thá-hmú*

adapter အဒပ်ပတာ *ădaq-păta*

address *n* နေရပ် လိပ်စာ *ne-yaq-leiq-sa*

admission ဝင်ခွင့် *win-gwín*

admitted ဝင်ခွင့်ပြု/ ဝန်ခံ *win-gwín-pyú/wum-k´an*

after ပြီးတော့ *pyì-dáw*

afternoon နေ့ခင်း/ မွန်းလွဲ *né-gìn/mùn-lwèh*

aftershave lotion မုတ်ဆိတ်ရိတ်ဆေးရည် *mouq-s'eiq-yeiq-s'è-ye*

again နောက်တစ်ကြိမ်/ ထပ်မံ *nauq-dăjein / t'aq-man*

against ဆန့်ကျင်ပြီး *s'án-cin-pyì*

age အသက် *ătheq*

air conditioning လေအေးပေးစက် *le-è-pè-zeq*

airmail လေယာဉ်နဲ့ပို့တဲ့စာ/ အမြန်ချောပို့ *le-yin-néh-pó-déh-sa/ămyan-ćàw-pó*

airplane လေယာဉ်ပျံ *le-yin-byan*

airport လေဆိပ် *le-zeiq*

aisle seat အစွန်ခုံ *ăsun-k'oun*

alarm clock အိပ်ရာနှိုးစက် *eiq-ya-hnò-zeq*

alcohol အရက် *ăyeq*

alcoholic *adj* အရက်စွဲနေတာ *ăyeq-swèh-ne-da*

allergic ဓာတ်မတည့် *daq-mătéh*

allergic reaction ဓာတ်မတည့်လို့ ဖြစ်တဲ့ တုန့်ပြန်မှု *daq-mătéh-ló-p'yiq-téh-toún-pyan-hmú*

alphabet အက္ခရာစာလုံး *eq-k'ăya-săloùn*

also လည်းပဲ *lèh-bèh*

alter *v* ပြောင်းလဲ/ ခြားနားစေ *pyaùn-lèh/ćà-nà-ze*

altitude sickness အမြင့်တက်ရင် မူးတတ်တယ် *ămyín-teq-yin-mù-daq-teh*

amazing အံ့သြစရာကောင်းတယ် *án-àw-zăya-kaùn-deh*

amber ပယင်း *păyìn*

ambulance လူနာတင်ကား *lu-na-tin-kà*

American အမေရိကန်လူမျိုး *Ăme-yí-kan-lu-myò*

amethyst ခရမ်းရောင် *k´ăyàn-yaun*

amount *n* **(money)** ပမာဏ (ငွေကြေး) *păma-ná (ngwe-cè)*

analgesic အကိုက်အခဲပျောက်ဆေး *pkaiq-ăk'èh-pyaq-s'è*

and နဲ့ *néh*

anesthetic ထုံဆေး/ မေ့ဆေး *t'oun-zè / mé-zè*

animal တိရိစ္ဆာန် *tăyeiq-s'an*

ankle ခြေကျင်းဝတ် *Će-jìn-wuq*

answer အဖြေ/ အဖြေပေး *ăp'ye- / ăp'ye-pè*

antibiotic ပိုးသတ်ဆေး *pò-thaq-s'è*

antidepressant စိတ်ကျရောဂါပျောက်ဆေး *seiq-cá-yàw-ga-pyauq-s'è*

antique ရှေးဟောင်းပစ္စည်း *shè-haùn-ptiq-sì*

antiques store ရှေးဟောင်းပစ္စည်း အရောင်းဆိုင် *shè-haùn-ptiq-sì-ăyaùn-zain*

antiseptic cream ပိုးသတ်တဲ့ လိမ်းဆေး *pò-thaq-téh-leìn-zè*

any ဘယ်ဟာဖြစ်ဖြစ်/ ဘာဖြစ်ဖြစ် *beh-ha-p'yiq-p'yiq*

anyone ဘယ်သူဖြစ်ဖြစ် *beh-dhu-p'yiq-p'yuq*

anything ဘယ်ဟာမဆို *beh-ha-măs'o*

anywhere ဘယ်နေရာမဆို *beh-ne-ya-măs'o*

apartment နေအိမ်တိုက်ခန်း *ne-ein-taiq-k'àn*

aperitif အစာမစားခင် စားသောက်ကောင်းဖို့ သောက်တဲ့အရက် *ăsa-măsà-gin-sà-thauq-kaùn-bó-thauq-téh-ăyeq*

appendix နောက်ဆက်တွဲ/ အူအတက် *nauq-s'eq-twèh / u-ăteq*

appliance ကိရိယာ တန်ဆာပလာ *kăyì-ya-dăza-băla*

adj	adjective	**BE**	British English	**prep**	preposition
adv	adverb	**n**	noun	**v**	verb

appointment ချိန်းဆိုချက် *ćeìn-s'o-jeq*
arcade ဈောင်းတန်း *zaùn-dàn*
architect ဗိသုကာပညာရှင် *bí-thú-ka-pyin-nya-shin*
arm လက်မောင်း *leq-maùn*
aromatherapy ရနံ့ကုထုံး *yănán-kú-t'oún*
around (approximately; around the corner) ပတ်လည် *paq*
arrival ဆိုက်ရောက်ရာ *s'aiq-yauq-ya*
arrive ဆိုက်ရောက်တယ် *s'aiq-yauq-teh*
art အနုပညာ *ănú-pyin-nya*
art gallery အနုပညာပြခန်း *ănú-pyin-nya-pyá-gàn*
aspirin အက်စ်ပရင် (အကိုက်အခဲပျောက်ဆေး) *Eq-s-păyin (ăkaiq-ăk'èh-pyauq-s'è*
assistance အကူအညီ *ăku-ănyi*
assorted အမျိုးစုံ *ămyò-zoun*
asthma အက်စ်မာ (ရင်ကျပ်ရောဂါ) *Eq-s-ma (yin-caq-yàw-ga)*
astringent ဖန်တာ/ ချုပ်စေတဲ့ *p'an-da / ćouq-se-déh*
at တွင်၊ မှာ၊ ၌ *twin/hma/hnaiq*
ATM ငွေထုတ်စက် *ngwe-t'ouq-seq*
attack *n* တိုက်ခိုက်တာ *taiq-k´aiq-ta*
attend တက်ရောက် *teq-yauq*
attractive ဆွဲဆောင်မှုရှိတယ် *s'wèh-s'aun-hmú-shí-deh*
audio guide နားကြပ်ဖြင့်နားထောင်ရတဲ့ အသံထွက်လမ်းညွှန် *năjaq-p'yín-nà-t'aun-yá-déh-ăthan-dweq-làn-hnyun*
Australia ဩစတြေးလျနိုင်ငံ *Àw-săte-lyá-nain-gan*
average ပျမ်းမျှ *pyán-hmyá*
away အဝေးသို့ / အဝေးမှာ *Ăwè-dhó / ăwè-hma*
awful ကြောက်စရာဘဲ *cauq-săya-bèh*

B

baby ကလေးငယ် *k´ălè-neh*
baby bottle ကလေးနို့ဗူး *k´ălè-nó-bù*
baby food ကလေးအစာ *k´ălè-ăsa*
baby wipes ကလေး အညစ်အကြေးသုတ်တဲ့ ဂွမ်းစတွေ *k´ălè-ănyiq-ăcè-thouq-téh-gùn-zá-dwe*
babysitter ကလေးထိန်း *k´ălè-deìn*
back နောက်ပြန်သွား/ အနောက်ဖက်/ ကျောကုန်း *nauq-pyan-thwà/ănauq-p'eq/càw-goùn*
backache ခါးနာတာ *k´à-na-da*
backpack ကျောပိုးအိတ် *càw-bò-eiq*
bad ဆိုးရွားတယ် *s'ò-ywà-deh*
bag (purse/ [handbag]); shopping အိတ် (ပိုက်ဆံအိတ် /ဟလက်ကိုင်အိတ်")/ (ဈေးဝယ်အိတ်) *eiq(paiq-s'an-eiq/leq-kain-eiq); (zè-weh-eiq)*
baggage [BE] ခရီးသွား အထုတ်အပို; *k'ăyì-thwà-ăt'ouq-ăpò*
baggage check ခရီးသွားအထုတ်အပိုး စစ်ဆေးတာ *k'ăyì-thwà-ăt'ouq-ăpò-siq-s'è-da*
baggage claim ခရီးသွားအထုတ်အပိုး ပြန်ထုတ်ခြင်း *k'ăyì-thwà-ăt'ouq-ăpò-pyan-t'ouq-ĉin*
bakery ပေါင်မုန့် / ကိတ်မုန့်ဖို *paun-moú/keiq-moún-p'o*
balance (finance) လက်ကျန် (ငွေကြေးဆိုင်ရာ အသုံးအနှုန်း) *leq-can (ngwe-cè-s'ain-ya-ăthoùn-ăhnoùn)*
balcony ဝရံတာ *wăyan-da*
ballet ballet ဘဲလေးအက *Bèh-lè-ăká*
bandage *n* ပတ်တီး *paq-tì*
bank (finance) ဘဏ် (ငွေကြေးဆိုင်ရာ အသုံးအနှုန်း) *ban (ngwe-cè-s'ain-ya-ăthoùn-ăhnoùn)*
bank note ဘဏ်ချလံ *ban-ćălan*
bar ဘား/ အရက်ဆိုင်/ အချောင်း/ တားဆီးတာ *bà/ăyeq-s'ain/ăćaùn/tà-s'ì-da*
barber ဆံပင်ညှပ်ဆိုင *zăbin-hnyaq-s'ain*
basket ဆွဲခြင်းတောင်း *s'wèh-ĵin-daùn*
basketball game ဘတ်စကက်ဘော ကစားပ *baq-săkeq-bàw-găzà-bwèh*
bath ရေချိုး *ye-ćò*
bathing suit ရေကူးဝတ်စုံ *ye-kù-wuq-soun*
bathrobe ရေချိုးပြီး ဝတ်တဲ့ဝတ်ရုံရှည် *ye-ćò-pyì-wuq-téh-wuq-youn-she*
bathroom ရေချိုးခန်း *ye-ćò-gàn*
battery ဘတ္တရီ *beq-t'ăyi*
battleground စစ်မြေပြင် *siq-mye-byin*
be ဖြစ်တာ/ ရှိတာ *p'yiq-ta / shí-da*
beach ball ကမ်းခြေဘောလုံးကစားနည်း *kàn-je-bàw-loùn-găzà-nì*
beard မုတ်ဆိတ်မွေး *mouq-s'eiq-mwè*
beautiful လှတယ် *hlá-deh*
beauty salon အလှပြင်ခန်း *ăhlá-pyin-gàn*
bed အိပ်ရာ *eiq-ya*
before (time) မတိုင်မီ (အချိန်) *mătain-mi (ăćein)*
begin အစ *ăsá*
behind အနောက်မှာ/ နောက်ကျတာ *ănauq-hma / nauq-cá-da*
beige အညိုဖျော့ရောင *ănyo-p'yáw-yaun*
bell ခေါင်းလောင်း *k´aùn-laùn*
below အောက်မှာ *auq-hma*
belt ခါးပတ် *găbaq*
berth သင်္ဘော/ လေယာဉ်ပျံပေါ်က အိပ်ခန်း *thin-bàw/le-yin-byan-baw-gá-eiq-k´àn*

better ပိုကောင်းတယ် *po-kaùn-deh*
between အကြား *ăcà*
bicycle စက်ဘီး *seq-beìn*
big ကြီးတာ *cì-da*
bike route စက်ဘီးလမ်းကြောင်း *seq-veìn-làn-jaùn*
bikini ဘီကီနီ (အမျိုးသမီးရေကူးဝတ်စုံ) *bi-ki-ni(ănyò-thămì-ye-kù-wuq-soun)*
bill (restaurant) ငွေတောင်းခံလွှာ (စားသောက်ဆိုင်)၊ ဘဏ်ချလံ *ngwe-taùn-k´àn-hlwa(sà-thauq-s'ain); ban-ćălan* ; **(bank note)**
binoculars အဝေးကြည့်မှန်ပြောင်း *ăwè-ćí-hman-byaùn*
bird ငှက် *hngeq*
birth ကလေးမွေး *k´ălè-mwè*
birthday မွေးနေ့ *mwè-nè*
black အနက်ရောင်/အမဲရောင် *ăneq-yaun / ămèh-yaun*
bladder ဆီးအိမ် *s'ì-ein*
blade ဓားသွား *dà-thwà*
blanket စောင် *saun*
bleach အရောင်ချွတ် *ăyaun-ćuq*
bleed သွေးထွက်တယ *thwè-t́weq-teh*
blind (window) နေကာ (ပြတင်းပေါက်) *ne-ga (bădìn-bauq)*
blister အရေကြည်ဖု *ăye-ci-bù*
blocked ပိတ်ဆို့တာ/ ဟန့်တားတာ *peiq-s'ó-da / hán-tá-da*
blood သွေး *thwè*
blood pressure သွေးပေါင် *thwè-baun*
blouse အမျိုးသမီးဝတ် အပေါ်အင်္ကျီ/ ဘလောက်စ်အင်္ကျီ *ămyò-thămì-wuq-ăpaw-ìn-ji / bălauq-ìn-ji*
blow dry လေနဲ့ခြောက်သွေ့အောင်လုပ်တာ *le-néh-ćauq-thwé-aun-louq-ta*
blue အပြာရောင် *ăpya-yaun*
boat လှေ *hle*
boat trip လှေခရီး *hle-k´ăyì*
body ခန္ဓာကိုယ် *k´an-da-ko*
bone အရိုး *ăyò*
book စာအုပ် *sa-ouq*
booklet (of tickets) စာအုပ်လေး (လက်မှတ်တွေပါတဲ့) *sa-ouq-lè (leq-hmaq-twe-pa-déh)*
bookstore စာအုပ်ဆိုင် *sa-ouq-s'ain*
boot ဘွတ်ဖိနပ် *buq-p'ănaq*
boring ပျင်းဖို့ကောင်းတယ် *pyìn-bó-kaùn-deh*
born မွေးတယ် *mwè-deh*
botanical garden ရုက္ခဗေဒဥယျာဉ် *youq-k´á-be-dá-ú-yin*
botany ရုက္ခဗေဒ ပညာရပ် *youq-k´á-be-dá-pyin-nya-yaq*
bother အနှောင့်အယှက်ပေးတာ/ ဖြစ်စေတာ *ăhnaún-ăsheq-pè-sa / p'yiq-se-da*
bottle ပုလင်း *pălìn*
bottle opener ပုလင်းဖွင့်တံ *pălìn-p'wín-dan*
bottom အောက်ခြေ *auq-će*
bowel ဝမ်းဗိုက်/ အူနဲ့ဆိုင်တဲ့ *wàn-baiq / u-néh-s'ain-déh*
bowl ဖလား။ခွက် *p'ălà*
box သေတ္တာ *thiq-ta*
boxing match လက်ဝှေ့ပွဲ *leq-hwé-bwèh*
boy ယောက်ျားလေး *yauq-cà-lè*
boyfriend ရည်းစား *yì-zà*
bra ဘရာစီယာ (အမျိုးသမီးအတွင်းခံအင်္ကျီ) *băya-si-ya (ămyò-thămì-ătwìn-gan-ìn-ji*
bracelet လက်ကောက် *leq-kauq*
brake *n* ဘရိတ်ခ် *băyeiq*
break (out of order) ပျက်စီး/ ဖျက်ဆီး/ ချိုး/ ကျိုးပဲ့ *pyeq-sì/p'yeq-s'ì/ćò/cò-péh*
breakdown (car) ပျက်သွားတာ (ကား) *pyeq-thwà-da (kà)*
breakfast မနက်စာ *măneq-sa*
breast ရင်သား *yin-dhà*
breathe အသက်ရှူ *ătheq-shu*
bridge တံတား *dădà*
bring ယူလာ/ ယူသွား *yu-la/yu-thwà*
bring down ယူသွားတာ *yu-thwà-da*
British (person) ဗြိတိသျှလူမျိုး *Byí-tí-shá-lu-myò*
broken ပျက်စီးနေတဲ့/ ကျိုးနေတဲ့/ ကွဲနေတဲ့ *pyeq-sì-ne-déh/cò-ne-déh/ kwéh-ne-déh*
brooch ရင်ထိုး *yin-dò*
broom တံမြက်စည်း *dăbyeq-sì*
brown အညိုရောင် *ănyo-yaun*
bruise သွေးခြည်ဥ *thwè-ji-ú*
brush *n* စုတ်တံ (ဘရပ်ရှ်)/ ဝက်မှင်ဘီး *souq-tan(băyaq) / weq-hmin-bì*
bucket ရေပုံး *ye-boùn*
bug ကြမ်းပိုး *Jăbò*
build တည်ဆောက် *ti-s'auq*
building အဆောက်အအုံ *ăs'auq-ăoun*
burn လောင်ကျွမ်း *laun-cwàn*
bus ဘတ်စ်ကား *baq-săkà*
bus station ဘတ်စ်ကားဂိတ် *baq-săkà-geiq*
bus stop ဘတ်စ်ကားမှတ်တိုင် *baq-săkà-hmaq-tain*
business card လုပ်ငန်းသုံးအမည်ကတ်/ လိပ်စာကတ် *louq-ngàn-dhoùn-ămyi-kaq/ leiq-sa-kaq*
business center (at hotel) လုပ်ငန်းသုံးစင်တာ

(ဘစ်စနက်စင်တာ) (ဟိုတယ်ရှိ) *louq-ngàn-dhoùn-sin-ta (biq-sǎneq-sin-ta) (ho-the-shí)*
business class အထူးတန်း *ǎtû-dàn*
business trip အလုပ်ကိစ္စနဲ့သွားတဲ့ခရီး *ǎlouq-keiq-sá-néh-thwà-déh-k´ǎyì*
busy အလုပ်များတယ် *ǎlouq-myà-deh*
but ဒါပေမယ့် *da-be-méh*
butane gas ဗျူတိန်းဓာတ်ငွေ့ *byu-teìn-daq-ngwé*
butcher သားသတ်သမား/ အသားရောင်းသူ *thà-thaq-thǎmà / ǎthà-yaùn-dhu*
button ကြယ်သီး *ceh-dhì*
buy ဝယ် *weh*

C

cabin (ship) (သင်္ဘော) ခေါင်းခန်း/ အိပ်ခန်း *(thin-bàw) gaùn-gàn / eiq-k´àn*
cafe ကော်ဖီဆိုင် *Kaw-p'i-zain*
calculator ဂဏန်းပေါင်းစက် *gǎnàn-paùn-seq*
calendar ပြက္ခဒိန် *pyeq-gǎdein*
call *n* **(phone);** *v*; **(summon)** ခေါ်ဆိုမှု (ဖုန်း)/ ခေါ်ဆို(ဆင့်ခေါ်တာ) *k´aw-s'o-hmú(p'oùn) / k´aw-s'o (s'ín-k´aw-da)*
calm ကြည်လင်သော/ တည်ငြိမ်သော *ci-lin-dhàw / ti-nyein-dhàw*
camera ကင်မရာ *kin-mǎya*
camera case ကင်မရာထည့်တဲ့ အိတ်/ ဗူး *kin-mǎya-t'éh-déh-eiq, bù*
camera shop ကင်မရာအရောင်းဆိုင် *kin-mǎya-ǎyaùn-zain*
can *v* **(be able to)** လုပ်နိုင် (တတ်နိုင်တယ်)၊ သံဗူး *louq-nain0taq-nain-deh) / than-bù* ; *n* **(container)**
Canada ကနေဒါနိုင်ငံ *kǎne-da-nain-gan(ngan)*
Canadian ကနေဒါလူမျိုး *Kǎne-da-lu-myò*
cancel ဖျက်သိမ်း *p'yeq-theìn*
candle ဖယောင်းတိုင် *p'ayaùn-dain*
candy store သကြားလုံးဆိုင် *dhǎjǎ-loùn-zain*
cap ဦးထုပ် *ouq-t'ouq*
car ကား *kà*
car hire [BE] အငှားကား *ǎhngà-kà*
car mechanic ကားပြင်ဆရာ *kà-pyin-s'ǎya*
car park [BE] ကားရပ်နားရန်နေရာ *kà-yaq-nà-yan-ne-ya*
car rental (with driver) ကားငှား (ကားမောင်းသူအပါ) *kà-hngà(kà-maùn-dhu-ǎpa)*
car seat ကားထိုင်ခုံ *kà-t'ain-goun*
carafe ရေပုလင်း *ye-bǎlìn*
card ဖဲ *p'èh*
card game ဖဲကစားခြင်း *p'èh-gǎzà-jìn*
cardigan သိုးမွေးအအင်္ကျီ (ရင်ကွဲသိုးမွေးအအင်္ကျီ) *thò-mwè-in-ji*
carry သယ် *theh*
cart တွန်းလှည် (တွန်းလှည်း) *tùn-hlèh*
carton (of cigarettes) ကာတွန်း (စီးကရက်) *ka-tùn (sì-kǎyeq)*
case (camera) အိတ်/ ဗူး (ကင်မရာ) (အိတ် (ကင်မရာ)) *eiq, bù (kin-mǎya)*
cash *v* ငွေပေး၊ ပိုက်ဆံ *ngwe-pè / paiq-s'an; n*
cashier ငွေလက်ခံသ *ngwe-leq-k´an-dhu*
casino ကာစီနို *ka-si-no*
castle slot; ရဲတိုက် အပေါက်ကျဉ်း *yèh-daiq-ǎpauq-cìn*
caution သတိပေး *dhǎdí-pè*
cave လှိုင်ဂူ *hlain-gu*
CD စီဒီ *si-di*
cell phone ဆဲလ်ဖုန်း/ လက်ကိုင်ဖုန်း *s'èh-(l)-p'oùn/ leq-kain-p'oùn*
cemetery သင်္ချိုင်း *thin-jaìn*
center of town မြို့လယ်ကောင် *myó-leh-gaun*
centimeter စင်တီမီတာ *sin-ti-mi-ta*
ceramics ကြွေထည်ပစ္စည်းတွေ *cwe-deh-pyiq-sì-dwe*
certain သေချာတယ *the-ja-deh*
certificate အောင်လက်မှတ်/ ထောက်ခံစာ *aun-leq-hmaq/t'auq-k´an-za*
chair ထိုင်ခုံ *tain-goun*
change n (money) အကြွေ (ငွေ)၊ လဲ (ငွေ)၊ လဲပေး (အဝတ်အစား၊ ကလေးအနှီး) *ǎcwe(ngwe)/ lèh(ngwe)/lèh-pè (ǎwuq-ǎsà/k´ǎlè-ǎhnì)* ; *v* **(money)** ; *v* **(clothes, diaper)**
charcoal မီးသွေး *mì-dhwè*
charge *n* အခကြေးငွေ/ စွပ်စွဲချက် ၊ တန်ဖိုးပြော/ စွပ်စွဲ *ǎk´á-cè-ngwe/suq-swèh-jeq tan-bò-pyàw / suq-swèh* ; *v*
cheap ဈေးသက်သာတာ *zè-theq-tha-da*
check (restaurant) *n* ; **(banking); v (someone, something)** ငွေစစ်ဆေးမှု (စားသောက်ဆိုင်)၊ ချက်လက်မှတ် (ဘဏ်နဲ့ပတ်သက်ပြီး)၊ စစ်ဆေး (တစ်စုံတစ်ယောက်၊ တစ်စုံတစ်ရာ) *ngwe-siq-s'è-hmú (sà-thauq-sain) / ćeq-leq-hmaq (ban-néh-paq-theq-pyì) siq-s'è (dǎzoun-tǎyauq/ dǎzoun-tǎya)*
check-in desk (airport) ချက်ခ်အင် လုပ်သည့်စားပွဲ (လေဆိပ်) *ćeq-in-louq-thí-zǎbwèh (le-zeiq)*

checking account လုပ်ငန်းသုံးအကောင့် (ဘဏ်စာရင်းရှင်) *louq-ngàn-dhoún-ăkaún*
check out *v* ချက်ခ်အောက်ထွက် *ćeq-auq-t́weq*
check-up (medical) (ဆေး) စစ် *(s'è) siq*
cheers ချီးယားစ် လုပ်/အားပေး/ဝမ်းသာအားရပြု *ĉi-yà-s-louq / à-pè / wàn-tha-à-yà-pyú*
chef စားဖိုမှူး *săp'o-hmù*
chemist [BE] ဓာတုဗေဒပညာရှင် *da-dú-be-dà-pyin-nya-shin*
cheque [BE] ချက်လက်မှတ် *ćeq-leq-hmaq*
chess ချက်ကစားနည်း *ćeq-găzà-nì*
chess set ချက်ကစားတဲ့ပစ္စည်းစုံ *ćeq-găzà-déh-pyiq-sì-zoun*
chest ရင်ပတ် *yin-baq*
chest pain ရင်ပတ်ထဲက အောင့်တာ *yin-baq-t́èh-gà-aún-da*
child ကလေး *k´ălè*
child's seat ကလေးထိုင်ခုံ *k´ălè-t́ain-goun*
children's clothing ကလေးအဝတ်အစား *k´ălè-ăwuq-ăsà*
children's portion ကလေးအချိုးစားစရာပမာဏ *k´ălè-ăćò-sà-zăya-păma-ná*
choice ရွေးချယ်မှု/ရွေးချယ်စရာ *ywè-ćeh-hmú / ywè-ćeh-săya*
church ဘုရားရှိခိုးကျောင်း *p'ăyà-shiq-k´ò-caùn*
cigar ဆေးပြင်းလိပ် *s'è-byìn-leiq*
cigarette စီးကရက် *sì-kăyeq*
cinema [BE] ရုပ်ရှင်ရုံ *youq-shin-youn*
classical ဂန္ထဝင်မြောက်တယ် *gan-dăwin-myauq-the*
clean *adj* သန့်ရှင်းတဲ့/ သန့်ရှင်း *thán-shìn-déh / than-shìn ; v*
cleansing cream မျက်နှာသန့်စင်ကရင်မ *myeq-hna-thán-sin-kăyin*
clear *v* ရှင်းလင်း *shin-lìn*
cliff ကမ်းပါးစောက် *găbà-zauq*
clip ကလစ် *kăliq*
clock နာရီ *na-yi*
close *v* ပိတ်တာ *peiq-ta*
closed ပိတ်ခဲ့/ပိတ်ထားတယ် *peiq-k´éh / peiq-t́à-deh*
cloth ပိတ်စ *peiq-sá*
clothing အဝတ်အစား *ăwuq-ăsà*
clothing store အဝတ်အစားရောင်းတဲ့ စတိုးဆိုင် *ăwuq-ăsà-yaùn-déh-sătò-zain*
cloud တိမ် *tein*
coat n (clothing) ကုတ်အင်္ကျီ (အဝတ်အစား) *kouq-ìn-ji (ăwuq-ăsà)*
coin အကြွေစေ့/ ဂိ၊ *ăcwe-sí / dìn-gà*
cold (illness) အအေးမိတာ (ဖျားနာမှု)၊ အေးတဲ့ *ăè-mí-da (p'yà-na-hmú)/è-déh ; adj*
collar ကော်လံ *kaw-la*
colleague လုပ်ဖော်ကိုင်ဖက် *louq-p'aw-kain-beq*
color အရောင် *ăyaun*
comb ဘီး *bì*
come လာတယ် *la-deh*
comedy ဟာသ *ha-thá*
commission (fee) ကော်မရှင်ခ (အခကြေးငွေ) *kaw-măshin-gá (ăk´á-cè-ngwe)*
common (frequent) ဖြစ်လေ့ရှိတဲ့ (မကြာခဏ) *p'yiq-lé-shí-déh (măca-k´ăná)*
compartment (train) အတွဲ (ရထား) *ătwèh (yăt́á)*
compass ကွန်ပတ်စ် (သံလိုက်အိမ်မြှောင်) *kun-paq-s (than-laiq-ein-hmyaun)*
complaint စွဲချက် *sáw-dăká*
computer (PC) ကွန်ပျူတာ (ပီစီ) *kun-pyu-ta(pi-si)*
concert ဖျော်ဖြေပွဲ/ ဂီတပွဲ *p'yaw-bye-bwèh/ gi-tá-bwh*
concert hall ဖျော်ဖြေပွဲ ကျင်းပတဲ့ခန်းမ *p'yaw-bye-bwèh-cìn-pá-déh-k´àn-má*
condom ကွန်ဒုံး *kun-doùn*
conference room ကွန်ဖရင့် အစည်းအဝေးခန်းမ *kun-p'ăyín-ăsì-ăwè-k´àn-má*
confirm အတည်ပြု *ăti-pyú*
confirmation အတည်ပြုမှု *ăti-pyú-hmú*
congratulations ချီးကျူးတယ်/ ချီးကျူးစကားများ *ĉi-kyù-deh/ĉi-kyù-zăgà-myà*
connect *v* ဆက်သွယ် *s'eq-thweh*
connection (transportation, internet) အဆက်အသွယ် (သယ်ယူပို့ဆောင်ရေး၊ အင်တာနက်) *ăs'eq-ăthweh(theh-yu-pó-s'aun-yè/in-ta-neq)*
constipation ဝမ်းချုပ်တဲ့ *wàn-ćouq-téh*
consulate ကောင်စစ်ဝန်ရုံး *kaun-siq-wun-yoùn*
contact lens မျက်ကပ်မှန်တေ *myeq-kaq-hman-dwe*
contagious ရောဂါကူးစက်တတ်တဲ့ *yàw-ga-kù-seq-taq-téh*
contain ပါဝင် *pa-win*
contraceptive ကိုယ်ဝန်တားဆေး *ko-wun-tà-zè*
contract ကျုံ့တယ်/ သဘောတူညီချက်စာချုပ်/ ရောဂါကူးစက်ခံရတယ် *coún-deh/dhăbàw-tu-nyi-jeq-sa-jouq/yàw-ga-kù-seq-k´an-yà-deh*
control ထိန်းချုပ် *t´èin-ćouq-the*
convention hall စည်းဝေးခန်းမ *sì-wè-k´àn-má*
copper ကြေးနီ *cè-ni*

corkscrew ပုလင်းဖော့ဆို့ဖွင့်တဲ့ဝက်အူလှည့်တံ *pălìn-p'áw-zó-p'wín-déh-weq-u-hléh-dan*
corner ထောင့် *daún*
cost *n* တန်ဖိုး ၊ ကျသင့်တယ် *tan-bò/cá-thín-deh; v*
cot ကလေးအိပ်ရာ/ ကုတင် *k´ălè-eiq-ya/gădin*
cotton ဂွမ်း *gùn(gwăn)*
cough *n* ချောင်းဆိုးတယ *ćaùn-s'ò-deh*
counter ကောင်တာ *kaun-ta*
country တိုင်းပြည် *taìn-pyi*
countryside ကျေးလက်ဒေသ *cè-leq-de-thá*
court (judicial) တရားရုံး (တရားဥပဒေနဲ့ဆိုင်တဲ့) *tăyà-yoùn (tăyà-ú-băde-néh-s'ain-déh)*
cover charge အားလုံးကာမိအောင်ပေးရတဲ့အခကြေးငွေ *á-loùn-ka-mi-aun-pè-yà-déh-ăk´á-cè-ngwe*
cramps ကြွက်တက်တာ၊ ကိုက်ခဲတာ *cweq-teq-ta / kaiq-k´èh-da*
crayon ရောင်စုံခဲတံ *yaun-zoun-k´èh-dan*
cream (toiletry) ကရင်မ် (အလှပြင်မှုဆိုင်ရာ) *kăyin-m(ăhlá-pyin-hmú-sain-ya)*
credit အကြွေး *ăcwè*
credit card အကြွေးဝယ်ကတ် *ăcwè-weh-kaq*
crib ကလေးပုခက် *k´ălè-păk´eq*
crockery [BE] အိုးခွက်ပန်းကန်တွေ *ò-k´weq-băgan-dwe*
crossing (maritime) ဖြတ်ကူးခြင်း (ပင်လယ်ရေကြောင်းနဲ့ဆိုင်တာ) *p'yaq-kù-jìn (pin-leh-ye-jaùn-néh-s'ain-da)*
crossroads လမ်းဆုံတွေ *làn-zoun-dwe*
crystal ကြည်လင်တဲ့ကျောက်တုံးပုံဆောင်ခဲ (ခရစ်စတယ်လ်) *ci-lin-déh-cauq-toùn-poun-s'aun-gèh (k´ăyiq-săteh-l)*
cufflink အမျိုးသားရှပ်အင်္ကျီလက်ကြယ်သီးတံ *ămyò-thà-shaq-ìn-ji-leq-ceh-dhì-dan*
cuisine အချက်အပြုတ်/ အစားအသောက် *ăćeq-ăpyouq/ăsà-ăthauq*
cup ခွက် *k´weq*
currency ငွေကြေး *ngwe-cè*
currency exchange office ငွေကြေးလဲလှယ်တဲ့ရုံး *ngwe-cè-lèh-hleh-déh-yoùn*
current (ocean) ရေစီးကြောင်း (သမုဒ္ဒရာ) *ye-zì-jaùn (thămouq-dăya)*
curtain ခန်းဆီး *k´àn-zì*
customs အကောက်ခွန်တွေ/ အခွန်ကောက်ခံမှုတွေ *ăkauq-k´un-dwe/ăk´un-kauq-k´an-hmú-dwe)*
customs declaration form အကောက်ခွန်ကြေငြာချက်ပုံစံ *ăkauq-k´un-ce-nya-jeq-poun-zan*
cut n (wound); ပြတ်ရှ (ဒဏ်ရာ)၊ ဖြတ် (ကပ်ကြေးနဲ့) *pyaq-shá(dan-ya)/p'yaq (kaq-cì-néh)* *v* **(with scissors)**
cycling စက်ဘီးစီး ။ခြင်း *seq-beìn-sì-jìn*

D

dairy ထောပတ်၊ ဒိန်ခဲ၊ နို့နဲ့ နို့ထွက်ပစ္စည်း *t´àw-baq, dein-gèh, nó-néh-nó-dweq-pyiq-sì*
damaged ပျက်စီးနေတဲ့ *pyeq-sì-ne-déh*
dance club အကခန်းမ/ ကလပ် *ăká-k´àn-má/kălaq*
dance *n* အက *ăká / ká-deh ; v*
danger အန္တရာယ် *an-dăyeh*
dangerous အန္တရာယ်ရှိတဲ့ *an-dăyeh-shì-déh*
Danish (person) ဒိန်းမတ် (လူမျိုး)၊ ဒိန်းမတ် (ဘာသာစကား) *Deìn-maq (lu-myò) deìn-maq (ba-dha-zăgà)*; **(language)** *adj*
dark မှောင်မိုက်တဲ့/ ရင့်တဲ့ *hmaun-maiq-téh/yín-déh*
date (appointment) ချိန်းဆိုမှု (အချိန်းအချက်)၊ နေ့စွဲ (နေ့) *ćeìn-s'o-hmú (ăćeìn-ăćeq)/né-zwèh (né)*; **(day)**
day နေ့ *né*
decision ဆုံးဖြတ်ချက် *s'oùn-p'yaq-ćeq*
deck (ship) ကုန်းပတ် (သင်္ဘော) *koùn-baq(thin-bàw)*
deck chair ကုန်းပတ်ကုလားထိုင် *koùn-baq-kălăťain*
declare (customs) ကြေငြာ (အခွန်နဲ့ဆိုင်တာ) *ce-nya (ăk´un-néh-s'ain-da)*
deep နက်တဲ့ *neq-téh*
degree (temperature) ဒီဂရီ (အပူချိန်) *di-găyi (ăpu-jein)*
delay နောက်ကျ *nauq-cá*
delicious အရသာရှိတဲ့ *ăyá-dha-shí-déh*
deliver ပေးပို့/ ဝေငှ *pè-pó/we-hngá*
delivery ပေးပို့မှု/ ဝေငှမှု *pè-pó-hmú/we-hngá-hmú*
denim ဂျင်းစတစ်မျိုး *n-zá-tămyò*
Denmark ဒိန်းမတ်နိုင်ငံ *Deìn-majq-nain-gan(ngan)*
dentist သွားဆရာဝန် *thwà-s'ăya-wun*
denture သွားတု *thwà-tú*
deodorant (ချွေး)အနံ့ပျောက်ဆေးတောင့် *(ćwè)ănán-pyauq-s'è-daún*
depart ခွဲခွာ/ ထွက်ခွာ *k´wèh-k´wa/ťweq-k´wa*
department (shop) ဌာန (ဆိုင်) *t´a-ná(s'ain)*
department store ဌာနမျိုးစုံပါတဲ့အရောင်းဆိုင် *t´a-ná-myò-zoun-pa-déh-ăyaùn-zain*
departure ထွက်ခွာ *t´weq-k´wa*
departure gate ထွက်ခွာရာဂိတ် *t´weq-k´wa-ya-geiq*

deposit n (bank) အပ်ငွေ (ဘဏ်)/ စရံငွေ *aq-ngwe(ban)/săyan-ngwe*; **(down payment)**
dessert အချိုပွဲ *ăćo-bwèh*
detergent ဆပ်ပြာမှုန့် *s'aq-pya-hmoún*
detour (traffic) လမ်းကြောင်းပြောင်းသွားတာ (ယာဉ်ကြောဆိုင်ရာ) *làn-gyaùn-pyaùn-thwà-da (yin-j-s'ain-ya)*
diabetic ဆီးချိုရောဂါရှိတဲ့/ဆီးချိုရောဂါသည *s'ì-jo-yàw-ga-shí-déh / s'ì-jo-yaw-ga-dheh*
diamond စိန *sein*
diaper ကလေးအနှီး *k'ălè-ăhnì*
diarrhea ဝမ်းလျှောတာ *wàn-shàw-da*
dictionary အဘိဓာန် *ăbí-dan*
diesel ဒီဇယ်ဆ *di-zeh-zi*
diet အစားလျှော့တယ်/ အစာ *ăsà-sháw-deh / ăsa*
difficult ခက်ခဲတဲ့ *k'eq-k'èh-déh*
digital ဒစ်ဂျစ်တယ် *diq-jiq-the*
dining car စားသောက်ခန်းတွဲ *sà-thauq-k'àn-dwèh*
dining room စားသောက်ခန်း *sà-thauq-k'àn*
dinner ညစာ *nyá-za*
direct *adj* တိုက်ရိုက်ဖြစ်တဲ့၊ လမ်းညွှန်/ပြ (တစ်စုံတစ်ယောက်အား) *daiq-yaiq-p'yiq-téh / làn-hnyun/pyá (dăzoun-tăyauq-à)*; *v* **(someone)**
direction လမ်းကြောင်း/ လမ်းညွှန်ချက် *làn-gyaùn / làn-hnyun-jeq*
directory (phone) (တယ်လီဖုန်း) လမ်းညွှန် *(the-li-p'oùn) làn-hnyun*
dirty ညစ်ပေတဲ့ *nyiq-pe-déh*
disabled မလုပ်နိုင် မကိုင်နိုင်တဲ့ *mălouq-nain-măkain-nain-déh*
disc (parking) ချပ်ပြားဝိုင်း (ပါကင်ထိုးတယ်) *jaq-pyà-wain (pa-kin-tò-deh)*
disconnect *v* **(computer)** ဆက်သွယ်မှုဖြတ်တောက် (ကွန်ပျူတာနှင့်ဆိုင်သော) *éq-thweh-hmú-p'yaq-tauq (kun-pyu-ta-hnín-s'ain-dhàw)*
discount ဈေးလျှော့ပေးတဲ့ *zè-sháw-pè-déh*
disease ရောဂါ *yàw-ga*
dish (food item) ဟင်းပွဲ (အစားအစာအမျိုးအမည်) *hìn-bwèh(ăsà-ăsa-ămyò-ămyi)*
dishes (plates) ပန်းကန်တွေ (ပန်းကန်ပြားများ) *băgan-dwe (băgan-byà-myà)*
dishwasher ပန်းကန်ဆေးစက် *băgan-s'è-zeq*
dishwashing detergent ပန်းကန်ဆေးတဲ့နေရာမှာ သုံးတဲ့ ဆပ်ပြာမှုန့် *băgan-s'è-déh-ne-ya-hma-thoùn-déh-s'aq-pya-hmoún*
disinfectant ရောဂါပိုးသေအောင်သုံးသည့် ဆေးရည်/ မှုန့် *yàw-ga-pò-the-aun-thoùn-dhí-s'è-yi / hmoún*
display case ခင်းကျင်းပြသတဲ့ဗီရို *k'ìn-cìn-pyá-déh-bi-do*
district (of town) ခရိုင် (မြို့တစ်မြို့ရဲ့) *k'ăyain (myó-tămyó-yéh)*
disturb နှောင့်ယှက *hnaún-sheq*
divorced ကွာရှင်းခဲ့တယ်/ တဲ့ *kwa-shìn-géh-deh / déh*
dizzy မူးဝေတယ်/ တဲ့ *mù-we-deh/déh*
doctor ဆရာဝန်/ ဒေါက်တာ *s'ăya-wun / dauq-ta*
doctor's office ဆရာဝန်ရုံးခန်း *s'ăya-wun-yoùn-gàn*
dog ခွေး *k'wè*
doll အရုပ်မ *ăyouq-má*
dollar (U.S.) ဒေါ်လာ (အမေရိကန်ပြည်ထောင်စု) *daw-la(ăme-yí-kan-pyi-daun-zú)*
domestic (airport terminal) ပြည်တွင်း (လေဆိပ်အဆောက်အဦး) *pyi-dwìn(le-zeiq-sauq-ăoun)*
domestic flight ပြည်တွင်းသွားလေယာဉ် *pyi-dwìn-thwà-le-yin*
double bed နှစ်ယောက်အိပ်ကုတင်/ အိပ်ရာ *hnăyauq-eiq-gădin / eiq-ya*
double room နှစ်ယောက်ခန်း *hnăyauq-k'an*
down အောက်ဖက် *auq-p'eq*
downtown area မြို့တွင်းပိုင်းဧရိယာ *myó-dwìn-bain-e-yi-ya*
dozen တစ်ဒါဇင် (ဆယ့်နှစ်ခု) *tăda-zin(s'ăhnăk'ú)*
dress *n* အဝတ်အစား *ăwuq-ăsà*
drink *n* သောက်စရာ (ကောက်တေးလ်)၊ သောက်တယ *thauq-săya(kauq-tè-l)/thauq-the* ; **(cocktail);** *v*
drinking water သောက်ရေ *thauq-ye*
drip အစက်ကျ *ăseq-cá*
drive မောင်းတယ် *maùn-deh*
driver's license ယာဉ်မောင်းလိုင်စင် *yin-maùn-lain-sin*
drop (liquid) အစက် (အရည်) *ăseq (ăye)*
drugstore ဆေးဆိုင် *s'è-zain*
dry ခြောက်/ အခြောက်လှမ်း *ćauq / ăćauq-hlàn*
dry cleaner အခြောက်လျှော်တဲ့နေရာ *ăćauq-shaw-déh-ne-ya*
dummy [BE] (baby's) ကစားစရာချိုလိမ် (ကလေးငယ်၏) *găzà-zăya-ćo-lein (k'ălè-ngeh-í)*
during အတောအတွင်း *ătàw-ătwìn*
duty (customs) အကောက်ခွန် (အခွန်အကောက်ဆိုင်တဲ့) *ăkauq-k'un(ăk'un-ăkauq-s'ain-déh)*
duty-free goods အကောက်ခွန်ကင်းလွတ်တဲ့

ပစ္စည်းတွေ *ăkauq-k´un-kìn-luq-téh-pyiq-sì-dwe*

duty-free shop အကောက်ခွန်ဆောင်ရန်မလိုသည့်ဆိုင် *ăkauq-k´un-s'aun-yan-mălo-dhí-s'ain*

dye ဆိုးဆေး *s'ò-zè*

E

each တစ်ခုစီ *tăk´ú-zi*

ear နား *nà*

ear drops နားတွင်းအစက်ချတဲ့ဆေးရည် *nà-dwìn-ăseq-ćá-déh-s'è-ye*

earache နားကိုက်ခြင်း *nà-kaiq-ĉin*

early စောစော *sàw-sàw*

earring နားကပ် *năgaq*

east အရှေ့ဘက် *ăshé-beq*

easy လွယ်ကူတဲ့ *lweh-ku-déh*

eat စားတယ် *sà-deh*

economy class *&dk;&dk;wef; yò-yò-dàn*

elastic ဆန့်နိုင်တဲ့ *s'án-nain-déh*

electric လျှပ်စစ်နဲ့ဆိုင်တဲ့ *hlyaq-siq-néh-s'ain-déh*

electrical outlet လျှပ်စစ်ဓာတ်အား ဆက်သွယ်ရရှိနိုင်တဲ့နေရာ *hlyaq-siq-daq-à-s'eq-thweh-yá-shí-nain-déh-ne-ya*

electricity လျှပ်စစ်အား *hlyaq-siq-à*

electronic လျှပ်စစ်ဆိုင်ရာပစ္စည်း *hlyaq-siq-s'ain-ya-puiq-sì*

elevator ဓာတ်လှေကား *daq-hle-gà*

e-mail အီးမေးလ် *Ì-mè-l-*

e-mail address အီးမေးလ် လိပ်စာ *Ì-mè-l-leiq-sa*

embassy သံရုံး *than-yòun*

embroidery ရွှေခြည်ထိုး ငွေခြည်ထိုး *shwe-ji-t'ò-ngwe-ji-t'ò*

emerald မြ *myá*

emergency အရေးပေါ် *ăyè-baw*

emergency exit အရေးပေါ်ထွက်ပေါက် *ăyè-baw-t'weq-pauq*

empty ဘာမျှမရှိအောင်လုပ်။သွန်ပစ် *ba-hmyá-măshí-aun-louq / thun-pyiq*

enamel သွားကို ကြွေရည်သုတ် *thaw-go-cwe-ye thouq*

end အဆုံးသတ်။ဆုံးစေ *ăs'òun-thaq / s'òun-ze*

engaged (phone) လိုင်းတိုက်နေတယ် (ဖုန်း) *lain-taiq-ne-deh(p'oùn)*

England အင်္ဂလန်နိုင်ငံ *In-gălan-nain-găn(ngan)*

English (language) အင်္ဂလိပ် (ဘာသာစကား)၊ (လူမျိုး) *In-găleiq(ba-dha-zăgà) / (lu-myò)*; **(person)**

enjoyable ကြည်နူးစရာကောင်းတဲ့ *ći-nù-zăya-kaùn-déh*

enlarge ကြီးစေ *ći-ze*

enough လုံလောက်တဲ့ *loun-lauq-téh*

enter *v* ဝင်ရောက် *win-yauq*

entrance ဝင်ပေါက် *win-bauq*

entrance fee ဝင်ခ/ဝင်ကြေး *win-gá / win-jè*

entry (access) ဝင်တယ် (လက်လှမ်းမှီ) *win-deh (leq-hlàn-hmi)*

envelope စာအိတ် *sa-eiq*

equipment ကိရိယာတန်ဆာပလာ *kăyí-ya-dăza-băla*

Europe ဥရောပ *Ú-yàw-pá*

European Union ဥရောပယူနီယမ်/ အဖွဲ့အစည်း *Ú-yàw-pá-u-ni-yan/ăp'wéh-ăsì*

evening ညနေ *nyá-ne*

every အရာရာ/ အသီးသီး *ăya-ya / ăthì-dhì*

everything အရာအားလုံး *ăya-à-loùn*

exchange rate ငွေလဲလှယ်နှုန်း *ngwe-lèh-hleh-hnoùn*

exchange *v* **(money)** လဲလှယ်ခြင်း (ငွေကြေး) *lèh-hleh-jìn (ngwe-cè)*

excursion လေ့လာရေးခရီး *lé-la-yè-k´ăyì*

excuse *v* ဆင်ခြေ/ အကြောင်းပြချက် ပေး *s'in-je/ăcaùn-pyá-jeq-pè*

exhibition ပစ္စည်း ပြပွဲ *pyiq-sì-pyá-pwèh*

exit *n* ထွက်ပေါက်၊ ထွက် (ကွန်ပျူတာနှင့်ဆိုင်သော) *t'weq-pauq/t'weq (kun-pyu- tà-hnín-s'ain-dhàw)* ; *v* **(computer)**

expect မျှော်လင့်တယ် *hmyaw-lín-deh*

expense ကုန်ကျစရိတ် *koun-cá-zăyeiq*

expensive ဈေးကြီးတဲ့ *zè-cì-déh*

express ဖော်ပြတယ်/ အမြန် *p'aw-pyá-deh/ămyan*

expression ဖော်ပြချက် *p'aw-pyá-jeq*

extension (phone) လိုင်းခွဲ (ဖုန်း) *lain-gwèh (p'oùn)*

extra အပို *ăpo*

eye မျက်လုံး *myeq-loùn*

eye drops မျက်စိအစက်ချဆေးရည် *myeq-sí-ăseq-ćá-s'e-ye*

eye shadow မျက်ခွံအရောင်တင်ဆေး *myeq-k'un-ăyoun-tin-zè*

eyesight မျက်စိအမြင် *myeq-sí-ămyin*

F

fabric (cloth) အစ (ပိတ်စ) *ăsá (peiq-sá)*

face မျက်နှာ *myeq-hna*

facial မျက်နှာဆေးကြော *myeq-hna-s'é-càw*

factory စက်ရုံ *seq-youn*

fair တရားမျှတတဲ့ *tăyà-hmyá-tá-déh*

fall *v* လျှော/ပြုတ် ကျ *shàw/pyouq-cà*

family မိသားစု *mí-thà-zú*

fan ပန်ကာ *pan-ka*

far ဝေးလံတဲ့ *wè-lan-déh*
fare (ticket) အခ (လက်မှတ်) *ăk´á (leq-hmaq)*
farm တောင်ယာ *taun-ya*
far-sighted အနီးမှုန်တာ *ănì-hmoun-da*
fast *adj* မြန်ဆန်တာ *myan-zan-da*
fast-food place အမြန်အစားအစာ ရနိုင်တဲ့နေရာ *ămyan-ăsà-ăsa-yá-nain-déh-ne-ya*
faucet ရေဘုံဘိုင်ခေါင်း *Ye-boun-bain-gaùn*
fax ဖက်စ် *p´eq-s*
fax number ဖက်စ်နံပါတ် *p´eq-s-nan-baq*
fee (commission) အခမဲ့ (ကော်မရှင်ပေးစရာမလို) *ăk´á-méh- (kaw-măshin-pè-zăya-mălo)*
feed *v* ကျွေးမွေး *cwè-mwè*
feel (physical state) ခံစားတယ် (ရုပ်ဝတ္ထုဆိုင်ရာ) *k´an-zà-deh (youq-wuq--t´ú-s'ain-ya)*
ferry ကူးတို့သင်္ဘော/ လှေ *gădó-thìn-bàw/hle*
fever အဖျား *ăp´yà*
few အနည်းငယ် *ănèh-ngeh*
field ကွင်းပြင် *Kwìn-byin*
file (for nails) ဖိုင် (လက်သည်းတိုက်သည့်အရာ) *p´ain (leq-thèh-taiq-thí-ăya)*
fill in (form) ဖြည့် (ပုံစံ) *p´yé (poun-zan)*
filling (tooth) ဖာ (သွား) *p´a (thwà)*
film [BE] ရုပ်ရှင် *youq-shin*
filter စစ်တဲ့အရာ/ရေစစ် *siq-téh-ăya/ye-ziq*
find *v* ရှာတွေ့/ ရှာဖွေ *sha-twé/sha-p´we*
fine (OK) ကောင်းတယ်(အိုကေ) *Kaùn-deh (o-ke)*
fine arts အသေးစိတ်အနုပညာ *ăthè-zeiq-ănú-pyin-nya*
finger လက်ချောင်း *leq-ćaùn*
fire မီး *mì*
fire escape မီးအရေးပေါ်လွတ်ပေါက် *mì-ăyè-baw-luq-pauq*
fire exit မီးအရေးပေါ်ထွက်ပေါက် *mì-ăyè-baw-t´weq-pauq*
first ပထမ *păt´ămá*
first-aid kit ရှေးဦးသူနာပြုပစ္စည်း *shè-ù-thu-na-pyú-pyiq-sì*
first class ပထမတန်း *păt´ămá-dàn*
first course ပထမဆုံးတည်ခင်းတဲ့အစာ *păt´ăm á-zoùn-the-k´ìn-déh-ăsa*
fishing ငါးမျှား/ခြင်း *ngà-hmyà-/jìn*
fit *v* ကျန်းမာ/ ဝတ်ကြည့် *càn-ma/wuq-cí*
fitting room အဝတ်လဲခန်း *ăwuq-lèh-gàn*
fix *v* ပြင်ဆင် *pyin-sin*
flashlight လက်နှိပ်ဓာတ်မီး *leq-hneiq-daq-mì*
flat [BE] (apartment) အခန်း (နေအိမ်တိုက်ခန်း) *ăk´àn (ne-ein-taiq-k´àn)*
flatware ဇွန်း၊ ခက်ရင်း၊ ဓား အစုံ *zùn-k´ăyìn-dà-ăsoun*
flea market ပစ္စည်းအဟောင်း ရောင်းတဲ့ဈေး *pyiq-sì-ăhaùn-yaùn-déh-zè*
flight လေယာဉ်ပျံ *le-yin-byan*
floor ကြမ်းပြင် *càn-pyin*
florist ပန်းစိုက်သူ/ပန်းရောင်းသူ *pàn-saiq-thu/pàn-yaùn-dhu*
flower ပန်း *Pàn*
flu ဗိုင်းရပ်စ် ပိုးကြောင့်ဖြစ်တဲ့ အအေးမိတဲ့ရောဂါတစ်မျိုး/ ဖလူးရောဂါ *baìn-yaq-s-pò-jaún-p´yiq—téh-ăè-mí-déh-yàw-ga-tămyò/p´ălù-yàw-ga*
fluid အရည် *ăye*
fog မြူ *myu*
follow လိုက်နာတယ်/ လိုက်တယ် *laiq-na-deh/laiq-the*
food အစားအစာ *ăsá-ăsa*
food poisoning အစာအဆိပ်သင့်မှု *ăsa-ăseiq-thín-hmú*
foot ခြေထောက် *ćè-dauq*
football [BE] ဘောလုံးကန်ခြင်း *bàw-loùn-kan-jìn*
for အတွက် *ătweq*
forbidden ပိတ်ပင်တားမြစ် *peiq-pin-tà-myiq*
forecast ခန့်မှန်းတယ် *k´án-hmàn-deh*
foreign မရင်းနှီးတာ/စိမ်းနေတာ *măyìn-hnì-da/seìn-ne-da*
forest သစ်တော *thiq-tàw*
forget မေ့လျော့ *mé-yáw*
fork ခက်ရင်း *k´ăyìn*
form (document) ပုံစံ (စာရွက်စာတမ်း) *poun-zan (sa-yweq-sa-dàn)*
fountain ရေပန်း *Ye-bàn*
frame (glasses) ဘောင် (မှန်များ) *baun (hman-myà)*
free လွတ်လပ်တဲ့ *luq-laq-téh*
freezer ရေခဲသေတ္တာ *ye-gè-thiq-ta*
fresh လတ်ဆတ်တဲ့ *laq-s'aq-téh*
friend မိတ်ဆွေ *meiq-s'we*
from မှ/ ထံမှ *hmá/t´an-hmá*
frying pan ကြော်လှော်တဲ့ယ်အိုး *caw-hlaw-déh-deh-ò*
full ပြည့်တာ *Pyí/pyé-da*
full-time အချိန်ပြည့် *ăćein-byé*
furniture ပရိဘောဂပစ္စည်း *Păyí-băw-gá-pyíq-sì*

G

gallery ပြခန်း *pyá-gàn*

game ကစားပွဲ *găzà-bwèh*
garage ဂိုဒေါင် *go-daun*
garbage အမှိုက် *ăhmaiq*
garden ပန်းခြံ *Pàn-jan*
gas ဂက်စ် (ဓာတ်ငွေ့) *geq-s (daq-ngwé)*
gasoline ဓာတ်ဆီ *daq-s´i*
gauze ဂွမ်း *gwàn (gùn)*
germ ပိုးမွှား *Pò-hmwà*
general သာမန်/ရိုးရိုး *tha-man/yò-yò*
general delivery ရိုးရိုးပို့ဆောင်မှု *yò-yò-pó-s´aun-hmú*
general practitioner [BE] ရိုးရိုးဆရာဝန် *yò-yò--s´ăya-wun*
genuine စစ်မှန်တာ/အစစ်အမှန် *siq-hman-da/ăsiq-ăhman*
get (find) ရရှိ (ရှာဖွေတွေ့ရှိ) *yá-shí (sha-p´we-twé-shí)*
get off ဆင်းတယ် *s'ìn-deh*
get up တက်/မတ်တပ်ရပ် *teq/meq-taq-yaq*
gift လက်ဆောင် *leq-s'aun*
gift shop လက်ဆောင်ရောင်းတဲ့ဆိုင် *leq-s'aun-yaùn-dèh-s'ain*
girl မိန်းကလေး *meìn-k´ălè*
girlfriend မိန်းကလေးမိတ်ဆွေ *meìn-k´ălè-meiq-s'we*
give ပေးတယ် *Pè-deh*
gland ဂလင်း *gălìn*
glass (drinking) ဖန်ခွက် (သောက်တဲ့) *p´an-gweq (thauq-téh)*
glasses (optical) မျက်မှန်တွေ (မျက်စိနဲ့ဆိုင်တာ) *myeq-hman-dwe (myeq-sí-néh-s'ain-da)*
glove လက်အိတ် *leq-eiq*
glue ကော် *kaw*
go away ဝေးဝေးသွား *wè-wè-thwà*
go back ပြန်သွားတာ *pyan-thwà-da*
go out အပြင်ထွက် *ăpyin-t´weq*
gold ရွှေ *shwe*
golf club ဂေါက်ကလပ် *gauq-kălaq*
golf course ဂေါက်ကွင်း *gauq-kwín*
golf tournament ဂေါက်ရိုက်ပြိုင်ပွဲ *gauq-yaiq-pyain-bwè*
good ကောင်းတာ/မင်္ဂလာရှိတာ *kaùn-da/min-găla-shí-da*
good afternoon မင်္ဂလာနေ့လည်ခင်းပါ *min-găla-né-leh-gìn-ba*
good evening မင်္ဂလာ ညနေခင်းပါ *min-găla-nyá-ne-gìn-ba*
good morning မင်္ဂလာ နံနက်ခင်းပါ *min-găla-nan-neq -k´ìn-ba*
good night မင်္ဂလာ ညချမ်းပါ *min-găla-nyá-jàn-ba*
goodbye နှုတ်ဆက်ပါတယ် *Hnouq-s'eq-pa-deh*
gram ဂရမ် (အလေးချိန်) *găyan (ălè-jein)*
grandchild မြေး *myè*
gray မီးခိုးရောင် *mì-gò-yaun*
great (excellent) သိပ်ကောင်းတယ် (အရမ်းကောင်းတယ်) *theq-kaùn-deh*
Great Britain ဂရိတ်ဗြိတိန်နိုင်ငံ *Găyeiq-Byí-tein-nain-gan (-ngan)*
green အစိမ်းရောင် *ăseìn-yaun*
greengrocer's [BE] ဟင်းသီးဟင်းရွက်ရောင်းသူ *hìn-dhì-hìn-yweq-yaùn-dhu*
greeting နှုတ်ခွန်းဆက်စကား *hnouq-k´ùn-s'eq-zăgà*
ground-floor room [BE] မြေညီထပ်အခန်း *mye-nyi-daq-ăk´àn*
group အုပ်စု *ouq-sú*
guesthouse ဧည့်ရိပ်သာ *éh-yeiq-tha*
guide dog လမ်းပြခွေး *làn-pyá-k´wè*
guide *n* လမ်းပြသူ/ဧည့်လမ်းညွှန် *làn-pyá-dhu/éh-làn-hnyun*
guidebook လမ်းညွှန်စာအုပ် *làn-hnyun-sa-ouq*
gym အားကစားလုပ်တဲ့အခန်း *à-găzà-louq-téh-ăk´àn*
gynecologist မီးယပ်အထူးကု *mì-yaq-ăt´ù-gú*

H

hair ဆံပင် *zăbin*
hair dryer ဆံပင်အခြောက်ခံတဲ့ကိရိယာ *zăbin-ăćauq-k´an-déh-kăyí-ya*
hairbrush ခေါင်းဖီးတဲ့ ဘီး *gaùn-p´ì-déh-bì*
haircut ဆံပင်ညှပ်တယ် *zăbin-hnyaq-teh*
hairdresser ဆံပင်ညှပ်ဆိုင် *zăbin-hnyaq-s'ain*
hairspray ဆံပင်ဖျန်းဆေး *zăbin-p´yàn-zè*
hall (room) ခန်းမ (အခန်း) *k´àn-má (ăk´àn)*
hammer တူ *tu*
hammock အဝတ်ပုခက် *ăwuq-păk´eq*
hand လက *leq*
hand cream လက်လိမ်းကရင်မ် *leq-leìn-kăyin-m*
hand washable လက်ဆေးနိုင်တဲ့ *leq-s'è-nain-déh*
handbag [BE] လက်ကိုင်အိတ် *leq-kain-eiq*
handicrafts လက်မှုပညာလက်ရာပစ္စည်းတွေ *leq-hmú-pyin-nya-leq-ya-pyiq-sì-dwe*
handkerchief လက်ကိုင်ပဝါ *leq-kain-păwa*
handmade လက်လုပ်ပစ္စည်း *leq-louq-pyiq-sì*
hanger အင်္ကျီချိတ် *ìn-ji-jeiq*
happy ပျော်တယ် *pyaw-deh*

harbor ဆိပ်ကမ်း *s'eiq-kàn*
hard မာတဲ့ *ma-déh*
hardware store ကွန်ပျူတာစက်ပစ္စည်းရောင်းဆိုင် *kun-pyu-ta-seq-pyiq-sì-yaùn-zain*
hare ယုန် *youn*
hat ဦးထုပ် *ouq-t´ouq*
have (must); possess ရမယ် (လုပ်ရမယ်)/ ရှိတယ် (ပိုင်ဆိုင်မှုပြ) *Yá-meh (louq-yá-meh)/shí-deh (pain-s'ain-hmú-pyá)*
hay fever ကောက်ရိုးခြောက်ချိန်တွင်ဖြစ်သောဓာတ်မတည့်သည့်ရောဂါ *Kauq-yò-ćauq-ćein-dwin-p´yiq-thaw-daq-mătéh-dhí-yàw-ga*
head ဦးခေါင်း *ù-gaùn*
headache ခေါင်းကိုက်ခြင်း *gaùn-kaiq-ĉìn*
headlight ကားရှေ့မီး *kà-shé-mì*
headphones နားကြပ် *năjaq*
health food store ကျန်းမာရေးနဲ့ ညီညွတ်တဲ့အစားအသောက် အရောင်းဆိုင် *càn-ma-yè-néh-nyi-nyuq-téh-ăsà-ăthouq-ăyaùn-zain*
health insurance ကျန်းမာရေးအာမခံ *càn-ma-yè-a-má-gan*
hearing-impaired အကြားအာရုံပျက်စီးခြင်း *Ăcà-a-youn-pyeq-sì-jìn*
heart နှလုံး *hnălouǹ*
heart attack နှလုံးရောဂါ *hnălouǹ-yàw-ga*
heat *v* အပူပေး *ăpu-pè*
heating အပူပေးခြင်း *ăpu-pè-jìn*
heavy လေးလံတယ် *lè-lan-deh*
hello ဟယ်လို (နှုတ်ခွန်းဆက်စကား) *Heh-lo (hnouq-k´ùn-s'eq-zăgà)*
helmet ဟဲလ်မက် (ဆိုင်ကယ်စီးဦးထုပ်) *hèh-l-meq (s'ain-keh-sì-ouq-t´ouq)*
help ကိုယ့်ဘာသာလုပ် (တစ်ဦးတည်း) *Kó-p´a-tha-louq (tăù-t´éh)*; **(oneself)**
here ဒီမှာ *di-hma*
hi ဟိုင်း (နှုတ်ခွန်းဆက်စကား) *Haìn (hnouq-k´ùn-s'eq-zăgà)*
high *adj* မြင့်တယ *myín-deh*
high tide ဒီရေ အမြင့်/အတက *di-ye-ămyín/ăteq*
highchair ထိုင်ခုံအမြင့် *t´ain-goun-ămyín*
highway ဟိုင်းဝေး (အဝေးပြေးလမ်းမ) *haìn-wè (ăwè-byè-làn-má)*
hill တောင်ကုန်း *taun-goùn*
hire [BE] *v* ငှားရမ်း *hngà-yàn*
history သမိုင်းကြောင်း *thămaìn-jaùn*
hole အပေါက် *ăpouq*
holiday အားလပ်ရက် *à-laq-yeq*; **[BE]**
home နေအိမ် *ne-ein*
horseback riding မြင်းစီးခြင်း *myìn-sì-jìn*
hospital ဆေးရုံ *s'è-youn*
hot (temperature) ပူတယ် (အပူချိန်) *pu-deh (ăpu-jein)*
hotel ဟိုတယ် *ho-teh*
hotel directory ဟိုတယ် လမ်းညွှန် *ho-teh-làn-hnyun*
hotel reservation ဟိုတယ် ကြိုတင်နေရာယူခြင်း *ho-teh-kyo-tin-ne-ya-yu-jìn*
hour (time) နာရီ (အချိန်) *na-yi (ăćein)*
house အိမ် *ein*
how ဘယ်လို *beh-lo*
how far ဘယ်လောက်ဝေးလ *beh-louq-wè-lèh*
how long ဘယ်လောက်ကြာလဲ *beh-louq-ca-lèh*
how many ဘယ်လောက်များလဲ *beh-louq-myà-lèh*
how much ဘယ်လောက်ကျလဲ *beh-louq-cá-lèh*
hug *v* ဖက်တယ် *p´eq-the*
humid စိုထိုင်းဆများ/စိုစွတ် *so-t´aìn-zá-myà/so-suq*
hungry ဆာလောင် *s'a-laun*
hunting အမဲလိုက် *ămè-laiq*
hurry အလျင်လို *ăyin-lo*
hurt နာကျင် *na-cin*
husband ခင်ပွန်း ယောကျ်ား *k´in-bùn/yauq-cà*

I

I ကျွန်ုပ် (ကျွန်တော်/ကျွန်မ) *cănouq (cănaw* **m**/ *cămá* **f**)
ice ရေခဲ *ye-gè*
icy (weather) ရေခဲတဲ့ (ရာသီဥတု) *ye-k´è-déh (ya-dhi-ú-dú)*
identification (card) သက်သေခံကတ်ပြား (ကတ်) *theq-the-gan-kaq-pyà (kaq)*
if တကယ်လို *dăgeh-ló*
ill [BE] ဖျားနာတယ *p´yà-na-deh*
illness ဖျားနာမှု *p´yà-na-hmú*
important အရေးကြီးတယ် *ăyè-ci-deh*
imported တင်သွင်း/ပို့ ထားတဲ့ *tin-thwìn/pó-t´à-déh*
impressive အထင်ကြီးစရာကောင်းတယ် *ăt´in-ci-zăya-kaùn-deh*
in အထဲမှာ *ăt´èh-hma*
include ပါဝင် *pa-win*
indoor အတွင်း/အမိုးအကာအောက်တွင်း *ătwìn/ămò-ăka-ouq-twìn*
inexpensive ဈေးမကြီးတဲ့ *zè-măci-déh*
infected ရောဂါကူးစက်ခံရ /တဲ့ *yàw-ga-kù-seq-*

k´an-yá-déh
infection ကူးစက်ရောဂါ *kù-seq-yàw-ga*
inflammation ရောင်ရမ်းခြင်း *yaun-yàn-jìn*
information စုံစမ်းမေးမြန်းမှု သတင်းအချက်အလက် *soun-zàn-mè-myàn-hmú/dhădìn-ăceq-ăleq*
information desk စုံစမ်းမေးမြန်းရန်စားပွဲ *soun-zàn-mè-myàn-yan-zăbwè*
injection ဆေးထိုးတယ်/ထိုးဆေး *s'è-t´ò-deh/t´ò-zè*
injure ဒဏ်ရာ ရ *dan-ya-yá*
injury ဒဏ်ရာ *dan-ya*
inn ထမင်းဆိုင် *t´ămìn-zain*
innocent အပြစ်မရှိဘူး *ăpyiq-măshí-bù*
inquiry စုံစမ်းတယ *soun-zàn-deh*
insect bite အင်းဆက်အကိုက်ခံရ *ìn-s'eq-ăkaiq-k´an-yá*
insect repellent အင်းဆက်ပြေးဆေး *ìn-s'eq-pyè-zè*
insect spray အင်းဆက်ဖျန်းဆေး *ìn-s'eq-p´yàn-zè*
inside အတွင်းဖက် *ătwìn-beq*
instant messenger ချက်ချင်းလက်ငင်း သတင်းပို့ပေးသူ *ćeq-ĉìn-leq-ngìn-dhădìn-pó-pè-dhu*
insurance အာမခံ *a-má-gan*
insurance claim အာမခံပေးရန် တောင်းဆို *a-má-gan-pè-yan-taùn-s'o*
interest (finance) အတိုး (ငွေကြေးဆိုင်ရာ) *ătò (ngwe-cè-s'ain-ya)*
interested စိတ်ဝင်စားတယ် *seiq-win-zà-deh*
interesting စိတ်ဝင်စားစရာကောင်းတဲ့ *seiq-win-zà-zăya-kaùn-déh*
international အပြည်ပြည်ဆိုင်ရာ/ပြည်ပ (လေဆိပ်အဆောက်အအုံ *ăpyi-pyi-s'ain-ya/pyi-pá (le-zeiq-ăs'auq-ăoun)*; **(airport terminal)**
international flight နိုင်ငံတကာလေယာဉ် *nain-gan (ngan)-dăga-le-yin*
internet အင်တာနက် *in-ta-neq*
internet cafe အင်တာနက်ကော်ဖီဆိုင် *in-ta-neq-kaw-p´i-zain*
interpreter စကားပြန်/ဘာသာပြန်ပေးသူ *zăgăbyan/ba-dha-pyan-pè-dhu*
intersection လမ်းဆုံ *làn-zoun*
introduce မိတ်ဆက် **meíq-s'eq**
introduction (social) မိတ်ဆက်စကား/အဖွင့်စကား (လူမှုရေးနှင့်ဆိုင်သော) *meíq-s'eq-zăgà/ăp´wín-zăgà (lu-hmú-yè-hnín-s'ain-dhàw)*
investment ရင်းနှီးမြှုပ်နှံမှု *yìn-hnì-hmyouq-hnan-hmú*
invitation ဖိတ်စာ *p´eiq-sa*
invite *v* ဖိတ်တယ် *p´eiq-teq*
invoice ငွေတောင်းခံလွှာ *ngwe-taùn-k´an-hlwa*
iodine အိုင်အိုဒင်း *ăin-o-dìn*
Ireland အိုင်ယာလန် နိုင်ငံ *ăin-ya-lan-nain-gan (ngan)*
Irish (person) အိုင်ယာလန် လူမျိုး/ စကား *ăin-ya-lan-lu-myò/zăgà; adj*
iron n (clothing) မီးပူ (အဝတ်အစား)/ မီးပူတိုက *mì-pu (ăwuq-ăsà)/mì-bu taiq;v*
itemized bill အမျိုးအစားအလိုက်ဖော်ပြတဲ့ ငွေတောင်းခံစာ *ămyò-ăsà-ălaiq-p´aw-pyá-déh-ngwe-taùn-k´an-sa*

J

jacket ဂျက်ကက်အင်္ကျီ *Jeq-keq-ìn-ji*
jade ကျောက်စိမ်း *cauq-seìn*
jar (container) ဖန်ရေတကောင်း (ထည့်စရာ) *p´an-ye-dăgaùn (t´éh-zăya)*
jaw မေးရိုး *mè-yò*
jeans ဂျင်း *Jìn*
jet ski ရေပေါ်ပြေးဆိုင်ကယ် *ye-baw-pyè-s'ain-keh*
jeweler လက်ဝတ်ရတနာ ပြုလုပ်သူ *leq-wuq-yădăna-pyú-louq-thu*
join *v* ပူးပေါင်းတယ် *pù-paùn-deh*
joint (anatomy) အဆစ် *ăs'iq*
journey ခရီး *k´ăyì*
just (only) မျှသာ (သာလျှင်) *hmyá-dha (dga-hyin)*

K

keep သိမ်းဆည်းထား *theìn-s'ì-t´à*
kerosene ရေနံဆီ *ye-nan-zi*
key သော့ *tháw*
key card သော့ကတ် *thàw-kaq*
kiddie pool ကလေးရေကူးကန် *k´ălè-ye-kù-gan*
kidney ကျောက်ကပ် *cauq-kaq*
kilogram ကီလိုဂရမ် *Ki-lo-găyan*
kilometer ကီလိုမီတာ *Ki-lo-mi-ta*
kind *adj* ကြင်နာတတ်တဲ့/ ကြင်နာတတ်ခြင်း *cin-na-daq-tèh/cin-na-daq-ĉìn; n*
kiss *v* နမ်းတယ် *nàn-deh*
knee ဒူးခေါင်း *dù-gaùn*
knife ဓားမြှောင် *dăhmyaun*
knitwear သိုးမွေးထည် *thò-mwè-t´eh*
knock တံခါးခေါက် *dăgà-k´auq*
know သိတယ် *thí-deh*

L

label တံဆိပ် *dăzeiq*
lace ဇာ *Za*
lactose intolerant နို့တွင်းပါသောဓာတ်တစ်မျိုးအား

ခံနိုင်ရည်မရှိမှု *nó-dwìn-pa-dhaw-daq-tămyò-à-k´an-nain-yi-măshí-hmú*
lake ရေကန် *ye-gan*
lamp မီးအိမ် *mì-eìn*
landscape နယ်မြေဒေသရှုခင်း *neh-mye-de-thá-shú-gín*
language ဘာသာစကား *ba-dha-zăgà*
lantern မှန်အိမ်/ မီးအိမ် *hman-ein/mì-eìn*
large ကြီးတယ် *cì-deh*
last နောက်ဆုံး *nauq-s'oùn*
late (time) နောက်ကျတယ် (အချိန်)/ (အချိန်ဆွဲတယ်) *nauq-cá-deh (ăcein)/(ăcein-s'wè-deh)*; **(delay)**
laugh ရယ်မော *yeh-màw*
launderette [BE] မိမိဘာသာ အဝတ်လျှော်မီးပူတိုက်နိုင် *mí-mí-p´a-dha-ăwuq-shaw-mì-bu-taiq-nain*
laundromat အဝတ်လျှော် မီးပူတိုက်ရန် နေရာအမှတ်အသား *ăwuq-shaw-mì-bu-taiq-yan-ne-ya-ăhmaq-ăthà*
laundry အဝတ်လျှော် မီးပူတိုက်ခြင်း *ăwuq-shaw-mì-bu-taiq-ĉin*
laundry ခေငူငအငနျူ အဝတ်လျှော် မီးပူတိုက်ရန် အထောက်အကူပစ္စည်းများ *ăwuq-shaw-mì-bu-taiq-yan-ăt´auq-ăku-pyiq-sì-myà*
laundry service ဒိုဘီဆိုင်ဝန်ဆောင်မှု *do-bi-zain-wun-s'aun-hmú*
lawyer ရှေ့နေ *Shé-ne*
laxative ဝမ်းပျော့ဆေး *wàn-pyàw-zè*
leather သားရေထည် *thăye-t´eh*
leave *v* ထွက်ခွာ/ ချန်ခဲ့ (နောက်တွင်) *t´weq-k´wa/ ćan-géh (nauq-twin)*; **(behind)**
left ဘယ်ဖက *f beh-beq*
leg ခြေထောက် *će-dauq*
lens (ခဓာနမင) မှန်ပြောင်းတွေ (ကင်မရာနဲ့ဆိုင်တာ)/ (မျက်မှန်တွေ) *hman-byaùn-dwe (kin-măya-néh-s'ain-da)/(myeq-hman-dwe)*; **(glasses)**
less ပိုနည်းတဲ့ *po-nèh-déh*
lesson သင်ခန်းစာ *thin-gàn-za*
letter စာ *sa*
library စာကြည့်တိုက် *sa-cí-daiq*
license (driving) လိုင်စင် (ယာဉ်မောင်း) *lain-sin (yin-maùn)*
life boat အသက်ကယ်လှေ *ătheq-keh-hle*
life guard (beach) (ကမ်းခြေစောင့်)အသက်ကယ်သူ *(kàn-je-saún) ătheq-keh-dhu*
life jacket အသက်ကယ်အင်္ကျီ *ătheq-keh-ìn-ji*
life preserver အသက်စောင့်သူ *ătheq-saún-dhu*
light (color) ဖျော့တာ (အရောင်)/ ပေါ့တာ (အလေးချိန်) *p´yáw-da (ăyaun)/páw-da (ălè-jein)*; **(weight)**
light bulb လျှပ်စစ်မီးသီး *hlyaq-siq-mì-dhì*
lighter ဓာတ်မီးခြစ် *daq-mì-jiq*
lightning လျှပ်စီးလက် *hlyaq-sì-leq*
like; (please) လုပ်/ လို ချင်တယ် (ကျေးဇူးပြုပြီး) *louq/lo-jin-deh (cè-zù-pyú-pyì)*
linen လီနင်စ *li-nin-sá*
lip နှုတ်ခမ်း *hnăk´àn*
lipstick နှုတ်ခမ်းနီ *hnăk´àn-ni*
liquor store အရက်ရောင်းတဲ့စတိုးဆိုင် *ăyeq-yaùn-déh-sătò-zain*
listen နားထောင် *nà-t´aun*
liter လီတာ (ပမာဏ) *li-ta (păma-ná)*
little (amount) အနည်းငယ် (ပမာဏ) *ănéh-ngeh (păma- ná)*
live *v* နေထိုင် *ne-t´ain*
local ဒေသဆိုင်ရာ *de-thá-s'ain-ya*
log off အင်တာနက်တွင်းဝင်ထားရာမှ ထွက် *in-ta-neq-twìn-win-t´à-ya-hmá-t´weq*
log on အင်တာနက်အတွင်း ဝင် *in-ta-neq-ătwì-win*
login ဝင် *win*
long ရှည်/ကြာတာ *she/ca-da*
long-sighted [BE] အနီးမှုန်တာ *ănì-hmoun-da*
look *v* ကြည့် *cí*
lose ပျောက် *pyauq*
loss ဆုံးရှုံး *s'oùn-shoùn*
lost ပျောက်ဆုံး *pyauq-s'oùn*
lost and found ပျောက်ပြီး ပြန်တွေ့ *pyauq-pyì-pyan-twé*
lost property office [BE] ပျောက်ဆုံးပစ္စည်း ရုံး *pyauq—s'oùn-pyiq-sì-yoùn*
lotion လိမ်းဆေးရည် *leìn-zè-ye*
loud (voice) ကြယ်လောင်တဲ့ (အသံ) *ceh-laun-dég (ăthan)*
love *v* ချစ်တယ် *ćiq-teh*
lovely ချစ်စရာကောင်းတဲ့ *ćiq-săya-kaùn-déh*
low နိမ့်တယ်/ နည်းတယ *neín-deh/néh-deh*
low tide ရေကျ/ဒီရေကျ *ye-cá/di-ye-cá*
luck ကုသိုလ်ကံ *kú-dho-kan*
luggage ခရီးဆောင်အထုတ်အပိုး *k´ăyì-zaun-ăt´ouq-ăpò*
luggage cart ခရီးဆောင်အထုတ်အပိုးတင်တွန်းလှည်း *k´ăyì-zaun-ăt´ouq-ăpò-tin-tùn-hlè*
lunch နေ့လည်စာ *né-leh-za*
lung အဆုတ် *ăs'ouq*

M

magazine မဂ္ဂဇင်း *meq-găzìn*
magnificent ခမ်းနား *k´án-nà*
maid အိမ်ဖော် *ein-baw*
mail *n* စာ/ စာပို့တယ် *sa/sa-pó-deh; v*
mailbox စာတိုက်သေတ္တာ *sa-daiq-thiq-ta*
make-up *n* မိတ်ကပ် *meiq-kaq*
mall ဈေးတန်း *zè-dàn*
mallet တင်းပုတ *tìn-bouq*
man ယောက်ျား *yauq-cà*
manager မန်နေဂျာ/စီမန်ခန့်ခွဲသူ *man-ne-ja/si-man-k´án-k´wèh-dhu*
manicure လက်သည်းထိုးခြင်း *leq-thè-t´ó-jìn*
many အများအပြား *ămyà-ăpyà*
map မြေပုံ *mye-boun*
market *n* ဈေး *zè*
married လက်ထပ်ခဲ့တယ/လက်ထပ်ထားတဲ့ *leq-t´aq-k´éh-deh/leq-t´aq-t´à-déh*
mass (religious service) ဆုတောင်းပွဲ (ဘာသာတရားဆိုင်ရာ ဆုတောင်းပွဲ) *s'ú-taùn-bwè (ba-dha-tăyà-s'ain-ya-s'u-taún-bwè)*
massage နှိပ်တာ *hneiq*
match n (sport) ပြိုင်ပွဲ (အားကစားဆိုင်ရာ) *pyain-bwè (à-găzà-s'ain-ya)*
material ရုပ်ဝတ္ထုနှင့်ဆိုင်တာ *youq-wuq-t´ú-hnín-s'ain-da*
matinée ဖြေဖျော်မှု *p´ye-p´yaw-hmú*
mattress မွေ့ယာ *mwé-ya*
may *v* ဖြစ်နိုင်ချေရှိ *p´yiq-nain-je-shí*
meadow မြက်ခင်းပြင် *myeq-k´ìn-byin*
meal အစာ *ăsa*
mean *v* ဆိုလို *s'o-lo*
measure တိုင်းတာ *taìn-ta*
measuring cup တိုင်းတာတဲ့ခွက် *taìn-ta-déh-k´weq*
measuring spoon တိုင်းတာတဲ့ဇွန်း *taìn-ta-déh-zùn*
mechanic စက်မှုပညာရှင် *seq-hmú-pyin-nya-shin*
medicine (drug) ဆေး *s'é*
meet တွေ့ဆုံ *Twé-s'oun*
memorial အထိမ်းအမှတ်ပွဲ *ăt´eìn-ăhmaq-pwè*
memory card မမ်မိုရီကတ်/မှတ်ဉာဏ်ကတ် *man-mo-yi-kaq/hmaq-nyan-kaq*
mend ပြုပြင် *pyú-pyin*
menu အစားအသောက်စာရင်း *ăsà-ăthaug-săyìn*
message သတင်း *dhădìn*
meter မီတာ *mi-ta*
middle အလယ် *ăleh*
midnight ညသန်းခေါင် *nyá-dhăgaun*
mileage မိုင်စုစုပေါင်း *mí-sú-zú-baún*
minute မိနစ် *mí-niq*
mirror မှန် *hman*
miscellaneous အထွေထွေ *ăt´we-t´we*
Miss မစ္စ *Miq-s*
miss *v* **(lacking)** လစ်လပ်နေတာပျောက်ဆုံးနေတာ *liq-laq-ne-da/pyauq-s'oùn-ne-da*
mistake အမှားအယွင်း *ăhmà-ăywìn*
mobile phone [BE] လက်ကိုင်ဖုန်း *leq-kain-p´oùn*
moisturizing cream အစိုဓာတ်ထိမ်းပေးသောကရင်မ် *ăso-daq-t´eìn-pè-dhàw-kăyin-m*
moment တခဏ/တဒင်္ဂအချိန် *tăk´ăná/tădin-gá-ăćein*
money ပိုက်ဆံ *paiq-s'an*
money order ငွေတောင်းခံလွှာ/ငွေပို့လွှာ *Ngwe-taùn -k´an-hlwa/ngwe-pó-hlwa*
month လ (အချိန်) *lá (ăćein)*
monument အထိမ်းအမှတ်အဆောက်အအုံ *ăt´eìn-ăhmaq-ăs'auq-ăoun*
moon လ *lá*
mop *n* တံမြက်စည်း *dăbyeq-sì*
moped တံမြက်စည်းလှည်းခဲ့တယ် *dăbyeq-sì-hlèh-géh-deh*
more ပိုပြီး *po-pyì*
morning နံနက်ခင်း *nan-neq-k´ìn*
mosque ဗလီ *băli*
mosquito net ခြင်ထောင် *ćin-daun*
motel မိုတယ *mo-teh*
motorboat မော်တော်ဘုတ် *maw-taw-bouq*
motorcycle မော်တော်ဆိုင်ကယ် *maw-taw-s'ain-keh*
moustache နှုတ်ခမ်းမွေး *hnăk´àn-mwè*
mouth ပါးစပ် *băzaq*
mouthwash ခံတွင်းသန့်ဆေးရည် *gădwìn-thán-s'è-yi (ye)*
move *v* ရွှေ့လျား *ywé-lyà*
movie ရုပ်ရှင် *youq-shin*
Mr. မစ္စတာ *Miq-săta*
Mrs. မစ္စစ် *Miq-siq*
much ပိုများတာ *po-myà-da*
mug *n* မတ်ခွက် *maq-k´weq*
mugging လမ်းဓားပြ *làn-dămyá*
muscle ကြွက်သား *cweq-thà*
museum ပြတိုက် *Pyá-daiq*
music ဂီတ *gi-tá*
musical ဂီတနဲ့ဆိုင်တာ *gi-tá-néh-s'ain-da*

must (have to) လုပ်ရမယ် (ရမယ်) *louq-yá-meh (yá-meh)*

N

nail (body) လက်သည်းခြေသည်း(ကိုယ်ခန္ဓာအစိတ်အပိုင်း) *leq-thèh-će-dhèh- (ko-k´an-da-ăseiq-ăpăin)*
nail clippers လက်သည်းညှပ်တဲ့ကိရိယာတွေ *leq-thèh-hnyaq-téh-kăyí-ya-dwe*
nail file လက်သည်းတိုက်တဲ့တံစဉ်း *leq-thèh-taiq-téh-dăzìn*
nail salon လက်သည်းခြေသည်းအလှပြုပြင်ခန်း *leq-thèh-će-dhèh-ăhlà-pyú-pyin-gàn*
name အမည် *ămyi*
napkin လက်သုတ်ပုဝါ *leq-thouq-păwa*
nappy [BE] ကလေးအနှီး *k´ălè-ăhnì*
narrow ကျဉ်းမြောင်းတဲ့ *cìn-myaùn-dèh*
nationality နိုင်ငံသား *nain-gan-dhà*
natural သဘာဝဖြစ်တဲ့ *dhăba-wá-p´yiq-téh*
nausea အန်ချင်တာ *an-jin-da*
near နီးကပ်တာ *nì-kaq-ta*
nearby အနီးတဝိုက် *ănì-tăwaiq*
near-sighted အဝေးမှုန် *ăwè-hmoun*
neck လည်ပင်း *leh-bìn*
necklace လည်ဆွဲ *leh-zwèh*
need *v* လိုအပ် *lo-aq*
needle အပ် *aq*
nerve အာရုံကြော *a-youn-jàw*
never ဘယ်တော့မှ *beh-dáw-hmá*
new အသစ် *ăthiq*
newspaper သတင်းစာ *dhădìn-za*
next နောက်ထပ် *nauq-t´aq*
next to ကပ်နေတဲ့ *kaq-ne-déh*
nice (beautiful) ကောင်းမွန်တဲ့ (လှပတဲ့) *kaùn-mun-déh (hlá-pá-déh)*
night ညဖက် *nyá-beq*
no မဟုတ်/ မရှိ *măhouq/măshí*
noisy ဆူညံတယ် *s'u-nyan-deh*
none တစ်ခုမှမဟုတ် *tăk´ú-hmyá-măhouq*
non-smoking ဆေးလိပ်မသောက်ရတဲ့ *s'è-leiq-măthauq-yá-déh*
noon မွန်းတည့် *mùn-déh*
normal သာမန်/ပုံမှန်/ရိုးရိုး *tha-man/poun-hman/yò-yò*
north မြောက်ဖက် *myauq-p´eq*
nose နှခေါင်း *hnăk´aùn*
not မဟုတ်/ မရှိ *măhouq/măshí*
note (bank note) ငွေစက္ကူ (ဘဏ်ထုတ်စက္ကူ) *ngwe-seq-ku (ban-douq-seq-ku)*
notebook မှတ်စုစာအုပ် *hmaq-sú-sa-ouq*
nothing ဘာမှမဟုတ်/ ဘာမှမရှိ *ba-hmyá-măhouq/ba-hmyá-măshí*
notice (sign) သတိပေးစာ (ဆိုင်းဘုတ်) *dhădí-pè-sa (s'aín-bouq)*
notify သတိပေး *dhădí-pè*
novice လူသစ်/ ရှင်သာမဏေ *lu-dhiq/shin-tha-măne*
now အခု *ăk´ú/ăgú*
number နံပါတ် *nan-baq*
nurse သူနာပြု *thu-na-byú*

O

o'clock နာရီတိတိ *na-yi-tí-dí*
occupation အလုပ်အကိုင် *ălouq-ăkain*
occupied နှစ်မြုပ်/နေထိုင် *hniq-hmyouq/ne-t´ain*
office ရုံးခန်း *yoùn-gàn*
off-licence [BE] လိုင်စင်ပြင်ပမှလုပ်ကိုင် *lain-sin-pyin-pá-hmá-louq-kain*
oil ဆီ *s'i*
old အိုတာ/ ဟောင်းတာ *o-da/haún-da*
old town မြို့ဟောင်း *myó-haún*
on အပေါ်မှာ *ăpaw-hma*
on time အချိန်မှီ *ăćein-hmi*
once တစ်ကြိမ် *dăjein*
one-way ticket အသွားတစ်ကြောင်းလက်မှတ် *ăthwà-dăjaùn-leq-hmaq*
only သာလျှင် *dha-hlyin*
open *adj* ပွင့်လင်းတာ/ ပွင့်နေ *pwín-lín-da/pwín-ne; v*
opera အော်ပရာ *aw-păya*
operation ပြုလုပ်ပုံ/ ခွဲစိတ်မှု *pyú-louq-poun/k´wèh-seiq-hmú*
operator အော်ပရေတာ *aw-păye-ta*
opposite ဆန့်ကျင်ဖက် *s'án-cin-beq*
optician မျက်မှန်ပညာရှင် *myeq-hman-pyin-nya-shin*
or ဒါမှမဟုတ် *da-hmá-măhouq*
orange (color) လိမ္မော်ရောင် (အရောင်) *lein-maw-yaun (ăyaun)*
orchestra သံစုံတီးဝိုင်း *than-zoun-tì-waìn*
order *n* အမိန့် / အမိန့်ပေး/မှာကြား *ămeín/ămeín-pè/hma-cà ; v*
out of order အစီအစဉ်အတိုင်းမဟုတ် *ăsi-ăsin-ătaìn-măhouq*
out of stock ပစ္စည်းပြတ်နေတာ *pyiq-sì-pyaq-ne-da*
outlet (electric) လျှပ်စစ်ဓာတ်အားထွက်ပေါက် *hlyaq-siq-daq-à-t´weq-pauq*

outside အပြင်ဖက် *ăpyin-beq*

oval ဘဲဥပုံ *bèh-ú-poun*

overlook *n* မျက်စိသျှန်း/ကျော်ကြည့် *myeq-sí-shàn/caw-cí*

oxygen treatment အောက်စီဂျင်ပေးပြီးကုသမှု *auq-si-jin-pè-pyì-kú-thá-hmú*

P

pacifier (baby's) နို့သီးခေါင်း/ချိုလိမ် (ကလေး၏) *nó-dhí-gaùn/ćo-lein (K´ălè-í-)*

packet အထုတ် *ăt´ouq*

pad (sanitary) အမျိုးသမီးလစဉ်သုံးပစ္စည်း(သန့်ရှင်းရေးပစ္စည်း) *ămyò-thămì-lá-zin-thoù-pyiq-sì-(thán-shìn-yè-pyiq-sì)*

pail ပုံး *poùn*

pain နာကျင်တယ်/နာကျင်မှု *na-cin-dah/na-cin-hmú*

painkiller အကိုက်အခဲပျောက်ဆေး/အနာပျောက်ဆေး *ăkaiq-ăk´èh-pyauq-s'è/ăna-pyauq-s'è*

paint *n* သုတ်ဆေး/ ဆေးသုတ်တယ် *thouq-s'è/s'è-thouq-teh ; v*

painting ဆေးသုတ်ခြင်း/သုတ်ဆေး *s'è-thouq-ĉìn/thouq-s'è*

pair အစုံ *ăsoun*

pajamas ညအိပ်ဝတ်စုံ *nyá-eiq-wuq-soun*

palace နန်းတော် *nàn-daw*

palpitations နှလုံးခုန်မြန်တာ *hnăloùn-k´oun-myan-da*

pants ဘောင်းဘီ *baùn-bi*

panty hose ခြေအိတ်ဘောင်းဘီရှည် *će-eiq-baùn-bi-she*

paper စက္ကူ/ စာရွက် *seq-ku/sa-yweq*

paper towel စက္ကူလက်သုတ်ပုဝါ *seq-ku-leq-thouq-păwa*

parcel [BE] ပါဆယ်ထုပ် *pa-s'eh-douq*

parents မိဘတွေ *mí-bá-dwe*

park *n* ပန်းခြံ။ကားရပ် *pàn-jan/kà-yaq ; v*

parking ကားရပ်တဲ့နေရာ *kà-yaq-tèh-ne-ya*

parking disc ကားရပ်တဲ့ အချပ်ဝိုင်း *kà-yaq-tèh-ăćaq-waìn*

parking garage ကားရပ်တဲ့ ဂိုဒေါင် *kà-yaq-tèh-go-daun*

parking lot ကားရပ်တဲ့ နေရာကျယ် *kà-yaq-tèh-ne-ya-ceh*

parking meter ကားရက်ချိန်မှတ်တဲ့မီတာ *kà-yaq-ćein-hmaq-téh-mi-ta*

part အစိတ်အပိုင်း *ăseiq-ăpaín*

part-time အချိန်ပိုင်း *ăćein-baìn*

party (social gathering) ပါတီ(လူမှုရေးဆိုင်ရာစုဝေးမှု) *pa-ti (lu-hmú-yè-s'ain-ya-sú-wè-hmú)*

passport နိုင်ငံကူးလက်မှတ် *nain-gan-gù-leq-hmaq*

passport control နိုင်ငံကူးလက်မှတ်ထိန်းချုပ်သည့်နေရာ *nain-gan-gù-leq-hmaq-t´eìn-ćouq-thí-ne-ya*

passport photo နိုင်ငံကူးလက်မှတ်ဓာတ်ပုံ/ပတ်စ်ပို့ဓာတ်ပုံ *nain-gan-gù-leq-hmaq-daq-poun/paq-săpó-daq-poun*

paste (glue) ကော်စေး (ကော်) *kaw-sè/sì (kaw)*

pastry shop ပေစထရီမုန့်ဆိုင် *pe-săt´ăyi-moún-zain*

patch ဖာထေးတဲ့အရာ *p´a-t´è-déh-ăya*

path လမ်းကြောင်း *làn-jaùn*

patient လူနာ *lu-na*

pattern နမူနာပုံစံ/ပုံစံ *nămu-na-poun-zan/poun-zan*

pay ပေး/ ငွေချေ *pè/ngwe-će*

payment ငွေပေးချေမှု *ngwe-pè-će-hmú*

peak n (mountain) ထိပ်ဖျား (တောင်) *t´eiq-p'yà (taun)*

pearl ပုလဲ *pălèh*

pedestrian လမ်းလျှောက်သွားသူ *làn-shauq-thwà-dhu*

pediatrician ကလေးအထူးကုဆရာဝန် *k´ălè-ăt'ù-kú-s'ăya-wun*

pedicure ခြေသည်းအလှပြုပြင်မှု *će-dhèh-ăhlá-pyú-pyin-hmú*

peg (tent) သစ်သားအထောက် (ရွက်ဖျင်တဲ) *thiq-thà-ăt´aunq (yweq-p´yin-dèh)*

pen ဘောပင် *bàw-pin*

pencil ခဲတံ *k´èh-dan*

pendant လော့ကက်သီး *láw-keq-thì*

penicillin ပင်နယ်ဆလင် *pin-ni-s'ălin*

per day တစ်နေ့လျှင် *tăné-hlyin*

per hour တစ်နာရီလျှင် *tăna-yi-hlyin*

per person လူတစ်ယောက်လျှင် *lu-tăyauq-hlyin*

per week တစ်ပတ်လျှင် *dăbaq-hlyin*

percentage ရာခိုင်နှုန်း *ya-gain-hnoùn*

perfume ရေမွှေး *ye-hmwè*

perhaps ဖြစ်တန်ရာ *p´yiq-tan-ya*

period (monthly) ရာသီ (လစဉ်) *ya-dhi (lá-zin)*

permit *n* **(fishing)** ခွင့်ပြုချက် (ငါးမျှားရန်)/(အမဲလိုက်ရန်) *k´wín-pyú-jeq (ngà-hmyà-yan)/(ămèh-laiq-yan);* **(hunting)**

person လူ *lu*

personal တစ်ဦးတစ်ယောက်ချင်းဆိုင်ရာ *tăù-*

tăyauq-ĉn-s'ain-ya
petite သေးသွယ်တယ် *thè-thweh-deh*
petrol [BE] ဓာတ်ဆီ *daq-s'i*
pewter ခဲနဲ့သံဖြူရောစပ်ထားတဲ့သတ္တု *k´èh-néh-than-p´yu-yàw-saq-t´à-déh-thaq-tú*
pharmacy ဆေးဆိုင် *s'è-zain*
phone card ဖုန်းကတ် *p´oùn-kaq*
photo ဓာတ်ပုံ *daq-poun*
photocopy *n* မိတ္တူ *meiq-tu*
photograph *n* ဓာတ်ပုံ/ ဓာတ်ပုံရိုက် *daq-poun/ daq-poun-yaiq*
photography ဓာတ်ပုံရိုက်ကူးမှု *daq-poun-yaiq-kù-hmú*
phrase စာပိုဒ် *sa-baiq*
pick up *v* **(go get)** သွားယူ (သွားပြီးယူ) *thawà-yu (thwà-pyì-yu)*
picnic ပျော်ပွဲစား *pyaw-bwè-zà*
picnic basket ပျော်ပွဲစားထွက်တဲ့အခါ သုံးတဲ့ခြင်း *pyaw-bwè-zà-t´weq-téh-ăk´a-thoùn-déh-ĉn*
piece အပိုင်းအစ *ăpaìn-asá*
pill ဆေးလုံး *s'è-loùn*
pillow ခေါင်းအုံး *gaùn-oùn*
PIN လျှို့ဝှက်နံပါတ် *shó-hweq-nan-baq*
pin n (brooch) ပင်အပ် (ရင်ထိုးမှ) *pin-aq (yin-dò-hmá)*
pink ပန်းရောင် *pán-yaun*
pipe ပိုက် *paiq*
place *n* နေရာ *ne-ya*
plane fly လေယာဉ်ပျံ *le-yin-byan*
plaster [BE] (bandage) ပလာစတာ (ပတ်တီး) *păla-sătą (paq-tì)*
plastic ပလပ်စတစ် *pălaq-sătiq*
plastic bag ပလပ်စတစ်အိတ် *pălaq-sătiq-eiq*
plastic wrap ပလပ်စတစ်အပတ် *pălaq-sătiq-ăpaq*
plate ပန်းကန်ပြား *băgan-byà*
platform [BE] (station) ပလက်ဖောင်း (ဘူတာရုံ) *păleq-p´aùn (bu-ta-youn)*
platinum ပလက်တီနမ် *păleq-ti-nan*
play *n* **(theatre)** သရုပ်ဆောင် (ဇာတ်ရုံ)၊ သရုပ်ဆောင်/ကစား *thăyouq-s'aun (zaq-youn)/ thăyouq-s'aun/găzà* ; *v*
playground ကစားကွင်း *găzà-gwìn*
playpen ကလေးငယ်များကစားရန်နေရာ *k´ălè-ngeh-myà-găzà-yan-ne-ya*
please ကျေးနပ်/ ကျေးဇူးပြုပြီး *ce-naq/cè-zù-pyú-pyì*
plug (electric) လျှပ်စစ်မီးခေါင်း *hlyaq-siq-mì-gaùn*
plunger စုပ်ခွက် *souq-k'weq*
pneumonia နျူမိုးနီးယား/ အဆုတ်အအေးပတ်ခြင်း *năyu-mò-nì-yà/ăs'ouq-ăè-paq-ĉn*
pocket အိတ်ထောင် *eiq-t´aun*
point of interest စိတ်ဝင်စားမှုဖြစ်စေတဲ့နေရာ *seiq-win-zá-hmú-p´yiq-se-d´eh-ne-ya*
point *v* ပွိုင့်/ အမှတ် *pwaín/ăhmaq*
poison အဆိပ် *ăs´eiq*
poisoning အဆိပ်သင့်ခြင်း *ăs´eiq-thín-jìn*
pole (ski) လက်ကိုင်တံ (စကိတ်စီးရာတွင်သုံး)၊ အလည်တိုင် (ရွက်ဖျင်တဲ) *leq-kain-dan (săkeiq-sì-ya-dwin-thoùn) ăleh-dain (yweq-p´yin-dèh)* **; (tent)**
police ရဲ *yèh*
police report ရဲအစီရင်ခံစာ *yèh-ăsi-yin-k´an-za*
police station ရဲစခန်း *yèh-săk´àn*
pond ရေအိုင် *ye-ain*
pool ရေကူးကန် *ye-kù-gan*
porcelain ကြွေထည် *cwe-deh*
port ဆိပ်ကမ်း *s'eiq-kàn*
portable အလွယ်တကူသယ်ယူသွားနိုင်တာ *ălweh-dăgu-theh-yu-thwà-nain-da*
porter ပေါ်တာ/ အထုတ်အပိုးသယ်သူ *paw-ta/ ăt´ouq—ăpò-theh-dhu*
portion အစိတ်အပိုင်း/ ဝေစု *ăseiq-ăpaìn/we-zú*
post [BE] *n* တာဝန်ကျရာနေရာ၊ စာပို့တယ် *ta-wun-cá-ya-ne-ya/sa-pó-deh* ; *v*
post office စာတိုက် *sa-daiq*
postage တံဆိပ်ခေါင်း *dăzeiq-gaùn*
postage stamp စာပို့တံဆိပ်ခေါင်း *sa-pó-dăzeiq-gaùn*
postcard ပို့စ်ကတ် *pó-săkaq*
pot အိုး *ò*
pottery မြေအိုး *mye-ò*
pound (British currency, weight) ပေါင် (ဗြိတိန်နိုင်ငံသုံးငွေကြေး၊ အလေးချိန်) *paun (byí-tein-nain-gan) dhoùn-ngwe-cè/ălè-jein)*
powder ပေါင်ဒါမှုန့် *paun-da-hmoún*
pregnant ကိုယ်ဝန်ရှိတာ *ko-wun-shí-da*
premium (gas/ petrol) အာမခံ/ ပရီမီယမ် (ဓာတ်ငွေ့၊ ဓာတ်ဆီ) *a-má-gan/păyi-mi-yan (daq-ngwé/daq-si)*
prescribe ဆေးညွှန်းတယ် *s'è-hnyùn-deh*
prescription ဆေးအညွှန်း *s'è-ăhnùn*
present *n* လက်ဆောင် *leq-s'aun*
press (iron) မီးပူ *mì-bu*
pressure ဖိအား *p´í-à*

pretty လှပချောမောတယ် *hlá-pá-c´áw-màw-deh*
price ဈေးနှုန်း *zè-hnoùn*
price-fixed menu ဈေးနှုန်းအတိအကျသတ်မှတ်ထားတဲ့ ပစ္စည်းစာရင်း *zè-hnoùn-ătí-ăcà-thaq-hmaq-t´à-déh-pyiq-sì-săyìn*
print *n* **(photo)** ပုံနှိပ် (ဓာတ်ပုံ)/ ပုံနှိပ်တယ် (စာရွက်စာတမ်း) *poun-hneiq (daq-poun)/poun-hneiq-teh (sa-yweq-sa-dàn); v* **(document)**
private သီးသန့်ဖြစ်သော *thì-thán-p´yiq-thàw*
profit *n* အမြတ်ငွေ *ămyaq-ngwe*
program (of events) ပရိုဂရမ်/အစီအစဉ် (အခမ်းအနားပွဲများ၏) *păyo-găyan/ăsi-ăsin (ăk´àn-ănà-bwèh-myà-í)*
pronounce *v* ထင်ရှားသိသာ *t´in-shà-thí-tha*
pronunciation *n* အသံထွက *ăthan-dweq*
provide အထောက်အပံ့ပေး *ăt'auq-ăpán-pè*
pull *v* ဆွဲတယ် *s'wè-deh*
pump စုပ်ထုတ *souq-t´ouq*
puncture ဖောက် *p´auq*
purchase *n* ဝယ်ယူမှု၊ ဝယ်ယ *weh-yu-hmú/weh-yu ;v*
pure စစ်မှန်တဲ့ *siq-hman-déh*
purple ခရမ်းရောင် *K´ăyán-yaun*
purse (handbag) ပိုက်ဆံအိတ် (လက်ကိုင်အိတ်) *paiq-s'an-eiq (leq-kain-eiq)*
push *v* တွန်း *tùn*
pushchair [BE] လက်တွန်းထိုင်ခုံ *leq-tù-t´ain-goun*
put ထား *t´à*

Q

quality အရည်အသွေး *ăyi-ăthwè*
quantity အရေအတွက် *ăye-ătweq*
question *n* မေးခွန်း *mè-gùn*
quick မြန်ဆန်တာ *myan-s'an-da*
quiet ငြိမ်သက်တာ *nyein-theq-ta*

R

race ပြိုင်ပ *pyain-bwéh*
race track ပြိုင်ပွဲလမ်းကြောင်း *pyain-bwéh-làn-jaùn*
racket (sport) တင်းနစ်/ ကြက်တောင်ရိုက်တဲ့ ရက်ကက် (အားကစားနဲ့ဆိုင်တာ) *ti`n-niq/ceq-taun-yaiq-téh-yeq-keq-cà-găzà-néh-s'ain-da*
radio ရေဒီယို *ye-di-yo*
railway station [BE] ရထားဘူတာရုံ *Yăt´à-bu-ta-youn*
rain မိုး *mò*
raincoat မိုးကာအင်္ကျီ *mò-ga-ìn-ji*
rape *n* အလိုမတူပဲ မတရား/မုဒိမ်းပြုကျင့်ခြင်း *ălo-mătu-béh-mătăyà-mădein pyù-cín-jìn*
rash အရေပြားနီနေတာ *ăye-byà-ni-ne-da*
rate *n* **(exchange)** နှုန်း (လဲလှယ်နှုန်း)၊ (ငွေကြေးတန်ဖိုး) *hnoùn (léh-hleh-hnoùn);* **(price)**
razor မုတ်ဆိတ်ရိတ်ဓါး *mouq-s'eiq-yeiq-tan*
razor blade မုတ်ဆိတ်ရိတ်တဲ့ဓား *mouq-s'eiq-yeiq-téh-dà*
ready အဆင်သင့်ဖြစ်တဲ့ *ăs'in-dhín-p´yiq-téh*
real (genuine) စစ်မှန်တယ် (မှန်ကန်တဲ့) *siq-hman-deh (hman-kan-déh)*
rear အနောက်ပိုင်း *ănouq-paín*
receipt ငွေလက်ခံဖြတ်ပိုင်း *ngwe-leq-k´an-p´yaq-pain*
reception ဧည့်ခံပွဲ/ဧည့်ခံကြိုဆိုတဲ့နေရာ *éh-kan-bwéh/éh-k´an-co-zo-déh-ne-ya*
receptionist ဧည့်ကြို *éh-jo*
recommend တိုက်တွန်း *taiq-tùn*
rectangular ထောင့်မှန်စတုဂံ *daún-hman-sătú-gan*
red အနီရောင် *ăni-yaun*
reduction လျှော့ချ *Shán-cá*
refrigerator ရေခဲသေတ္တာ *ye-géh-thiq-ta*
refund *v* ပြန်အမ်း *pyan-àn*
regards ဆက်စပ်ပြီး *s'eq-saq-pyí*
region နေရာဒေသ *ne-ya-de-thá*
registered mail မှတ်ပုံတင်စာ *hmaq-poun-tin-sa*
registration မှတ်ပုံတင်ခြင်း *hmaq-poun-tin-jìn*
regular (gas / petrol) ပုံမှန် (ဓာတ်ငွေ့/ဓာတ်ဆီ) *poun-hman (daq-ngwé/daq-s'i)*
relationship ဆက်စပ်မှု *s'eq-saq-hmú*
reliable ယုံကြည်စရာကောင်းတာ *youn-ci-săya-kaùn-da*
religion ဘာသာတရား *ba-dha-tăyà*
rent *v* ငှားရမ်းတယ် *hngà-yàn-deh*
rental ငှားရမ်းတဲ့ *hngà-yàn-déh*
rental car အငှားကား *ăhngà-kà*
repair *n* ပြုပြင်မှု/ ပြုပြင် *pyù-pyin-hmú/pyú-pyin; v*
repeat *v* ထပ်လုပ်/ပြန်လုပ် *t´aq-louq/pyan-louq*
report (theft) အစီရင်ခံတယ် (ခိုးယူမှု) *ăsi-yni-k´an-deh (k´ò-yu-hmú)*
request *n* ခွင့်တောင်းမှု/ ခွင့်တောင်း *k´wín-taún-hmú/k´wín-taún; v*
required လိုအပ်တယ် *lo-aq-the*
requirement လိုအပ်ချက် *lo-aq-ćeq*
reservation ကြိုတင်နေရာယူထားမှု *co-tin-ne-ya-yu-t´à-hmú*

reservations office ကြိုတင်နေရာယူရန်ရုံး *co-tin-ne-ya-yu-yan-yoùn*
reserve ဖယ်ထား *p´eh-t´à*
reserved ဖယ်ထားတာ *p´eh-t´à-da*
rest *n* အနားယူ *ăna-yu*
restaurant စားသောက်ဆိုင် *sà-thauq-s'ain*
restroom အနားယူဖို့နေရာ/အိမ်သာ *ănà-yu-bó-ne-ya/ein-dha*
retired ပင်စင်ယူခဲ့တယ်/ပင်စင်ယူထားတဲ့ *pin-sin-yu-géh-deh/pin-sin-yu-t´à-déh*
return (come back); (give back) ပြန်လာ၊ ပြန်ပေး *pyan-la/pyan-pé*
return ticket [BE] အပြန်လက်မှတ် *ăpyan-leq-hmaq*
rib နံရိုး *nan-yó*
ribbon ဖဲကြိုး *p´éh-jò*
right (correct) အမှန်(ပြင်ဆင်)/ ညာဖက် (ဦးတည်ရာ) *ăhman (pyin-s'in)/nya-beq (ù-ti-ya)*; **(direction)**
ring (jewelry); (bell) လက်စွပ် (လက်ဝတ်ရတနာ)၊ ခေါင်းလောင်းထိုး *leq-suq (leq-wuq-yădăna), k´aùn-laùn-t´ò*
river မြစ် *myiq*
road လမ်းမ *làn-má*
road assistance လမ်းအကူ *làn-ăku*
road map လမ်းမြေပုံ *làn-mye-boun*
road sign လမ်းကြောင်းပြဆိုင်းဘုတ် *làn-jaùn-byá-s'aìn-bouq*
robbery ဓားပြတိုက်မှု *dămyá-taiq-hmú*
romantic စိတ်ကူးယဉ်တဲ့/ ရင်ခုန်စရာကောင်းတဲ့ *seiq-kù-yin-déh/yin-k´oun-săya-kaùn-déh*
room (hotel); (space) အခန်း (ဟိုတယ်ခန်း)/ (နေရာ) *ăk´àn (ho-the-gàn)/(ne-ya)*
room number အခန်းနံပါတ် *ăkan-nan-baq*
room service အခန်းတွင်းဝန်ဆောင်မှု *ăkan-dwìn-wun-s'aun-hmú*
room temperature အခန်းအပူချိန် *ăkan-ăpu-jein*
rope ကြိုး *cò*
round လုံးဝန်းတာ *loùn-wùn-da*
round (golf) အပတ် (ဂေါက်သီးရိုက်သောအပတ်) *ăpaq (gauq-thì-yaiq-thàw-ăpaq)*
round-trip ticket အသွား–အပြန်လက်မှတ် *ăthwà-ăpyan-leq-hmaq*
route လမ်းကြောင်း *làn-jaùn*
rowboat လှော်သောလှေ *hlaw-dhăw-hle*
rubber (material) ရာဘာ *ya-ba*
rubbish [BE] အမှိုက်သရိုက် *ăhmaiq-thăyaiq*
ruby ပတ္တမြား *bădămyà*

S

safe n (vault) မီးခံသေတ္တာ၊ လုံခြုံတဲ့ *mì-gan-thaq-loun-joun-déh*
; (not in danger)
safety pin လုံခြုံရေးတွယ်အပ် *loun-joun-yé-tweh-aq*
safari park ဆာဖာရီပန်းခြံ *s'a-p´a-yi-pàn-jan*
sailboat ရွက်လှေ *yweq-hle*
sale *n* ရောင်းချတာ၊ ဈေးလျှော့ပေးမှု *yaùn-ćá-da/zé-sháw-pé-hmú*; **(bargains)**
same အတူတူ/ တူညီတာ *sătu-tu/tu-nyi-da*
sand သဲ *théh*
sandal ကွင်းထိုးဖိနပ် *gwín-dó-p´ănaq*
sanitary napkin သန့်ရှင်းရေးပဝါ (အမျိုးသမီးလစဉ်သုံးပစ္စည်း) *than-shìn-yé-pàwa (ămyò-thămì-lá-zin-thoùn-pyiq-sì)*
sapphire မြ *myá*
sarong လုံချည်/ ထဘီ *loun-ji/t´ămein*
satin ဖဲ *p´é*
saucepan လက်ကိုင်ပါတဲ့ ဒယ်အိုးသေး *leq-kain-pa-déh-deh-ò-dhé*
saucer ခွက်တင်ပန်းကန်ပြားသေး *keh-tin-deh*
sauna ချွေးထုတ်ခန်း *ćwè-t´ouq-k´àn*
save *v* ကယ်တင်တယ် *keh-tin-deh*
savings account ငွေစုစာရင်း *ngwe-sú-săyìn*
scarf လည်စည်း *leh-zì*
scenery မြင်ကွင်း/ ရှုခင်း *myin-gwin/shú-gìn*
scenic route မြင်ကွင်း/ ရှုခင်းကောင်းတဲ့လမ်းကြောင်း *myin-gwin/shú-gìn-kaùn-déh-làn-jaùn*
school ကျောင်း *caùn*
scissors ကပ်ကြေး *kaq-cé*
scooter စကူတာ *săku-ta*
Scotland စကော့တလန်နိုင်ငံ *Săkáw-tălan-nain-gan*
screwdriver ဝက်အူလှည့် *weq-u-hléh*
sculpture ပန်းပု *băbú*
sea ပင်လယ် *pin-leh*
season ရာသီ *ya-dhi*
seat ထိုင်ခုံ *t´ain-goun*
seat belt ထိုင်ခုံခါးပတ် *t´ain-goun-găbaq*
second ဒုတိယ *dú-tí-yá*
second class ဒုတိယတန်း *dú-tăyá-dàn*
second-hand shop အဟောင်းပစ္စည်းဆိုင် *ăhaùn-pyiq-sì-zain*
section အခန်းကဏ္ဍ/ ဌာနစိတ် *ăk´àn-kan-dá/t´a-ná-zeiq*
see မြင် *myin*

sell ရောင်း *yau`n*
send ပို့ *pó*
senior citizen အသက်အရွယ်ကြီးသူ *ätheq-äyweh-cì-dhu*
sentence ဝါကျ/ ထောင်ချ *weq-cá/t´aun-ćá*
separated (relationship) ကွဲတယ် (လင်မယားဆက်ဆံရေး) *kwéh-deh (lin-măyà-s'eq-s'an-yé*
serious လေးနက်တာ/ပြင်းထန်တာ *lé-neq-ta/pyìn-t´an-da*
serve (meal) တည်ခင်း (အစားအစာ) *the-k´ìn (ăsà-ăsa)*
service (restaurant) ဝန်ဆောင်မှု (စားသောက်ဆိုင်) *wun-s'aun-hmù (sà-thauq-s'ain)*
set menu ကြိုတင်စီစဉ်တွဲထားတဲ့အစားအသောက်စာရင်း *co-tin-si-sin-twéh-t´à-déh-ăsà-ăthauq-săyìn*
sew ချုပ်လုပ် *ćouq-louq*
shampoo ခေါင်းလျှော်ရည် *gaùn-shaw-ye*
shape ပုံသဏ္ဍာန်/ အသွင်အပြင် *poun-dhădan/ăthwin-ăpyin*
sharp (pain) စူးရှတဲ့ (နာကျင်မှု) *sù-shà-déh (na-cin-hmú)*
shave *n* (အမွေးအမှင်)ရိတ်ခြင်း *(ămwé-ăhmyin) yeiq-ćin*
shaving brush အမွေးရိတ်ဘီး *ămwé-yeiq-bì*
shaving cream အမွေးရိတ်သုံးတဲ့ကရင်မ် *ămwé-yeiq-thoùn-déh-kăyin-m*
shelf စင် *sin*
ship *n* သင်္ဘော/ တင်ပို့တယ် *thin-bàw/tin-pó-deh: v*
shirt ရှပ်အင်္ကျီ *shaq-in-ji*
shoe ရှူးဖိနပ် *shù-p´ănaq*
shoe store ရှူးဖိနပ်အရောင်းဆိုင် *shù-p´ănaq-äyaùn-zain*
shop *n* ဈေးဆိုင် *zé-zain*
shopping ဈေးဝယ်ခြင်း *zé-weh-jìn*
shopping area ဈေးဝယ်နိုင်တဲ့ ဧရိယာ *zé-weh-nain-déh-e-yí-ya*
shopping centre [BE] ဈေးဝယ်စင်တာ *zé-weh-sin-ta*
shopping mall ဈေးဝယ်နိုင်တဲ့အဆောက်အအုံ/ မောလ် *zé-weh-nain-déh-ăs'auq-ăoun/măw-l*
short တိုတယ် *to-teh*
shorts ဘောင်းဘီတို *baùn-bi-do*
short-sighted [BE] အဝေးမှုန် *äwèh-hmoun*
shoulder ပုခုံး *păk´oùn*
shovel *n* ဂေါ်ပြား *gaw-byà*
show *n* ပြပွဲ၊ ပြသ *pyá-bwéh/pyá-thá; v*
shower (stall) ရေပန်းနဲ့ရေချိုးခန်း (အခန်း) *ye-bàn-néh-ye-ćò-gàn (ăk´àn)*
shrine ပုထိုး/စေတီ/ဘုရားစင် *pă-t´ò/ze-di/p´äyà-zin*
shut ပိတ် *peiq*
shutter (window) တရုတ်ကပ် (တံခါး) *tăyouq-kaq (dăgà)*
side ဖက်/ ဘေးဖက *beq/bè-beq*
sightseeing လှည့်လည်ကြည့်ရှုခြင်း *hléh-leh-cí-shú-jìn*
sightseeing tour လှည့်လည်ကြည့်ရှုတဲ့ခရီးစဉ် *hléh-leh-cí-shú-déh-k´äyì-zin*
sign ဆိုင်းဘုတ်/ လက္ခဏာ/ ဆိုင်းထိုး လက်မှတ်ထိုး *s'aìn-bouq/leq-k´ăna/s'aìn-t´ò/leq-hmaq-t´ò*
sign (notice) *v* ဆိုင်းဘုတ် (သတိပေးချက်) *s'aìn-bouq (dhădí-pè-jeq)*
signature ဆိုင်း/ လက်မှတ် *s'aìn/leq-hmaq*
silk ပိုးစ *pò-zá*
silver ငွေ **ngwe**
silverware ငွေထည်ပစ္စည်း *ngwe-deh-pyiq-sì*
since ကတည်းက *gădà-gá*
sing သီချင်းဆို *thăcîn-s'o*
single *n* **(ticket); (unmarried** တစ်ကြောင်း (လက်မှတ်)၊ တစ်ကိုယ်တည်း (လက်ထပ်မထားသူ) *dăjaùn (leq-hmaq)/dăgo-déh (leq-t´aq-măt´à-dhu)*
single room တစ်ယောက်စာအခန်း *tăyauq-sa-ăk'àn*
size; (clothes); (shoes) အရွယ်အစား/ ဆိုက်ဇ် (အဝတ်အစား) ၊ (ရှူးဖိနပ်) *äyweh-ăsà/s'aiq-z (ăwuq-ăsà) (shù-p´ănaq)*
skin အရေပြား *äye-byà*
skirt စကပ် *săkaq*
sky ကောင်းကင် *kaùn-kin*
sleep *v* အိပ် *eiq*
sleeping bag အိပ်ရာလိပ *eiq-ya-leiq*
sleeping car အိပ်ခန်းပါတဲ့ကား *eiq-k´àn-pa-déh-kà*
sleeping pill အိပ်ဆေး *eiq-s'è*
sleeve အင်္ကျီလက *f`in-ji-leq*
slice *n* အချပ်/ အလွှာ *ăcaq/ăhlwa*
slide (photo) အချပ် (ဓာတ်ပုံ) *ăcaq (daq-poun)*
slipper ဖိနပ်ပြား/ ခြေညှပ်ဖိနပ *p´ănaq-pyà/će-hmyaq-p´nănaq*
slow နှေးကွေးတယ် *hné-kwe`-deh*
small သေးငယ်တယ် *thé-ngeh-deh*
smoke မီးခိုး/ ဆေးလိပ်သောက် *mì-gò/s'è-leiq-thauq*
smoker ဆေးလိပ်သောက်သူ *s'è-leiq-thauq-thu*
snack သွားရည်စာ *thăye-za*
snack bar စနက်ဘား *săneq-bà*

sneaker အားကစားဖိနပ် *ă-găzà-p´ănaq*
snorkeling equipment ရေငုပ်တဲ့အခါ သုံးတဲ့ ကိရိယာတန်ဆာပလာ *ye-ngouq-téh-ăk´a-thoùn-déh-kăyí-ya-dăza-băla*
snow နှင်း *hnìn*
soap ဆပ်ပြာ *s'aq-pya*
soccer ဘောလုံးကန်ကစားခြင်း *bàw-loùn-kan-găzà-jìn*
soccer match ဘောလုံးကစားပြိုင်ပွဲ *bàw-loùn-găzà-pyain-bwéh*
sock ခြေအိတ် *će-eiq*
socket (electric) လျှပ်စစ်ပလပ်ခေါင်း *hlyaq-siq-pălaq-gaùn*
soft နူးညံ့တယ် *nù-nyán-deh*
sold out ရောင်းကုန်သွား *yaùn-koun-thwà*
someone တစ်စုံတစ်ယောက် *dăzoun-tăyauq*
something တစ်စုံတစ်ရာ *dăzoun-tăya*
song သီချင်း *thăĉin*
soon မကြာမီ *măca-mi*
sore (painful) အနာ (နာကျင်တာ) *ăna (na-cin-da)*
sore throat လည်ချောင်းနာခြင်း *leh-jaùn-na-jìn*
sorry ဝမ်းနည်းပါတယ် *wàn-néh-ba-deh*
sort (kind) အမျိုးအစား *ămyò-ăsà*
south တောင်ဖက် *taun-beq*
souvenir အမှတ်တရပစ္စည်း *ăhmaq-tăyá-pyiq-sì*
souvenir shop အမှတ်တရပစ္စည်းအရောင်းဆိုင် *ăhmaq-tăyá-pyiq-sì-ăyaùn-zain*
spa စပါ/ရေပူစမ်း *spa/ye-bu-sàn*
spatula ဆေးများရောနှောရာတွင်အသုံးပြုသည့်အတံ/ ကော်သည့်အတံ *s'é-myà-yàw-hnàw-ya-dwin-ăthoùn-pyú-dhí-ătan/kaw-dhí-ătan*
speak *v* စကားပြော *zăgà-pyàw*
special အထူး *ăt´ù*
specialist အထူးကု/ အထူးကျွမ်းကျင်သူ *ăt´ù-gú/ ăt´ù-cw-cin-dhu*
speciality အထူးပြုဌာန *ăt´ù-pyú-t´a-ná*
spell *v* စာလုံးပေါင်း *sa-loùn-paùn*
spend ကုန်ဆုံးစေ *koun-s'oùn-ze*
spine ကျောရိုး *càw-yò*
sponge ရေမြှုပ် *ye-hmyouq*
spoon ဇွန်း *zùn*
sport အားကစား *ă-găzà*
sporting goods store အားကစားပစ္စည်းအရောင်းဆိုင် *ă-găzà-pyiq-sì-ăyaùn-zain*
sprained အဆစ်လွဲဒဏ်ရာရခဲ့ *ăs'iq-dan-ya-yá-géh*
square (shape) စတုရန်း (ပုံသဏ္ဍာန်) *sătú-yàn (poun-dhădan)*
stadium အားကစားရုံ *ă-găzà-youn*
staff ဝန်ထမ်း *wun-dàn*
stain ဆေးစွန်းတယ် *s'é-sùn-deh*
stainless steel အစွန်းအပြောက်မထင်တဲ့စတီး *ăsùn-ăpyauq-măt´in-déh-sătì*
stairs လှေကားထစ်တွေ *hle-gădiq-twe*
stamp *n* **(postage)** တံဆိပ်ခေါင်း (စာပို့တံဆိပ်ခေါင်း)/ တုံးထု (လက်မှတ်) *dăzeiq-gaùn (da-pó-dăzeiq-gaùn)/toùn-t´ú (leq-hmaq)*; *v* **(ticket)**
staple ချုပ်စက် *ćouq-seq*
star ကြယ် *ceh*
start စတင် *sá-tin*
starter [BE] (meal) ပထမဆုံးစတင်တည်ခင်းတဲ့အရာ (အစာ) *păt´ămá-zoùn-sá-tin-the-k´ìn-déh-ăya (ăsa)*
station (train) ဘူတာရုံ (ရထား)/ (မြေအောက်ရထား) *bu-ta-youn (yăt´à)/(mye-aunq-yăt´à)*; **(subway)**
stationery store စက္ကူနှင့်စာရေးကိရိယာပစ္စည်း အရောင်းဆိုင် *seq-ku-hnín-sa-yè-kăyí-ya-pyiq-sì-ăyaùn-zain*
stay (trip) ခေတ္တနေ (ခရီးစဉ်အတွင်း)/ တည်းရှိနေ၊ နေထိုင် *k´iq-tá-ne (k´ăyì-zin-ătwìn)/ti-shí-ne/ ne/-t´ain*; *v* **(remain)**; *v* **(reside)**
steal ခိုးယူ *k´ó-yu*
sterling silver စတာလင်ငွေထည် *săta-lin-ngwe-deh*
sting *n* ပျားဆိပ်၊ ပျားတုပ် *pyà-s'eiq/pyà-touq*; *v*
stockings ခြေအိတ်ရှည် *će-eiq-she*
stomach အစာအိမ် *ăsa-ein*
stomachache ဗိုက်အောင့်ခြင်း *baiq-aún-jìn*
stop (bus) မှတ်တိုင် (ဘတ်စ်ကား)၊ ရပ်တန့် *hmaq-tain (baq-săkà)/yaq-tán*; *v* **stop**
store (shop) စတိုးဆိုင်/အရောင်းဆိုင် *sătò-zain/ ăyaùn-zain*
stove မီးဖို *mì-bo*
straight ahead တည့်တည့်သွား *téh-déh-thwà*
strange ထူးဆန်းတယ် *t´ù-s'àn-deh*
street လမ်းသွယ် *làn-dhweh*
street map လမ်းမြေပုံ *làn-mye-boun*
string ကြိုး *cò*
stroller လက်တွန်းလှည်း *leq-tùn-hlè*
strong သန်မာတာ/သန်စွမ်းတာ *than-ma-da/than zwàn-da*
student ကျောင်းသား *caùn-dhà*
study *v* သင်ယူလေ့လာ *thin-yu-lé-la*
stunning အံ့အားသင့်စေ *án-à-thín-ze*
sturdy သန်မာကြံ့ခိုင်တဲ့ *than-ma-cán-k´ain-déh*
suit (man's) ဝတ်စုံ (အမျိုးသား)/ (အမျိုးသမီး) *wuq-soun (ămyò-thà) (ămyò-thămì)*; **(woman's)**

suitcase ခရီးဆောင်အိတ် *k'ăyì-zaun-eiq*
sun နေ *ne*
sunburn နေလောင်ခြင်း *ne-loun-jìn*
sunglasses နေကာမျက်မှန် *ne-ga-myeq-hman*
sunstroke နေအပူကြောင့် လေဖြတ်ခြင်း *ne-ăpu-jaún-le-p'yaq-ĉin*
sun-tan lotion နေလောင်စေတဲ့/ အသားညိုစေတဲ့ လိမ်းဆေးရည် *ne-laun-ze-déh/ăthà-nyo-ze-déh-leì-zè-ye*
super (gas/ petrol) စူပါ (ဓာတ်ငွေ့/ ဓာတ်ဆီ) *su-pa (daq-ngwé/daq-si)*
supermarket စူပါမားကတ် *su-pa-mà-kaq*
supplement *n* အားဖြည့်တဲ့အရာ *à-p'yé-déh-ăya*
suppository စအိုထဲထည့်သွင်းတဲ့ဆေးတောင့် *săo-dèh-t'éh-thwìn-déh-s'è-daún*
surgery [BE] ခွဲစိတ်မှု/ ခွဲစိတ်ကုသခြင်း *k'wèh-seiq-hmú/k'wèh-seiq-kú-thá-jìn*
surname မိဘမျိုးရိုးအမည် *mí-bá-myò-yò-ămyi*
swallow မျိုချတယ် *myo-ćá-deh*
sweater ဆွယ်တာ/အနွေးထည် *s'weh-ta/ănwè-deh*
sweatshirt အားကစားလုပ်ချိန်မှာ ဝတ်တဲ့အနွေးထည် *ă-găzà-louq-ćein-hma-wuq-téh-ănwè-deh*
sweet ချိုတယ် *ćo-deh*
swell ဖောင်းတယ် *p'aùn-deh*
swelling ရောင်ပြီးဖောင်းနေခြင်း *yaun-pyì-p'aùn-ne-jìn*
swim *v* ရေကူးတယ် *ye-kù-deh*
swimming ရေကူးခြင်း *ye-kù-jìn*
swimming pool ရေကူးကန် *ye-kù-gan*
swimming trunks ရေကူးဘောင်းဘီ *ye-kù-baùn-bi*
swollen ရောင်ပြီးဖောင်းနေတဲ့ *youn-pyì-p'aùn-ne-déh*
symbol သင်္ကေတ *thin-ke-ta'*
synagogue ဂျူးဘုရားရှိခိုကျောင်း *Jù-p'ăyà-shiq-k'ò-caùn*
synthetic အရာဝတ္ထုတွေ ပေါင်းစပ်ထုတ်လုပ်ထားတဲ့ *ăya-wuq-t'ú-dwe-paùn-saq-t'ouq-louq-t'à-déh*
system စနစ် *săniq*

T

table စားပွဲ *zăbwèh*
tablet (medical) ဆေးလုံး (ဆေးနဲ့ဆိုင်တာ) *s'è-loùn (s'è-néh-s'ain-da)*
tailor အပ်ချုပ်သမား *aq-ćouq-thămà*
take ယူ *yu*
take away *v* **[BE]** အပြင်သို့ယူသွား *ăpyin-dhó-yu-thwà*
taken (occupied) ယူပြီးပြီ (ပြည့်သွားပြီ) *yu-pyì-byi (pyé-thwà-byi)*
tampon တန်ပွန် (အမျိုးသမီးသုံးပစ္စည်း) *tan-pun (ămyà-thì-thoùn-pyiq-sì)*
tap (water) ရေပိုက်ခေါင်း (ရေ) *ye-paiq-gaùn (ye)*
tax အခွန် *ăk'un*
taxi အငှားကား/ တက်စီ *ăhngà-kà/teq-si*
taxi rank [BE] တက္ကစီရပ်တဲ့နေရာ *teq-si-yaq-téh-ne-ya*
taxi stand တက္ကစီတန်းစီတဲ့နေရာ *teq-si-tàn-si-déh-ne-ya*
team အဖွဲ့ *ăp'wéh*
tear *v* စုတ်ဖြတ်တယ် *s'ouq-p'yèh-deh*
teaspoon လက်ဖက်ရည်ဇွန်း *lăp'eq-ye-zùn*
telephone booth တယ်လီဖုန်းပြောတဲ့နေရာ *teh-li-p'oùn-pyàw-déh-ne-ya*
telephone directory တယ်လီဖုန်းလမ်းညွှန် *teh-li-p'oùn-làn-hnyun*
telephone *n* တယ်လီဖုန်း/ တယ်လီဖုန်းဆက် *teh-li-p'oùn-/ teh-li-p'oùn-s'eq; v*
telephone number တယ်လီဖုန်းနံပါတ် *teh-li-p'oùn-nan-baq*
tell ပြောတယ် *pyàw-deh*
temperature အပူချိန် *ăpu-jein*
temple ဘုရားကျောင်း *p'ăyà-caùn*
temporary ခဏတစ်ဖြုတ် *k'năná-tăp'youq*
tennis court တင်းနစ်ကွင်း *tìn-niq-kwìn*
tennis match တင်းနစ်ပြိုင်ပွဲ *tìn-niq-pyain-bwèh*
tennis racket တင်းနစ်ရိုက်တံ *tìn-niq-yaiq-tan*
tent ရွက်ဖျင်တဲ *yweq-p'yin-dèh*
terminal အဆောက်အအုံ *ăs'auq-ăoun*
terrace ဝရန်တာ *wăyan-da*
terrible ဆိုးဝါးတဲ့/ ကြောက်စရာကောင်းတဲ့ *s'ò-wá-déh/cauq-săya-kau`nh-déh*
terrifying ကြောက်ရွံ့ဖွယ်ဖြစ်တဲ့ *cauq-yún-bweh-p'yiq-téh*
thank ကျေးဇူးတင် *cè-zù-tin*
thank you ကျေးဇူးတင်ပါတယ် *cè-zù-tin-ba-deh*
theater ဇာတ်ရုံ *zaq-youn*
theft ခိုးယူမှု *k'ò-yu-hmú*
then ပြီးတော့ *pyì-dáw*
there ဟိုမှာ *ho-hma*
thermometer သာမိုမီတာ အပူချိန်တိုင်းကိရိယာ *tha-mo-mi-ta/ăpu-jein-taìn-kăyí-ya*
thief သူခိုး *thăk'ò*
thigh ပေါင *paun*
thin ပိန်တယ် *pein-deh*
think (believe) တွေးတောယူဆ (ယုံကြည်) *twè-táw-yu-s'á (youn-ci)*

thirsty ရေဆာတယ် *ye-s'a-deh*
thread အပ်ချည် *aq-ći*
throat လည်ချောင်း *leh-jaùn*
through ဖြတ်ပြီး *p´yaq-pyì*
thumb လက်မ *leq-má*
thunder မိုးခြိမ်းသံ *mò-ćoùn-dhan*
thunderstorm မိုးသည်းထန်စွာရွာသွန်း/ မိုးကြိုးပစ် *mò-thè-t´an-zwa-ywa-thùn/mò-jò-pyiq*
ticket လက်မှတ် *leq-hmaq*
ticket office လက်မှတ်ရုံ *leq-hmaq-youn*
tide ဒီရေ *di-ye*
tie ချည်နှောင် *ći-hnaun*
tie clip ချည်တဲ့ကလစ် *ći-déh-kăliq*
time *n* အချိန် (ပြန်ဖြစ်တဲ့ အဖြစ်အပျက်) *ăćein (pyan-p´yiq-tà-ăp´yiq-ăpyeq)*
; (recurrent occasion)
timetable [BE] အချိန်ဇယား *ăćein-zăyà*
tin [BE] (container) သံဗူး (ထည့်တဲ့အရာ) *than-bù (t´éh-déh-ăya)*
tin opener [BE] သံဗူးဖွင့်တံ *than-bù-p´wín-dan*
tire ကားတိုင်ယာ *Kà-ta-ya*
tired နွမ်းနယ်တယ် *nwàn-neh-deh*
tissue တစ်ရှူး *tiq-shù*
to သို့/ကို *dhó/go(ko)*
tobacco ဆေးရွက်ကြီး *s'è-yweq-cì*
tobacconist ဆေးရွက်ကြီး ဆေးလိပ်ရောင်းသူ *s'è-yweq-cì-s'è-leiq-yaùn-dhu*
today ဒီနေ့ *di-né*
toe ခြေချောင်း *će-jaùn*
toilet [BE] အိမ်သာ *ein-dha*
toilet paper အိမ်သာသုံးစက္ကူ *ein-dha-thoùn-seq-ku*
toiletry အလှပြင်အသုံးအဆောင် *ăhlá-pyin-ăthoùn-ăs'aun*
tomb ဂူ *gu*
tomorrow မနက်ဖြန် *măneq-p'yan*
tongue လျှာ *sha*
tonight ဒီနေ့ည *di-né-nyá*
too (also) လည်း/ပဲ (လည်း) *lèh/bèh (lèh)*
too much အရမ်းများတယ် *ăyàn-myà-deh*
tool ကိရိယာတန်ဆာပလာ *kăyí-ya-dăza-băla*
tooth သွား *thwà*
toothache သွားကိုက်ခြင်း *thwà-kaiq-ĉin*
toothbrush သွားတိုက်တံ *thwà-daiq-tan*
toothpaste သွားတိုက်ဆေး *thwà-daiq-s'é*
torn (clothes) ပြဲနေတဲ့ (အဝတ်စတွေ) *pyèh-ne-déh (ăwuq-sá-dwe)*
touch *v* ထိတယ *t'í-deh*
tour ခရီးသွားလာခြင်း/လည်ပတ်ခြင်း *k´ăyì-thwà-la-jìn/leh-paq-ĉin*
tourist office ကမ္ဘာလှည့်ခရီးသည်ရုံး *găba-hlèh-k´ăyì-deh-yoùn*
tow truck ကားကိုကြိုးနဲ့ဆွဲယူတဲ့ထရပ်ကား *kà-go-cò-néh-s'wèh-yu-dèh-t´ăyaq-kà*
towards ဆီသို့ *s'i-dhó*
towel တဘက် *tăbeq*
tower မျှော်စင် *hmyaw-zin*
town မြို့ *myó*
town hall မြို့တော်ခန်းမ *myó-daw-k´àn-má*
toy ကစားစရာ *găzá-săya*
track (train) လမ်း (ရထား) *lán (yăt´á)*
traffic light မီးပွိုင့် *mì-pwaín*
trail လမ်းကြောင်း/တန်းလန်းလိုက် *làn-jaùn/tán-lán-laiq*
trailer ကားနောက်မှာဆွဲတဲ့လှည်း/ နမူနာရုပ်ရှင် *ká-nauq-hma-s'wèh-dèh-hlèh/nămu-na-youq-shin*
train ရထား *yăt´à*
tram ဓာတ်ရထား *daq-yăt'à*
tranquillizer စိတ်ငြိမ်ဆေး *seiq-nyein-zè*
transfer (money) လွှဲပို့တယ် (ပိုက်ဆံ) *hlèh-pó-deh (paiq-s'an)*
translate ဘာသာပြန် *ba-dha-pyan*
travel ခရီးသွားတယ် *k´ăyì-thwà-deh*
travel agency ခရီးသွားအေဂျင်စီ *k´ăyì-thwà-e-jin-si*
travel guide ခရီးသွားလမ်းညွှန် *k´ăyì-thwà-làn-hnyun*
travel sickness ခရီးသွားတဲ့အခါ မူးဝေတတ်မှုကားမူးတတ်ခြင်း *k´ăyì-thwà-déh-ăk´a-mù-we-daq-hmú/kà-mù-daq-ĉin*
traveler's check ခရီးသွားချက်လက်မှတ် *k´ăyì-thwà-ćeq-leq-hmaq*
treatment ကုသမှု *kú-thá-hmú*
tree သစ်ပင် *thiq-pin*
trim ဖြတ်/တိ *p´yaq/tí*
trip ခရီး *K´ăyì*
trolley တွန်းလှည်း *tùn-hlèh*
trousers [BE] ဘောင်းဘီရှည် *baùn-bi-she*
T-shirt တီရှပ်အကျီ *t-shàq-ìn-ji*
tube ရေပိုက်/ပြွန် *ye-paiq/pyun*
turn (change direction) လှည့်တယ် (ဦးတည်ရာပြောင်းတယ်) *hléh-deh (ù-ti-ya-pyaùn-deh)*
TV တီဗွီ *ti-bwi*
tweezers မွေးညှပ် *mwè-hnyaq*

U

ugly ရုပ်ဆိုးတယ် *youq-s'ò-deh*
umbrella ထီး (ကမ်းခြေ) *t'ì (kán-je)* **; (beach)**
unconscious သတိမရ/ သတိလက်လွတ်ဖြစ် *dhădí-măyá/dhădí-leq-luq-p'yiq*
under အောက်မှာ *ouq-hma*
underpants အောက်ခံဘောင်းဘီ *ouq-k'an-baùn-bi*
undershirt အောက်ခံရှပ်အင်္ကျီ *ouq-k'an-shaq-ìn-ji*
understand နားလည်တယ် *nà-leh-deh*
undress အဝတ်အစားချွတ် *ăwuq-ăsà-ćuq*
United States အမေရိကန်ပြည်ထောင်စု *ăme-yí-kan-pyi-daun-zú*
university တက္ကသိုလ် *teq-kătho*
unleaded (fuel) ခဲမပါတဲ့ (လောင်စာဆီ) *k'-măpa-déh (laun-za-zi)*
until အထိ *ăt'í*
up အထက် *ăt'eq*
upstairs အပေါ်ထပ် *ăpaw-daq*
urgent အဆောတလျင် *ăs'àw-tălyin*
use အသုံးပြု *ăthoùn-pyú*
usually အမြဲလိုလို *ămyèh-lo-lo*

V

vacancy လစ်လပ်နေတဲ့နေရာ *liq-laq-ne-déh-ne-ya*
vacant လစ်လပ်နေတယ် *liq-laq-ne-deh*
vacation အပမ်းဖြေအားလပ်ရက် *ăpán-p'ye-à-laq-yeq*
vaccinate ကာကွယ်ဆေးထိုး *ka-kweh-s'è-t'ò*
vacuum cleaner အမှိုက်စုပ်စက် *ăhmaiq-souq-seq*
valley တောင်ကြား *taun-jà*
value တန်ဖိုး *tan-bò*
value-added tax [BE] တန်ဖိုးပေါ်မှထပ်ပေါင်းထည့်ထားတဲ့အခွန် *tan-bò-baw-hmá-t'aq-paùn-t'éh-t'à-déh-ăk'un*
vegetarian ဟင်းသီးဟင်းရွက်သာစားသူ/ အသားမစားသူ *hìn-dhì-hìn-yweq-sà-dhu/ăthá-măsá-dhu*
vein သွေးပြန်ကြော *thwè-byan-jàw*
very အလွန် *ălun*
veterinarian တိရိစ္ဆာန်ဆေးကုဆရာဝန် *tăyeiq-s'an-s'è-kù-s'ăya-wun*
video camera ဗွီဒီယို ကင်မရာ *bwi-di-yo-kin-măya*
view (panorama) မြင်ကွင်း (ကျယ်ပြန့်တဲ့မြင်ကွင်း) *myin-gwìn (ceh-pyàn-déh-myin-gwìn)*
village ကျေးရွာ *cè-ywa*
visit *n* အလည် *ăleh; v*
visiting hours လည်ပတ်နိုင်တဲ့အချိန် *leh-paq-nain-déh-ăćein*
visually impaired အမြင်အာရုံချွတ်ယွင်းနေတာ *ămyin-a-youn-ćuq-ywìn-ne-da*
V-neck ဗွီပုံစံလည်ပင်း *bwi-poun-zan-leh-bìn*
voltage ဗို့အား/လျှပ်စစ်အား *bó-á/hlyaq-siq-à*
vomit *v* အန် *an*

W

wait *v* စောင့်ဆိုင်း *saún-s'aìn*
waiter စားပွဲထိုး *zăbèh-dò*
waiting room စောင့်ဆိုင်းတဲ့ အခန်း *saún-s'aìn-déh-ăk'àn*
waitress စားပွဲထိုးမိန်းကလေး *zăbèh-dò-meìn-k'ălè*
wake အိပ်ရာမှနိုး *eiq-ya-hmá-nò*
wake-up call မနက်အိပ်ရာမှနှိုးတဲ့ဖုန်း *măneq-eiq-ya-hmá-hnò-déh-p'oùn*
Wales ဝေလနိုင်ငံ *We-lá-nain-gan*
walk *n* လမ်းလျှောက်ခြင်း *làn-shauq-ĉìn*
wall နံရံ *nan-yan*
wallet အိတ်ဆောင်ပိုက်ဆံအိတ် *eiq-s'aun-paiq-s'an-eiq*
want လိုအပ်/အလိုရှိ *lo-aq/ălo-shí*
warm (temperature) နွေးထွေးတယ် (အပူချိန်)/ အပူပေး (ပြန်လည်အပူပေး/နွှေးတယ်) *nwè-t'wè-deh (ăpu-jein)/ăpu-pè (pyan-leh-ăpu-pè/hmwè-deh); v* **(reheat)**
wash ဆေးကြော/လျှော်ဖွတ် *s'è-càw/shaw-p'uq*
washing machine အဝတ်လျှော်စက် *ăwuq-shaw-zeq*
watch *n* လက်ပတ်နာရီ *leq-paq-na-yi*
water ရေ *ye*
waterfall ရေတံခွန် *ye-dăgun*
waterproof ရေမဝင်နိုင် *ye-măwin-nain*
water-ski ရေပေါ်မှာစကိတ်စီးခြင်း *ye-baw-hma-săkeiq-sì-ĵìn*
wave *n* လှိုင်း *hlaìn*
way လမ်းကြောင်း *làn-jaùn*
weather ရာသီဥတု *Ya-dhi-ú-du'-*
weather forecast ရာသီဥတု ကြိုတင်ခန့်မှန်းချက် *ya-dhi-ú-du'-co-tin-k'àn-hmán-jeq*
week ရက်သတ္တပတ် *yeq-thaq-dăbaq*
weekend ရုံးပိတ်ရက် စနေ တနင်္ဂနွေ *yoùn-peiq-yeq-Săne-Tănìn-gănwe*
well ကောင်းမွန်တယ် *kaùn-mun-deh*
west အနောက်အရပ *ănauq-ăyaq*

what ဘာလဲ *Ba-lèh*
wheel ဘီး *bì (beìn)*
wheelchair ဘီးတပ်ထိုင်ခုံ *beìn-taq-t´ain-goun*
when ဘယ်အချိန်လဲ *beh-ăc´ein-lèh*
where ဘယ်နေရာလဲ *beh-ne-ya-lèh*
which ဘယ်ဟာလဲ *beh-ha-lèh*
white အဖြူရောင် *ăp´yu-yaun*
who ဘယ်သူလဲ *beh-dhu-lèh*
whole တစ်ခုလုံး *tăk´ú-loùn*
why ဘာကြောင့်လJ *ba-jaún-lèh*
wide ကျယ်ဝန်းတယ် *ceh-wùn-deh*
widow (female) မုဆိုးမ (အမျိုးသမီး)/ မုဆိုးဖို (အမျိုးသား) *mouq-s'ò-má (ămyò-thámì)/mouq-s'ò-bo (ămyò-thá)*; **(male)**
wife ဇနီးမယား *zănì-măyà*
wind လေ *le*
window ပြတင်းပေါက် (ဈေးဆိုင်) *bădìn-bauq (zè-zain)*; **(shop)**
window seat ပြတင်းပေါင်ခုံ *bădìn-baun-k´oun*
windsurfer လေဟုန်စီးသူ *le-houn-sì-dhu*
wine list ဝိုင်စာရင်း *wain-săyìn*
wireless ကြိုးမဲ့ *cò-méh*
wish *v* ဆန္ဒပြု/ ရှိ *s'an-dá-pyú/shí*
with နဲ့အတူ *néh-ătu*
withdraw (banking) ပြန်ထုတ်ယူ (ဘဏ်လုပ်ငန်းနဲ့ဆိုင်တာ) *pyan-t´ouq-yu (ban-louq-ngàn-néh-s'ain-da)*
without မပါရှိပဲ *măpa-shí-bèh*
woman မိန်းမ *meìn-¬á*
wonderful အံ့အားသင့်ဖွယ်ကောင်းတာ *án-à-thín-bweh-kaùn-da*
wood သစ်သား/သစ်တော *thiq-thà/thiq-tàw*
wool သိုးမွေး *thò-mwè*
word စကားလုံး *zăgăloùn*
work *v* အလုပ်လုပ် *ălouq-louq*
worse ပိုဆိုးတာ *po-s'ò-da*
wound ဒါဏ်ရာ *dan-ya*
write ရေးတယ် *yè-deh*
wrong မှားယွင်း *hmà-ywì*

X

X-ray ဓာတ်မှန် *daq-hman*

Y

year နှစ် *hniq*
yellow အဝါရောင် *ăwa-yaun*
yes ဟုတ်ကဲ့ *houq-kéh*
yesterday မနေ့က *măné-gá*
yet အထိ/ မရောက်သေး *ăt´í/măyauq-thè*
young ငယ်ရွယ်တဲ့ *ngeh-yweh-déh*

Z

zero သုံည *thoun-nyá*
zip(per) ဇစ် *ziq*

Burmese – English

A

ă-găzà အားကစား sport

à-găzà-louq-téh-ăk´àn အားကစားလုပ်တဲ့အခန်း gym

ă-găzà-p´ănaq အားကစားဖိနပ် sneaker

á-loùn-ka-mi-aun-pè-yà-déh-ăk´á-cè-ngwe အားလုံးကာမိအောင်ပေးရတဲ့ အခကြေးငွေ cover charge

a-má-gan အာမခံ insurance

a-má-gan-pè-yan-taùn-s'o အာမခံပေးရန် တောင်းဆို insurance claim

a-youn-jàw အာရုံကြော nerve

ăbí-dan အဘိဓာန် dictionary

ăc´eq-ăleq-thiq-myà-yá-shí-nain-déh-ne-ya/ dhădìn-za-yaùn-déh-ne-ya အချက်အလက်သစ်များရရှိနိုင်တဲ့နေရာ/ သတင်းစာရောင်းတဲ့နေရာ newsstand

ăcà အကြား between

Ăcà-a-youn-pyeq-sì-jìn အကြားအာရုံပျက်စီးခြင်း hearing-impaired

ăcaq (daq-poun) အချပ် (ဓာတ်ပုံ) slide (photo)

ăcaq/ăhlwa အချပ်။အလွှာ slice *n*

ăćauq-shaw-déh-ne-ya အခြောက်လျှော်တဲ့နေရာ dry cleaner

ăćein (pyan-p´yiq-tà-ăp´yiq-ăpyeq) အချိန် (ပြန်ဖြစ်တဲ့ အဖြစ်အပျက်) time *n*; **(recurrent occasion)**

ăćein-baìn အချိန်ပိုင်း *part-time*

ăćein-byé အချိန်ပြည့် full-time

ăćein-hmi အချိန်မှီ on time

ăćo-bwèh အချိုပွဲ dessert

ăcwè အကြွေး credit

ăcwe-sí / dìn-gà အကြွေစေ့/ ဒင်္ဂါး coin

ăcwè-weh-kaq အကြွေးဝယ်ကတ် credit card

ăcwe(ngwe)/lèh(ngwe)/lèh-pè (ăwuq-ăsà/ k´ălè-ăhnì) အကြွေ(ငွေ)၊ လဲ (ငွေ)၊ လဲပေး (အဝတ်အစား၊ကလေးအနှီး) change *n* (money); *v* (money); *v* (clothes, diaper)

ădaq-păta အဒပ်ပတာ adapter

ăè-mí-da (p'yà-na-hmú)/è-déh အအေးမိတာ (ဖျားနာမှု)/ အေးတဲ့ cold (illness); *adj*

ăhaùn-pyiq-sì-zain အဟောင်းပစ္စည်းဆိုင် second-hand shop

ăhlá-pyin-ăthoùn-ăs'aun အလှပြင်အသုံးအဆောင် toiletry

ăhlá-pyin-gàn အလှပြင်ခန်း beauty salon

ăhmà-ăywìn အမှားအယွင်း mistake

ăhmaiq အမှိုက် garbage

ăhmaiq-thăyaiq အမှိုက်သရိုက် rubbish [BE]

ăhman (pyin-s'in)/nya-beq (ù-ti-ya) အမှန်(ပြင်ဆင်)/ ညာဖက် (ဦးတည်ရာ) right (correct); (direction)

ăhmaq-tăyá-pyiq-sì-ăyaùn-zain အမှတ်တရပစ္စည်းအရောင်းဆိုင် souvenir shop

ăhnaún-ăsheq-pè-sa / p'yiq-se-da အနှောင့်အယှက်ပေးတာ/ဖြစ်စေတာ bother

ăhngà-kà အငှားကား car hire [BE]

ăhngà-kà အငှားကား rental car

Ain-o-dìn အိုင်အိုဒင်း iodine

Ain-ya-lan-lu-myò/zăgà အိုင်ယာလန် လူမျိုး/ စကား Irish (person); *adj*

Ain-ya-lan-nain-gan (ngan) အိုင်ယာလန် နိုင်ငံ Ireland

ăk´á (leq-hmaq) အခ (လက်မှတ်) fare (ticket)

ăk´á-méh- (kaw-măshin-pè-zăya-mălo) အခမဲ့ (ကော်မရှင်ပေးစရာမလို) fee (commission)

ăk´àn (ho-the-gàn)/(ne-ya) အခန်း (ဟိုတယ်ခန်း)/ (နေရာ) *room (hotel); (space)*

ăk´àn (ne-ein-taiq-k´àn) အခန်း (နေအိမ်တိုက်ခန်း) flat [BE] (apartment)

ăk´àn-kan-dá/t´a-ná-zeiq အခန်းကဏ္ဍ/ဌာနစိတ် section

ăk´ú/ăgú အခု now

ăk´un အခွန် tax

ăká / ká-deh အက dance n; v

ăk´á-cè-ngwe/suq-swèh-jeq tan-bò-pyàw / suq-swèh အခကြေးငွေ/စွပ်စွဲချက် ၊ တန်ဖိုးပြော/ စွပ်စွဲ charge *n*

ăká-k´àn-má/kălaq အကခန်းမ/ ကလပ် dance club

ăkaiq-ăk´èh-pyauq-s'è/ăna-pyauq-s'è အကိုက်အခဲပျောက်ဆေး/အနာပျောက်ဆေး painkiller

ăkan-ăpu-jein အခန်းအပူချိန် မသသာ temperature

ăkan-dwìn-wun-s'aun-hmú အခန်းတွင်းဝန်ဆောင်မှု room service

ăkan-nan-baq အခန်းနံပါတ် room number

ăkauq-k´un-ce-nya-jeq-poun-zan အကောက်ခွန်ကြေငြာချက်ပုံစံ customs declaration form

ăkauq-k´un-dwe/ăk´un-kauq-k´an-hmú-dwe) အကောက်ခွန်တွေ/အခွန်ကောက်ခံမှုတွေ customs
ăkauq-k´un-kìn-luq-téh-pyiq-sì-dwe အကောက်ခွန်ကင်းလွတ်တဲ့ ပစ္စည်းတွေ duty-free goods
ăkauq-k´un-s'aun-yan-mălo-dhí-s'aintaumu fçနှ် ဆောင်ရန်မလိုသည့်ဆိုင် duty-free shop
ăkauq-k´un(ăk´un-ăkauq-s'ain-déh) အကောက်ခွန် (အခွန်အကောက်ဆိုင်တဲ့) duty (customs)
ăku-ănyi အကူအညီ assistance
ăleh အလယ် middle
ăleh အလည် visit *n; v*
ălo-mătu-béh-mătăyà-mădein pyù-cín-jìn အလိုမတူပဲ မတရား/မုဒိမ်းပြုကျင့်ခြင်း rape *n*
ălouq-ăkain အလုပ်အကိုင် occupation
ălouq-keiq-sá-néh-thwà-déh-k´ăyì အလုပ်ကိစ္စနဲ့သွားတဲ့ခရီး business trip
ălouq-louq အလုပ်လုပ် work *v*
ălouq-myà-deh အလုပ်များတယ် *busy*
ălouq-youn, louq-ngàn-myà-shí-déh-k´ăyain-de-thá အလုပ်ရုံ/လုပ်ငန်းများရှိတဲ့ခရိုင်ဒေသ business district
ălweh-dăgu-theh-yu-thwà-nain-da အလွယ်တကူသယ်ယူသွားနိုင်တာ portable
ămè-laiq အမဲလိုက် hunting
Ăme-yí-kan-lu-myò အမေရိကန်လူမျိုး American
ămeín/ămeín-pè/hma-cà အမိန့်/ အမိန့်ပေး/မှာကြား order *n; v*
ămwé-yeiq-bì အမွေးရိတ်ဘီး shaving brush
ămwé-yeiq-thoùn-déh-kăyin-m အမွေးရိတ်သုံးတဲ့ကရင်မ် shaving cream
ămyò-ăsà-ălaiq-p´aw-pyá-déh-ngwe-taùn-k´an-sa အမျိုးအစားအလိုက်ဖော်ပြတဲ့ငွေတောင်းခံစာ itemized bill
ăwuq-ăsà အဝတ်အစား clothing
ăwuq-ăsà-yaùn-déh-sătò-zain အဝတ်အစားရောင်းတဲ့ စတိုးဆိုင် clothing store
ămyà-ăpyà အများအပြား many
ămyan-ăsà-ăsa-yá-nain-déh-ne-ya အမြန်အစားအစာ ရနိုင်တဲ့နေရာ fast-food place
ămyaq-ngwe အမြတ်ငွေ profit *n*
ămyèh-lo-lo အမြဲလိုလို *usually*
ămyi အမည် name
ămyin-a-youn-ćuq-ywìn-ne-da အမြင်အာရုံချွတ်ယွင်းနေတာ visually impaired
ămyín-teq-yin-mù-daq-teh tjrifhwuf&if မူးတတ်တယ် altitude sickness
ămyò-ăsà အမျိုးအစား၂သမအ (ညှိ)
ămyò-thà-shaq-ìn-ji-leq-ceh-dhì-dan အမျိုးသားရှပ်အင်္ကျီ လက်ကြယ်သီးတံ cufflink
ămyò-thămì-lá-zin-thoù-pyiq-sì- (thán-shìn-yè-pyiq-sì) အမျိုးသမီးလစဉ်သုံးပစ္စည်း(သန့်ရှင်းရေးပစ္စည်း) pad (sanitary)
ămyò-thămì-wuq-ăpaw-ìn-ji / bălauq-ìn-ji အမျိုးသမီးဝတ် အပေါ်အင်္ကျီ။ဘလောက်စ်အင်္ကျီ blouse
ămyò-zoun အမျိုးစုံ assorted
(ćwè) ănán-pyauq-s'è-daún (acR;) အနံ့ပျောက်ဆေးတောင့် deodorant
(kàn-je-saún) ătheq-keh-dhu (ကမ်းခြေစောင့်) အသက်ကယ်သူ life guard (beach)
an အန် vomit *v*
án-à-thín-ze အံ့အားသင့်စေ stunning
án-àw-zăya-kaùn-deh အံ့သြစရာကောင်းတယ် amazing
an-dăyeh အန္တရာယ် danger
an-dăyeh-shì-déh အန္တရာယ်ရှိတဲ့ dangerous
an-jin-da အန်ချင်တာ nausea
ăna (na-cin-da) အနာ (နာကျင်တာ) sore (painful)
ănà-yu-bó-ne-ya/ein-dha အနားယူဖို့နေရာ/အိမ်သာ restroom
ănauq-ăyaq အနောက်အရပ် west
ănauq-hma / nauq-cá-da အနောက်မှာ/နောက်ကျတာ behind
ănèh-ngeh အနည်းငယ် few
ănéh-ngeh (păma- ná) အနည်းငယ် (ပမာဏ) little (amount)
ăneq-yaun / ămèh-yaun အနက်ရောင်/အမဲရောင် black
ănì-hmoun-da အနီးမှုန်တာ far-sighted
ănì-hmoun-da အနီးမှုန်တာ long-sighted [BE]
ănì-tăwaiq အနီးတဝိုက် nearby
ăni-yaun အနီရောင် red
ănouq-paín အနောက်ပိုင်း rear
ănú-pyin-nya t နုပညာ art
ănú-pyin-nya-pyá-gàn အနုပညာပြခန်း art gallery
ănyo-p'yáw-yaun အညိုဖျော့ရောင် beige
ănyo-yaun အညိုရောင် brown
ăp´wéh အဖွဲ့ team
ăp´yà အဖျား fever
ăp´yu-yaun အဖြူရောင် white

ăpaìn-asá အပိုင်းအစ piece
ăpán-p´ye-à-laq-yeq အပမ်းဖြေအားလပ်ရက် vacation
ăpaq (gauq-thì-yaiq-thàw-ăpaq) အပတ် (ဂေါက်သီးရိုက်သောအပတ်) round (golf)
ăpaw-hma အပေါ်မှာ on
ăpo အပို extra
ăpo-pyiq-sì အပိုပစ္စည်း accessory
ăpouq အပေါက် hole
ăpu-jein အပူချိန် temperature
ăpu-pè အပူပေး heat *v*
ăpya-yaun အပြာရောင် blue
ăpyan-leq-hmaq အပြန်လက်မှတ် return ticket [BE]
ăp'ye- / ăp'ye-pè အဖြေ/ အဖြေပေး answer
ăpyi-pyi-s'ain-ya/pyi-pá (le-zeiq-ăs'auq-ăoun) အပြည်ပြည်ဆိုင်ရာ/ပြည်ပ(လေဆိပ်အဆောက်အအုံ) international; (airport terminal)
ăpyin-beq အပြင်ဖက် outside
ăpyin-dhó-yu-thwà အပြင်သို့ယူသွား take away *v* [BE]
ăpyin-t´weq အပြင်ထွက် go out
ăpyiq-măshí-bù အပြစ်မရှိဘူး innocent
aq အပ် needle
aq-ći အပ်ချည် thread
aq-ćouq-thămà အပ်ချုပ်သမား tailor
aq-ngwe(ban)/săyan-ngwe အပ်ငွေ (ဘဏ်)/ စရံငွေ deposit *n* (bank)
aq-saiq-kú-thá-hmú အပ်စိုက်ကုသမှု acupuncture
ăs´eiq အဆိပ် poison
ăs´eiq-thín-jìn အဆိပ်သင့်ခြင်း poisoning
ăsa အစာ meal
ăsá အစ begin
ăsá (peiq-sá) အစ (ပိတ်စ) fabric (cloth)
ăsá-ăsa အစားအစာ food
ăsa-ăseiq-thín-hmú အစာအဆိပ်သင့်မှု food poisoning
ăsà-ăthaug-săyìn အစားအသောက်စာရင်း menu
ăsa-ein အစာအိမ် stomach
ăsa-măsà-gin-sà-thauq-kaùn-bó-thauq-téh-ăyeq အစာမစားခင် စားသောက်ကောင်းဖို့သောက်တဲ့အရက် aperitif
ăsà-sháw-deh / ăsa အစားလျှော့တယ်/အစာ diet
ăs'auq-ăoun အဆောက်အအုံ building
ăs'auq-ăoun အဆောက်အအုံ terminal
ăseìn-yaun အစိမ်းရောင် green
ăseiq-ăpaín အစိတ်အပိုင်း part
ăseiq-ăpaìn/we-zú အစိတ်အပိုင်း/ဝေစု portion
ăseq (ăye) အစက် (အရည်) drop (liquid)
ăs'eq-ăthweh(theh-yu-pó-s'aun-yè/in-ta-neq) အဆက်အသွယ် (သယ်ယူပို့ဆောင်ရေး၊ အင်တာနက်) connection (transportation, internet)
ăseq-cá အစက်ကျ drip
ăshé-beq အရှေ့ဘက် east
ăsi-ăsin-ătaìn-măhouq အစီအစဉ်အတိုင်းမဟုတ် out of order
ăsi-yni-k´an-deh (k´ò-yu-hmú) အစီရင်ခံတယ် (ခိုးယူမှု) report (theft)
ăs'in-dhín-p´yiq-téh အဆင်သင့်ဖြစ်တဲ့ ready
ăs'iq (k´an-da-be-dá-s'ain-ya) အဆစ် (ခန္ဓာဗေဒဆိုင်ရာ) joint (anatomy)
ăs'iq-dan-ya-yá-géh အဆစ်ဒဏ်ရာရခဲ့ sprained
ăso-daq-t´eìn-pè-dhàw-kăyin-m အစိုဓာတ်ထိမ်းပေးသောကရင်မ် moisturizing cream
ăsoun အစုံ pair
ăs'oùn-thaq / s'oùn-ze အဆုံးသတ်/ဆုံးစေ end
ăs'ouq အဆုတ် lung
ăsùn-ăpyauq-măt´in-déh-sătì အစွန်းအပြောက်မထင်တဲ့စတီး stainless steel
ăsun-k'oun အစွန်ခုံ aisle seat
ăt´èh-hma အထဲမှာ in
ăt´eìn-ăhmaq-ăs'auq-ăoun အထိမ်းအမှတ်အဆောက်အအုံ monument
ăt´eìn-ăhmaq-pwè အထိမ်းအမှတ်ပွဲ memorial
ăt´eq အထက် up
ăt´í အထိ until
ăt´í/măyauq-thè အထိ/မရောက်သေး yet
ăt´in-cì-zăya-kaùn-deh အထင်ကြီးစရာကောင်းတယ် impressive
ăt´ouq အထုပ် packet
ăt´ù အထူး special
ăt´ù-gú/ăt´ù-cw-cin-dhu အထူးက/ အထူးကျွမ်းကျင်သူ specialist
ăt´ù-pyú-t´a-ná အထူးပြုဌာန speciality
ăt´we-t´we အထွေထွေ miscellaneous
ăt'auq-ăpán-pè အထောက်အပံ့ပေး provide
ătàw-ătwìn အတောအတွင်း during
ăthan-dweq အသံထွက် pronunciation *n*
ăthè-zeiq-ănú-pyin-nya အသေးစိတ်အနုပညာ fine arts
ătheq အသက် age
ătheq-ăyweh-cì-dhu အသက်အရွယ်ကြီးသူ senior citizen

ătheq-keh-hle အသက်ကယ်လှေ life boat
ătheq-keh-ìn-ji အသက်ကယ်အင်္ကျီ life jacket (preserver US)
ătheq-shu အသက်ရှူ breathe
ăthiq အသစ် new
ăthoùn-pyú အသုံးပြု use
ăthwà-ăpyan-leq-hmaq အသွား–အပြန်လက်မှတ round-trip ticket
ăthwà-dăjaùn-leq-hmaq အသွားတစ်ကြောင်းလက်မှတ် one-way ticket
ăti-pyú အတည်ပြု confirm
ăti-pyú-hmú အတည်ပြုမှု confirmation
ătò (ngwe-cè-s'ain-ya) အတိုး (ငွေကြေးဆိုင်ရာ) interest (finance)
ăťù-dàn အထူးတန်း business class
ătu-tu/tu-nyi-da အတူတူ/တူညီတာ same
ătwèh (yăťá) အတွဲ (ရထား) compartment (train)
ătweq အတွက် for
ătwìn-beq အတွင်းဖက် inside
ătwìn/ămò-ăka-ouq-twìn အတွင်း/ အမိုးအကာအောက်တွင်း indoor
aun-leq-hmaq/ťauq-k´an-za အောင်လက်မှတ်/ ထောက်ခံစာ certificate
auq-će အောက်ခြေ bottom
auq-hma အောက်မှာ below
auq-p'eq အောက်ဖက် down
auq-si-jin-pè-pyì-kú-thá-hmú အောက်စီဂျင်ပေးပြီးကုသမှု oxygen treatment
aw-păya အော်ပရာ opera
aw-păye-ta အော်ပရေတာ operator
Àw-săte-lyá-nain-gan ဩစတြေးလျနိုင်ငံ Australia
ăwa-yaun အဝါရောင် yellow
ăwè-cí-hman-byaùn အဝေးကြည့်မှန်ပြောင်း binoculars
Ăwè-dhó / ăwè-hma အဝေးသို့/အဝေးမှာ away
ăwè-hmoun အဝေးမှုန် near-sighted
ăwèh-hmoun အဝေးမှုန် short-sighted [BE]
ăwuq-ăsà အဝတ်အစား dress *n*
ăwuq-lèh-gàn အဝတ်လဲခန်း fitting room
ăwuq-păk´eq အဝတ်ပုခက် hammock
ăwuq-shaw-mì-bu-taiq-ćìn အဝတ်လျှော် မီးပူတိုက်ခြင်း laundry
ăwuq-shaw-mì-bu-taiq-yan-ăt´auq-ăku-pyiq-sì-myà အဝတ်လျှော် မီးပူတိုက်ရန် အထောက်အကူပစ္စည်းများ laundry facilities
ăwuq-shaw-mì-bu-taiq-yan-ne-ya-ăhmaq-ăthà အဝတ်လျှော် မီးပူတိုက်ရန် နေရာအမှတ်အသား laundromat
ăwuq-shaw-zeq အဝတ်လျှော်စက် washing machine
ăya-à-loùn အရာအားလုံး everything
ăyá-dha-shí-déh အရသာရှိတဲ့ delicious
ăya-ya / ăthì-dhì အရာရာ/ အသီးသီး every
ăyaun အရောင် color
ăyaun-ćuq အရောင်ချွတ် bleach
ăye အရည် fluid
ăye-ătweq အရေအတွက် quantity
ăyè-baw အရေးပေါ် emergency
ăyè-baw-ťweq-pauq အရေးပေါ်ထွက်ပေါက် emergency exit
ăye-byà အရေပြား skin
ăye-byà-ni-ne-da အရေပြားနီနေတာ rash
ăyè-cì-deh ta&;MuD;w,f important
ăyeq အရက် alcohol
ăyeq-swèh-ne-da အရက်စွဲနေတာ alcoholic *adj*
ăyeq-yaùn-déh-sătò-zain အရက်ရောင်းတဲ့စတိုးဆိုင် liquor store
ăyi-ăthwè အရည်အသွေး quality
ăyin-lo အလျင်လို hurry
ăyò အရိုး bone
ăyouq-má အရုပ်မ doll
ăyweh-ăsà/s'aiq-z (ăwuq-ăsà) (shù-p´ănaq) အရွယ်အစား/ ဆိုက်ဇ် (အဝတ်အစား) ၊ (ရှူးဖိနပ်) size; (clothes); (shoes)
à-laq-yeq အားလပ်ရက် holiday ; [BE]
à-p´yé-déh-ăya အားဖြည့်တဲ့အရာ supplement *n*

B

ba-dha-pyan ဘာသာပြန် translate
ba-dha-tăyà ဘာသာတရား religion
ba-dha-zăgà ဘာသာစကား language
ba-hmyá-măhouq/ba-hmyá-măshí ဘာမှမဟုတ်/ ဘာမှမရှိ nothing
ba-hmyá-măshí-aun-louq / thun-pyiq ဘာမျှမရှိအောင်လုပ်/ သွန်ပစ် empty
ba-jaún-lèh ဘာကြောင့်လဲ why
Ba-lèh ဘာလဲ what
bà/ăyeq-s'ain/ăćaùn/tà-s'ì-da ဘား/အရက်ဆိုင်/ အချောင်း/တားဆီးတာ bar
băbú ပန်းပု sculpture
bădămyà ပတ္တမြား ruby
bădìn-baun-k´oun ပြတင်းပေါက်ခုံ window seat

bădìn-bauq (zè-zain) ပြတင်းပေါက် (ဈေးဆိုင်) window; (shop)
băgan-byà ပန်းကန်ပြား plate
băgan-dwe (băgan-byà-myà) ပန်းကန်တွေ (ပန်းကန်ပြားများ) dishes (plates)
băgan-s'è-déh-ne-ya-hma-thoùn-déh-s'aq-pya-hmoún ပန်းကန်ဆေးတဲ့နေရာမှာ သုံးတဲ့ ဆပ်ပြာမှုန့် dishwashing detergent
băgan-s'è-zeq ပန်းကန်ဆေးစက် dishwasher
baìn-yaq-s-pò-jaún-p´yiq—téh-ăè-mí-déh-yàw-ga-tămyò/p´ălù-yàw-ga ဗိုက်အောင့်ခြင်း stomachache
băli ဗလီ mosque
ban (ngwe-cè-s'ain-ya-ăthoùn-ăhnoùn) ဘဏ် (ငွေကြေးဆိုင်ရာ အသုံးအနှုန်း) bank (finance)
ban-ćălan ဘဏ်ချလံ bank note
baq-săkà ဘတ်စ်ကား bus
baq-săkà-geiq ဘတ်စ်ကားဂိတ် bus station
baq-săkà-hmaq-tain ဘတ်စ်ကားမှတ်တိုင် bus stop
baq-săkeq-bàw-găzà-bwèh ဘတ်စကက်ဘော ကစားပွဲ basketball game
baun (hman-myà) ဘောင် (မှန်များ) frame (glasses)
baùn-bi ဘောင်းဘီ pants
baùn-bi-do ဘောင်းဘီတို shorts
bàw-loùn-găzà-pyain-bwéh ဘောလုံးကစားပြိုင်ပွဲ soccer match
bàw-loùn-kan-găzà-jìn ဘောလုံးကန်ကစားခြင်း soccer
bàw-loùn-kan-jìn ဘောလုံးကန်ခြင်း football [BE]
bàw-pin ဘောပင် pen
băya-si-ya (ămyò-thămì-ătwìn-gan-ìn-ji ဘရာစီယာ (အမျိုးသမီးအတွင်းခံအင်္ကျီ) bra
băyeiq ဘရိတ်ခ် brake *n*
băzaq ပါးစပ် mouth
beh-ăc´ein-lèh ဘယ်အချိန်လဲ when
beh-beq ဘယ်ဖက် left
beh-dáw-hmá ဘယ်တော့မှ never
beh-dhu-lèh ဘယ်သူလဲ who
beh-dhu-p'yiq-p'yuq ဘယ်သူဖြစ်ဖြစ် anyone
beh-ha-lèh ဘယ်ဟာလဲ which
beh-ha-măs'o ဘယ်ဟာမဆို anything
beh-ha-p'yiq-p'yiq ဘယ်ဟာဖြစ်ဖြစ်/ဘာဖြစ်ဖြစ em any
Bèh-lè-ăká ဘဲလေးအက ballet
beh-lo ဘယ်လို how
beh-louq-ca-lèh ဘယ်လောက်ကြာလဲ how long
beh-louq-cá-lèh ဘယ်လောက်ကျလဲ how much
beh-louq-myà-lèh ဘယ်လောက်များလဲ how many
beh-louq-wè-lèh ဘယ်လောက်ဝေးလဲ how far
beh-ne-ya-lèh ဘယ်နေရာလဲ where
beh-ne-ya-măs'o ဘယ်နေရာမဆို anywhere
bèh-ú-poun ဘဲဥပုံ oval
beq-t'ăyi ဘတ္တရီ battery
beq/bè-beq ဖက်/ဘေးဖက် side
bì ဘီး comb
bì (beìn) ဘီး wheel
bi-ki-ni(ănyò-thămì-ye-kù-wuq-soun) ဘီကီနီ (အမျိုးသမီးရေကူးဝတ်စုံ) bikini
bí-thú-ka-pyin-nya-shin ဗိသုကာပညာရှင် architect
bu-ta-youn (yăt´à)/(mye-aunq-yăt´à) ဘူတာရုံ (ရထား)/ (မြေအောက်ရထား) station (train)
buq-p'ănaq ဘွတ်ဖိနပ် boot
bwi-di-yo-kin-măya ဗွီဒီယို ကင်မရာ video camera
bwi-poun-zan-leh-bìn ဗွီပုံစံလည်ပင်း V-neck
Byí-tí-shá-lu-myò ဗြိတိသျှလူမျိုး British (person)
byu-teìn-daq-ngwé ဗျူတိန်းဓာတ်ငွေ့ butane gas

C

càn-ma-yè-a-má-gan ကျန်းမာရေးအာမခံ health insurance
càn-ma-yè-néh-nyi-nyuq-téh-ăsà-ăthouq-ăyaùn-zain ကျန်းမာရေးနဲ့ ညီညွတ်တဲ့ အစားအသောက် အရောင်းဆိုင် health food store
càn-ma/wuq-cí ကျန်းမာ/ဝတ်ကြည့် fit *v*
càn-pyin ကြမ်းပြင် floor
cănouq (cănaw/cămá) ကျွန်ုပ် (ကျွန်တော်/ ကျွန်မ) I
caùn ကျောင်း school
caùn-dhà ကျောင်းသား student
ćaùn-s'ò-deh ချောင်းဆိုးတယ် cough *n*
ćauq / ăćauq-hlàn ခြောက်/အခြောက်လှမ်း dry
cauq-kaq ကျောက်ကပ် kidney
cauq-săya-bèh ကြောက်စရာဘဲ awful
cauq-seìn ကျောက်စိမ်း jade
cauq-yún-bweh-p´yiq-téh ကြောက်ရွံ့ဖွယ်ဖြစ်တဲ့ terrifying
càw-bò-eiq ကျောပိုးအိတ် backpack
caw-hlaw-déh-deh-ò ကြော်လှော်တဲ့ဒယ်အိုး frying pan
caw-jaw / ăt'eq ကျော်ကျော်/အထက် above
càw-yò ကျောရိုး spine
će-dauq ခြေထောက် leg
ćè-dauq ခြေထောက် foot
će-dhèh-ăhlá-pyú-pyin-hmú ခြေသည်းအလှပြုပြင်မ pedicure

će-eiq ခြေအိတ် sock
će-eiq-baùn-bi-she ခြေအိတ်ဘောင်းဘီရှည် panty hose
će-eiq-she ခြေအိတ်ရှည် stockings
će-jaùn ခြေချောင်း toe
Će-jìn-wuq ခြေကျင်းဝတ် ankle
cè-leq-de-thá ကျေးလက်ဒေသ countryside
ce-naq/cè-zù-pyú-pyì ကျေနပ်/ကျေးဇူးပြုပြီး please
cè-ni ကြေးနီ copper
ce-nya (ăk´un-néh-s'ain-da) ကြေငြာ (အခွန်နဲ့ဆိုင်တာ) **declare (customs)**
cè-ywa ကျေးရွာ village
cè-zù-tin ကျေးဇူးတင် thank
cè-zù-tin-ba-deh ကျေးဇူးတင်ပါတယ် thank you
ceh ကြယ် star
ceh-dhì ကြယ်သီး button
ceh-laun-dég (ăthan) ကြယ်လောင်တဲ့ (အသံ) loud (voice)
ceh-wùn-deh ကျယ်ဝန်းတယ wide
ćeìn-s'o-jeq ချိန်းဆိုချက် appointment
ćeìn-s'o-hmú (ăćeìn-ăćeq)/né-zwèh (né) ချိန်းဆိုမှု (အချိန်းအချက်)/ နေ့စွဲ (နေ့) date (appointment); (day)
ćeq-auq-t'weq ချက်ခ်အောက်ထွက် check out *v*
ćeq-ĉin-leq-ngìn-dhădìn-pó-pè-dhu ချက်ချင်းလက်ငင်း သတင်းပို့ပေးသူ instant messenger
ćeq-găzà-déh-pyiq-sì-zoun ချက်ကစားတဲ့ပစ္စည်းစုံ chess set
ćeq-găzà-nì ချက်ကစားနည်း chess
ćeq-in-louq-thí-zăbwèh (le-zeiq) ချက်ခ်အင်လုပ်သည့်စားပွဲ (လေဆိပ်) check-in desk (airport)
ćeq-leq-hmaq ချက်လက်မှတ် cheque [BE]
ćeq-pyouq-p'ó-ăt'auq-ăku-pyiq-sì-dwe ချက်ပြုတ်ဖို့ အထောက်အကူပစ္စည်းတွေ cooking facilities
cí ကြည့် look *v*
cì-da ကြီးတာ big
cì-deh ကြီးတယ် large
ći-déh-kăliq ချည်တဲ့ကလစ် tie clip
ći-hnaun ချည်နှောင် tie
ĉi-kyù-deh/ĉi-kyù-zăgà-myà ချီးကျူးတယ်/ ချီးကျူးစကားများ congratulations
ĉi-kyù-deh/ĉi-kyù-zăgà-myà ချီးကျူးတယ်/ ချီးကျူးစကားများ congratulations
ci-lin-déh-cauq-toùn-poun-s'aun-gèh (k´ăyiq-săteh-l) ကြည်လင်တဲ့ကျောက်တုံးပုံဆောင်ခဲ (ခရစ်စတယ်လ်) crystal
ci-lin-dhàw / ti-nyein-dhàw ကြည်လင်သော/ တည်ငြိမ်သော calm
cì-nù-zăya-kaùn-déh ကြည်နူးစရာကောင်းတဲ့ enjoyable
ĉi-yà-s-louq / à-pè / wàn-tha-à-yà-pyú ချီးယားစ် လုပ်/ အားပေး/ ဝမ်းသာအားရပြု cheers
cì-ze ကြီးစေ enlarge
ćin-daun ခြင်ထောင် mosquito net
cìn-myaùn-dèh ကျဉ်းမြောင်းတဲ့ narrow
cin-na-daq-tèh/cin-na-daq-ĉìn ကြင်နာတတ်တဲ့/ ကြင်နာတတ်ခြင်း kind *adj; n*
ćiq-săya-kaùn-déh ချစ်စရာကောင်းတဲ့ lovely
ćiq-teh ချစ်တယ် love *v*
cò ကြိုး rope
cò ကြိုး string
ćo-deh ချိုတယ် sweet
cò-méh ကြိုးမဲ့ wireless
co-tin-ne-ya-yu-t´à-hmú ကြိုတင်နေရာယူထားမှု reservation
co-tin-ne-ya-yu-yan-yoùn ကြိုတင်နေရာယူရန်ရုံး reservations office
co-tin-si-sin-twéh-t´à-déh-ăsà-ăthauq-săyìn ကြိုတင်စီစဉ်တွဲထားတဲ့ အစားအသောက်စာရင်း set menu
coún-deh/dhăbàw-tu-nyi-jeq-sa-jouq/ yàw-ga-kù-seq-k´an-yà-deh ကျုံ့တယ်/ သဘောတူညီချက်စာချုပ်/ရောဂါကူးစက်ခံရတယ် contract
ćouq-louq ချုပ်လုပ် sew
ćouq-seq ချုပ်စက် staple
cwe-deh ကြွေထည် porcelain
cwe-deh-pyiq-sì-dwe ကြွေထည်ပစ္စည်းတွေ ceramics
cwè-mwè ကျွေးမွေး feed *v*
ćwè-t´ouq-k´àn ချွေးထုတ်ခန်း sauna
cweq-teq-ta / kaiq-k´èh-da ကြွက်တက်တာ၊ ကိုက်ခဲတာ cramps
cweq-thà ကြွက်သား muscle

D

da-be-méh ဒါပေမယ့် but
da-dú-be-dà-pyin-nya-shin ဓာတုဗေဒပညာရှင် chemist [BE]; pharmacy [US]
da-hmá-măhouq ဒါမှမဟုတ် **or**

dà-thwà ဓားသွား blade
dăbaq-hlyin တစ်ပတ်လျှင် per week
dăbyeq-sì တံမြက်စည်း broom
dăbyeq-sì တံမြက်စည်း mop *n*
dăbyeq-sì-hlèh-géh-deh တံမြက်စည်းလှည်းခဲ့တယ် moped
dădà တံတား bridge
dăgà-k´auq တံခါးခေါက် knock
dăgeh-ló တကယ်လို့ if
dăhmyaun ဓားမြှောင် knife
daiq-yaiq-p'yiq-téh / làn-hnyun/pyá (dăzoun-tăyauq-à) တိုက်ရိုက်ဖြစ်တဲ့၊ လမ်းညွှန်/ပြ (တစ်စုံတစ်ယောက်အား) direct *adj; v* (someone)
dăjaùn (leq-hmaq)/dăgo-déh (leq-t´aq-măt´à-dhu) တစ်ကြောင်း (လက်မှတ်)၊ တစ်ကိုယ်တည်း (လက်ထပ်မထားသူ) single *n* (ticket); (unmarried)
dăjein တစ်ကြိမ် once
dămyá-taiq-hmú ဓားပြတိုက်မှု robbery
dan-ya ဒဏ်ရာ injury
dan-ya ဒဏ်ရာ wound
dan-ya-yá ဒဏ်ရာ ရ injure
daq-hle-gà ဓာတ်လှေကား elevator
daq-hlew-gà ဒာတ်လှေကား lift [BE] elevator
daq-hman ဓာတ်မှန် X-ray
daq-mătéh ဓာတ်မတည့် allergic
daq-mătéh-ló-p'yiq-téh-toún-pyan-hmú ဓာတ်မတည့်လို့ ဖြစ်တဲ့ တုန့်ပြန်မှု allergic reaction
daq-mì-jiq ဓာတ်မီးခြစ် lighter
daq-poun ဓာတ်ပုံ photo
daq-poun-yaiq-kù-hmú ဓာတ်ပုံရိုက်ကူးမှု photography
daq-poun/daq-poun-yaiq ဓာတ်ပုံ။ဓာတ်ပုံရိုက် photograph *n*
daq-s´i ဓာတ်ဆီ gasoline [US]; petrol [BE]
daún ထောင့် corner
daún-hman-sătú-gan ထောင့်မှန်စတုဂံ rectangular
daw-la(ăme-yí-kan-pyi-daun-zú) ဒေါ်လာ (အမေရိကန်ပြည်ထောင်စု) dollar (U.S.)
dăzeiq တံဆိပ် label
dăzeiq-gaùn တံဆိပ်ခေါင်း postage
dăzeiq-gaùn (da-pó-dăzeiq-gaùn)/toùn-t´ú (leq-hmaq) တံဆိပ်ခေါင်း (စာပို့တံဆိပ်ခေါင်း)၊ တုံးထု (လက်မှတ်) stamp *n* (postage); *v* (ticket)
dăzoun-tăya တစ်စုံတစ်ရာ something
dăzoun-tăyauq တစ်စုံတစ်ယောက် someone
de-thá-s'ain-ya ဒေသဆိုင်ရာ local
Deìn-majq-nain-gan(ngan) ဒိန်းမတ်နိုင်ငံ Denmark
Deìn-maq (lu-myò) deìn-maq (ba-dha-zăgà) ဒိန်းမတ် (လူမျိုး)၊ ဒိန်းမတ် (ဘာသာစကား) Danish (person)
dha-hlyin သာလျှင် only
dhăba-wá-p´yiq-téh သဘာဝဖြစ်တဲ့ natural
dhădí-pè သတိပေး caution
dhădí-pè သတိပေး notify
dhădí-pè-sa (s'aín-bouq) သတိပေးစာ (ဆိုင်းဘုတ်) notice (sign)
dhădìn သတင်း message
dhădìn-za သတင်းစာ newspaper
dhăjă-loùn-zain သကြားလုံးဆိုင် candy store
dhó/go(ko) သို့/ကို to
di-găyi (ăpu-jein) ဒီဂရီ (အပူချိန်) degree (temperature)
di-hma ဒီမှာ here
di-né ဒီနေ့ today
di-né-nyá ဒီနေ့ည tonight
di-ye ဒီရေ tide
di-ye-ămyín/ăteq ဒီရေ အမြင့်/အတက် high tide
di-zeh-zi ဒီဇယ်ဆီ diesel
diq-jiq-the ဒစ်ဂျစ်တယ် digital
do-bi-zain-wun-s'aun-hmú ဒိုဘီဆိုင်ဝန်ဆောင်မှု laundry service
dù-gaùn ဒူးခေါင်း knee
dú-tăyá-dàn ဒုတိယတန်း second class
dú-tí-yá ဒုတိယ second

E

éh-jo ဧည့်ကြို receptionist
éh-kan-bwéh/éh-k´an-co-zo-déh-ne-ya ဧည့်ခံပွဲ။ဧည့်ခံကြိုဆိုတဲ့နေရာ reception
éh-yeiq-tha ဧည့်ရိပ်သာ guesthouse
ein အိမ် house
ein-baw အိမ်ဖော် maid
ein-dha အိမ်သာ toilet [BE]
ein-dha-thoùn-seq-ku အိမ်သာသုံးစက္ကူ toilet paper
eiq အိပ် sleep *v*
eiq-k´àn-pa-déh-kà အိပ်ခန်းပါတဲ့ကား sleeping car
eiq-s'aun-paiq-s'an-eiq အိတ်ဆောင်ပိုက်ဆံအိတ် wallet
eiq-s'è အိပ်ဆေး sleeping pill
eiq-t´aun အိတ်ထောင် pocket

eiq-ya အိပ်ရာ bed
eiq-ya-hmá-nò အိပ်ရာမှနိုး wake
eiq-ya-hnò-zeq အိပ်ရာနှိုးစက် alarm clock
eiq-ya-leiq အိပ်ရာလိပ် sleeping bag
eiq, bù (kin-măya) အိတ်/ဗူး (ကင်မရာ) (အိတ် (ကင်မရာ)) case (camera)
eq-k'ăya-săloùn အက္ခရာစာလုံး alphabet
Eq-s-ma (yin-caq-yàw-ga) အက်စ်မာ (ရင်ကျပ်ရောဂါ) asthma
Eq-s-păyin (ăkaiq-ăk'èh-pyauq-s'è အက်စ်ပရင် (အကိုက်အခဲပျောက်ဆေး) aspirin
éq-thweh-hmú-p'yaq-tauq (kun-pyu-ta-hnín-s'ain-dhàw) ဆက်သွယ်မှုဖြတ်တောက် (ကွန်ပျူတာနှင့်ဆိုင်သော) disconnect *v* (computer)

G

găbà-zauq ကမ်းပါးစောက် cliff
găbaq ခါးပတ် belt
gădà-gá ကတည်းက since
gădó-thìn-bàw/hle ကူးတို့သင်္ဘော/လှေ ferry
gădwìn-thán-s'è-yi (ye) ခံတွင်းသန့်ဆေးရည် mouthwash
gălìn ဂလင်း gland
gan-dăwin-myauq-the ဂန္ထဝင်မြောက်တယ် classical
gănàn-paùn-seq ဂဏန်းပေါင်းစက် calculator
(thin-bàw) gaùn-gàn / eiq-k´àn (သင်္ဘော) ခေါင်းခန်း/အိပ်ခန်း cabin (ship)
gaùn-kaiq-ćin ခေါင်းကိုက်ခြင်း headache
gaùn-oùn ခေါင်းအုံး pillow
gaùn-p´ì-déh-bì ခေါင်းဖီးတဲ့ ဘီး hairbrush
gaùn-shaw-ye ခေါင်းလျှော်ရည် shampoo
gauq-kălaq ဂေါက်ကလပ် golf club
gauq-kwín ဂေါက်ကွင်း golf course
gauq-yaiq-pyain-bwè ဂေါက်ရိုက်ပြိုင်ပွဲ golf tournament
gaw-byà ဂေါ်ပြား shovel
găyan (ălè-jein) ဂရမ် (အလေးချိန်) gram
Găyeiq-Byí-tein-nain-gan (-ngan) ဂရိတ်ဗြိတိန်နိုင်ငံ Great Britain
găzà-bwèh ကစားပွဲ game
găzà-gwìn ကစားကွင်း playground
găzá-săya ကစားစရာ toy
găzà-zăya-ćo-lein (k´ălè-ngeh-í) ကစားစရာချိုလိမ် (ကလေးငယ်၏) dummy [BE] (baby's)
geq-s (daq-ngwé) ဂက်စ် (ဓာတ်ငွေ့) gas
gi-tá ဂီတ music
go-daun ဂိုဒေါင် garage
gu ဂူ tomb
gùn(gwăn) ဂွမ်း cotton
gwàn (gùn) ဂွမ်း gauze
gwín-dó-p´ănaq ကွင်းထိုးဖိနပ် sandal

H

ha-thá ဟာသ comedy
Haìn (hnouq-k´ùn-s'eq-zăgà) ဟိုင်း (နှုတ်ခွန်းဆက်စကား) hi
haìn-wè (ăwè-byè-làn-má) ဟိုင်းဝေး (အဝေးပြေးလမ်းမ) highway
hèh-l-meq (s'ain-keh-sì-ouq-t´ouq) ဟဲလ်မက် (ဆိုင်ကယ်စီးဦးထုပ်) helmet
Heh-lo (hnouq-k´ùn-s'eq-zăgà) ဟယ်လို (နှုတ်ခွန်းဆက်စကား) hello
hìn-bwèh(ăsà-ăsa-ămyò-ămyi) ဟင်းပွဲ (အစားအစာအမျိုးအမည်) dish (food item)
hlá-deh လှတယ် beautiful
hlá-pá-c´áw-màw-deh လှပချောမောတယ် pretty
hlaìn လှိုင်း wave *n*
hlain-gu လှိုင်ဂူ cave
hlaw-dhăw-hle လှော်သောလှေ rowboat
hle လှေ boat
hle-gădiq-twe လှေကားထစ်တွေ stairs
hle-k´ăyì လှေခရီး boat trip
hléh-deh (ù-ti-ya-pyaùn-deh) လှည့်တယ် (ဦးတည်ရာပြောင်းတယ်) turn (change direction)
hléh-leh-cí-shú-déh-k´ăyì-zin လှည့်လည်ကြည့်ရှုတဲ့ခရီးစဉ် sightseeing tour
hléh-leh-cí-shú-jìn လှည့်လည်ကြည့်ရှုခြင်း ျငါအျနနငညါ
hlèh-pó-deh (paiq-s'an) လွှဲပို့တယ် (ပိုက်ဆံ) transfer (money)
hlyaq-sì-leq လျှပ်စီးလက် lightning
hlyaq-siq-à လျှပ်စစ်အား electricity
hlyaq-siq-daq-à-s'eq-thweh-yá-shí-nain-déh-ne-ya လျှပ်စစ်ဓာတ်အား ဆက်သွယ်ရရှိနိုင်တဲ့နေရာ electrical outlet
hlyaq-siq-daq-à-t´weq-pauq လျှပ်စစ်ဓာတ်အားထွက်ပေါက် outlet (electric)
hlyaq-siq-mì-dhì လျှပ်စစ်မီးသီး light bulb
hlyaq-siq-mì-gaùn လျှပ်စစ်မီးခေါင်း plug (electric)
hlyaq-siq-néh-s'ain-déh လျှပ်စစ်နဲ့ဆိုင်တဲ့ electric
hlyaq-siq-pălaq-gaùn လျှပ်စစ်ပလပ်ခေါင်း socket (electric)
hlyaq-siq-s'ain-ya-puiq-sì လျှပ်စစ်ဆိုင်ရာပစ္စည်း electronic

hmá/t´an-hmá မ/ထံမှ from
hman မှန် mirror
hman-byaùn-dwe (kin-măya-néh-s'ain-da)/(myeq-hman-dwe) မှန်ပြောင်းတွေ (ကင်မရာနဲ့ဆိုင်တာ)/ (မျက်မှန်တွေ) lens (camera); (glasses)
hman-ein/mì-eìn မှန်အိမ်/မီးအိမ် lantern
hmaq-poun-tin-sa မှတ်ပုံတင်စာ registered mail
hmaq-sú-sa-ouq မှတ်စုစာအုပ် notebook
hmaun-maiq-téh/yín-déh မှောင်မိုက်တဲ့/ရင့်တဲ့ dark
hmyá-dha (dga-hyin) မျှသာ (သာလျှင်) just (only)
hmyaw-lín-deh မျှော်လင့်တယ် expect
hmyaw-zin မျှော်စင် tower
hnăk´àn နှုတ်ခမ်း lip
hnăk´àn-mwè နှုတ်ခမ်းမွေး moustache
hnăk´àn-ni နှုတ်ခမ်းနီ lipstick
hnăk´aùn နှာခေါင်း nose
hnăloùn နှလုံး heart
hnăloùn-k´oun-myan-da နှလုံးခုန်မြန်တာ palpitations
hnăloùn-yàw-ga နှလုံးရောဂါ heart attack
hnaún-sheq နှောင့်ယှက် disturb
hnăyauq-eiq-gădin / eiq-ya နှစ်ယောက်အိပ်ကုတင်/အိပ်ရာ double bed
hnăyauq-k´an နှစ်ယောက်ခန်း double room
hné-kwe`-deh နှေးကွေးတယ် slow
hneiq နှိပ်တာ massage
hngà-yàn ငှားရမ်း hire [BE] *v*
hngà-yàn-deh ငှားရမ်းတယ် rent *v*
hngà-yàn-déh ငှားရမ်းတဲ့ rental
hngeq ငှက bird
hnìn နှင်း snow
hniq နှစ် year
hniq-hmyouq/ne-t´ain နှစ်မြုပ်/နေထိုင် occupied
hnoùn (léh-hleh-hnoùn) နှုန်း (လဲလှယ်နှုန်း)၊ (ငွေကြေးတန်ဖိုး) rate *n* (exchange); (price)
hnouq-k´ùn-s'eq-zăgà နှုတ်ခွန်းဆက်စကား greeting
Hnouq-s'eq-pa-deh နှုတ်ဆက်ပါတယ် goodbye
ho-hma ဟိုမှာ there
ho-teh ဟိုတယ် hotel
ho-teh-kyo-tin-ne-ya-yu-jìn ဟိုတယ်ကြိုတင်နေရာယူခြင်း hotel reservation
houq-kéh ဟုတ်ကဲ့ yes

I

Ì-mè-l- အီးမေးလ် e-mail
Ì-mè-l-leiq-sa အီးမေးလ် လိပ်စာ e-mail address
In-gălan-nain-găn(ngan) အင်္ဂလန်နိုင်ငံ England
In-găleiq(ba-dha-zăgà) / (lu-myò) အင်္ဂလိပ် (ဘာသာစကား)/ (လူမျိုး) English (language)
Ìn-ji-jeiq အင်္ကျီချိတ် hanger
ìn-ji-leq အင်္ကျီလက် sleeve
Ìn-s'eq-ăkaiq-k´an-yá အင်းဆက်အကိုက်ခံရ insect bite
Ìn-s'eq-p´yàn-zè အင်းဆက်ဖျန်းဆေး insect spray
Ìn-s'eq-pyè-zè အင်းဆက်ပြေးဆေး insect repellent
in-ta-neq-kaw-p´i-zain အင်တာနက်ကော်ဖီဆိုင် internet cafe
in-ta-neq-twìn-win-t´à-ya-hmá-t´weq အင်တာနက်တွင်းဝင်ထားရာမှ ထွက် log off
ìn-zá-tămyò ဂျင်းစတစ်မျိုး denim

J

Jăbò ကြမ်းပိုး bug
Jeq-keq-ìn-ji ဂျက်ကက်အင်္ကျီ jacket
Jìn ဂျင်း jeans

K

k´ălè-ăhnì ကလေးအနှီ; nappy [BE]; diaper [US]
k´ălè-ăt'ù-kú-s'ăya-wun ကလေးအထူးကုဆရာဝန် pediatrician
k´ălè-ngeh-myà-găzà-yan-ne-ya ကလေးငယ်များကစားရန်နေရာ playpen
k´ălè-ye-kù-gan ကလေးရေကူးကန် kiddie pool
k´án-hmàn-deh ခန့်မှန်းတယ် forecast
k´àn-má (ăk´àn) ခန်းမ (အခန်း) hall (room)
k´án-nà ခမ်းနား magnificent
k´an-zà-deh (youq-wuq--t´ú-s'ain-ya) ခံစားတယ် (ရုပ်ဝတ္ထုဆိုင်ရာ) feel (physical state)
K´ăyán-yaun ခရမ်းရောင် purple
k´ăyì ခရီး journey
K´ăyì ခရီး trip
k´ăyì-zaun-ăt´ouq-ăpò-tin-tùn-hlè ခရီးဆောင်အထုတ်အပိုးတင်တွန်းလှည်း luggage cart
k'ăyì-thwà-ăt'ouq-ăpò-pyan-t'ouq-ćin ခရီးသွားအထုတ်အပိုး ပြန်ထုတ်ခြင်း baggage claim
k'ăyì-thwà-ăt'ouq-ăpò-siq-s'è-da ခရီးသွားအထုတ်အပိုး စစ်ဆေးတာ baggage check
k´ăyì-thwà-ćeq-leq-hmaq ခရီးသွားချက်လက်မှတ် traveler's check

k´ăyì-thwà-deh ခရီးသွားတယ် travel
k´ăyì-thwà-e-jin-si ခရီးသွားအေဂျင်စီ travel agency
k´ăyì-thwà-la-jìn/leh-paq-ćin ခရီးသွားလာခြင်း/ လည်ပတ်ခြင်း tour
k´ăyì-thwà-làn-hnyun ခရီးသွားလမ်းညွှန် travel guide
k´ăyì-zaun-ăt´ouq-ăpò ခရီးဆောင်အထုတ်အပိုး luggage
k´ăyì-zaun-eiq ခရီးဆောင်အိတ် suitcase
k´ăyìn ခက်ရင်း fork
k´èh-dan ခဲတံ pencil
k´èh-néh-than-p´yu-yàw-saq-t´à-déh-thaq-tú ခဲနဲ့သံဖြူရောစပ်ထားတဲ့သတ္တု pewter
k´in-bùn/yauq-cà ခင်ပွန်း ယောကျ်ား husband
k´iq-tá-ne (k´ăyì-zin-ătwìn)/ti-shí-ne/ne/-t´ain ခေတ္တနေ (ခရီးစဉ်အတွင်း)၊ တည်ရှိနေ၊ နေထိုင် stay (trip); *v* (remain);*v* (reside)
k´năná-tăp´youq ခဏတစ်ဖြုတ် temporary
k´ó-yu ခိုးယူ steal
k´ò-yu-hmú ခိုးယူမှု theft
k´wín-pyú-jeq (ngà-hmyà-yan)/(ămèh-laiq-yan) ခွင့်ပြုချက် (ငါးမျှားရန်)၊ (အမဲလိုက်ရန်) permit *n* (fishing); (hunting)
k´wín-taún-hmú/k´wín-taún ခွင့်တောင်းမှု၊ ခွင့်တောင်း request *n; v*
k´ăyì-thwà-ăťouq-ăpò ခရီးသွား အထုတ်အပိုး baggage [BE]
kà ကား **car**
kà-hngà(kà-maùn-dhu-ăpa) ကားငှား (ကားမောင်းသူအပါ) car rental (with driver)
ka-kweh-s'è-t´ò ကာကွယ်ဆေးထိုး vaccinate
k´à-na-da ခါးနာတာ backache
ká-nauq-hma-s'wèh-dèh-hlèh/nămu-na-youq-shin ကားနောက်မှာဆွဲတဲ့လှည်း/ နမူနာရုပ်ရှင် trailer
kà-pyin-s'ăya ကားပြင်ဆရာ car mechanic
kà-shé-mì ကားရှေ့မီး headlight
ka-si-no ကာစီနို casino
Kà-ta-ya ကားတိုင်ယာ tire
kà-ťain-goun ကားထိုင်ခုံ car seat
ka-tùn (sì-kăyeq) ကာတွန်း (စီးကရက်) carton (of cigarettes)
kà-yaq-ćein-hmaq-téh-mi-ta ကားရက်ချိန်မှတ်တဲ့မီတာ parking meter
kà-yaq-nà-yan-ne-ya ကားရပ်နားရန်နေရာ car park [BE]
kà-yaq-tèh-ne-ya ကားရပ်တဲ့နေရာ parking
kaiq-k'èh-hmú ကိုက်ခဲမှု ache
k´ălè-ăćò-sà-zăya-păma-ná ကလေးအချိုးစားစရာပမာဏ children's portion
k´ălè-ăhnì ကလေးအနှီး diaper
k´ălè-ănyiq-ăcè-thouq-téh-gùn-zá-dwe ကလေး အညစ်အကြေးသုတ်တဲ့ ဂွမ်းစတွေ baby wipes
k´ălè-ăsa ကလေးအစာ baby food
k´ălè-ăwuq-ăsà ကလေးအဝတ်အစား children's clothing
k´ălè-deìn ကလေးထိန်း babysitter
k´ălè-eiq-ya/gădin ကလေးအိပ်ရာ/ ကုတင် cot
k´ălè-mwè ကလေးမွေး birth
k´ălè-neh ကလေးငယ baby
k´ălè-păk´eq ကလေးပုခက် crib
k´ălè-ťà-déh-ne-ya ကလေး ထားတဲ့နေရာ child barn
k´ălè-ťain-goun ကလေးထိုင်ခုံ child's seat
kăliq ကလစ် clip
k´an-da-ko ခန္ဓာကိုယ် body
k´án-hmàn-je (zè-hnoùn-k´án-hmàn-je) ခန့်မှန်းချေ/ (ဈေးနှုန်းခန့်မှန်းချေ) estimate n; (quotation)
kàn-je-bàw-loùn-găzà-nì ကမ်းခြေဘောလုံးကစားနည်း beach ball
k´àn-zì ခန်းဆီး curtain
Kăne-da-lu-myò ကနေဒါလူမျိုး Canadian
kăne-da-nain-gan(ngan) ကနေဒါနိုင်ငံ Canada
kaq-cé ကပ်ကြေး scissors
kaq-ne-déh ကပ်နေတဲ့ next to
kaùn-da/min-găla-shí-da ကောင်းတာ/ မင်္ဂလာရှိတာ good
Kaùn-deh (o-ke) ကောင်းတယ်(အိုကေ) fine (OK)
kaùn-kin ကောင်းကင် sky
k´aùn-laùn ခေါင်းလောင်း bell
kaùn-mun-deh ကောင်းမွန်တယ် well
kaùn-mun-déh (hlá-pá-déh) ကောင်းမွန်တဲ့ (လှပတဲ့) nice (beautiful)
kaun-siq-wun-youn ကောင်စစ်ဝန်ရုံး consulate
kaun-ta ကောင်တာ counter
kauq-yò-ćauq-ćein-dwin-p´yiq-thaw-daq-mătéh-dhí-yàw-ga ကောက်ရိုးခြောက်ချိန်တွင်ဖြစ်သော ဓာတ်မတည့်သည့်ရောဂါ hay fever
kaw ကော် glue
kaw-la ကော်လံ collar

kaw-măshin-gá (ăk´á-cè-ngwe) ကော်မရှင်ခ (အခကြေးငွေ) commission (fee)
Kaw-p'ï-zain ကော်ဖီဆိုင် cafe
kaw-sè/sì (kaw) ကော်စေး (ကော်) paste (glue)
k´aw-s'o-hmú(p'òun) / k´aw-s'o (s'ín-k´aw-da) ခေါ်ဆိုမှု (ဖုန်း)/ ခေါ်ဆို(ဆင့်ခေါ်တာ) call (phone); *v*; (summon)
k´ăyain (myó-tămyó-yéh) ခရိုင် (မြို့တစ်မြို့ရဲ့) district (of town)
k´ăyàn-yaun ခရမ်းရောင amethyst
kăyí-ya-dăza-băla ကိရိယာတန်ဆာပလာ equipment
kăyí-ya-dăza-băla ကိရိယာတန်ဆာပလာ tool
kăyì-ya-dăza-băla ကိရိယာ တန်ဆာပလာ appliance
kăyin-m(ăhlá-pyin-hmú-sain-ya) ကရင်မ် (အလှပြင်မှုဆိုင်ရာ) cream (toiletry)
k´èh-byeq ခဲဖျက် eraser
keh-tin-deh ခွက်တင်ပန်းကန်ပြားသေး saucer
keh-tin-deh ကယ်တင်တယ် save *v*
k´eq-k´èh-déh ခက်ခဲတဲ့ difficult
Ki-lo-găyan ကီလိုဂရမ် kilogram
Ki-lo-mi-ta ကီလိုမီတာ kilometer
k´ìn-cìn-pyá-déh-bi-do ခင်းကျင်းပြသတဲ့ဗီရို display case
kin-măya ကင်မရာ camera
kin-măya-ăyaùn-zain ကင်မရာအရောင်းဆိုင f camera shop
kin-măya-t'éh-déh-eiq, bù ကင်မရာထည့်တဲ့ အိတ်/ ဗူး camera case
Kó-p´a-tha-louq (tăù-t´éh) ကိုယ့်ဘာသာလုပ် (တစ်ဦးတည်း) help; (oneself)
ko-wun-shí-da ကိုယ်ဝန်ရှိတာ pregnant
ko-wun-tà-zè ကိုယ်ဝန်တားဆေး contraceptive
koùn-baq-kălăt'ain ကုန်းပတ်ကုလားထိုင် deck chair
koùn-baq(thin-bàw) ကုန်းပတ် (သင်္ဘော) deck (ship)
koun-cá-zăyeiq ကုန်ကျစရိတ် expense
koun-s'oùn-ze ကုန်ဆုံးစေ spend
kouq-ìn-ji (ăwuq-ăsà) ကုတ်အင်္ကျီ (အဝတ်အစား) coat *n* (clothing)
kú-dho-kan ကုသိုလ်ကံ luck
kú-thá-hmú ကုသမှု treatment
kù-seq-yàw-ga ကူးစက်ရောဂါ infection
kun-doùn ကွန်ဒုံး condom
kun-paq-s (than-laiq-ein-hmyaun) ကွန်ပတ်စ် (သံလိုက်အိမ်မြှောင်) compass
kun-p'ăyín-ăsì-ăwè-k´àn-má ကွန်ဖရင့် အစည်းအဝေးခန်းမ conference room
kun-pyu-ta(pi-si) ကွန်ပျူတာ (ပီစီ) computer (PC)
kwa-shìn-géh-deh / déh ကွာရှင်းခဲ့တယ်/ တဲ့ divorced
k´wè ခွေး dog
kwéh-deh (lin-măyà-s'eq-s'an-yé ကွဲတယ် (လင်မယားဆက်ဆံရေး) separated (relationship)
k´wèh-k´wa/t'weq-k´wa ခွဲခွာ/ ထွက်ခွာ depart
k´weq ခွက် cup
Kwìn-byin ကွင်းပြင် field

L

lá လ moon
lá (ăćein) လ (အချိန်) month
la-deh လာတယ် come
lain-gwèh (p'oùn) လိုင်းခွဲ (ဖုန်း) extension (phone)
lain-sin (yin-maùn) vdkifpif (,mOfarmif;) license (driving)
lain-sin-pyin-pá-hmá-louq-kain လိုင်စင်ပြင်ပမှလုပ်ကိုင် off-licence [BE]
lain-taiq-ne-deh(p'oùn) လိုင်းတိုက်နေတယ် (ဖုန်း) engaged (phone)
laiq-na-deh/laiq-the လိုက်နာတယ်/လိုက်တယ် follow
lán (yăt´á) လမ်း (ရထား) track (train)
làn-ăku လမ်းအကူ road assistance
làn-dămyá လမ်းဓားပြ mugging
làn-dhweh လမ်းသွယ် street
làn-gyaùn / làn-hnyun-jeq လမ်းကြောင်း/ လမ်းညွှန်ချက် direction
làn-gyaùn-pyaùn-thwà-da (yin-j-s'ain-ya) လမ်းကြောင်းပြောင်းသွားတာ (ယာဉ်ကြောဆိုင်ရာ) detour (traffic)
làn-hnyun-sa-ouq လမ်းညွှန်စာအုပ် guidebook
làn-jaùn လမ်းကြောင်း path
làn-jaùn လမ်းကြောင်း route
làn-jaùn လမ်းကြောင်း way
làn-jaùn-byá-s'aìn-bouq လမ်းကြောင်းပြဆိုင်းဘုတ် road sign
làn-jaùn/tán-lán-laiq လမ်းကြောင်း/ တန်းလန်းလိုက် trail

(the-li-p'òun) làn-hnyun (တယ်လီဖုန်း) လမ်းညွှန် directory (phone)
làn-má လမ်းမ road
làn-mye-boun လမ်းမြေပုံ road map
làn-mye-boun လမ်းမြေပုံ street map
làn-pyá-dhu/éh-làn-hnyun လမ်းပြသူ/ ဧည့်လမ်းညွှန် guide *n*
làn-pyá-k´wè လမ်းပြခွေး guide dog
làn-shauq-ćìn လမ်းလျှောက်ခြင်း walk *n*
làn-shauq-thwà-dhu လမ်းလျှောက်သွားသူ pedestrian
làn-zoun လမ်းဆုံ intersection
làn-zoun-dwe လမ်းဆုံတွေ crossroads
lăp´eq-ye-zùn လက်ဖက်ရည်ဇွန်း teaspoon
laq-s'aq-téh လတ်ဆတ်တ fresh
laun-cwàn လောင်ကျွမ်း burn
láw-keq-thì လော့ကက်သီး pendant
le လေ wind
le-è-pè-zeq လေအေးပေးစက် air conditioning
le-houn-sì-dhu လေဟုန်စီးသူ windsurfer
lé-la-yè-k´ăyì လေ့လာရေးခရီး excursion
lè-lan-deh လေးလံတယ် heavy
le-mwè-ya လေမွေ့ယာ air mattress
le-néh-ćauq-thwé-aun-louq-ta လေနဲ့ခြောက်သွေ့အောင်လုပ်တာ blow dry
lé-neq-ta/pyìn-t´an-da လေးနက်တာ/ပြင်းထန်တာ serious
le-yin-byan လေယာဉ်ပျံ airplane
le-yin-byan လေယာဉ်ပျံ flight
le-yin-byan လေယာဉ်ပျံ စူညေနှ့ပ
le-yin-néh-pó-déh-sa/ămyan-ćàw-pó လေယာဉ်နဲ့ပို့တဲ့စာ/အမြန်ချောပို့ airmail
le-zeiq လေဆိပ် airport
lèh-bèh လည်းပဲ also
leh-bìn လည်ပင်း neck
lèh-hleh-jìn (ngwe-cè) လဲလှယ်ခြင်း (ငွေကြေး) exchange v (money)
leh-jaùn လည်ချောင်း throat
leh-jaùn-na-jìn လည်ချောင်းနာခြင်း sore throat
leh-paq-nain-déh-ăćein လည်ပတ်နိုင်တဲ့အချိန် visiting hours
leh-zì လည်စည်း scarf
leh-zwèh လည်ဆွဲ necklace
lèh/bèh (lèh) လည်း/ပဲ (လည်း) too (also)
lein-maw-yaun (ăyaun) လိမ္မော်ရောင် (အရောင်) orange (color)
leìn-zè-ye လိမ်းဆေးရည် lotion
leq လက် ညေ
leq-can (ngwe-cè-s'ain-ya-ăthoùn-ăhnoùn) လက်ကျန် (ငွေကြေးဆိုင်ရာ အသုံးအနှုန်း) balance (finance)
leq-ćaùn လက်ချောင်း finger
leq-eiq လက်အိတ် glove
leq-hlàn-hmi လက်လှမ်းမှီ access *n*
leq-hmaq လက်မှတ် ticket
leq-hmaq-youn လက်မှတ်ရုံ ticket office
leq-hmú-pyin-nya-leq-ya-pyiq-sì-dwe လက်မှုပညာလက်ရာပစ္စည်းတွေ handicrafts
leq-hneiq-daq-mì လက်နှိပ်ဓာတ်မီး flashlight
leq-hwé-bwèh လက်ဝှေ့ပွဲ boxing match
leq-kain-eiq လက်ကိုင်အိတ် handbag [BE]
leq-kain-p´oùn လက်ကိုင်ဖုန်း mobile phone [BE]
leq-kain-pa-déh-deh-ò-dhé လက်ကိုင်ပါတဲ့ ဒယ်အိုးသေး saucepan
leq-kain-păwa လက်ကိုင်ပဝါ handkerchief
leq-k´an/k´wí-pyú လက်ခံ/ ခွင့်ပြု accept *v* (approval)
leq-kauq လက်ကောက် bracelet
leq-leìn-kăyin-m လက်လိမ်းကရင်မ် hand cream
leq-louq-pyiq-sì လက်လုပ်ပစ္စည်း handmade
leq-má လက်မ အကာဘ
leq-maùn လက်မောင်း arm
leq-paq-na-yi လက်ပတ်နာရီ watch *n*
leq-s'aun လက်ဆောင် gift
leq-s'aun-yaùn-dèh-s'ain လက်ဆောင်ရောင်းတဲ့ဆိုင် gift shop
leq-s'aun လက်ဆောင် present *n*
leq-s'è-nain-déh လက်ဆေးနိုင်တဲ့ hand washable
leq-suq (leq-wuq-yădăna), k´aùn-laùn-t´ò လက်စွပ် (လက်ဝတ်ရတနာ)၊ ခေါင်းလောင်းထိုး ring (jewelry); (bell)
leq-t´aq-k´éh-deh/leq-t´aq-t´à-déh လက်ထပ်ခဲ့တယ်/ လက်ထပ်ထားတဲ့ married
leq-thè-t´ó-jìn လက်သည်းထိုးခြင်း manicure
leq-thèh-će-dhèh-ăhlà-pyú-pyin-gàn လက်သည်းခြေသည်းအလှပြုပြင်ခန်း nail salon
leq-thèh-taiq-téh-dăzìn လက်သည်းတိုက်တဲ့တံစဉ်း nail file
leq-thouq-păwa လက်သုတ်ပဝါ napkin
leq-tù-t´ain-goun လက်တွန်းထိုင်ခုံ pushchair [BE]
leq-tùn-hlè လက်တွန်းလှည်း stroller; pushchair [BE]
leq-wuq-yădăna-pyú-louq-thu လက်ဝတ်ရတနာပြုလုပ်သ l jeweler
li-nin-sá လီနင်စ linen

li-ta (păma-ná) လီတာ (ပမာဏ) liter; litre [BE]
liq-laq-ne-da/pyauq-s'oùn-ne-da လစ်လပ်နေတာ/ ပျောက်ဆုံးနေတာ miss *v* (lacking)
liq-laq-ne-deh လစ်လပ်နေတယ် vacant
liq-laq-ne-déh-ne-ya လစ်လပ်နေတဲ့နေရာ vacancy
lo-aq လိုအပ် need *v*
lo-aq-ćeq လိုအပ်ချက် requirement
lo-aq-the လိုအပ်တယ် required
lo-aq/ălo-shí လိုအပ်/အလိုရှိ want
loun-ji/t´ămein လုံချည်/ထဘီ sarong
loun-joun-yé-tweh-aq လုံခြုံရေးတွယ်အပ် safety pin
loun-lauq-téh လုံလောက်တဲ့ enough
loùn-wùn-da လုံးဝန်းတာ round
louq-nain0taq-nain-deh) / than-bù လုပ်နိုင် (တတ်နိုင်တယ်)၊ သံဗူး can *v* (be able to); *n* (container)
louq-ngàn-dhoún-ăkaún လုပ်ငန်းသုံးအကောင့် (ဘဏ်စာရင်းရှင်) checking account
louq-ngàn-dhoùn-ămyi-kaq/ leiq-sa-kaq လုပ်ငန်းသုံးအမည်ကတ်/လိပ်စာကတ် business card
louq-ngàn-dhoùn-sin-ta (biq-săneq-sin-ta) (ho-the-shí) လုပ်ငန်းသုံးစင်တာ (ဘစ်စနက်စင်တာ) (ဟိုတယ်ရှိ) business center (at hotel)
louq-p'aw-kain-beq လုပ်ဖော်ကိုင်ဖက် colleague
louq-yá-meh (yá-meh) လုပ်ရမယ် (ရမယ်) must (have to)
louq/lo-jin-deh (cè-zù-pyú-pyì) လုပ်/လိုချင်တယ် (ကျေးဇူးပြုပြီး) like; (please)
lu လူ person
lu-dhiq/shin-tha-măne လူသစ်/ရှင်သာမဏေ novice
lu-na လူနာ patient
lu-na-tin-kà လူနာတင်ကား ambulance
lu-tăyauq-hlyin လူတစ်ယောက်လျှင် per person
luq-laq-téh လွတ်လပ်တဲ့ free
lweh-ku-déh လွယ်ကူတဲ့ easy

M

ma-déh မာတဲ့ hard
măca-mi မကြာမီ soon
măhouq/măshí မဟုတ်/မရှိ no
măhouq/măshí မဟုတ်/မရှိ not
mălouq-nain-măkain-nain-déh မလုပ်နိုင်မကိုင်နိုင်တဲ့ disabled
man-mo-yi-kaq/hmaq-nyan-kaq မမ်မိုရီကတ်/မှတ်ဉာဏ်ကတ် memory card
man-ne-ja/si-man-k´án-k´wèh-dhu မန်နေဂျာ/စီမံခန့်ခွဲသူ manager
măneq-eiq-ya-hmá-hnò-déh-p´oùn မနက်အိပ်ရာမှနှိုးတဲ့ဖုန်း wake-up call
măneq-p'yan မနက်ဖြန် tomorrow
măneq-sa မနက်စာ breakfast
măpa-shí-bèh မပါရှိပဲ without
mătain-mi (ăćein) မတိုင်မီ (အချိန်) before (time)
mătaw-tăs'-t'í-k´aiq-hmú မတော်တဆထိခိုက်မှု accident
maùn-deh မောင်းတယ် drive
maw-taw-bouq မော်တော်ဘုတ် motorboat
maw-taw-kà-làn မော်တော်ဝေး/ ကားလမ်း motorway [BE]
maw-taw-s'ain-keh မော်တော်ဆိုင်ကယ် motorcycle
măyìn-hnì-da/seìn-ne-da မရင်းနှီးတာ/ စိမ်းနေတာ foreign
mè-gùn မေးခွန်း question *n*
mé-yáw မေ့လျော့ forget
mè-yò မေးရိုး jaw
meìn-k´ălè မိန်းကလေး girl
meìn-k´ălè-meiq-s'we မိန်းကလေးမိတ်ဆွေ girlfriend
meìn-má မိန်းမ woman
meiq-kaq မိတ်ကပ် make-up n
meíq-s'eq မိတ်ဆက် introduce
meiq-s'we မိတ်ဆွေ friend
meiq-tu မိတ္တူ photocopy *n*
meq-găzìn မဂ္ဂဇင်း magazine
mì မီး fire
mì-ăyè-baw-dăgăbauq မီးအရေးပေါ်တံခါးပေါက် fire door
mì-ăyè-baw-luq-pauq မီးအရေးပေါ်လွတ်ပေါက် fire escape
mì-ăyè-baw-t´weq-pauq မီးအရေးပေါ်ထွက်ပေါက် *fire exit*
mí-bá-dwe မိဘတွေ စမေနညအျ
mí-bá-myò-yò-ămyi မိဘမျိုးရိုးအမည် surname
mì-bu မီးပူ press (iron)
mì-dhwè မီးသွေး charcoal
mì-eìn မီးအိမ် lamp
mì-gan-thaq-loun-joun-déh မီးခံသေတ္တာ၊

လုံခြုံတဲ့ safe *n* (vault); (not in danger)
mì-gò-yaun မီးခိုးရောင် gray
mì-gò/s'è-leiq-thauq မီးခိုး/ဆေးလိပ်သောက် smoke
mí-mí-p´a-dha-ăwuq-shaw-mì-bu-taiq-nain မိမိဘာသာ အဝတ်လျှော်မီးပူတိုက်နိုင် launderette [BE]
mí-niq မိနစ် minute
mì-pu (ăwuq-ăsà)/mì-bu-taiq မီးပူ (အဝတ်အစား)၊ မီးပူတိုက် iron n (clothing); v
mì-pwaín မီးပွိုင့် traffic light
mí-sú-zú-baún မိုင်စုစုပေါင်း mileage
mi-ta မီတာ meter
mí-thà-zú မိသားစု family
mì-yaq-ăt´ù-gú မီးယပ်အထူးက gynecologist
min-găla-nan-neq -k´ìn-ba မင်္ဂလာ နံနက်ခင်းပါ good morning
min-găla-nyá-jàn-ba မင်္ဂလာ ညချမ်းပါ good night
min-găla-nyá-ne-gìn-ba မင်္ဂလာ ညနေခင်းပါ good evening
Miq-s မစ္စ Miss
Miq-săta မစ္စတာ Mr.
Miq-siq မစ္စစ် Mrs.
mò မိုး rain
mò-ćoùn-dhan မိုးခြိမ်းသံ thunder
mò-ga-ìn-ji မိုးကာအင်္ကျီ raincoat
mò-thè-t´an-zwa-ywa-thùn/mò-jò-pyiq မိုးသည်းထန်စွာရွာသွန်း/မိုးကြိုးပစ် thunderstorm
mouq-s'eiq-yeiq-s'è-ye မုတ်ဆိတ်ရိတ်ဆေးရည် aftershave lotion
mouq-s'eiq-yeiq-tan မုတ်ဆိတ်ရိတ်တံ razor
mouq-s'eiq-yeiq-téh-dà မုတ်ဆိတ်ရိတ်တဲ့ဓား razor blade
mouq-s'ò-má (ămyò-thámì)/mouq-s'ò-bo (ămyò-thá) မုဆိုးမ (အမျိုးသမီး)/ မုဆိုးဖို (အမျိုးသား) widow (female); (male)
mù-we-deh/déh မူးဝေတယ်/တဲ့ dizzy
mùn-déh မွန်းတည့် noon
mwè-deh မွေးတယ် born
mwè-nè မွေးနေ့ birthday
mwé-ya မွေ့ယာ mattress
myá မြ emerald
myá မြ sapphire
myan-s'an-da မြန်ဆန်တာ quick
myan-zan-da မြန်ဆန်တာ fast *adj*
myauq-p´eq မြောက်ဖက် north
myè မြေး grandchild
mye-boun မြေပုံ map
mye-nyi-daq-ăk´àn မြေညီထပ်အခန်း ground-floor room [BE]
mye-ò မြေအိုး pottery
myeq-hman-dwe (myeq-sí-néh-s'ain-da) မျက်မှန်တွေ (မျက်စိနဲ့ဆိုင်တာ) glasses (optical)
myeq-hman-pyin-nya-shin မျက်မှန်ပညာရှင် optician
myeq-hna မျက်နှာ face
myeq-hna-s'é-càw မျက်နှာဆေးကြော facial
myeq-hna-thán-sin-kăyin မျက်နှာသန့်စင်ကရင်မ် cleansing cream
myeq-k'un-ăyoun-tin-zè မျက်ခွံအရောင်တင်ဆေး eye shadow
myeq-kaq-hman-dwe မျက်ကပ်မှန်တွေ contact lens
myeq-loùn မျက်လုံး eye
myeq-sí-ămyin မျက်စိအမြင် eyesight
myeq-sí-ăseq-ćá-s'e-ye မျက်စိအစက်ချဆေးရည် eye drops
myeq-sí-shàn/caw-cí မျက်စိသျှန်း/ ကျော်ကြည့် overlook *n*
myin မြင် see
myín-deh မြင့်တယ် high *adj*
myin-gwìn (ceh-pyàn-déh-myin-gwìn) မြင်ကွင်း (ကျယ်ပြန့်တဲ့မြင်ကွင်း) view (panorama)
myin-gwin/shú-gìn မြင်ကွင်း/ရှုခင်း scenery
myin-gwin/shú-gìn-kaùn-déh-làn-jaùn မြင်ကွင်း/ရှုခင်း ကောင်းတဲ့လမ်းကြောင်း scenic route
myìn-sì-jìn မြင်းစီးခြင်း horseback riding
myiq မြစ် river
myó မြို့ town
myo-ćá-deh မျိုချတယ် swallow
myó-dwìn-baìn-e-yi-ya မြို့တွင်းပိုင်းဧရိယာ downtown area
myó-haún မြို့ဟောင်း old town
myó-leh-gaun မြို့လယ်ကောင် center of town
myu မြူ fog

N

nà နား **ear**
na-cin နာကျင် hurt

na-cin-dah/na-cin-hmú နာကျင်တယ်/နာကျင်မှု pain
nà-dwìn-ăseq-ćá-déh-s'è-ye နားတွင်းအစက်ချတဲ့ဆေးရည် ear drops
nà-kaiq-ćìn နားကိုက်ခြင်း earache
nà-t´aun နားထောင် listen
na-yi နာရီ clock
na-yi (ăćein) နာရီ (အချိန်) hour (time)
na-yi-tí-dí နာရီတိတိ o'clock
năgaq နားကပ် earring
nain-gan (ngan)-dăga-le-yin နိုင်ငံတကာလေယာဉ် international flight
nain-gan-dhà နိုင်ငံသား nationality
nain-gan-gù-leq-hmaq နိုင်ငံကူးလက်မှတ် passport
nain-gan-gù-leq-hmaq-daq-poun/paq-săpó-daq-poun နိုင်ငံကူးလက်မှတ်ဓာတ်ပုံ/ပတ်စ်ပို့ဓာတ်ပုံ passport photo
nain-gan-gù-leq-hmaq-t´eìn-ćouq-thí-ne-ya နိုင်ငံကူးလက်မှတ်ထိန်းချုပ်သည့်နေရာ passport control
năjaq နားကြပ် headphones
năjaq-p'yín-nà-t'aun-yá-déh-ăthan-dweq-làn-hnyun နားကြပ်ဖြင့်နားထောင်ရတဲ့ အသံထွက်လမ်းညွှန် audio guide
nămu-na-poun-zan/poun-zan နမူနာပုံစံ/ပုံစံ pattern
nan-baq နံပါတ် number
nàn-daw နန်းတော် palace
nàn-deh နမ်းတယ် kiss *v*
nan-neq-k´ìn နံနက်ခင်း morning
nan-yan နံရံ wall
nan-yó နံရိုး rib
nauq-cá နောက်ကျ delay
nauq-cá-deh (ăćein)/(ăćein-s'wè-deh) နောက်ကျတယ် (အချိန်)/ (အချိန်ဆွဲတယ်) late (time); (delay)
nauq-dăjein / t'aq-man နောက်တစ်ကြိမ်/ထပ်မံ *again*
nauq-pyan-thwà/ănauq-p'eq/càw-goùn နောက်ပြန်သွား/အနောက်ဖက်/ကျောကုန်း back
nauq-s'eq-twèh / u-ăteq နောက်ဆက်တွဲ/အူအတက် appendix
nauq-s'oùn နောက်ဆုံး last
nauq-t´aq နောက်ထပ် next
năyu-mò-nì-yà/ăs'ouq-ăè-paq-ćìn နျူမိုးနီးယား/အဆုတ်အအေးပတ်ခြင်း pneumonia
ne နေ sun
né နေ့ day
ne-ăpu-jaún-le-p'yaq-ćìn နေအပူကြောင့်လေဖြတ်ခြင်း sunstroke
ne-ein နေအိမ် home
ne-ein-taiq-k'àn နေအိမ်တိုက်ခန်း apartment
ne-ga (bădìn-bauq) နေကာ (ပြတင်းပေါက်) blind (window)
ne-ga-myeq-hman နေကာမျက်မှန် sunglasses
né-gìn/mùn-lwèh နေ့ခင်း/မွန်းလွဲ afternoon
ne-laun-ze-déh/ăthà-nyo-ze-déh-leì-zè-ye နေလောင်စေတဲ့/အသားညိုစေတဲ့ လိမ်းဆေးရည် sun-tan lotion
né-leh-za နေ့လည်စာ lunch
ne-loun-jìn နေလောင်ခြင်း sunburn
ne-t´ain နေထိုင် live *v*
ne-ya နေရာ place *n*
ne-ya-de-thá နေရာဒေသ **region**
ne-yaq-leiq-sa နေရပ် လိပ်စာ address *n*
néh နဲ့ and
néh-ătu နဲ့အတူ with
neh-mye-de-thá-shú-gín နယ်မြေဒေသရှုခင်း landscape
neín-deh/néh-deh နိမ့်တယ်/နည်းတယ် low
neq-téh နက်တဲ့ deep
ngà-hmyà-/jìn ငါးမျှားခြင်း fishing
ngeh-yweh-déh ငယ်ရွယ်တဲ့ young
ngwe ငွေ silver
ngwe-cè ငွေကြေး currency
ngwe-cè-lèh-hleh-déh-yoùn ငွေကြေးလဲလှယ်တဲ့ရုံး currency exchange office
ngwe-deh-pyiq-sì ငွေထည်ပစ္စည်း silverware
ngwe-lèh-hleh-hnoùn ငွေလဲလှယ်နှုန်း exchange rate
ngwe-leq-k´an-p´yaq-pain ငွေလက်ခံဖြတ်ပိုင်း receipt
ngwe-leq-k´an-dhu ငွေလက်ခံသူ cashier
ngwe-pè / paiq-s'an ငွေပေး/ ပိုက်ဆံ cash *v; n*
ngwe-pè-će-hmú ငွေပေးချေမှု payment
ngwe-seq-ku (ban-douq-seq-ku) ငွေစက္ကူ (ဘဏ်ထုတ်စက္ကူ) note (bank note)
ngwe-sú-săyìn ငွေစုစာရင်း savings account
Ngwe-taùn-k´an--hlwa/ngwe-pó-hlwa ငွေတောင်းခံလွှာ/ ငွေပို့လွှာ money order
ngwe-taùn-k´an-hlwa ငွေတောင်းခံလွှာ invoice

ngwe-t'ouq-seq ငွေထုတ်စက် ATM
ngwe-zăyìn ငွေစာရင်း account
nì-kaq-ta နီးကပ်တာ near
nó-dhí-gaùn/ćo-lein (K´ ălè-í-) နို့သီးခေါင်း/ ချိုလိမ် (ကလေး၏) pacifier (baby's)
nó-dwìn-pa-dhaw-daq-tămyò-à-k´an-nain-yi-măshí-hmú နို့တွင်းပါသောဓာတ်တစ်မျိုးအား ခံနိုင်ရည်မရှိမှု lactose intolerant
nù-nyán-deh နူးညံ့တယ် soft
nwè-t´wè-deh (ăpu-jein)/ăpu-pè (pyan-leh-ăpu-pè/hmwè-deh) နွေးထွေးတယ် (အပူချိန်)/ အပူပေး (ပြန်လည်အပူပေး/ နွှေးတယ်) warm (temperature); *v* (reheat)
nyá-beq ညဖက် night
nyá-dhăgaun ညသန်းခေါင် midnight
nyá-eiq-wuq-soun ညအိပ်ဝတ်စုံ pajamas
nyá-ne ညနေ *evening*
nyá-za ညစာ dinner
nyein-theq-ta ငြိမ်သက်တာ *quiet*
nyiq-pe-déh ညစ်ပေတဲ့ dirty

O

ò အိုး pot
o-da/haún-da အိုတာ/ ဟောင်းတာ old
ò-k´weq-băgan-dwe အိုးခွက်ပန်းကန်တွေ crockery [BE]
ouq-sú အုပ်စု group
ouq-t´ouq ဦးထုပ် hat
ouq-t'ouq ဦးထုပ cap

P

p´a (thwà) ဖာ (သွား) filling (tooth)
p´a-t´è-déh-ăya ဖာထေးတဲ့အရာ patch
p´ain (leq-thèh-taiq-thí-ăya) ဖိုင် (လက်သည်းတိုက်သည့်အရာ) file (for nails)
p´an-gweq (thauq-téh) ဖန်ခွက် (သောက်တဲ့) glass (drinking)
p´an-ye-dăgaùn (t´éh-zăya) ဖန်ရေတကောင်း (ထည့်စရာ) jar (container)
p´ănaq-pyà/će-hmyaq-p´nănaq ဖိနပ်ပြား/ ခြေညှပ်ဖိနပ် slipper
p´aùn-deh ဖောင်းတယ် swell
p´auq ဖောက် puncture
p´ăyà-caùn ဘုရားကျောင်း temple
p´é ဖဲ satin
p´éh-jò ဖဲကြိုး ribbon
p´eh-t´à ဖယ်ထား reserve
p´eiq-sa ဖိတ်စာ invitation
p´eiq-teq ဖိတ်တယ် invite *v*
p´eq-s ဖက်စ် fax
p´eq-s-nan-baq ဖက်စ်နံပါတ် fax number
p´eq-the ဖက်တယ် hug *v*
p´í-à ဖိအား pressure
p´oùn-kaq ဖုန်းကတ် phone card
p´yà-na-deh ဖျားနာတယ် ill [BE]
p´yà-na-hmú ဖျားနာမှု illness
p´yaq-pyì ဖြတ်ပြီး through
p´yaq/tí ဖြတ်/တိ trim
p´yé (poun-zan) ဖြည့် (ပုံစံ) fill in (form)
p´ye-p´yaw-hmú ဖြေဖျော်မှု matinée
p´yiq-nain-je-shí ဖြစ်နိုင်ချေရှိ may *v*
p´yiq-tan-ya ဖြစ်တန်ရာ perhaps
p'yiq-ta / shí-da ဖြစ်တာ/ရှိတာ *be*
p'aw-pyá-deh/ămyan ဖော်ပြတယ်/အမြန် express
p'aw-pyá-jeq ဖော်ပြချက် *expression*
pa-s'eh-douq ပါဆယ်ထုပ် parcel [BE]
pă-t´ò/ze-di/p´ăyà-zin ပုထိုး/စေတီ/ဘုရားစင် shrine
pa-ti ပါတီ party (social gathering)
pa-win ပါဝင် contain
pa-win ပါဝင် include
paiq ပိုက် pipe
paiq-s'an-eiq (leq-kain-eiq) ပိုက်ဆံအိတ် (လက်ကိုင်အိတ်) purse (handbag)
paiq-s'an ပိုက်ဆံ money
păk´oùn ပုခုံး shoulder
p'ălà ဖလား။ခွက် bowl
păla-săta (paq-tì) ပလာစတာ (ပတ်တီး) plaster [BE] (bandage)
pălaq-sătiq ပလပ်စတစ် plastic
pălaq-sătiq-ăpaq ပလပ်စတစ်အပတ် *plastic wrap*
pălaq-sătiq-eiq ပလပ်စတစ်အိတ် plastic bag
pălèh ပုလဲ pearl
păleq-p´aùn (bu-ta-youn) ပလက်ဖောင်း (ဘူတာရုံ) platform [BE] (station)
păleq-ti-nan ပလက်တီနမ် platinum
pălìn ပုလင်း bottle
pălìn-p'áw-zó-p'wín-déh-weq-u-hléh-dan ပုလင်းဖော့ဆို့ဖွင့်တဲ့ ဝက်အူလှည့်တံ corkscrew
pălìn-p'wín-dan ပုလင်းဖွင့်တံ bottle opener
păma-ná (ngwe-cè) ပမာဏ (ငွေကြေး) amount *n* (money)
pàn ပန်း flower
p'an-da / ćouq-se-déh ဖန်တာ/ချုပ်စေတဲ့

astringent
pàn-jan ပန်းခြံ garden
pàn-jan/kà-yaq ပန်းခြံ/ကားရပ် park *n; v*
pan-ka ပန်ကာ fan
pàn-saiq-thu/pàn-yaùn-dhu ပန်းစိုက်သူ/ပန်းရောင်းသူ florist
pán-yaun ပန်းရောင် pink
paq-leh(nì-pà) / (daún-jò-paq-leh) ပတ်လည် (နီးပါး)/ (ထောင့်ချိုးပတ်လည်) around (approximately); (around the corner)
paq-tì ပတ်တီး bandage *n*
păt´ămá ပထမ first
păt´ămá-dàn ပထမတန်း first class
păt´ămá-zoùn-sá-tin-the-k´ìn-déh-ăya (ăsa) ပထမဆုံးစတင်တည်ခင်းတဲ့အရာ (အစာ) starter [BE] (meal)
paun ပေါင် thigh
paun (byí-tein-nain-gan) dhoùn-ngwe-cè/ălè-jein) ပေါင် (ဗြိတိန်နိုင်ငံသုံးငွေကြေး၊ အလေးချိန်) pound (British currency, weight)
paun-da-hmoún ပေါင်ဒါမှုန့် powder
paun-moú/keiq-moún-p'o ပေါင်မုန့်/ကိတ်မုန့်ဖို bakery
paw-ta/ăt´ouq-ăpò-theh-dhu ပေါ်တာ/အထုတ်အပိုးသယ်သူ porter
p'ăyà-shiq-k´ò-caùn ဘုရားရှိခိုးကျောင်း church
p'ayaùn-dain ဖယောင်းတိုင် candle
Păyí-băw-gá-pyíq-sì ပရိဘောဂပစ္စည်း furniture
păyìn ပယင်း amber
păyo-găyan/ăsi-ăsin (ăk´àn-ănà-bwèh-myà-í) ပရိုဂရမ်/အစီအစဉ် (အခမ်းအနားပွဲများ၏) program (of events)
Pè-deh ပေးတယ် give
pè-pó-hmú/we-hngá-hmú ပေးပို့မှု/ဝေငှမှု delivery
pè-pó/we-hngá ပေးပို့/ဝေင deliver
pè/ngwe-će ပေး/ငွေချေ pay
p'èh ဖဲ card
p'èh-găzà-jìn ဖဲကစားခြင်း card game
p´eh-t´à-da ဖယ်ထားတာ reserved
pein-deh ပိန်တယ် thin
peiq ပိတ် shut
peiq-k´éh / peiq-t'à-deh ပိတ်ခဲ့/ပိတ်ထားတယ် closed
peiq-pin-tà-myiq ပိတ်ပင်တားမြစ် forbidden
peiq-s'ó-da / hán-tá-da ပိတ်ဆို့တာ/ဟန့်တားတာ blocked
peiq-ta ပိတ်တာ close *v*
pin-aq (yin-dò-hmá) ပင်အပ် (ရင်ထိုးမှ) pin *n* (brooch)
pin-leh ပင်လယ် sea
pin-ni-s'ălin ပင်နယ်ဆလင် penicillin
pin-sin-yu-géh-deh/pin-sin-yu-t´à-déh ပင်စင်ယူခဲ့တယ်/ပင်စင်ယူထားတဲ့ retired
pkaiq-ăk'èh-pyaq-s'è အကိုက်အခဲပျောက်ဆေး analgesic
pó ပို့ send
Pò-hmwà ပိုးမွှား germ
po-kaùn-deh ပိုကောင်းတယ် better
po-myà-da ပိုများတာ much
po-nèh-déh ပိုနည်းတဲ့ less
po-pyì ပိုပြီး more
pó-săkaq ပို့စ်ကတ် postcard
po-s'ò-da ပိုဆိုးတာ worse
pò-thaq-s'è ပိုးသတ်ဆေး antibiotic
pò-thaq-téh-leìn-zè ပိုးသတ်တဲ့ လိမ်းဆေး *antiseptic cream*
pò-zá ပိုးစ silk
poùn ပုံး pail
poun-dhădan/ăthwin-ăpyin ပုံသဏ္ဌာန်/အသွင်အပြင် shape
poun-hneiq (daq-poun)/poun-hneiq-teh (sa-yweq-sa-dàn) ပုံနှိပ် (ဓာတ်ပုံ)/ ပုံနှိပ်တယ် (စာရွက်စာတမ်း) print *n* (photo); *v* (document)
poun-zan (sa-yweq-sa-dàn) ပုံစံ (စာရွက်စာတမ်း) form (document)
pu-deh (ăpu-jein) ပူတယ် (အပူချိန်) hot (temperature)
pù-paùn-deh ပူးပေါင်းတယ် join *v*
pwaín/ăhmaq ပွိုင့်/အမှတ် point *v*
pwín-lín-da/pwín-ne ပွင့်လင်းတာ/ပွင့်နေ open *adj; v*
pyá-bwéh/pyá-thá ပြပွဲ/ ပြသ *show n; v*
Pyá-daiq ပြတိုက် museum
pyá-gàn ပြခန်း gallery
pyà-s'eiq/pyà-touq ပျားဆိပ်/ ပျားတုပ် sting *n; v*
pyain-bwè (à-găzà-s'ain-ya) ပြိုင်ပွဲ (အားကစားဆိုင်ရာ) match *n* (sport)
pyan-àn ပြန်အမ်း refund *v*
pyán-hmyá ပျမ်းမျှ average
pyan-la/pyan-pé ပြန်လာ၊ ပြန်ပေး return (come back); (give back)
pyan-t´ouq-yu (ban-louq-ngàn-néh-s'ain-da)

ပြန်ထုတ်ယူ (ဘဏ်လုပ်ငန်းနဲ့ဆိုင်တာ) withdraw (banking)
pyan-thwà-da ပြန်သွားတာ go back
p'yaq-kù-jìn (pin-leh-ye-jaùn-néh-s'ain-da) ဖြတ်ကူးခြင်း (ပင်လယ်ရေကြောင်းနဲ့ဆိုင်တာ) crossing (maritime)
pyaùn-lèh/ćà-nà-ze ပြောင်းလဲ/ခြားနားစေ alter *v*
pyauq ပျောက် lose
pyauq-pyì-pyan-twé ပျောက်ပြီး ပြန်တွေ့ lost and found
pyauq-s'oùn ပျောက်ဆုံး lost
pyauq—s'oùn-pyiq-sì-youn ပျောက်ဆုံးပစ္စည်းရုံး lost property office [BE]
pyaw-bwè-zà aysmfyGJpm; picnic
pyaw-bwè-zà-t´weq-téh-ăk´a-thoùn-déh-ĉin ပျော်ပွဲစားထွက်တဲ့အခါ သုံးတဲ့ခြင်း picnic basket
p'yaw-bye-bwèh-cìn-pá-déh-k´àn-má ဖျော်ဖြေပွဲ ကျင်းပတဲ့ခန်းမ concert hall
pyaw-deh ပျော်တယ် happy
pyàw-deh ပြောတယ် tell
pyeq-gădein ပြက္ခဒိန် calendar
pyeq-sì-ne-déh ပျက်စီးနေတဲ့ damaged
pyeq-sì-ne-déh/cò-ne-déh/ kwéh-ne-déh ပျက်စီးနေတဲ့/ကျိုးနေတဲ့/ကွဲနေတဲ့ broken
pyeq-sì/p'yeq-s'ì/ćò/cò-péh ပျက်စီး/ဖျက်ဆီး/ချိုး/ကျိုးပဲ့ break (out of order)
p'yeq-theìn ဖျက်သိမ်း cancel
pyeq-thwà-da (kà) ပျက်သွားတာ (ကား) breakdown (car)
pyì-dáw ပြီးတော့ after
pyì-dáw ပြီးတော့ then
pyi-dwìn-thwà-le-yin ပြည်တွင်းသွားလေယာဉ် domestic flight
pyi-dwìn(le-zeiq-sauq-ăoun) ပြည်တွင်း (လေဆိပ်အဆောက်အဦး) domestic (airport terminal)
Pyí/pyé-da ပြည့်တာ full
pyìn-bó-kaùn-deh ပျင်းဖို့ကောင်းတယ် boring
pyin-sin ပြင်ဆင် fix *v*
pyiq-sì-pyá-pwèh ပစ္စည်း ပြပွဲ exhibition
pyiq-sì-pyaq-ne-da ပစ္စည်းပြတ်နေတာ out of stock
pyú-louq-poun/k´wèh-seiq-hmú ပြုလုပ်ပုံ/ခွဲစိတ်မှု operation
pyú-pyin ပြုပြင် mend
pyù-pyin-hmú/pyú-pyin ပြုပြင်မှု/ ပြုပြင် repair *n; v*

S

Sa စာ letter
sa-baiq စာပိုဒ် phrase
sa-cí-daiq စာကြည့်တိုက် library
sa-daiq စာတိုက် post office
sa-daiq-thiq-ta စာတိုက်သေတ္တာ mailbox
sà-deh စားတယ် eat
sa-eiq စာအိတ် envelope
s'a-laun ဆာလောင် hungry
sa-loùn-paùn စာလုံးပေါင်း spell *v*
sa-ouq စာအုပ် book
sa-ouq-lè (leq-hmaq-twe-pa-déh) စာအုပ်လေး (လက်မှတ်တွေပါတဲ့) booklet (of tickets)
sa-ouq-s'ain စာအုပ်ဆိုင် bookstore
sa-pó-dăzeiq-gaùn စာပို့တံဆိပ်ခေါင်း postage stamp
sà-thauq-k´àn-dwèh စားသောက်ခန်းတွဲ dining car
sà-thauq-s'ain စားသောက်ဆိုင် restaurant
sá-tin စတင် start
sa/sa-pó-deh pm? စာပို့တယ် mail *n; v*
s'aìn-bouq (dhădí-pè-jeq) ဆိုင်းဘုတ် (သတိပေးချက်) sign (notice) *v*
s'aìn-bouq/leq-k´ăna/s'aìn-t´ò/leq-hmaq-t´ò ဆိုင်းဘုတ်/လက္ခဏာ/ဆိုင်းထိုး/လက်မှတ်ထိုး sign
s'aìn/leq-hmaq ဆိုင်း/လက်မှတ် signature
s'aiq-yauq-teh ဆိုက်ရောက်တယ် arrive
s'aiq-yauq-ya ဆိုက်ရောက်ရာ arrival
săkaq စကပ် skirt
Săkáw-tălan-nain-gan စကော့တလန်နိုင်ငံ Scotland
săku-ta စကူတာ scooter
s'án-cin-beq ဆန့်ကျင်ဖက် opposite
s'án-cin-pyì ဆန့်ကျင်ပြီး against
s'án-nain-déh ဆန့်နိုင်တဲ့ elastic
săneq-bà စနက်ဘား snack bar
săniq စနစ် system
săo-dèh-t´éh-thwìn-déh-s'è-daún စအိုထဲထည့်သွင်းတဲ့ဆေးတောင့် suppository
săp'o-hmù စားဖိုမှူး chef
s'aq-pya ဆပ်ပြာ soap
s'aq-pya-hmoún ဆပ်ပြာမှုန့် detergent
săta-lin-ngwe-deh စတာလင်ငွေထည် sterling silver
sătò-zain/ăyaùn-zain စတိုးဆိုင်/အရောင်းဆိုင် store (shop)
sătú-yàn (poun-dhădan) စတုရန်း (ပုံသဏ္ဍာန်)

square (shape)
saun စောင် blanket
saún-s'àin စောင့်ဆိုင်း wait *v*
sáw-dăká စွေ့ဒက complaint
sàw-sàw စောစော early
s'ăya-wun / dauq-ta ဆရာဝန / ဒေါက်တာ doctor
s'ăya-wun-yoùn-gàn ဆရာဝန်ရုံးခန်း doctor's office
s'é ဆေး medicine (drug)
s'è-ăhnùn ဆေးအညွှန်း prescription
s'è-byìn-leiq ဆေးပြင်းလိပ် cigar
s'è-hnyùn-deh ဆေးညွှန်းတယ် prescribe
s'è-leiq-măthauq-yá-déh ဆေးလိပ်မသောက်ရတဲ့ non-smoking
s'è-leiq-thauq-thu ဆေးလိပ်သောက်သူ smoker
s'è-loùn ဆေးလုံး pill
s'è-loùn (s'è-néh-s'ain-da) ဆေးလုံး (ဆေးနဲ့ဆိုင်တာ) tablet (medical)
s'é-sùn-deh ဆေးစွန်းတယ stain
s'è-t´ò-deh/t´ò-zè aဆေးထိုးတယ်/ထိုးဆေး injection
s'è-thouq-ĉin/thouq-s'è ဆေးသုတ်ခြင်း/သုတ်ဆေး painting
s'è-youn ဆေးရုံ hospital
s'è-yweq-cì ဆေးရွက်ကြီး tobacco
s'è-yweq-cì-s'è-leiq-yaùn-dhu ဆေးရွက်ကြီးဆေးလိပ်ရောင်းသူ tobacconist
s'è-zain ဆေးဆိုင် drugstore
s'è-zain ဆေးဆိုင် pharmacy
s'èh-(l)-p'oùn/leq-kain-p'oùn ဆဲလ်ဖုန်း/လက်ကိုင်ဖုန်း cell phone
sein စိန် diamond
seiq-cá-yàw-ga-pyauq-s'è စိတ်ကျရောဂါပျောက်ဆေး **antidepressant**
s'eiq-kàn ဆိပ်ကမ်း port
seiq-kù-yin-déh/yin-k´oun-săya-kaùn-déh စိတ်ကူးယဉ်တဲ့/ရင်ခုန်စရာကောင်းတဲ့ romantic
seiq-nyein-zè စိတ်ငြိမ်ဆေး tranquillizer
seiq-win-zà-deh စိတ်ဝင်စားတယ် interested
seiq-win-zà-zăya-kaùn-déh စိတ်ဝင်စားစရာကောင်းတဲ့ interesting
seq-bèin စက်ဘီး bicycle
seq-bèin-sì-jìn စက်ဘီးစီး /ခြင်း cycling
seq-hmú-pyin-nya-shin စက်မှုပညာရှင် mechanic
seq-ku-leq-thouq-păwa စက္ကူလက်သုတ်ပုဝါ paper towel
seq-ku/sa-yweq စက္ကူ/စာရွက် paper
s'eq-saq-hmú ဆက်စပ်မှု relationship
s'eq-saq-pyí ဆက်စပ်ပြီး regards
s'eq-thweh ဆက်သွယ် connect v
seq-vein-làn-jaùn စက်ဘီးလမ်းကြောင်း bike route
seq-youn စက်ရုံ factory
sha လျှာ tongue
sha-twé/sha-p´we ရှာတွေ့/ရှာဖွေ find *v*
Shán-cá လျှော့ချ reduction
shaq-in-ji ရှပ်အင်္ကျီ shirt
shàw/pyouq-cà လျှော/ပြုတ် ကျ fall *v*
shè-haùn-ptiq-sì ရှေးဟောင်းပစ္စည်း antique
Shé-ne ရှေ့နေ lawyer
shè-ù-thu-na-pyú-pyiq-sì ရှေးဦးသူနာပြုပစ္စည်း first-aid kit
she/ca-da ရှည်/ကြာတာ long
shó-hweq-nan-baq လျှို့ဝှက်နံပါတ် PIN
shù-p´ănaq ရှူးဖိနပ် shoe
shù-p´ănaq-ăyaùn-zain ရှူးဖိနပ်အရောင်းဆိုင် **shoe store**
shwe ရွှေ gold
shwe-ji-tò-ngwe-ji-tò ရွှေခြည်ထိုး ငွေခြည်ထိုး embroidery
s'i ဆီ oil
s'i-dhó ဆီသို့ towards
si-di စီဒီ CD
s'ì-ein ဆီးအိမ် bladder
s'i-jo-yàw-ga-shí-déh / s'ì-jo-yaw-ga-dheh ဆီးချိုရောဂါရှိတဲ့/ဆီးချိုရောဂါသည် diabetic
sì-kăyeq စီးကရက် cigarette
s'ìn-deh ဆင်းတယ် get off
s'in-je/ăcaùn-pyá-jeq-pè ဆင်ခြေ/အကြောင်းပြချက် ပေး excuse *v*
sin-ti-mi-ta စင်တီမီတာ centimeter
(s'è) siq (ဆေး) စစ် check-up (medical)
siq-hman-da/ăsiq-ăhman စစ်မှန်တာ/အစစ်အမှန် genuine
siq-hman-déh စစ်မှန်တဲ့ pure
siq-hman-deh (hman-kan-déh) စစ်မှန်တယ် (မှန်ကန်တဲ့) real (genuine)
siq-mye-byin စစ်မြေပြင် battleground
siq-téh-ăya/ye-ziq စစ်တဲ့အရာ/ရေစစ် filter
s'o-lo ဆိုလ mean *v*
so-t´àin-zá-myà/so-suq စိုထိုင်းဆများ/စိုစွတ် humid
s'ò-wá-déh/cauq-săya-kau`nh-déh ဆိုးဝါးတဲ့/ကြောက်စရာကောင်းတဲ့ terrible
s'ò-ywà-deh ဆိုးရွားတယ bad
s'ò-zè ဆိုးဆေး dye
s'oùn-p'yaq-ćeq ဆုံးဖြတ်ချက် decision

s'oùn-shoùn ဆုံးရှုံး loss
soun-zàn-deh စုံစမ်းတယ် inquiry
soun-zàn-mè-myàn-hmú/dhădìn-ăceq-ăleq စုံစမ်းမေးမြန်းမှု/သတင်းအချက်အလက် information
soun-zàn-mè-myàn-yan-zăbwè စုံစမ်းမေးမြန်းရန်စားပွဲ information desk
souq-k'weq စုပ်ခွက် plunger
s'ouq-p'yèh-deh စုတ်ဖြဲတယ် tear *v*
soun-zàn-mè-myàn-yan-zăbwè စုံစမ်းမေးမြန်းရန်စားပွဲ information desk
souq-tan(băyaq) / weq-hmin-bì စုတ်တံ (ဘရပ်ရှ်)/ဝက်မှင်ဘီး brush *n*
soun-zàn-mè-myàn-yan-zăbwè စုံစမ်းမေးမြန်းရန်စားပွဲ information desk
spa/ye-bu-sàn စပါ/ရေပူစမ်း spa
s'u-nyan-deh ဆူညံတယ် noisy
su-pa-mà-kaq စူပါမားကတ် supermarket
sù-shà-déh (na-cin-hmú) စူးရှတဲ့ (နာကျင်မှု) sharp (pain)
s'ú-taùn-bwè (ba-dha-tăyà-s'ain-ya-s'u-taún-bwè) ဆုတောင်းပွဲ (ဘာသာတရားဆိုင်ရာ ဆုတောင်းပွဲ) mass (religious service)
s'wè-deh ဆွဲတယ် pull *v*
s'wèh-jìn-daùn ဆွဲခြင်းတောင်း basket
s'wèh-s'aun-hmú-shí-deh ဆွဲဆောင်မှုရှိတယ် attractive
s'weh-ta/ănwè-deh ဆွယ်တာ/အနွေးထည် sweater

T

t´à ထား put
t´ain-goun ထိုင်ခုံ seat
t´ain-goun-ămyín ထိုင်ခုံအမြင့် highchair
t´ain-goun-găbaq ထိုင်ခုံခါးပတ် seat belt
t´aq-louq/pyan-louq ထပ်လုပ်/ပြန်လုပ် repeat *v*
t´àw-baq, dein-gèh, nó-néh-nó-dweq-pyiq-sì ထောပတ်၊ ဒိန်ခဲ၊ နို့နဲ့ နို့ထွက်ပစ္စည်း dairy
t´eìn-ćouq-the ထိန်းချုပ် control
t´eiq-p'yà (taun) ထိပ်ဖျား (တောင်) peak *n* (mountain)
t´ìn-shà-thí-tha ထင်ရှားသိသာ pronounce *v*
t´ù-s'àn-deh ထူးဆန်းတယ် strange
t´weq-k´wa/ćan-géh (nauq-twin) ထွက်ခွာ/ချန်ခဲ့ (နောက်တွင်) leave *v*; (behind)
t´weq-k´wa ထွက်ခွာ departure
t´weq-k´wa-ya-geiq ထွက်ခွာရာဂိတ် departure gate
t'í-deh ထိတယ် touch *v*
t'weq-pauq/t'weq (kun-pyu- tà-hnín-s'ain-dhàw) ထွက်ပေါက်၊ ထွက် (ကွန်ပျူတာနှင့်ဆိုင်သော) exit *n; v* (computer)
ta-wun-cá-ya-ne-ya/sa-pó-deh တာဝန်ကျရာနေရာ၊ စာပို့တယ် post [BE] *n; v*
tăbeq တဘက် towel
tain-goun ထိုင်ခုံ chair
taìn-pyi တိုင်းပြည် country
taìn-ta တိုင်းတာ measure
taìn-ta-déh-k´weq တိုင်းတာတဲ့ခွက် measuring cup
taìn-ta-déh-zùn တိုင်းတာတဲ့ဇွန်း measuring spoon
taiq-k´aiq-ta တိုက်ခိုက်တာ attack *n*
taiq-tùn တိုက်တွန်း recommend
tăk´ú-hmyá-măhouq တစ်ခုမှမဟုတ် none
tăk´ú-loùn တစ်ခုလုံး whole
tan-bò-baw-hmá-t´aq-paùn-t´éh-t´à-déh-ăk´un တန်ဖိုးပေါ်မှထပ်ပေါင်းထည့်ထားတဲ့အခွန် value-added tax [BE]
tan-pun (ămyà-thì-thoùn-pyiq-sì) တန်ပွန် (အမျိုးသမီးသုံးပစ္စည်း) tampon
tăna-yi-hlyin တစ်နာရီလျှင် per hour
tăné-hlyin တစ်နေ့လျှင် per day
tăù-tăyauq-ćìn-s'ain-ya တစ်ဦးတစ်ယောက်ချင်းဆိုင်ရာ personal
taun-beq တောင်ဖက် south
taun-goùn တောင်ကုန်း hill
taun-ya တောင်ယာ farm
tăyà-youn (tăyà-ú-băde-néh-s'ain-déh) တရားရုံး (တရားဥပဒေနဲ့ဆိုင်တဲ့) court (judicial)
tăyauq-sa-ăk'àn တစ်ယောက်စာအခန်း single room
tăyeiq-s'an တိရိစ္ဆာန် animal
tăyeiq-s'an-s'è-kù-s'ăya-wun တိရိစ္ဆာန်ဆေးကုဆရာဝန် veterinarian
tăyouq-kaq (dăgà) တရုတ်ကပ် (တံခါး) shutter (window)
teh-li-p'oùn-/ teh-li-p'oùn-s'eq တယ်လီဖုန်း/တယ်လီဖုန်းဆက် telephone *n; v*
teh-li-p'oùn-làn-hnyun တယ်လီဖုန်းလမ်းညွှန် telephone directory
teh-li-p'oùn-nan-baq တယ်လီဖုန်းနံပါတ် telephone number
teh-li-p'oùn-pyàw-déh-ne-ya တယ်လီဖုန်းပြောတဲ့နေရာ telephone booth
tein တိမ် cloud

teq-kătho တက္ကသိုလ် university
teq-si-tàn-si-déh-ne-ya တက္ကစီတန်းစီတဲ့နေရာ taxi stand
teq-si-yaq-téh-ne-ya တက္ကစီရပ်တဲ့နေရာ taxi rank [BE]
teq-yauq တက်ရောက် attend
teq/meq-taq-yaq တက်/မတ်တပ်ရပ် get up
tha-man/poun-hman/yò-yò သာမန်/ပုံမှန်/ရိုးရိုး normal
tha-man/yò-yò သာမန်/ရိုးရိုး general
tha-mo-mi-ta/ăpu-jein-taìn-kăyí-ya သာမိုမီတာ/အပူချိန်တိုင်းကိရိယာ thermometer
thăĉin သီချင်း song
thăĉin-s'o သီချင်းဆို sing
thăk´ò သူခိုး thief
thămaìn-jaùn သမိုင်းကြောင်း history
than-bù-p´wín-dan သံဘူးဖွင့်တံ tin [BE]; can [US] opener
than-ma-cán-k´ain-déh သန်မာကြံ့ခိုင်တဲ့ sturdy
than-ma-da/than-zwàn-da သန်မာတာ/သန်စွမ်းတာ strong
thán-shìn-déh / than-shìn သန့်ရှင်းတဲ့/သန့်ရှင်း clean *adj; v*
than-shìn-yé-pàwa (ămyò-thămì-lá-zin-thoùn-pyiq-sì) သန့်ရှင်းရေးပဝါ sanitary napkin; -towel [BE]
than-yoùn သံရုံး embassy
than-zoun-tì-waìn သံစုံတီးဝိုင်း orchestra
thauq-săya(kauq-tè-l)/thauq-the သောက်စရာ (ကောက်တေးလ်)/ သောက်တယ် drink *n*; (cocktail); *v*
thauq-ye သောက်ရေ drinking water
tháw သော့ key
thaw-go-cwe-ye-thouq သွားကို ကြွေရည်သုတ် enamel
thàw-kaq သော့ကတ် key card
thawà-yu (thwà-pyì-yu) သွားယူ (သွားပြီးယူ) pick up *v* (go get)
thăye-t´eh သားရေထည် leather
thăye-za သွားရည်စာ snack
thăyouq-s'aun (zaq-youn)/ thăyouq-s'aun/ găzà သရုပ်ဆောင် (ဇာတ်ရုံ)/ သရုပ်ဆောင်/ကစား play *n* (theatre; *v*)
the-ja-deh သေချာတယ် certain
the-k´in (ăsà-ăsa) တည်ခင်း (အစားအစာ) serve (meal)
thé-ngeh-deh သေးငယ်တယ် small
thè-thweh-deh သေးသွယ်တယ် petite
theh သယ် carry
théh သဲ sand
theìn-s'ì-t´à သိမ်းဆည်းထား keep
theq-kaùn-deh သိပ်ကောင်းတယ် (အရမ်းကောင်းတယ်) great (excellent)
theq-the-gan-kaq-pyà (kaq) သက်သေခံကတ်ပြား (ကတ်) identification (card)
thí-deh သိတယ် know
thì-thán-p´yiq-thàw သီးသန့်ဖြစ်သော private
thin-bàw/tin-pó-deh သင်္ဘော/ တင်ပို့တယ် ship *n; v*
thin-gàn-za သင်ခန်းစာ lesson
thin-jaìn သင်္ချိုင်း cemetery
thin-ke-ta' သင်္ကေတ symbol
thin-yu-lé-la သင်ယူလေ့လာ study *v*
thiq-pin သစ်ပင် tree
thiq-ta သေတ္တာ box
thiq-thà/thiq-tàw သစ်သား/သစ်တော wood
thò-mwè သိုးမွေး wool
thò-mwè-ìn-ji သိုးမွေးအင်္ကျီ (ရင်ကွဲသိုးမွေးအင်္ကျီ) cardigan
thoun-nyá သုံည zero
thouq-s'è/s'è-thouq-teh သုတ်ဆေး၊ ဆေးသုတ်တယ် paint *n; v*
thu-na-byú သူနာပြု *nurse*
thwà သွား tooth
thwà-daiq-s'é သွားတိုက်ဆေး toothpaste
thwà-daiq-tan သွားတိုက်တံ toothbrush
thwà-kaiq-ĉin သွားကိုက်ခြင်း toothache
thwà-s'ăya-wun သွားဆရာဝန် dentist
thwà-tú သွားတု denture
thwè သွေး blood
thwè-baun သွေးပေါင် blood pressure
thwè-byan-jàw သွေးပြန်ကြော vein
thwè-ji-ú သွေးခြည်ဥ bruise
thwè-t'weq-teh သွေးထွက်တယ် bleed
t´ì (kán-je) ထီး (ကမ်းခြေ) umbrella; (beach)
t-shàq-ìn-ji တီရှပ်အင်္ကျီ T-shirt
ti-bwi တီဗွီ TV
ti-s'auq တည်ဆောက် build
tìn-niq-yaiq-tan တင်းနစ်ရိုက်တံ tennis racket
tìn-niq-kwìn တင်းနစ်ကွင်း tennis court
tin-thwìn/pó-t´à-déh တင်သွင်း/ပို့ ထားတဲ့ imported
tiq-shù တစ်ရှူး tissue
to-teh တိုတယ် short
t'oun-zè / mé-zè ထုံဆေး/မေ့ဆေး anesthetic

tu တူ hammer
tùn တွန်း push *v*
tùn-hlèh တွန်းလှည်း trolley; cart [US]
Twé-s'oun တွေ့ဆုံ meet
twè-táw-yu-s'á (youn-ci) တွေးတောယူဆ (ယုံကြည်) think (believe)
twin/hma/hnaiq တွင်၊ မှာ၊ ၌ at

U

ù-gaùn ဦးခေါင်း head
Ú-yàw-pá ဥရောပ Europe
Ú-yàw-pá-u-ni-yan/ăp'wéh-ăsì ဥရောပယူနီယမ်/ အဖွဲ့အစည်း European Union

W

wain-săyìn ဝိုင်စာရင်း wine list
wàn-baiq / u-néh-s'ain-déh ဝမ်းဗိုက /အူနဲ့ဆိုင်တဲ့ bowel
wàn-ćouq-téh ဝမ်းချုပ်တဲ့ constipation
wàn-néh-ba-deh ဝမ်းနည်းပါတယ sorry
wàn-pyàw-zè ဝမ်းပျော့ဆေး laxative
wàn-shàw-da ဝမ်းလျှောတာ diarrhea
wăyan-da ဝရံတာ balcony
wăyan-da ဝရန်တာ terrace
We-lá-nain-gan ဝေလနိုင်ငံ Wales
wè-lan-déh ဝေးလံတဲ့ far
wè-wè-thwà ဝေးဝေးသွား go away
weh ဝယ် buy v
weq-cá/t´aun-cá ဝါကျ/ထောင်ချ sentence
weq-u-hléh ဝက်အူလှည့် screwdriver
win ဝင် login
win-bauq ဝင်ပေါက် entrance
win-deh (leq-hlàn-hmi) ဝင်တယ် (လက်လှမ်းမှီ) entry (access)
win-gá / win-jè ဝင်ခ/ဝင်ကြေး entrance fee
win-gwín ဝင်ခွင့် admission
win-gwín-pyú/wum-k´an ဝင်ခွင့်ပြု/ ဝန်ခံ admitted
win-yauq ဝင်ရောက် enter *v*
wun-dàn ဝန်ထမ်း staff
wuq-soun ဝတ်စုံ suit (man's/ woman's)

Y

ya-ba ရာဘာ rubber (material)
ya-dhi ရာသီ season
ya-dhi (lá-zin) ရာသီ (လစဉ်) period (monthly)
Ya-dhi-ú-du´- ရာသီဥတ weather
ya-dhi-ú-du´-co-tin-k´àn-hmán-jeq ရာသီဥတုကြိုတင်ခန့်မှန်းချက် weather forecast
ya-gain-hnoùn ရာခိုင်နှုန်း percentage
Yá-meh (louq-yá-meh)/shí-deh (pain-s'ain-hmú-pyá) ရမယ် (လုပ်ရမယ်)/ ရှိတယ် (ပိုင်ဆိုင်မှုပြ) have (must); (possess)
yănán-kú-ťoún ရနံ့ကုထုံး aromatherapy
yăt´à ရထား train
Yăt´à-bu-ta-youn ရထားဘူတာရုံ railway station [BE]
yau`n ရောင်း sell
yaun-pyì-p´aùn-ne-jìn ရောင်ပြီးဖောင်းနေခြင်း swelling
yaun-yàn-jìn ရောင်ရမ်းခြင်း inflammation
yaun-zoun-k´èh-dan ရောင်စုံခဲတံ crayon
yauq-cà ယောကျ်ား man
yauq-cà-lè ယောကျ်ားလေး boy
yàw-ga ရောဂါ disease
yàw-ga-kù-seq-k´an-yá-déh ရောဂါကူးစက်ခံရ / တဲ့ infected
yàw-ga-kù-seq-taq-téh ရောဂါကူးစက်တတ်တဲ့ contagious
yàw-ga-pò-the-aun-thoùn-dhí-s'è-yi / hmoún ရောဂါပိုးသေအောင်သုံးသည့် ဆေးရည်/မှုန့် disinfectant
ye ရေ water
ye-bălìn ရေပုလင်း carafe
Ye-bàn ရေပန်း fountain
ye-bàn-néh-ye-ćò-gàn (ăk´àn) ရေပန်းနဲ့ရေချိုးခန်း (အခန်း) shower (stall)
ye-baw-hma-săkeiq-sì-jìn ရေပေါ်မှာစကိတ်စီးခြင်း water-ski
ye-baw-pyè-s'ain-keh ရေပေါ်ပြေးဆိုင်ကယ် jet ski
ye-boùn ရေပုံး bucket
Ye-boun-bain-gaùn ရေဘုံဘိုင်ခေါင်း faucet
ye-cá/di-ye-cá ရေကျ/ ဒီရေကျ low tide
ye-ćò ရေချိုး bath
ye-ćò-gàn ရေချိုးခန်း bathroom
ye-ćò-pyì-wuq-téh-wuq-youn-she ရေချိုးပြီးဝတ်တဲ့ဝတ်ရုံရှည် bathrobe
ye-dăgun ရေတံခွန် waterfall
yè-deh ရေးတယ် write
ye-di-yo ရေဒီယို radio
ye-gan ရေကန် lake
ye-gè ရေခဲ ice
ye-gè-thiq-ta ရေခဲသေတ္တာ freezer
ye-géh-thiq-ta ရေခဲသေတ္တာ refrigerator
ye-hmwè ရေမွှေး perfume
ye-hmyouq ရေမြှုပ် sponge
ye-kù-baùn-bi ရေကူးဘောင်းဘီ swimming trunks

ye-kù-deh ရေကူးတယ် swim *v*
ye-kù-gan ရေကူးကန် pool
ye-kù-gan ရေကူးကန swimming pool
ye-kù-jìn ရေကူးခြင်း swimming
ye-kù-wuq-soun ရေကူးဝတ်စုံ bathing suit
ye-măwin-nain ရေမဝင်နိုင် waterproof
ye-nan-zi ရေနံဆီ kerosene
ye-ngouq-téh-ăk´a-thoùn-déh-kăyí-ya-dăza-băla ရေငုပ်တဲ့အခါ သုံးတဲ့ ကိရိယာတန်ဆာပလာ snorkeling equipment
ye-paiq-gaùn (ye) ရေပိုက်ခေါင်း (ရေ) tap (water)
ye-s'a-deh ရေဆာတယ f thirsty
ye-zì-jaùn (thămouq-dăya) ရေစီးကြောင်း (သမုဒ္ဒရာ) current (ocean)
yèh ရဲ police
yèh-ăsi-yin-k´an-za ရဲအစီရင်ခံစာ police report
yeh-màw ရယ်မော laugh
yèh-săk´àn ရဲစခန်း police station
yeq-thaq-dăbaq ရက်သတ္တပတ် week
yì-zà ရည်းစား boyfriend
yin-baq ရင်ပတ် chest
yin-baq-tèh-gà-aún-da ရင်ပတ်ထဲက အောင့်တာ chest pain
yin-dhà ရင်သား breast
yin-dò ရင်ထိုး brooch
yìn-hnì-hmyouq-hnan-hmú ရင်းနှီးမြှုပ်နှံမှု investment
yin-maùn-lain-sin ယာဉ်မောင်းလိုင်စင် driver's license
yò-yò-dàn ရိုးရိုးတန်း; economy class
youn-ci-săya-kaùn-da ယုံကြည်စရာကောင်းတာ reliable
yoùn-gàn ရုံးခန်း office
yoùn-peiq-yeq-Săne-Tănìn-gănwe ရုံးပိတ်ရက် စနေ တနင်္ဂနွေ weekend
youn-pyì-p´aùn-ne-déh ရောင်ပြီးဖောင်းနေတဲ့ swollen
youq-k´á-be-dá-ú-yin ရုက္ခဗေဒဥယျာဉ် botanical garden
youq-shin ရုပ်ရှင film [BE]
youq-shin ရုပ်ရှင် movie
youq-shin-youn ရုပ်ရှင်ရုံ cinema [BE]
youq-s'ò-deh ရုပ်ဆိုးတယ် ugly
youq-wuq-t´ú-hnín-s'ain-da ရုပ်ဝတ္ထုနှင့်ဆိုင်တာ material
yu ယူ take
yu-la/yu-thwà ယူလာ/ ယူသွား bring
ywé-lyà ရွေ့လျား move *v*
yweq-hle ရွက်လှေ sailboat

Z

Za ဇာ lace
zăbèh-dò စားပွဲထိုး waiter
zăbèh-dò-mein-k´ălè စားပွဲထိုးမိန်းကလေး waitress
zăbin ဆံပင် hair
zăbin-ăćauq-k´an-déh-kăyí-ya ဆံပင်အခြောက်ခံတဲ့ကိရိယာ hair dryer
zăbin-hnyaq-s'ain ဆံပင်ညှပ်ဆိုင် barber
zăbin-hnyaq-s'ain ဆံပင်ညှပ်ဆိုင် hairdresser
zăbin-hnyaq-teh ဆံပင်ညှပ်တယ် hair cut
zăbin-p´yàn-zè ဆံပင်ဖျန်းဆေး hairspray
zăbwèh စားပွဲ table
zăgà-pyàw စကားပြော speak *v*
zăgăbyan/ba-dha-pyan-pè-dhu စကားပြန/ဘာသာပြန်ပေးသူ interpreter
zăgăloùn စကားလုံး word
zănì-măyà ဇနီးမယား wife
zaq-youn ဇာတ်ရုံ theater
zè ဈေး market *n*
zè-cì-déh ဈေးကြီးတဲ့ expensive
zè-dàn ဈေးတန်း mall
zè-hnoùn ဈေးနှုန်း price
zè-hnoùn-ătí-ăcà-thaq-hmaq-t´à-déh-pyiq-sì-săyìn ဈေးနှုန်းအတိအကျသတ်မှတ်ထားတဲ့ ပစ္စည်းစာရင်း price-fixed menu
zè-măcì-déh ဈေးမကြီးတဲ့ inexpensive
zè-sháw-pè-déh ဈေးလျှော့ပေးတဲ့ discount
zè-theq-tha-da ဈေးသက်သာတာ cheap
zé-weh-jìn ဈေးဝယ်ခြင်း shopping
zé-weh-nain-déh-e-yí-ya ဈေးဝယ်နိုင်တဲ့ ဧရိယာ shopping area
zé-zain ဈေးဆိုင် shop *n*
ziq ဇစ် zip(per)
zùn ဇွန်း spoon

Burmese

phrase book & dictionary

Never be lost for words with Berlitz®

- **Over 8,000 words and phrases** communicate with ease in every situation
- **Color-coded sections organized by theme** go from the airport to the hotel, shopping
- **Easy pro** speak wit with simp
- **Menu re** order the
- **Free app** access all available time of d

US$9.99/£6.99

ISBN 978-178-004-510-8

www.berlitzpublishing.c